# GCSE LAW

4th edition

Jacqueline Martin

HODDER
EDUCATION
AN HACHETTE UK COMPANY

Orders: please contact Bookpoint Ltd, 130 Milton Park, Abingdon, Oxon OX14 4SB.
Telephone: (44) 01235 827720.
Fax: (44) 01235 400454.
Lines are open from 9.00–5.00, Monday to Saturday, with a 24 hour message answering service. You can also order through our website www.hoddereducation.co.uk

If you have any comments to make about this, or any of our other titles, please send them to
educationenquiries@hodder.co.uk

*British Library Cataloguing in Publication Data*

A catalogue record for this title is available from the British Library

ISBN: 978 0 340 98377 5

First Edition Published 1995

Second Edition Published 2001

Third Edition Published 2005

This Edition Published 2009

Impression number      10 9 8 7 6 5 4 3

Year                    2013 2012 2011 2010

Hachette UK's policy is to use papers that are natural, renewable and recyclable products and made from wood grown in sustainable forests. The logging and manufacturing processes are expected to conform to the environmental regulations of the country of origin.

Artwork by Ian Foulis

Cover photo © Lew Long/Corbis

Typeset by Dorchester Typesetting Group Ltd

Printed and bound in Italy for Hodder Education, an Hachette UK Company, 338 Euston Road, London NW1 3BH

# CONTENTS

# PREFACE

This edition of GCSE Law has been extensively re-written and the material extended to cover both AQA and OCR GCSE specifications that start teaching from 2009. The arrangement of the chapters has been altered. In particular the longer chapters in the previous editions have been split into shorter chapters in order to make it easier for students to grasp each topic. This also aids ease of reference for the different topics covered by each board. The grid below shows the relevant chapters for each Unit of both AQA and OCR GCSE.

| AQA | Unit 1 | Chapters 1 to 4 and 7 to 15 |
|-----|--------|------------------------------|
|     | Unit 2 | Chapters 17 to 30, 32 and 34 to 40 |
| OCR | Unit B141 | Chapters 1 to 6 and 9 and 10 |
|     | Unit B142 | Chapters 7, 8, 11, 12 and 38 to 40 |
|     | Unit B143 | Chapters 34 to 37 |
|     | Unit B144 | Chapters 17, 18 and 29 to 33 |

This text is also suitable for other courses with a law element or any introductory level law course.

The text assumes no prior knowledge. The vocabulary is relatively straightforward, but specialised legal vocabulary is introduced as necessary. Summary charts and aids such as flow charts are used throughout the book in order to provide additional help for students. There are suggested activities and exercises for students to do. Simple problem situations are given in many sections on substantive sections for the students to practise applying the law.

Throughout the book for simplicity of language the forms of he, him and his are used in preference to the phrases 'he or she', 'him or her', 'his or hers'. This is in line with legal practice as the Interpretation Act 1978 states that in all Acts of Parliament 'he' includes 'she' etc.

The law is as I believe it to be on 2 April 2009, save that I have anticipated the fact that the House of Lords will be replaced by the Supreme Court from October 2009 and used Supreme Court when explaining the court structure and appeals.

*Jacqueline Martin*

# ACKNOWLEDGEMENTS

The author and publishers would like to thank the following for permission to reproduce copyright material:

*Daily Mail* for articles on pages 6, 7, 35, 252 and 283; *Daily Express* for the articles on pages 6 and 217; articles on pages 26 and 36 © Telegraph Media Group Limited 2008; Picture on page 33 © Nils Jorgensen/Rex Features; Citizens Advice for logo on page 45; picture on page 83 © Stockdisc/Corbis; picture on page 85 © Peter Dazeley/Photographer's Choice/Getty Images; picture on page 96 © rnl-Fotolia.com; picture on page 105 © Richard Sowersby/Rex Features; picture on page 112 © Ian Nicholson/PA Photos; article on page 179 © Fran Yeoman, NI Syndication Limited, 21 October 2008; article on page 202 © Russell Jenkins, NI Syndication Limited, 11 November 2008;  picture on page 235 © Gari Wyn Williams/Alamy; article on page 282 © NI Syndication Limited, 27 November 2008; picture on page 296 © OJO Images/Rex Features; picture on page 298 © Andreas M. Gross/WestEnd61/Rex Features; article on page 321 © Ben Hoyle, NI Syndication Limited; Oxford, Cambridge and RSA Examinations for OCR examination questions, AQA examination materials are reproduced by permission of the Assessment and Qualifications Alliance; © Crown copyright material is reproduced with the permission of the controller of HMSO.

Every effort has been made to track and acknowledge ownership of copyright. The publishers will be glad to make suitable arrangements with any copyright holders whom it has not been possible to contact.

# CHAPTER 1

# INTRODUCING LAW

*Gambler jailed*

Murder charge

Killer given life!

Headlines like these often provide the main source of information about law for the ordinary person, together, of course, with TV programmes such as *The Bill* or *Crimewatch*. People do not usually stop to think about law; it just exists. So the first question to ask is:

## What is law?

It is difficult to give a short simple answer to this question. There is no generally agreed definition, though many legal writers have attempted to define law. For example an English legal writer, Sir John Salmond, defined law as 'the body of principles recognised and applied by the State in the administration of justice'.

A simpler definition is that law is a set of rules. Many organisations, however, have rules and there are also rules of morality. So what makes law different from these? Rules become law when they are created or recognised by the Government. The rules will then be enforced by the courts. In other words, they are 'recognised and applied by the State'.

A rule in an organisation is a private matter and is not in force throughout the community. A moral rule is a matter for people's consciences; it will not be enforced by the Government.

In this country there is a complicated legal system to make sure that laws are obeyed; that is a system concerned with the 'administration of justice'.

## Why we need law

There are several reasons why it is necessary to have law. The main reasons are:

- to keep public order
- to protect individual freedoms
- to regulate relationships
- to set standards
- to provide solutions for legal problems.

## Keeping public order

There are people who believe that there should be no laws at all. These people are called anarchists, but it is difficult to imagine how any society would operate without at least some rules. What if there were no law against stealing; or assault; or murder? What do you think society would be like? It has been said that without law, man's life would be 'brutish, nasty and short'. These are very obvious examples of why we have law, but there are many other examples.

Try imagining what traffic conditions would be like if there were no law about which side of the road you should drive on ... or ... if everyone could ignore traffic lights! Most people will agree that this would lead to traffic chaos, numerous accidents and injuries.

So it is easy to see that rules (laws) are needed to keep public order.

## Protecting individual freedoms

The law recognises that individuals have rights. These are set out in the European Convention on Human Rights. This lists the freedoms and rights that everyone should have. These include:

- the right to liberty
- freedom of movement
- freedom from discrimination.

There are many others (see Chapter 38 for more details on human rights). However, without laws recognising these freedoms, they could be ignored. It is clearly important to protect individuals from being locked up for no reason. Of course, the law does recognise that there are occasions when people must lose their liberty, for example those sent to prison for committing crimes.

Many laws are concerned with protecting our rights and freedoms. In employment law there are laws forbidding discrimination against people on the basis of their gender, race, religion or age.

## Regulating relationships

In any society, people need to operate together in a wide variety of matters, so it is necessary to have laws to regulate these relationships. For example, when items are bought and sold, there must be rules as to what should happen if the item is faulty. Another example is when two people marry. There must be some rules, for example should there be a minimum age at which they can marry? If they divorce, how should their property be divided?

In the world of business, laws on a number of points are needed. How do you form a company and what are the rules about contracts and employment?

All these show that a modern society needs laws and the more complex society becomes, the more laws it will need. If you lived alone on a

desert island it would not be necessary to have any laws.

## Setting standards

In our increasingly complex and technological society, it is important that there are standards for many areas of everyday life. For example, it is important that there are standards for traffic. These are needed to prevent accidents. So this means that there are laws on many points to do with vehicles and roads. There are speed limits, set standards for the tyres and lights used on vehicles, limits on weight carried by vehicles and many, many more. Without these there would be far more accidents causing injury or death.

In some cases it does not matter what the rule is, as long as there is a law. The side of the road on which we drive is not important. What is important is that all traffic in the country drives on the same side. In the United Kingdom traffic drives on the left side of the road. In many other countries, traffic drives on the right side of the road.

Another area where it is important to have standards is in the production and sale of food. This is to prevent food being sold which is unfit for people to eat. If there were no such regulations, there would be many cases of food poisoning causing illness and in some cases death.

Yet another major area is in health and safety, especially at work. In the nineteenth century, when there were few rules about safety at work, large numbers of workers were killed in the course of their work. Since then many laws have been passed to make employers use safe working systems and protect workers from the risk of injury or death.

## Providing solutions for legal problems

It is also necessary to have a method of providing solutions for legal problems. The court system allows those with a legal problem to take the matter to court for a decision on it. Having a set of laws also allows lawyers to advise on any legal problems that arise.

### ACTIVITY

Make a list of areas of life in which you think it is necessary to have laws, and compare your list with other people's.

## Classification of law

From the references already made to various laws, it is obvious that there are many different types of law in England and Wales. Law can be divided up in several ways.

## International and national law

First there is an important distinction between international law – which governs disputes occurring between nations – and national law, which is concerned only with the rules of one country – in our case England and Wales. Scotland has its own municipal law. That is why there have already been references to England and Wales in this book, rather than Great Britain or the United Kingdom.

## Public and private law

The second main division is between public and private law; public law involves the State or Government in some way while private law (often called civil law) is concerned only with disputes between private individuals or businesses. If you bought a DVD player which did not work you would certainly want to have it changed for one that did work or to have your money back. This type of dispute comes under private law since it concerns only you and the shop.

Both public law and private law can be further divided. Public law may be divided into:

(a) constitutional law – dealing with the method of government, for example laws setting out who has the right to vote at a general election
(b) administrative law – which governs how public bodies such as local councils should operate
(c) criminal law – which states what behaviour is forbidden at risk of punishment; it involves the State on one side and one or more individuals accused of a particular crime on the other side. The headlines at the beginning of this chapter all involved criminal law.

Private (civil) law has many branches. Look at the following situations, all of which are covered by different areas of civil law:

- John is behind with the hire-purchase payments on his car – contract law
- Imran is injured in a car crash caused by Leanne – tort law
- Sheila and Henry decide their marriage has broken down – family law
- Alysha wants to start a new company – company law
- David claims he has been unfairly dismissed from work – employment law
- William has died and not left his wife any money – inheritance law.

These are just a few examples of civil law. It covers a wide variety of situations.

Figure 1.1 below summarises the different divisions of law.

## Differences between civil and criminal law

For our purposes the distinction between civil and criminal law is the most important division in law. It is important to know whether a case is civil or criminal as it affects how the case is started, who starts it, in which court it will be heard and what powers are available to the judge.

## Criminal cases

Criminal cases are where the State accuses someone of a crime. The case is usually taken (prosecuted) by the Crown Prosecution Service. The case takes place in the Magistrates' Court or the Crown Court. The purpose of the trial is to decide whether the defendant is guilty or not guilty. Quite often the defendant will admit his or her guilt by pleading guilty. When someone admits their guilt or is found guilty by a court, they are sentenced. There are a number of different ways in which a court can deal with a person who is guilty of a crime. For example, the court may send them to prison, give them work to do in the community or fine them.

The criminal law has developed to protect the community. There are several different types of crime. For example, there are offences against the person, such as assault; offences against property, such as theft; and offences against public order, such as riot.

## Civil cases

These are cases taken by individual people or businesses in order to claim or enforce a right. The person starting the case is called the claimant. There are different types of civil case. For example, there may be a breach of contract (see Sources D and E in Activity 3) or there may be a claim for damage done through the negligence of another person (this is known as a civil wrong or tort). Usually the person making the claim wants money to compensate for what has happened.

In civil cases the main purpose is to investigate disputes between the parties and decide whether the defendant is liable to pay compensation. There is no 'punishment' involved. The court is trying to put the people back in the position they would have been in if the contract had been carried out properly or the tort not happened.

Figure 1.2 gives a summary of some of the most important differences between civil and criminal law.

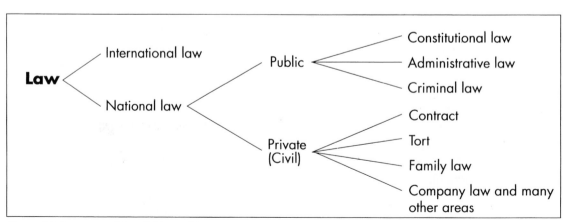

Figure 1.1 Summary of the divisions of law

# Case name

The name of the case will usually tell you if the case is criminal or civil. In the examples at the bottom of Figure 1.2 'R' stands for Rex (which means King) or Regina (which means Queen), showing that the case has been started by the State. Some criminal cases will be started by the Director of Public Prosecutions and this is always written as DPP in a case name. It is also possible to have a criminal case taken by the Attorney-General.

In each case name, the small 'v' between the names means 'versus' (Latin for against). The year of the case is given after the names. So, later in this book you will see the case of *R v Moloney* (1985). This is a criminal case.

In the civil cases the surname of the person starting the case is given first, then the surname of the person being sued (taking the case against). If a company is involved in a case, then the company's name is used. The legal term for the person starting the case is the *claimant*. Later in this book you will find the case of *Beale v Taylor* (1967). This is a civil case.

## ACTIVITY

### Activity 1

Find the cases of *R v Moloney* (1985) and the case of *Beale v Taylor* (1967). There is a case index at the back of the book. Write the facts of the two cases in your own words. Explain why *R v Moloney* (1985) is a criminal case and why *Beale v Taylor* (1967) is a civil case.

| | CRIMINAL<br>Public law | CIVIL<br>Private law |
|---|---|---|
| Purpose of the law | To maintain law and order<br>To protect society<br>To punish offenders | To uphold individual's rights<br>To compensate the individual |
| Purpose of the trial | To decide if the defendant is guilty | To decide if there is a breach of rights |
| Person starting the case | The State, usually through the Crown Prosecution Service | The individual whose rights have been affected |
| Legal name for person starting case | Prosecutor | Claimant |
| Courts used to hear cases | Magistrates' Court OR Crown Court | County Court OR High Court |
| Person/persons making the decision | Magistrates OR Jury | Judge<br>Very rarely a jury |
| Standard of proof | Beyond reasonable doubt | On the balance of probabilities |
| Decision | The defendant is found guilty or not guilty | The claimant wins or loses case<br>The defendant may be liable to pay compensation |
| Powers of the court | Prison, fine, discharge, community order | Award of damages (money), injunction |
| Name of the case | *R v Smith*<br>*DPP v Smith* | *Jones v Smith*<br>*XYZ Company Ltd v Smith* |

Figure 1.2 Differences between civil and criminal law

# The standard of proof

Another important difference between civil and criminal cases is what is called the burden of proof or the standard to which the case has to be proved. In criminal cases this standard is a high one, *beyond reasonable doubt*, since a conviction could result in the defendant going to prison for a long time. In civil cases the standard is lower, *on balance of probabilities*. This is because the judge has to decide for one party or the other and so gives judgment for the party he or she thinks is most probably right.

## ACTIVITY

### Activity 2

Sources A, B and C are newspaper extracts about criminal cases. Read the sources and answer the questions below.

### Source A

**Gang smile in court as they are jailed for killing homeowner who caught them burgling**

Three youths smirked in court as they were jailed for life for the murder of a father of three. Mark Witherall, 47, was kicked and stamped to death after he found the gang burgling his house.

A judge said they had turned on their victim 'like a pack of hyenas'. There was applause in the public gallery of Maidstone Crown Court as the three were led away to start their sentences.

Curtis Delima, 19, 21-year-old Mark Elliott and Gerry Cusden, 16 – all from Whitstable, Kent – had been found guilty of murdering Mr Witherall last month following a nine-week trial.

*(Source: an article by Christian Gysin, Mail Online, 19 April 2008)*

### Source B

**Ellie death: Grandmother acquitted**

The grandmother of dog attack victim Ellie Lawrenson has been acquitted of her manslaughter. The jury of seven men and five women at Liverpool Crown Court found Jacqueline Simpson, 45, innocent after a six-day trial.

Ellie was killed by her uncle Kiel Simpson's pit bull terrier on New Year's Eve after Simpson, who had smoked 10 joints and drunk two bottles of wine, let it in. Ellie, killed at Simpson's home in St Helens, Merseyside, had 72 injuries.

The maximum sentence for manslaughter is life imprisonment. Hearing the verdict, Simpson wiped her eyes.

Speaking to the jury, the judge said: 'This is an unusual case which had given rise to very strong emotions. Suffice to say, the greatest sentence passed in this case is a life sentence of regret this lady has passed on herself.'

*(Source: Daily Express, 11 September 2007)*

### Source C

**Dyer sentenced for club burglary**

A footballer was sentenced for a burglary of a nightclub staffroom during which cash and mobile phones were stolen.

Southampton midfielder, Nathan Dyer, pleaded guilty at Portsmouth Magistrates' Court to the charge of non-dwelling burglary and was ordered to carry out 60 hours of community service.

The 20-year-old said he was ashamed after he admitted rummaging through bags belonging to staff at the Bar Bluu club on Southsea seafront on February 28. He said he did not steal any of the items during the incident, which involved four other men.

Chairman of the Bench Christopher Malone also ordered Dyer, who was dressed in a dark suit with black tie, to pay a total of £392.50 compensation to the four victims as well as £65 costs.

He warned Dyer that if he did not complete the 60 hours of unpaid work satisfactorily within a 12-month period he could face imprisonment.

*(Source: Daily Express, 25 July 2008)*

## Questions

1. In which courts were the cases in the three sources heard?
2. In which case was the defendant found not guilty?
3. In which case did the defendant plead guilty?
4. What different punishments were used in the cases in Sources A and C?

## ACTIVITY

### Activity 3

Sources D and E are newspaper extracts about civil cases. Read them and answer the questions below.

### Source D

**Cheating husband loses bid to claim back £3,000 he spent on his former mistress**

A cheating husband who tried to reclaim £3,000 from his mistress after their affair turned sour has lost his court battle for a refund.

Health and safety consultant Geoffrey Fitch, 60, embarked on a two-year relationship with Gillian Mitchell, who visited lonely hearts websites.

A judge heard that he gave the 53-year-old divorced mother-of-three jewellery and took her on dinner dates, visits to the theatre and trips abroad.

But only two weeks after they moved in together their on-off relationship ended when Mr Fitch accused Mrs Mitchell of cheating on him.

'She constantly took telephone calls from another man, or men, which reinforces my claim that she has a number of different partners.'

Mr Fitch, of Ringmer, East Sussex, said he gave Mrs Mitchell a £2,000 loan to pay off a council tax bill and paid off an £800 debt and £157 garage bill. He launched legal action to try to recoup the cash.

*(Source: Mail Online, 1 September 2008)*

### Source E

**Rapper Rhymes wins court battle to perform**

American rap star Busta Rhymes today won his High Court battle for the right to perform at a charity concert tonight.

Rhymes, real name Trevor George Smith Jr, was refused permission to enter the UK at London City Airport yesterday morning because of criminal convictions in the USA.

The 36-year-old rapper is performing tonight at the Orange RockCorps gig at the Royal Albert Hall.

The concert was due to start at 7–7.30 pm

and this afternoon Rhymes won his race against time to get the legal all-clear to perform.

The Judge emphasised the extraordinary nature of the case and stressed that he was acting so as not to disappoint the thousands of fans who, even as he was giving his judgment, were heading to the Royal Albert Hall.

*(Source: The Independent, 26 September 2008)*

Questions

1. In which courts were the cases in Sources D and E heard? Are they different from the courts mentioned in Sources A, B and C in the previous activity?

2. In Source D, explain in your own words who took the case to court and why.

3. Did the claimant in Source D win or lose the case?

4. Did the claimant in Source E win or lose the case?

## Double liability

Sometimes one action can be in breach of two types of law. This gives rise to what is known as double liability; that means that two separate court cases may take place. Double liability can occur wherever there is a crime and, in the course of that crime, an individual's rights are affected. The most common occurrence of this is where there is a road traffic offence (involving criminal law) and someone is injured as a result so that he wants to claim damages (under the civil law called *tort*).

Let us take an imaginary example. Mr Brown drives through a red traffic light and crashes into Mrs Green's car, damaging her car and causing minor injuries to her.

First, Mr Brown has committed a crime by going through the red light. This is the criminal case and will be started by the police and then taken over by the Crown Prosecution Service. Mr Brown will be summonsed to appear at the Magistrates' Court. If he disputes the case by claiming the lights were green, the magistrates will hear evidence and decide if he is guilty or not guilty. If they decide he is guilty, they have the powers to order him to pay a fine, put penalty points on his driving licence or even disqualify him from driving. In other words they are punishing him for his bad driving.

Second, Mrs Green will want to claim compensation, both to pay the cost of repairing her car and for her injuries. This means she will have to start another case against Mr Brown in the County Court to make her claim. This is the civil case. The judge will have to decide if Mr Brown was negligent and caused her injuries. If he decides this is so, then he will award damages to Mrs Green. This will be money to pay for the repairs to her car and another sum of money as compensation for her injuries.

So the one act of driving through red lights by Mr Brown means that he has two cases taken against him in two different courts. This is why it is called double liability.

### BRIEF SUMMARY OF CHAPTER

**Definition of law**
■ set of rules applied by the State

**Reasons for having law**
■ keeps public order
■ protects individual freedoms and rights
■ regulates life, for example business, family

**Civil and criminal law**
■ have different purposes and different courts

# CHAPTER 2

# THE HIERARCHY OF THE COURTS

In Chapter 1 we looked at what law is and why we need to have laws. Where there is a system of law, there must a system of courts to enforce that law.

In Chapter 1 we also saw that there are criminal cases and civil cases and that each of these are dealt with in their own separate courts. For both criminal and civil cases there are courts where cases are dealt with originally in the first instance and a decision made.

In every fair legal system there also needs to be a method of appealing against a decision made by the original court. In England and Wales there are courts of appeal for both criminal and civil cases.

## Criminal courts

The two criminal courts where defendants are tried for crimes are:

- Magistrates' Courts
- Crown Court.

## Magistrates' Courts

There are about 400 Magistrates' Courts throughout England and Wales. Cases are tried either by a professional judge, known as a District Judge, or by a panel of non-lawyers known as lay magistrates. These are ordinary people from the local community who have been appointed to sit as magistrates. There is more detail about Magistrates' Courts in Chapter 3.

## Crown Court

There are about 90 Crown Courts in major towns and cities throughout England and Wales.

Cases at the Crown Court are tried by a judge and jury. The jury has 12 ordinary people on it. The judge decides any points of law. The jury decides whether, on the facts of the case, the defendant is guilty or not guilty. There is more detail about the Crown Court in Chapter 4.

### ACTIVITY

**Activity 1**

**Find out which is your nearest:**

(a) Magistrates' Courts

(b) Crown Court

## Criminal appeal courts

The courts which hear appeals on criminal cases are:

- Crown Court (for most appeals from the Magistrates' Courts)
- High Court Administrative Court (for appeals from the Magistrates' Courts on points of law)
- Court of Appeal (Criminal Division) for appeals from the Crown Court
- Supreme Court for a further appeal from the Court of Appeal (NB This used to be the House of Lords).

The highest appeal court is the Supreme Court. This only hears appeals on important points of law. The structure of the criminal courts is shown in Figure 2.1.

Further detail on appeals from the Magistrates' Courts is given in Chapter 3. Further detail on appeals from the Crown Court is given in Chapter 4.

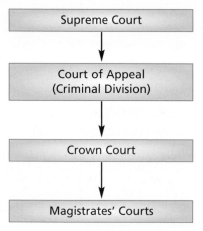

**Figure 2.1** The hierarchy of the criminal courts

## Civil courts

The two civil courts where a civil case can be heard for the first time are:

• County Court
• High Court.

The civil court in which a particular case is dealt with depends mainly on the amount of money claimed and/or the complexity of the case.

### County Court

There are about 200 County Courts in towns and cities throughout England and Wales. Cases are decided by judges. It is very, very rare for any case in the County Court to be decided by a jury.

District judges deal with smaller claims. Circuit judges deal with larger claims.

### High Court

The High Court is based in London. However, judges from the High Court in London also go to some of the major cities such as Bristol,

Birmingham, Manchester or Newcastle to deal with cases.

The High Court deals with claims of more than £15,000. It does not hear anything smaller than this. Usually claims in the High Court are for much larger amounts of money or for cases which are very complicated or involve a point of law.

The High Court has three Divisions. Each Division specialises in different types of civil case. The Divisions are:

• Chancery Division – specialising in company law, partnerships and land law
• Queen's Bench Division – specialising in cases on contract law and tort
• Family Division – specialising in family cases.

## Civil appeal courts

There are also courts to hear appeals on civil cases. These are:

• High Court – for appeals from the County Court
• Court of Appeal (Civil Division) – for appeals from the High Court
• Supreme Court – for a further appeal from the Court of Appeal (NB This used to be the House of Lords).

The structure of the civil courts is shown in Figure 2.2.

**Figure 2.2** The hierarchy of the civil courts

Details of what cases are heard in each court and how civil cases are started are given in Chapter 7.

## ACTIVITY

### Activity 2

Fill in the gaps in the description of the court structure by selecting the appropriate word or phrase from the list in the box below the text. Note that you may need to use some words or phrases more than once.

There are two types of court which hear criminal cases in England and Wales. These are the Magistrates' Courts and the ...................................... . Lay ...................................... hear cases in the Magistrates' Courts. A jury decides whether the defendant is guilty or not guilty in the ...................................... .

Appeals from the Magistrates' Courts are usually made to the ......................................, but it is possible to appeal on ...................................... to the High Court (Administrative Court).

There are two types of court which hear civil cases in England and Wales. These are the ...................................... and the High Court. The High Court has three divisions, the ...................................... Division, the Queen's Bench Division and the Family Division.

An appeal from the High Court is made to the ...................................... . A further appeal can be made to the ...................................... . This is the highest court in our legal system.

| a point of law | Appeal Court |
| Chancery | County Court |
| Court of Appeal (Civil Division) | |
| Court of Appeal (Criminal Division) | |
| Crown Court | magistrates |
| jury | Magistrates' Courts |
| sentence | Supreme Court |

|  | CRIMINAL COURTS | CIVIL COURTS |
|---|---|---|
| Courts of trial | Magistrates' Courts<br>*tries lower level of offences* | County Court<br>*deals with smaller claims and less complex cases* |
|  | Crown Court<br>*tries more serious offences* | High Court<br>*hears claims for large amounts of money and complex cases* |
| Courts of Appeal | Crown Court<br>*normal route of appeal from the Magistrates' Courts* | High Court<br>*hears appeals from the County Court* |
|  | High Court Administrative Court<br>*hears appeals from Magistrates' Courts on points of law* | Court of Appeal (Civil Division)<br>*hears appeals from High Court cases* |
|  | Court of Appeal (Criminal Division)<br>*hears appeals from cases tried in the Crown Court* | |
| Further appeal | Supreme Court | Supreme Court |

Figure 2.3 Summary of criminal and civil courts

## BRIEF SUMMARY OF CHAPTER

**Criminal courts where defendants are tried for crimes**

- Magistrates' Courts – less serious offences
- Crown Court – more serious offences

**Courts which hear appeals on criminal cases**

- Crown Court – appeals from the Magistrates' Courts
- High Court Administrative Court – appeals from the Magistrates' Courts on a point of law
- Court of Appeal (Criminal Division) – appeals from the Crown Court
- Supreme Court – appeals from the Court of Appeal

**Civil courts where a civil case can be heard for the first time**

- County Court
- High Court
- The court used depends on the amount claimed and the complexity of the case

**Courts which hear appeals on civil cases**

- High Court – appeals from the County Court
- Court of Appeal (Civil Division) – appeals from the High Court
- Supreme Court – appeals from the Court of Appeal

# CHAPTER 3

# CRIMINAL COURTS: MAGISTRATES' COURTS

Before a defendant is tried at a Magistrates' Court or the Crown Court, there are a number of events which must occur. These are known as pre-trial matters.

## Pre-trial

### Summons or arrest

Criminal cases are started in one of two ways. The accused person may be either:

- summoned to court, or
- arrested by the police and charged with an offence.

### Summons

A summons is a document sent by post to the accused person. It tells them they must attend at court on the date given in the letter. This method of starting criminal proceedings is used for less serious offences. For example, many driving offences are started in this way.

A summons can only be used where the offender's name and address are known.

### Arrest

For more serious offences, the suspected person will be arrested by the police. The police will investigate the matter by interviewing the suspect and witnesses. The police may also take fingerprints and DNA samples from the suspect.

When the police believe they have enough evidence against the suspect, they will charge him or her with the relevant offence or offences. If the case is complicated, then the police will consult a member of the Crown Prosecution Service before charging the suspect with an offence.

### Police bail

After the suspect has been charged the police may decide to allow them bail. This means the police tell the accused that they can go free but must attend at the Magistrates' Courts on a certain date.

The police can place conditions on bail. For example, they can order the accused person to hand over his or her passport. This is to try to ensure that the person does not leave the country. Or they can order the person to report once or twice a week to a local police station. This also is a way of making sure that the person has not run away and will go to court on the set date. There are other conditions that can be imposed. These are explained below.

If the police feel that the accused is too dangerous to release on bail, or is likely to run away and not attend court, the police will take the accused to the local Magistrates' Courts as soon as possible. This usually within 24 hours.

The magistrates will then decide whether the accused should be allowed bail while awaiting trial or whether he or she should be kept in custody. There is more information on bail below.

## The Crown Prosecution Service

The Crown Prosecution Service (CPS) is responsible for prosecuting most cases in the criminal courts.

Some CPS staff work in key police stations in what are known as Criminal Justice Units, so that they can advise the police at early stages of cases. In particular CPS staff advise on the correct charges when the police charge the suspect.

After the defendant has been charged all the information the police have collected is sent to the Crown Prosecution Service. A CPS case worker will decide if there is enough evidence for the case to go ahead.

## Code for Crown Prosecutors

There is a Code for Crown Prosecutors to help them decide when to prosecute. In making this decision the two key tests are:

1. the evidential test – is there a realistic prospect of conviction?
2. whether it is in the public interest to prosecute.

The Code also places emphasis on fairness and the interests of justice as the most important principles. The views of the victim should be taken into account when considering whether it is in the public interest to prosecute. But this is only one factor, and Crown Prosecutors must balance all factors for and against prosecution carefully and fairly. About one in eight cases are discontinued.

When the CPS decide that the case should go ahead, then the CPS will arrange for a lawyer to prosecute the case at court. This may be a lawyer from the CPS or they may instruct an independent lawyer to act as prosecutor.

## Duty solicitors

While a suspect is being held by the police at a police station, he or she has the right to consult a lawyer. The suspect can ask to see their own lawyer, if they have one, but most suspects will consult with a duty solicitor.

When someone is arrested and taken to a police station, the custody officer at that police station must tell the person about the duty solicitor scheme. This is a rota system of solicitors on call in the area who can give advice to anyone in police custody. Advice may be given over the phone or for some cases a lawyer may go to the police station. This service is free to the defendant.

There is also a duty solicitor scheme for Magistrates' Courts, so that a defendant who attends court without his or her own lawyer has the chance to get advice about their case. This service is also free.

## Bail

There are various stages in the process when a person may be granted bail. Bail means being allowed to be at liberty, rather than being held in custody, while awaiting the next stage in the criminal process.

### Police bail

The first point at which an arrested person may be given bail is during the police investigation. The police may bail a suspect with a condition that he or she return to the police station on a set date.

The second point at which the police may give bail to a suspect is when they have charged him or her. In this instance he or she is given a date when they must attend court.

### Bail at court

Where the police are not willing to bail an accused person, the police must arrange for that person to appear before a Magistrates' Court as soon as possible. If, as happens in most cases, the court cannot deal with the whole case at that first hearing, the magistrates will then make the decision on whether the accused should be given bail or stay in custody until the next court hearing. If an accused person is not given bail it is said that they are *remanded in custody*.

The main rules about bail are set out in the Bail Act 1976. This Act starts with the presumption that bail should be granted. However, if good reasons are shown, bail may be refused.

Bail can be refused if there are substantial reasons for believing that the defendant, if released on bail, would:

**(a)** fail to surrender, that is, not attend court for the next hearing
**(b)** commit further offences
**(c)** interfere with witnesses.

When making their decision the magistrates look at various factors. These include:

**(a)** the nature and seriousness of the offence
**(b)** the past record of the defendant
**(c)** the defendant's ties with the community; for example, does he or she live in the area?
**(d)** whether the defendant has previously 'jumped' bail. In other words, whether he or she has failed to attend court when bailed to do so on a previous occasion.

If the magistrates decide not to grant bail they must give their reasons for the refusal.

## Conditions

When the police or the magistrates decide to grant bail they may impose conditions on that bail. Such conditions can include an order that:

• the accused must hand in his passport
• the accused must live at a bail hostel, or
• the accused must report to the police at set times.

In addition it is possible to ask for a *surety*. A surety is another person who is prepared to promise that they will pay the court a certain sum of money if the defendant fails to attend court. No money is paid unless the accused fails to answer to his bail.

This system is different from that in other countries, especially the USA, where the surety must pay the money into court before the defendant is released on bail, but gets the money back when the defendant attends court as required.

## ACTIVITY

### Activity 1

Explain whether the defendant in each of the following situations is likely to be given bail or not.

1. Felicity is accused of the theft of £2,000. She is married and lives locally. She has one previous conviction for theft.

2. William is accused of robbery. During the robbery it is alleged that he threatened the victim with a gun. He has no previous convictions.

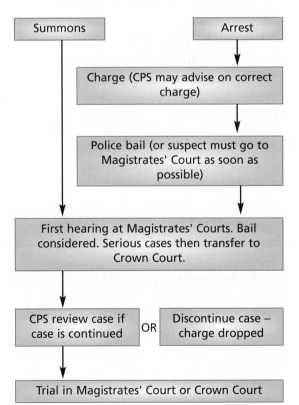

**Figure 3.1** Flow chart of pre-trial matters in criminal cases

## Classification of offences

We have seen that there are two types of court which deal with criminal cases: the Magistrates' Court and the Crown Court. To understand the way cases are allocated to these courts it is necessary to understand how crimes are classified. This is done by dividing crimes into minor crimes, middle-range crimes and serious crimes and making different arrangements for each group.

In legal terms these three categories of crime are called:

- summary offences (minor crimes)
- offences triable either way (middle-range crimes)
- indictable offences (serious crimes).

The differences between these three categories of crime are summarised below in Figure 3.2.

### Summary offences

Summary offences are offences that can be tried only in a Magistrates' Court and are the least serious crimes. There are many different offences in this category, including nearly all driving offences. Other examples are taking a vehicle without consent, minor assaults and being found drunk in a public place.

## Offences triable either way

These are offences that can be tried either in the Magistrates' Court or in the Crown Court. They are the middle range of crimes and include theft and assault causing actual bodily harm.

If a defendant is pleading not guilty to a triable either way offence he has the right to ask for the case to be tried by a judge and jury at the Crown Court, or he can agree to the case being tried by the magistrates at the Magistrates' Court.

The magistrates can also decide if the case is suitable for them to try. If they think it is too serious then they can send the defendant to the Crown Court for trial.

To explain how these provisions work, let's use theft as an example. Theft can be of small items from a shop: this type of case is clearly suitable for magistrates to try, but the defendant can still choose to be tried at the Crown Court.

However, theft can be of very much larger items or amounts of money. If the defendant was charged with stealing £50,000 from his employer, then the magistrates would decide that this was too serious for them to deal with. The magistrates would send the case to the Crown Court. The defendant could not choose to be tried by the magistrates.

| Category of offence | Place of trial | Examples of offence |
|---|---|---|
| Summary | Magistrates' Court | Driving without insurance<br>Taking a vehicle without consent<br>Common assault |
| Triable either way | Magistrates' Court<br>OR<br>Crown Court | Theft<br>Assault causing actual bodily harm |
| Indictable | Crown Court | Murder<br>Manslaughter<br>Rape |

Figure 3.2 The three categories of offence

# Indictable offences

These are offences that can be tried only at the Crown Court by a judge and jury. They are the more serious offences and include murder, manslaughter, rape and robbery. These offences are called indictable (pronounced in-dye-table) offences because they are tried on indictment (pronounced in-dye-t-ment), that is, the document on which the charges are written down.

## ACTIVITY

### Activity 2

Decide whether the following statements are true or false.

1. The police prosecute criminal cases in the courts. TRUE/FALSE
2. The police are advised on what charge to make against an offender by the Crown Prosecution Service. TRUE/FALSE
3. The Crown Prosecution Service will decide if it is in the public interest to prosecute. TRUE/FALSE
4. A summons is a document ordering the defendant to attend court. TRUE/FALSE
5. Suspects held at a police station always have to pay for advice from a lawyer. TRUE/FALSE
6. The police cannot bail a defendant. TRUE/FALSE
7. Magistrates can place conditions on bail. TRUE/FALSE

## The trial at the Magistrates' Court

At the start of any case the clerk of the court will check the defendant's name and address and then ask whether he or she pleads guilty or not guilty. (Remember that summary offences have to be tried at the Magistrates' Court.) Over 90 per cent of defendants plead guilty and the following is a short summary of the normal procedure in such cases.

# Guilty plea

1. The court will be given a brief summary of the facts of the case by the CPS prosecutor.
2. The defendant is asked if he or she agrees with those facts (if he does not the magistrates may have to hold an enquiry as to the facts).
3. The defendant's past record of convictions, if any, is given to the court.
4. Information about the defendant's financial position is given to the magistrates. This is very important if the magistrates decide to fine the defendant.
5. Any relevant reports are given to the court; for example there may be a pre-sentence report prepared by a probation officer or a medical report.
6. The defendant or his lawyer can then explain anything he wants to about the reasons for committing the crime or his personal circumstances. This is called making a speech in mitigation.
7. The magistrates decide the sentence.

## Not guilty plea

When a defendant pleads not guilty the case, naturally, is longer and more complicated since both sides will want to call witnesses. As the prosecution have to prove the charge, they always start the procedure, usually making a short speech explaining to the magistrates what the case is about and how they hope to prove it.

Then the prosecution calls their witnesses and asks them questions about what they saw or heard. The defence are allowed to cross-examine the witnesses in order to try to show that their evidence is not reliable.

Once all the prosecution witnesses have given evidence, then the defence calls its witnesses, including the defendant if he wishes to give evidence. The procedure follows the same pattern as for prosecution witnesses, this time with the defence asking the questions first and the prosecution cross-examining afterwards.

When all the evidence has been given the defence will make a speech to the magistrates, trying to persuade them that the case has not been proved 'beyond reasonable doubt', pointing out the weaknesses in the prosecution evidence.

The magistrates then decide whether the defendant is guilty or not guilty.

If the magistrates find the defendant guilty, they hear about his past convictions, if any, and his background and financial situation. They may also look at reports about the defendant. The defence can make a speech in mitigation.

Finally the magistrates decide what sentence they will impose on the defendant.

Figure 3.3 is a flow chart of the proceedings in the Magistrates' Court. It shows what happens for cases in which the defendant pleads guilty and for cases where the defendant pleads not guilty.

## The magistrates' role

In cases in the Magistrates' Courts where a defendant pleads not guilty, the magistrates who hear the case have two roles.

1. They decide if the defendant is guilty or not guilty.
2. If they find the defendant guilty, they decide on sentence.

This is different to cases in the Crown Court where the jury decide if the defendant is guilty or not guilty and then the judge decides the sentence.

As lay magistrates are not lawyers, they have a magistrates' clerk (legal adviser) at court to help them with any points of law that have to be decided.

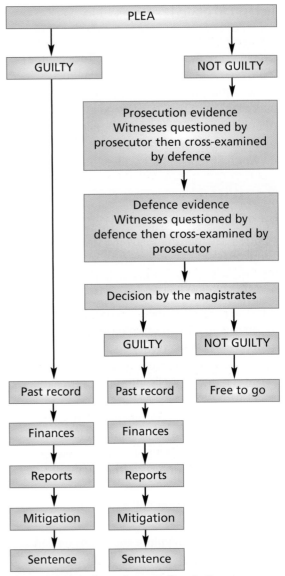

Figure 3.3 Flow chart of proceedings in the Magistrates' Court

## Post-trial

After a trial where a defendant has been found guilty there are two matters which arise. The first is that the magistrates have to sentence the defendant. This will happen in every case where the defendant is guilty.

The second post-trial matter is whether the defendant or the prosecution wish to appeal against the decision of the magistrates.

## Sentencing

Before magistrates sentence a defendant, they will hear about the defendant's past convictions, if any, and his or her background and financial situation. They may also have a pre-sentence report prepared by a probation officer or a medical report about the defendant.

The defendant or his or her lawyer can make a speech explaining to the magistrates any reasons, such as family circumstances – perhaps he or she has a disabled child – or other reasons why they should be lenient.

The magistrates then have to decide what sentence to pass on the defendant. The main sentences available to them are:

- custody (sending the defendant to prison)
- a community order
- a fine
- a discharge.

For driving cases the magistrates can also disqualify the defendant from driving for a set amount of time.

## Custody

Prison is only available for offenders aged 21 and over. Offenders aged 18 to 20 are sent to a Young Offenders' Institution as a custodial sentence.

A defendant can only be sent to prison for a maximum of 6 months by magistrates for one offence or 12 months for two or more offences. If the magistrates feel that the defendant should be given a longer sentence then they must send the defendant to the Crown Court for sentencing.

## Community orders

The court can make a community order on offenders aged 16 and over. This is a sentence which is carried out in the community. The magistrates can impose various requirements on the defendant. These include:

- an unpaid work requirement
- a curfew requirement
- a supervision requirement
- a drug rehabilitation requirement
- an alcohol treatment requirement.

The magistrates can 'mix and match' requirements allowing them to create a 'package' which fits the case.

## Unpaid work requirement

An offender can be ordered to do up to 300 hours' work on community projects. This might involve painting school buildings or gardening for elderly people. The offender will usually work an eight-hour day on Saturday or Sunday until the number of hours set by the court is completed.

## Curfew requirement

An offender is required to stay at a set address during certain hours (usually 6 pm to 6 am). They are usually tagged so that it is easy to check if they are obeying the curfew. A curfew cannot be for more than 12 hours in any day and it is for a maximum of six months.

## Supervision requirement

For this requirement the offender is placed under the supervision of a probation officer for a period of up to three years. During the period of supervision the offender must attend appointments with the supervising officer or with any other person decided by the supervising officer.

## Drug rehabilitation and alcohol treatment

Much crime is linked to drug and alcohol abuse and the idea behind these two requirements is to tackle the causes of crime, hopefully preventing further offences.

## Fines

Magistrates can fine up to a maximum of £5,000. For those under 18 years old there are lower maximum fines. In deciding the amount of a fine the court must take into account both the seriousness of the offence and the financial circumstances of the offender. Fines are the most common method of sentencing a defendant in the Magistrates' Courts. Over 70 per cent of guilty defendants are dealt with in this way.

## Discharges

For minor offences and particularly for first time offenders the courts can decide not to punish them but to discharge them, either conditionally or absolutely.

A conditional discharge carries the condition that the offender must not re-offend within a certain time, up to three years; if he or she breaks this condition he or she can be resentenced for the original offence.

An absolute discharge means that there are no conditions attached. The reason for using discharges is that the majority of first time offenders will be sufficiently punished by the fact that they have appeared in court and are unlikely to commit any further offences.

Discharges can be used for offenders of any age (over the age of 10) and are very common for younger offenders.

## Sentencing handbook

Magistrates have a sentencing handbook which suggests the type of sentence that is suitable in certain circumstances.

# Appeals

The defendant has the right to appeal against both conviction and/or sentence after a trial in the Magistrates' Court.

The defendant has a choice of two different appeal routes. These are:
• to the High Court Administrative Court, or
• to the Crown Court.

An appeal to the High Court Administrative Court can only be made when the appeal is about a point of law. In such cases there is no dispute about the facts of the case. The facts will be set out by the Magistrates' Court and sent to the High Court Administrative Court. The judges in this court then consider the law and decide how it operates on the facts as stated by the Magistrates' Court. Appeals on points of law only happen in about 50 or 60 cases a year.

The normal appeal route is to the Crown Court where the case is retried by a judge sitting with two magistrates. After this there is normally no further appeal. The only exception is if there then is a point of law in dispute. In these cases there is a possible appeal to the High Court Administrative Court. This is very rarely used. It only happens in about 10 to 20 cases a year.

## Further appeal

When the High Court Administrative Court has decided an appeal, there is a possible further appeal to the Supreme Court. Such an appeal has to be on point of law of general importance and it is also necessary to get permission to appeal.

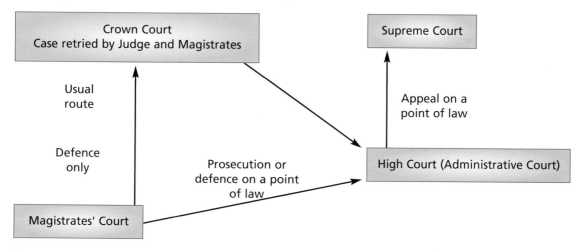

Figure 3.4 Appeals from the Magistrates' Courts

## BRIEF SUMMARY OF CHAPTER

**Criminal Cases**

- Criminal cases are started by either summonsing or arresting the defendant

**Crown Prosecution Service**

- The Crown Prosecution Service is responsible for prosecuting cases in the criminal courts

**Duty Solicitor**

- A defendant may ask to see a duty solicitor either at the police station or at court

**Bail**

- A defendant will either be bailed to the next court appearance or remanded in custody

- The Bail Act 1976 has a presumption that bail should be granted, but bail can be refused for good reason

**The three categories of crime**

- summary offences (minor crimes)

- offences triable either way (middle-range crimes)

- indictable offences (serious crimes)

**The ways to try a case**

- Summary offences can only be tried in the Magistrates' Courts

- Triable either way offences can be tried in either the Magistrates' Courts or the Crown Court

- Indictable offences can only be tried at the Crown Court

- In the Magistrates' Courts the cases are tried by magistrates

- In the Crown Court the cases are tried by a judge and a jury of 12

**The main sentences available to punish a guilty defendant**

- custody (sending the defendant to prison)

- community orders

- fines

- discharges

## EXAMINATION QUESTION

Identify **four** different bail conditions which can be imposed by the police or in court.

(4 marks)

*AQA Specimen Paper*

# CHAPTER 4

# CRIMINAL COURTS: CROWN COURT

## The Crown Court

The Crown Court hears all indictable criminal cases as well as any triable either way cases that are sent from the Magistrates' Court for trial at the Crown Court. The total number of cases tried at the Crown Court each year is about 80,000. The court sits in some 90 towns and cities throughout England and Wales.

## Trial on indictment

At the Crown Court the defendant is tried on indictment (pronounced in-dye-t-ment). An indictment is the document setting out the charges against the defendant; if the defendant is accused of committing only one crime, the indictment will contain only that charge or count. If the defendant is accused of committing several crimes then the indictment will list each one. Figure 4.1 shows a sample indictment.

---

**BARCHESTER CROWN COURT**

The Queen v Anthony Absolute charged as follows:

STATEMENT OF OFFENCE
Theft contrary to section 1(1) of the Theft Act 1968

PARTICULARS OF OFFENCE
Anthony Absolute on the 2nd day of March 2009 stole a gold watch belonging to Donald Duck

---

Figure 4.1 A sample indictment

## Role of the judge

### Before the trial

The defendant will appear before a judge alone to start with. The defendant will be asked whether he pleads guilty or not guilty. If he is pleading not guilty he will have to be tried by a jury.

The judge will give directions about what witnesses should attend the trial and make sure that any other evidence the prosecution or defence wish to produce is ready for the trial.

### Guilty plea

If a defendant pleads guilty a jury will not be used, but a judge will hear information about both the crime and the defendant and will decide on the sentence. Over six out of every ten defendants pleads guilty at the Crown Court.

### At the trial

When a defendant is tried at the Crown Court, the trial is held with a judge and a jury. The judge makes all decisions about points of law. For example, the judge will decide if evidence is admissible or not (ie if it is legally allowed to be used in the trial).

The procedure is similar to that in the Magistrates' Court. The prosecution call their evidence first as it is for the prosecution to prove the charge against the defendant. All prosecution witnesses can be cross-examined by the defence.

If the prosecution do not have sufficient evidence the defence will ask the judge to rule that there is insufficient evidence for the case to go to the jury. About one in five of all trials at the Crown Court are stopped by the judge for this reason at the end of the prosecution case and the judge directs the jury to acquit the defendant.

At the end of the trial the judge will sum up the case to the jury. The judge does this by reminding them of the evidence. This is particularly important if the trial has been a very long one, when the first witnesses may have given evidence several weeks earlier.

The judge will explain any law the jury need to know and how it applies to the case. The judge will remind the jury that they must only convict the defendant if they are sure beyond reasonable doubt that the defendant committed the offence. The judge then sends the jury out to consider their verdict.

## Sentencing

If the jury find the defendant guilty, then the judge decides what sentence the defendant should be given.

## Role of the jury

The jury will consist of 12 people. Their role is to decide the verdict. Is the defendant guilty or not guilty?

The jury listen to the whole case. They hear all the witnesses give evidence. They look at any important items which are part of the evidence. For example, if the case involved a shooting, then the jury will see the gun that was used. If the case involved a stabbing, the jury may see the knife which the prosecution allege was used.

In other cases, such as fraud, the jury may have to look at a lot of documents and accounts.

At the end of the case after the judge has summed up to the jury, the jury then leave the court room and are taken to a smaller room where they will discuss the case and make their decision.

Only the 12 jury members are allowed to be present at their discussion of the case. No one else is allowed in the room while that discussion is going on. This is to prevent anyone else trying to influence their decision.

## Majority verdicts

When the jury are first sent to consider the verdict they will be told they must come to a verdict on which they are all agreed. However, if the jury take a long time discussing the case, the judge may tell them that they can have a majority verdict.

At least 10 of the jury must agree on the verdict. So a majority verdict can be 11 to 1 or 10 to 2.

## Sentencing in the Crown Court

Where the jury find the defendant guilty (or if a defendant pleaded guilty) the last stage at the Crown Court is that the judge must decide on the sentence.

Before the judge sentences the defendant, he will hear about the defendant's past convictions, if any, and the defendant's background and financial situation. There may also be a pre-sentence report prepared by a probation officer or a medical report about the defendant.

The defendant or his lawyer can make a speech explaining to the judge any reasons, such as family circumstances – perhaps he has a disabled child – or other reasons why the judge should be lenient.

| Trial in the Crown Court | |
|---|---|
| **Judge's role** | **Jury's role** |
| **Pre-trial** <br> Deals with preliminary issues <br> These include <br> • the defendants' plea: and <br> • making sure the case is ready for trial | |
| **At the trial** <br> • decides points of law <br> • can stop case at end of prosecution evidence and direct an acquittal <br> • sums up the case for the jury <br> • explains to them the standard of proof – beyond reasonable doubt | **At the trial** <br> • listen to all the evidence <br> • decide the facts <br> • decide whether the defendant is guilty or not guilty <br> The verdict can be unanimous or by a majority of 10-2 or 11-1 |
| **Post-trial** <br> Decides sentence if the defendant is found guilty | |

Figure 4.2 Summary of the roles of judge and jury in the Crown Court

The same basic range of penalties as in the Magistrates' Courts are available for sentencing in the Crown Court. These are:

• custody (sending the defendant to prison)
• a community order
• a fine
• a discharge.

## Custody

Prison is only available for offenders aged 21 and over. Offenders aged 18 to 20 are sent to a Young Offenders' Institution as a custodial sentence.

For murder the only sentence the judge can pass is life imprisonment. The judge cannot do anything else. However, the judge can set a minimum number of years which the defendant must serve before being considered for parole. This is often 30 years and cannot be less than 15 years. This minimum term does not mean that the defendant will be released then; it only means that parole for the defendant (when he is

let out on licence) cannot be considered before then.

For other very serious offences, including manslaughter, rape and robbery, the maximum prison sentence the judge can give is life, but the judge does not have to give it. The sentence can be shorter, for example 12 years or 5 years.

Other less serious offences have a maximum term of imprisonment and the judge cannot give more than that. For example, the maximum term for theft is seven years. This means the judge can send the defendant to prison for any length of time up to seven years. In fact, the maximum is very rarely given; the sentence is likely to be a lot shorter unless the theft is exceptionally large (say of a million pounds). For less serious thefts, the judge can even give a non-custodial sentence.

A custodial sentence is the most common punishment in the Crown Court. About 60 per cent of guilty defendants in the Crown Court are sent to prison.

### Activity 1

Read the following newspaper article and answer the questions below.

**Gunman jailed for life for shooting dead boxer**

A gunman who shot dead a former British boxing champion in a row over smoking has been jailed for life.

Kanyana Mulenga, 23, was told he must spend at least 28 years in jail after being convicted of the 'senseless' murder of father-of-three James Oyebola.

He gunned down Mr Oyebola with a converted replica automatic pistol three weeks after the ban on lighting up in public places came into force in July last year.

The 46-year-old was shot through the back of the neck at the Chateau 6 bar in Fulham Broadway, west London, after asking a group of men to stop smoking.

*(Source: taken from an article in the Daily Telegraph, 9 October 2008)*

### Questions

1. What offence was Mulenga convicted of?
2. What sentence was he given?
3. What was the minimum number of years he must serve in prison?
4. Explain whether he will be automatically released from prison after this time.

## Community orders

The court can impose a community order on offenders aged 16 and over. This is a sentence which is carried out in the community. The judge can impose various requirements on the defendant. These include:

- an unpaid work requirement
- a curfew requirement
- a supervision requirement
- a drug rehabilitation requirement
- an alcohol treatment requirement.

## Fines

The judge can fine a defendant. There is no limit on the amount of the fine. For those under 18 years old there are lower maximum fines. In deciding the amount of a fine the court must take into account both the seriousness of the offence and the financial circumstances of the offender.

## Discharge

This sentence is not used very often in the Crown Court as the offences the court is dealing with are usually too serious for a discharge. But it is possible for the judge to impose a discharge if the case is suitable. This means the defendant must not commit any further offences within a set time, usually three years. If he or she does not commit any offence in this time, then that is the end of the matter.

## Appeals from the Crown Court

If the defendant was tried in the Crown Court, then the only appeal route is to the Court of Appeal (Criminal Division). The appeal can be against conviction and/or against sentence.

## Further appeal

After the Court of Appeal it is possible to appeal to the Supreme Court if there is a point of law of general importance at issue in the case. It is also necessary to get permission from the Supreme Court for the appeal to go ahead.

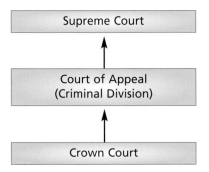

Figure 4.3 Appeal routes following a trial in the Crown Court

## ACTIVITY

### Activity 2

Answer the following questions.

1. What is meant by an indictment?

2. What categories of offence are dealt with in the Crown Court?

3. Explain the role of the judge in the Crown Court.

4. How many people are there on a jury in the Crown Court?

5. Explain the role of the jury in the Crown Court.

6. What is meant by a 'unanimous verdict'?

7. What is meant by a 'majority verdict'?

8. What type of sentence is the one most often given in the Crown Court?

9. To which court can a convicted defendant appeal after trial in the Crown Court?

10. A second appeal to the Supreme Court can be made in some cases. What two conditions are there for such an appeal to take place?

## BRIEF SUMMARY OF CHAPTER

**Offences tried at Crown Court**
- all indictable offences and some either way offences

**Judge's role**
- deals with preliminary issues
- decides facts
- sums up to the jury
- passes sentence on the defendant

**Jury's role**
- decide verdict

**Sentencing**
- custodial sentences are the most used
- but can also give community order, fine, discharge

**Appeals**
- to the Court of Appeal (Criminal Division)
- further appeal to the Supreme Court

# CHAPTER 5

# SENTENCING

When judges or magistrates pass sentence on a defendant they will consider several matters. These include:

- the aim or purpose of the sentence – what they are trying to achieve with that particular sentence
- the facts of the offence – is it a particularly serious offence of its kind – what role did the defendant play in the offence
- the background of the defendant – has he or she any previous convictions – has he or she a drug habit or any mental health problems
- whether the defendant pleaded guilty to the offence.

## Aims of sentencing

The Criminal Justice Act 2003 sets out the purposes of sentencing for those aged 18 and over. It says that a court must have regard to:

- the punishment of offenders
- the reduction of crime (including its reduction by deterrence and its reduction by the reform and rehabilitation of offenders)
- the protection of the public, and
- the making of reparation by offenders to persons affected by their offences.

Let's look at each of these aims or purposes in turn.

## Punishment

This is where a defendant is given a sentence simply because he deserves punishment. An important point about punishment is that it

should be proportionate to the offence committed.

## Proportionality or 'just deserts'

This is the idea that the defendant should only be punished to the extent that his crime deserves – no more, no less – and has led to the idea of tariff sentences, that is, that each crime has a set punishment.

In some American states this idea of tariff sentencing means that the judge has very little discretion over sentencing. The exact number of months of imprisonment to be served is set down and the judge can only make minor variations from this.

In this country the Sentencing Guidelines Council give sentencing guidelines for some offences. These state what they consider to be the correct range of punishments for types of offences.

The Council's basic guidelines for robbery are set out in Figure 5.1.

## Deterrence

This is where the sentence is aimed at deterring or 'putting off' the defendant from committing any more offences. The deterrence may be aimed at the offender as an individual or it may be aimed generally at the reduction of crime.

### Individual deterrence

This aims to punish the offender in such a way that he or she will never repeat the criminal

**EXAMPLE**

One of the offences that the Sentencing Guidelines Council has issued guidelines for is robbery. Robbery carries a maximum penalty of life imprisonment.

| Type/nature of activity | Starting point | Sentencing range |
| --- | --- | --- |
| The offence includes the threat or use of minimal force and removal of property. | 12 months' custody | Up to 3 years' custody |
| A weapon is produced and used to threaten, and/or force is used which results in injury to the victim. | 4 years' custody | 2–7 years' custody |
| The victim is caused serious physical injury by the use of significant force and/or use of a weapon. | 8 years' custody | 7–12 years' custody |

Figure 5.1 Sentencing guidelines for adults convicted of robbery

conduct because of fear of further punishment. Prison is supposed to have this effect. However, 65 per cent of those sent to prison re-offend within two years of release so that it does not appear to have as big a deterrent effect as one might think.

Another penalty based on this theory is a suspended prison sentence. This means that the offender is given a prison sentence but does not go to prison unless he or she commits a further offence during a period of time (maximum two years) fixed by the court. The idea is that the sentence 'hangs over' the offender as he or she knows he or she will go to prison if he or she commits another offence. This is intended to deter him or her from further offending.

## General deterrence

The aim of this approach is to punish one (or more) offenders so severely that other potential offenders are deterred from committing similar offences.

The death penalty is viewed in this way. Potential murders will be put off committing murder because they know they will lose their own life. However, there is no evidence that this idea works. In the USA, where some states have kept the death penalty while others have abolished it, there is little difference in the numbers of murders committed.

Long prison sentences are also sometimes given as a warning to others who might be likely to commit the same type of offence, especially when a particular type of crime is on the increase.

## Reform of the offender

Another name for this aim is rehabilitation. It involves looking at the individual offender's needs in terms of a sentence. The emphasis is on the offender rather than the offence. The aim is to reform the offender's behaviour and rehabilitate him or her back into society.

Reformation is considered the most important element when dealing with young offenders but can also be important for some adult offenders.

Community orders are the main sentence for achieving reform. For example, a requirement that the offender should receive treatment for drug abuse or alcohol abuse may be used by the court where the defendant has a drug or drink problem that causes them to commit crimes.

For this aim it is important that the court has information about the defendant's background. The court will want a report from a probation officer and, where appropriate, a medical report.

The main criticism of this approach is that it leads to inconsistency in sentencing. Offenders who have committed exactly the same type of offence may be given different sentences because the court is concentrating on the offender and the possibility of reforming him or her.

## Protection of society

This is where the defendant is felt to be too dangerous to be left at liberty in society. Society needs to be protected from the defendant. Long prison sentences are used for this purpose, especially where the defendant has committed serious violent or sexual offences.

Another method of protecting the public is to impose a curfew order on the offender ordering him to remain at home for certain times of the day or night. The curfew can be monitored by an electronic tag, which should trigger an alarm if the offender leaves his home address during a curfew period.

There are also lower levels of sentence which have some effect of protecting society. For example banning people from driving is another punishment where the courts are trying to protect society, in this case from being at risk as a result of the defendant's driving.

## Reparation

This is the idea of doing something to make up for the offence and, where possible, make reparation to the victim. Reparation can be by doing unpaid work for the community in general or for the victim in particular. There are schemes which bring the offender and the victim together so that the offender can understand the distress they have caused the victim and can apologise.

| Aim of sentence | Explanation/examples of sentence |
|---|---|
| Punishment | Proportionate punishment for offence |
| Deterrence | Individual – punish severely to 'put off' from committing other offences<br>• immediate custodial sentence<br>• suspended prison sentence |
| Reform/rehabilitation | Reform the offender's behaviour<br>• community order |
| Protection of society | Make offender incapable of committing further offences<br>• long prison sentence<br>• curfew<br>• ban from driving |
| Reparation | Offender has to do something to make amends for the offence committed<br>• unpaid work in the community<br>• direct reparation to victim<br>• pay compensation |

**Figure 5.2** Summary of the aims of sentencing

## Factors taken into account in sentencing

### The offence

In looking at the offence, the most important point to establish is how serious was it, of its type? Theft of a pair of jeans from a shop is obviously much less serious than theft of £50,000 from an employer. An assault that seriously injures the victim is more serious than one where the victim is only slightly bruised.

The court will also consider what role the defendant played in the offence – was he or she the ringleader? If so, he is likely to receive a more severe sentence than someone who only played a small part.

### EXAMPLE

#### Robbery

In Figure 5.1 we saw that the Sentencing Guidelines Council has issued guidelines on the level of sentence for different levels of seriousness of robbery. The Council also pointed out that there are factors which made a robbery more serious and could increase the sentence. These included:

- the offence was pre-planned
- wearing a disguise
- the offence was committed at night
- a vulnerable victim (ie very young or very elderly or disabled) targeted.

### Racially aggravated offences

There will a heavier sentence if the offence was racially or religiously aggravated. This means that if the defendant has assaulted someone because of their race, the sentence will be more severe than for other assaults.

### The background of the defendant

If the defendant has previous convictions, then the sentence is likely to be greater than for a first time offender. The court may also want a pre-sentence report on the defendant and his background. Where appropriate, the court may also want a medical report on the defendant.

### Reduction for guilty plea

There can be a reduction in sentence for a guilty plea, particularly where made early in the proceedings. This mainly applies to custodial sentences.

In such a case the judge can take off up to one third of the sentence he would normally have imposed. So, if the judge would normally have given a three-year custodial sentence, then he can take off one year and pass a sentence of two years.

## Custodial sentences

There are different custodial sentences available for different age groups. Young offenders can only be given custodial sentences in extreme cases and are always held in separate units from adult offenders.

### Prison sentences

Prison is only available for offenders aged 21 and over. For the crime of murder the only sentence possible is imprisonment for life. For other crimes Parliament sets out the maximum possible period of imprisonment for each crime; for example, the maximum for theft is seven years while the maximum for rape is life imprisonment. It is rare for an offender to be given the maximum sentence available, especially for theft and other crimes against property.

In the guidelines of suggested 'entry points' published by the Magistrates' Association a custodial sentence is advised for offences such as aggravated vehicle taking, assaulting a police officer and burglary of a residential property. Magistrates' maximum sentence for one offence is six months.

The United Kingdom has a higher percentage of its population in prison than any other European Union country. Many prisons are old, overcrowded and lacking in facilities. Critics point out that prison fails to deter or reform the majority of prisoners. Indeed there are frequent reports about the misuse of drugs in prison and the high levels of violence.

Reformers argue that it is unnecessary for so many offenders to be imprisoned, particularly those who are not dangerous and have committed crimes such as theft.

Prisoners do not serve the whole of the sentence passed by the court. Anyone sent to prison for less than four years is automatically released after they have served half of the sentence and may be released before the half way point if they are electronically tagged. Long-term prisoners serving four years or more are automatically released after they have served half of their sentence.

## Minimum sentences

Since 1997 there have been minimum sentences for burglars and drug dealers who repeatedly offend.

Anyone aged 18 or over who is convicted on three separate occasions of burglary must be given a minimum sentence of three years. Anyone aged 18 or over who is convicted on three separate occasions of dealing in class A drugs must be given a minimum sentence of seven years.

## Suspended prison sentences

An offender may be given a suspended prison sentence – of up to two years (six months maximum in the Magistrates' Court) – but the serving of that sentence is suspended for a period of time of up to two years.

Inside of a prison

If during this period of suspension the defendant does not commit any further crimes the original period of imprisonment will not be served. If, however, the offender does commit another offence during the period of suspension the original sentence is 'activated': that is, he or she automatically serves that sentence plus any extra given for the new offence.

Suspended prison sentences should only be given where the offence is so serious that an immediate custodial sentence would have been appropriate but there are exceptional circumstances in the case to justify suspending the sentence.

Suspended sentences can have requirements such as doing unpaid work added to them. A suspended sentence can only be used where the offender is aged 21 or over.

## Young Offenders' Institutions

Offenders aged 18 to 20 can be sent to a Young Offenders' Institution as a custodial sentence. The minimum sentence is 21 days and the maximum is the maximum allowed for the particular offence. If the offender becomes 21 years old while serving the sentence, he or she will be transferred to an adult prison.

## Detention and training orders

Offenders aged 15 to 17 can be sentenced to a detention and training order as a custodial sentence. The minimum is 4 months and the maximum 24 months. This sentence can also be given to those aged 12 to 14 but only if they are persistent offenders.

## Detention

For very serious offences committed by people under the age of 18, offenders can be detained for longer periods. This is possible where the crime they have committed carries a maximum prison sentence for adults of at least 14 years.

This applies to crimes such as manslaughter, rape and wounding with intent.

Also any offender aged 10 to 17 who is convicted of murder is detained during Her Majesty's Pleasure. This is an 'open-ended' sentence.

## Community orders

Judges and magistrates can give the defendant a community order. This can have different requirements attached to it.

The full list of requirements available to the courts is:

**(a)** an unpaid work requirement
**(b)** an activity requirement
**(c)** a programme requirement
**(d)** a prohibited activity requirement
**(e)** a curfew requirement
**(f)** an exclusion requirement
**(g)** a residence requirement
**(h)** a mental health treatment requirement
**(i)** a drug rehabilitation requirement
**(j)** an alcohol treatment requirement
**(k)** a supervision requirement, and
**(l)** in the case where the offender is aged under 25, an attendance centre requirement.

Most are self-explanatory from their name, such as drug rehabilitation and alcohol treatment. Much crime is linked to drug and alcohol abuse and the idea behind these two requirements is to tackle the causes of crime, hopefully preventing further offences.

Mental health treatment is also aimed at the cause of the offender's behaviour. The main other requirements are explained briefly below.

The sentencers can 'mix and match' requirements allowing them to fit the restrictions and rehabilitation to the offender's needs. The sentence is available for offenders age 16 and over.

## Unpaid work requirement

An offender can be ordered to do up to 300 hours' work on community projects. This might involve painting school buildings or gardening for elderly people. The offender will usually work an eight-hour day on Saturday or Sunday until the number of hours set by the court is completed.

## Programme requirement

Under this requirement, the court can order the offender to take part in a programme, for example for anger management. This is intended to help the offender manage his or her behaviour better so that he or she will not re-offend.

## Prohibited activity requirement

Under this the court can order the offender not to do certain things. For example, someone who has used a spray can to write graffiti on a wall (criminal damage) can be banned from carrying any spray cans in a public place.

It is also possible to order that the offender does not contact the victim. This may be used where the offender has repeatedly targeted one person.

## Curfew requirement

An offender is required to stay at a set address during certain hours (usually 6 pm to 6 am). They are usually tagged so that it is easy to check if they are obeying the curfew. A curfew cannot be for more than 12 hours in any day and it is for a maximum of 6 months.

## Exclusion requirement

Under this an offender can be banned from going to certain places such as a football ground when matches are being played there. This would be suitable where the offence was committed in connection with a football match. It can also be used to ban a defendant from all pubs in a particular area. This would be suitable

if the offender was committing offences after drinking in local pubs. The ban can be for up to two years.

## Supervision requirement

For this requirement the offender is placed under the supervision of a probation officer for a period of up to three years. During the period of supervision the offender must attend appointments with the supervising officer or with any other person decided by the supervising officer.

Perhaps next time you'll think before you steal my apples.

### ACTIVITY

#### Activity 1

Read the two following extracts from newspaper articles and answer the questions below.

#### Article 1

**Doherty given community order**

Troubled rock star Pete Doherty was given a 12-month community order today after admitting a series of drug offences.

The 26-year-old Babyshambles front man and former boyfriend of Kate Moss was sentenced at Ealing Magistrates' Court in west London after earlier pleading guilty to seven charges of possessing illegal substances.

The singer was also ordered to take part in a drug rehabilitation programme for 12 months and warned that if he breached this order, he could face a custodial sentence.

*(Source: Daily Mail, 9 February 2006)*

## Article 2

**Spurned lecturer Paul Kavanagh stalked student with hundreds of emails and calls**

A university law lecturer bombarded a female student with hundreds of love letters, emails, telephone calls and text messages after being spurned for another man, a court has heard.

Paul Kavanagh, 46, has been made the subject of a restraining order after magistrates heard how he besieged Jacqueline Pickstock, with more than 300 text messages in one weekend as part of a campaign of harassment which continued even after a police warning.

He denied a charge of harassment but was found guilty following a trial in June of this year. Magistrates have now imposed a restraining order preventing him from contacting Miss Pickstock.

He was also given a 12 month community order with 200 hours of community work to carry out as well as £625 costs to pay.

*(Source: taken from an article by John Bingham, Daily Telegraph, 9 October 2008)*

## Questions

1. In what type of court were both these cases heard?

2. In article 1, what requirement was added to the community order imposed on Pete Doherty?

3. What aim do you think the court had when it imposed this requirement?

4. If he breached that requirement what could happen to him?

5. In article 2, what requirements were added to the community order imposed on the defendant?

6. What aim do you think the court had when it imposed these requirements?

## Fines

The courts have the power to fine an offender for any crime. The Crown Court theoretically has no limits on the amount it can fine and in some company fraud cases there have been fines of over a million pounds.

The Magistrates' Court is limited to a maximum fine of £5,000. For those under 18 years old there are lower maximum fines. In deciding the amount of a fine the court must take into account both the seriousness of the offence and the financial circumstances of the offender.

## Discharges

For minor offences and particularly for first time offenders the courts can decide not to punish them but to discharge them, either conditionally or absolutely.

A conditional discharge carries the condition that the offender must not re-offend within a certain time, up to three years; if he or she breaks this condition he or she can be re-sentenced for the original offence.

An absolute discharge means that there are no conditions attached. The reason for using discharges is that the majority of first time offenders will be sufficiently punished by the fact that they have appeared in court and are unlikely to commit any further offences. Discharges can be used for offenders of any age. They are very common for younger offenders.

Figure 5.3 shows in simple diagram form the seriousness of the different levels of punishment.

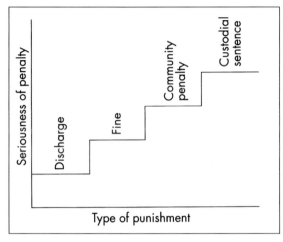

**Figure 5.3** Levels of punishment

## ACTIVITY

### Activity 2

Look for newspaper articles giving details of sentences passed on offenders by the courts.

You can do this online by searching national newspapers and/or you can look at local newspapers which are likely to report on cases heard in your local Magistrates' Court.

Compare the type of offence/offender and the nature of the sentence in each case.

(This work could be used towards coursework on sentencing.)

## Young offenders

### Youth rehabilitation order

This is a community sentence for those under the age of 18. The court can attach a variety of requirements to the order. These are similar to the requirements that can be attached to a Community Order for those aged 18 and over.

In addition, a youth rehabilitation order may also impose an education requirement making specific arrangements for education. A Youth Rehabilitation Order can also include intensive supervision and surveillance or an order that the young offender be placed with foster parents.

### Reparation orders

Under the Powers of Criminal Courts (Sentencing) Act 2000 an offender below the age of 18 can be ordered to make reparation for his or her offence, either to the victim or to the community. The order is for a maximum of 24 hours' work and the reparation order must be completed under supervision within 3 months. An order for direct reparation to a victim can only be made with that person's consent.

### Referral to a youth offender panel

Instead of passing a sentence the court can refer a young offender to a youth offender panel. This panel will work with the offender to prevent him or her re-offending.

The panel agrees a programme of behaviour with the young offender. This is called a youth offender contract. Agreement may be made about a number of different matters such as making reparation, attending rehabilitation sessions, carrying out unpaid work in the community or staying away from certain places or people.

## ACTIVITY

### Activity 3

Suggest one suitable punishment for each of the following cases and explain what the aim of the punishment is.

1. Marie, aged 18, has been found guilty of stealing a pair of jeans from a shop. It is her first offence.

2. Peter, aged 27, has been found guilty of an assault causing grievous bodily harm. He has three previous convictions for violence.

3. Susan, aged 22, has been found guilty of taking and driving away a car without the consent of the owner and causing criminal damage to it. She has one previous conviction for a similar crime.

## BRIEF SUMMARY OF CHAPTER

**The aims of sentencing**
■ punishment of offenders
■ reduction of crime (reduction by deterrence and reduction by reform/rehabilitation of offenders)
■ protection of the public
■ making of reparation by offenders to persons affected by their offences

**Other factors taken into account in sentencing**
■ the offence
■ the background of the defendant, including previous convictions
■ whether the defendant has pleaded guilty

**Types of sentences**
■ custodial sentences
■ community orders
■ fines
■ discharges

# CHAPTER 6

# POLICE POWERS

In order to detect and prosecute criminals it is necessary for the police to have powers to stop, search and arrest people. On the other hand it is important that police actions are controlled in order to protect citizens from harassment and pressure.

To try and achieve this balance Parliament passed the Police and Criminal Evidence Act 1984. This Act is usually referred to as PACE. The Act also allows the Home Secretary to issue Codes of Practice on such matters as searching, detaining, questioning and identifying suspects.

## Powers to stop and search

Section 1 of PACE gives the police the right to stop and search people and vehicles in a public place.

A police officer can only use this power if he or she has reasonable grounds for suspecting that the person stopped is in possession of, or the vehicle stopped contains, stolen goods or prohibited articles. Prohibited articles include such items as offensive weapons and articles for use in connection with burglary or theft.

## Public place

'Public place' includes all roads and streets and public squares and parks. It also includes areas like pub car parks and can even include private gardens if the officer has good reasons for believing the person does not live at that address.

## Safeguards

As this power to stop and search members of the general public is quite a wide one, the Act contains certain conditions as safeguards. The main ones are that the police officer must give his or her name and station and tell the person stopped the reason for the search.

If the officer is not in uniform, he or she must also produce documentary evidence to show that he or she is a police officer. Plain clothes police have no right to stop a vehicle under PACE.

During a search of a person in public, the only clothing a police officer can ask that person to remove is a coat, jacket or gloves. As soon as possible after the search, the police officer must make a written report about it.

I thought the police could only ask for the removal of coat and gloves.

The Police Code of Practice A under PACE contains guidance on when the powers to stop and search should be used. The Code stresses that powers to stop and search must be used fairly, responsibly, with respect for people being searched and without unlawful discrimination.

This means that the police cannot stop people just because of their race or age or because they are known to have a previous conviction. The police must have another reason for stopping the person.

## Other powers to stop and search

Although PACE contains the main right to stop and search there are other Acts which also give this power in special circumstances, for instance the Misuse of Drugs Act 1971 allows the police to search for controlled drugs.

## Powers of arrest

### Arrest under PACE

Section 24 of PACE sets out the powers the police have to arrest suspects. It gives police officers the right to arrest in the following circumstances.

(a) anyone who is about to commit an offence
(b) anyone who is in the act of committing an offence
(c) anyone whom he has reasonable grounds for suspecting to be about to commit an offence
(d) anyone whom he has reasonable grounds for suspecting to be committing an offence.

The next part of s 24 gives a police officer power to arrest if the officer has reasonable grounds for suspecting that an offence has been committed. In this instance he may arrest anyone whom he has reasonable grounds to suspect of being guilty of it.

Also, if an offence has been committed, a constable may arrest anyone who is guilty of the offence or anyone whom he has reasonable grounds for suspecting to be guilty of it.

Figure 6.1 gives a summary of these powers of arrest.

These are very wide powers of arrest, but there is a necessity test which sets limits on when an officer has the power to arrest. However, these limitations are not thought to be adequate.

## Necessity test

An arresting officer can only arrest if he has reasonable grounds for believing that it is necessary to make the arrest for one of the following reasons:
• to enable the person's name or address to be ascertained
• to prevent the person:
  – causing physical injury to himself or any other person
  – suffering physical injury
  – causing loss of or damage to property
  – committing an offence against public decency
  – causing an unlawful obstruction of the highway
• to protect a child or other vulnerable person
• to allow the prompt and effective investigation of the offence or of the conduct of the person
• to prevent any prosecution for the offence from being hindered by the disappearance of the person in question.

These reasons given in the necessity test are clearly sensible ones. For example, it would be ridiculous if the police were not able to arrest someone who was causing injury to another person. Also the police need to be able to arrest someone who is running away from the scene of a crime.

**Timing of offence**          **Powers – can arrest:**

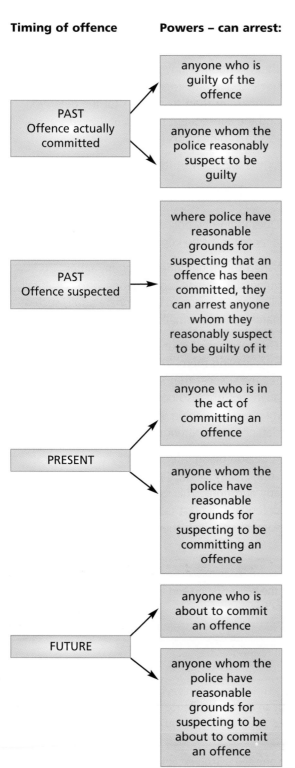

Figure 6.1 Police powers of arrest

## Safeguards

A police officer can only use reasonable force to make an arrest. The officer also has to inform the person that they are being arrested. This can be done in everyday language, for example saying 'you're nicked' is sufficient. The person also has to be told the reason for the arrest.

An arrested person has to be taken to a police station as soon as possible.

### ACTIVITY

#### Activity 1

In each situation state whether there has been a lawful arrest. Give reasons for your answer.

1  Kate is arrested by a police officer when a store manager told the officer that Kate had stolen a pair of jeans from the shop. The store manager was mistaken.

2  Hari is arrested by a police officer when the officer recognises him from a photo of a suspect wanted for murder.

3  A police officer arrests David when he sees David trying the door handles of several cars in the local car park.

## Powers of detention

Once a suspected person is arrested and taken to a police station, PACE and the Code of Practice drawn up by the Home Secretary under PACE state that the custody officer at that station must inform the suspect of his or her rights. These are:

(a) to have someone informed of his or her arrest;

(b) to consult privately with a solicitor, and to be told that independent legal advice is available free of charge;

(c) to be able to consult the Code of Practice.

Where the arrest is for an indictable offence, the right to a and b above may be delayed for 36 hours.

The custody officer must also keep a custody record noting all the events that occur while the arrested person remains at the police station.

## Detention time limits

For most offences the police can only hold a person for a maximum of 36 hours. Then the person must either be charged with an offence or released.

For indictable offences the rules are different. Here the person may be detained for up to 36 hours. Then the police can apply to detain him or her further. This application has to be made to magistrates.

There will be a hearing in a Magistrates' Court where the detained person has the right to be represented and to put his or her side of events. Magistrates may authorise the police to extend the detention for up to 96 hours in total. After this the suspect must either charged or released.

The only exception to these time limits is where someone is arrested for terrorism offences. In such cases it is possible for the suspect to be held for up to 28 days.

## Review of detention

The Police and Criminal Evidence Act states that the detention of any arrested person must be 'reviewed' at set intervals. The first review must be not later than six hours after the detention and the subsequent reviews at intervals of not less than nine hours.

Figure 6.2 sets out the time limits on detention.

## Interviews

Questioning by police may be tape recorded and a record must be kept of all interviews.

When someone under 17 or any other vulnerable person (eg someone who is mentally ill) is interviewed, an appropriate adult, such as a parent, must normally be present.

The police must caution all suspects before interviewing them. This means the police must tell the suspect that they do not have to say anything, but also pointing out that a failure to mention something which is later used in their defence could strengthen the case against them.

A person being interviewed by the police can, of course, stay silent; they do not have to answer any questions. This means that the fact that the defendant did not tell the police about something which they might have been

| Time factor | |
|---|---|
| Start of detention | The arrested person arrives at the police station and the custody officer decides there is reason to detain him or her |
| 6 hours | First review |
| 15 hours and every 9 hours afterwards | Second review and subsequent reviews |
| 36 hours | Police must charge or release arrested person unless he or she is being interviewed in connection with an indictable offence<br>Police may apply to magistrates to extend the period of detention for an indictable offence |
| 96 hours | Maximum time for holding an arrested person except for terrorist offences |

Figure 6.2 Time limits on detention

expected to mention, but then uses that point in their defence at court, can be considered by the court as part of the evidence against them.

## Searches, finger prints and samples

The police may search a person when they arrest them. When an arrested person is brought to the police station, the custody officer must record all the property they have on them and may also decide that it is necessary to search them.

In some cases, the police may make a strip search. This can only take place if it is necessary to remove an article which a person in detention should not be allowed to keep, and there is reasonable suspicion that the person might have such an article concealed on their person.

Such searches should not take place in an area where the search can be seen by any person who does not need to be present. No member of the opposite sex should be present during a strip search. Suspects should not normally be required to remove all their clothing at the same time. A man should be allowed to put his shirt back on before he removes his trousers and a woman should be given a robe or similar garment to wear once she has removed her top garment.

### Fingerprints

The police may take finger prints without the person's consent. Records of any fingerprints taken can be kept on the police databases, even if the defendant is not charged with an offence.

### Samples

The police can take samples, such as hair or samples of saliva, from a detained person without the person's consent. Records of these can also be kept on the police databases, even if the defendant is not charged with an offence.

**ACTIVITY**

### Activity 2

State whether each of the following statements is TRUE or FALSE.

1. Police cannot stop and search a person who is in a private garden.
2. The police cannot ask a person to take off a coat when stopping and searching them.
3. There must have been an offence committed for the police to have the right to arrest someone.
4. A person who has been arrested for an indictable offence cannot be held for more than 96 hours.
5. There must be a review after a person has been detained at a police station for six hours.
6. Only those under the age of 16 need to have an appropriate adult present when the police interview them.
7. The police must tape-record all interviews with a suspect at a police station.
8. A person held at a police station has the right to have someone informed of his or her arrest.
9. The police must have consent of the suspect before they take their fingerprints.
10. The custody officer can search a detained person when they are brought into the police station.

## The balance between police powers and individual rights

It is obvious that the police must be able to hold a suspected person while they investigate the offence. They may need to wait for the results of a DNA test to see if the suspect is linked to the crime. They need to be able to question the suspect and ask for explanations of certain things.

If the police could not do this, then it would be difficult to obtain evidence to convict those guilty of offences. However, at the same time, the individual's rights have to be protected.

Police Code of Practice C gives protection to suspects who are being questioned in regard to the physical conditions of the interview. For example, the Code states that interview rooms and cells must be adequately lit, heated and ventilated.

It also says that suspects who are being questioned must be given adequate breaks, usually about every two hours. The detained person must also be given meals, refreshments and the chance to sleep.

While a suspect is being detained at a police station, the treatment of that suspect must be monitored by the custody officer. The custody officer has to keep records of all happenings during the detention period. This will include the length and timing of interviews and other matters such as visits of police officers to the defendant's cell. This also helps to protect the suspect.

## Legal advice

Another important safeguard of individual rights is the fact that a person held at a police station has the right to consult a lawyer. This can be their own lawyer or they can ask for the duty solicitor. The duty solicitor scheme gives free legal advice to anyone detained in a police station.

### BRIEF SUMMARY OF CHAPTER

PACE sets down rules for stop and search, arrest and detention.

Codes of practice are also produced to give more detail on the carrying out of these powers.

**Stop and search**
- Officer must have reasonable grounds for suspecting the person is in possession of stolen goods or other prohibited articles
- Officer must give name and station and the reason for stopping
- Only coat, jacket and gloves can be removed during search

**Powers of detention**
- Normal maximum time of detention is 36 hours but this can be extended by magistrates for indictable offences
- Custody officer must keep record of detention and review it regularly

**Suspect's rights**
- to have someone informed of his or her arrest
- to see a lawyer
- to be able to consult the codes of practice

**Interviews**
- must be tape recorded
- Those under 17 or vulnerable must have an appropriate adult present

**Searches**
- Police can search arrested person at time of arrest or they can be searched at the police station
- A strip search can be made if necessary but there are strict rules about this

**Samples**
- Police can take fingerprints and samples

**Balance of rights**
- Police need to be able to investigate crime by arresting and taking fingerprints and samples
- but individual rights need to be protected by making sure an arrested person is held in proper conditions, has meals and rest, and can contact a lawyer

# CHAPTER 7

# CIVIL COURTS

## Civil claims

As we saw in Chapter 1, civil law is quite separate from criminal law and has its own courts and procedure. It involves individuals or companies who wish to make a claim because their rights have been affected in some way. Common examples of the sorts of cases that could go to a civil court are:

**(a)** a television rental company claiming for money not paid on a TV renting agreement

**(b)** a claim for the cost of repairing damage caused to a car because of the other person's negligent driving

**(c)** a family claiming compensation for being put in sub-standard accommodation on a holiday package they paid for in this country

**(d)** a landlord claiming for unpaid rent and for an order that the tenant leave the property

**(e)** a workman claiming for injuries he suffered at work because of faulty machinery.

In civil cases most people will try to come to an agreement rather than start court proceedings. Court cases cost money. To start a case, even without consulting a solicitor, means paying a court fee; using a solicitor costs more and there is never any guarantee that you will win your case. Even if you do win, the other party may not have enough money to pay the claim and your costs. If the case is complicated it could last years and cost hundreds of thousands of pounds.

In most cases it is sensible to write to the other person, making it clear what is being claimed and the reasons for the claim. It may be possible to negotiate a settlement of the claim.

It is only when the other person disputes the claim, or will not reply at all, that court proceedings should be considered.

## Getting advice

Before staring a court case, it is sensible to get legal advice. This can be obtained from a number of places.

### Citizens Advice Bureaux

Citizens Advice Bureaux (CAB) exist in most towns. They issue general advice to anyone on a variety of points including legal matters, but the staff are not usually legally qualified.

They can also provide a list of local solicitors and information on which ones do legal aid work. The bureaux have schemes under which they can refer people to certain solicitors who are prepared to offer a short interview at a very low cost or even free and some CABs have an arrangement where local solicitors take it in turn to attend once a week or fortnight at the Citizens Advice Bureau to give advice to people.

Some CABs have contracts with the Legal Services Commission to provide legal help under Government-funded schemes.

## Law centres

Law centres are intended to provide a community or neighbourhood service in poorer areas, especially inner city areas. Law centres are staffed by full-time paid lawyers.

The areas of work most commonly done by law centres include matters concerning housing (for example, tenants' rights), social security and other welfare rights, employment problems, planning and environmental issues and women's rights. In most of these areas legal aid is not available. Law centres will advise and represent people both in court and before tribunals.

## Other organisations

For some problems it may be possible to get advice from a related organisation; in particular trade unions will help their members in work-related matters, while organisations such as the Automobile Association will help their members in motoring cases.

Charities may also give legal advice on areas connected to the charity. For example, Shelter may help with housing problems, while Age Concern may advise elderly people on benefit rights.

## Internet sites

There are websites where it is possible to get basic advice on legal problems. One of these is provided by the Community Legal Service. This website is at www.clsdirect.org.uk. It provides a wide range of advice on how to deal with different legal problems.

## Funding a civil case

If you decide you are going to make a claim, an important point is to know how it can be financed. Taking a case to court can be expensive. If it is a complicated case and you use a lawyer, then you have to pay the lawyer's fees. There are also court fees to be paid at each stage of the case.

It is impossible to know how long the case will last or what the final amount of cost will be.

If you win the case you may get back most of these costs from the other person, but if you lose the case you will have to pay the other person's costs as well as your own. Case costs can run into hundreds of thousands of pounds, so arranging for funding of the case is very important.

## Private funding

If you have enough money you can fund the case yourself. However, most people cannot afford to take a big case to court, so there are other ways in which the case costs can be covered. These are:

• conditional fees
• insurance
• public funding.

## Conditional fees

This is where the solicitor and client agree on the fee which would normally be charged for such a case. The agreement also states what the solicitor's 'success fee' will be. This can be an 'uplift' of up to 100 per cent of the agreed normal fee.

If the solicitor does not win the case, then the client pays nothing. If the solicitor is successful then the client pays the normal fee plus the success fee. This is why these agreements are often called 'no-win, no-fee' agreements.

If you win the case you can claim your lawyer's costs from the losing party. So, although you have had to pay a success fee on top of normal legal fees, you will be able to get most of your costs back.

This type of agreement allows a person taking a case in court to know exactly what his or her lawyer's fees will be.

## Insurance

There are two ways in which it is possible to ensure against having to pay legal costs.

The first is 'before the event' insurance. This is where insurance is paid on something such as a house or a car and the insurance policy also covers the possibility of legal costs.

For example, most motor insurance policies offer cover (for a small amount extra) for help with legal fees in cases arising from road accidents. This is 'before the event' as there has not been any problem when the insurance policy is issued. It is covering a possible future event.

The other type of legal insurance policy is 'after the event' insurance. This is where you are about to start a claim against another person (or a claim is being made against you). You now know that there is a legal case and you want to protect against losing that case. As there is already a case, the cost of this type of insurance premium can be quite high.

## Public funding

The Community Legal Service provides help for legal disputes. This may include representation by a lawyer in a case in the County Court or the High Court.

However, certain types of civil cases are not funded by the Community Legal Service Fund. Cases for which funding is NOT available include:

- claims for personal injury, or death or damage to property through someone else's negligence
- defamation or malicious falsehood cases
- claims for amounts of less than £5,000
- most tribunal hearings, except for cases in the

Mental Health Tribunal and Immigration Tribunals.

Even if your case is one for which funding from the Community Legal Service is available, there are several restrictions on whether the case will be funded.

First, there are strict financial limits on who can be given help under the Community Legal Service. You have to be quite poor to qualify for funding.

Also the Service will not fund your case unless there is a realistic chance of the case succeeding. Finally, the cost of bringing the case must not be greater than the likely damages (amount of money the court will award).

### ACTIVITY

**Activity 1**

**Fill in the gaps with the appropriate word or phrase from the box below.**

Advice and funding in civil cases

If a person has a legal problem there are several places where they can get advice. ............................................... Bureaux give advice, in particular on debt, welfare or housing problems. In some areas there are also ......................... Centres which can help. There are other specialist organisations such as .................. which advise on work related problems. It is even possible to look for advice on the ............................. .

If you decide to take a case to court, you will need to be able to fund it. If you pay your legal costs yourself, this is known as .................. funding. If you get help from the Community Legal Service, this is known as ................... funding.

You may be able to make a ........................ fee agreement with a solicitor, in which he will only charge you if you win the case. He will then charge the normal fee plus a

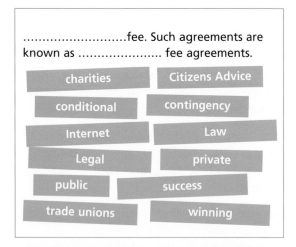

..........................fee. Such agreements are known as ...................... fee agreements.

charities

Citizens Advice

conditional

contingency

Internet

Law

Legal

private

public

success

trade unions

winning

## Bringing a civil claim

The first decision when making a claim is which court to use. The two main courts that deal with civil cases are:

• the County Court
• the High Court.

The amount claimed is usually the deciding factor in where to start a case, but the seriousness and difficulty of the case will also be considered.

Most civil cases can be started in either court, but claims for less than £15,000 must be started in the County Court. Also claims under £25,000 are normally dealt with in the County Court.

Claims for £25,000 to £50,000 can be started and dealt with in either the County Court or the High Court. The exception is cases of personal injuries. If the claim for compensation for those injuries is less than £50,000 the case must be started in the County Court.

For claims over £50,000 it is more usual to go to the High Court although the County Court can deal with larger claims.

In civil cases the person making the claim is called the claimant and the other party is the defendant.

NB For some family matters, such as custody of children, it is possible to go to the Magistrates' Courts. But note that Magistrates' Courts do NOT deal with divorce cases.

## The claim form

The first stage is to get a claim form from the court (see Figure 7.1), fill it in and take or send it to the court and pay the court fee. The court then sends the claim by post to the defendant.

When filling in the form, the important points are to make it clear who is claiming, how much is claimed and why the claim is being made.

The cost of issuing a claim form depends on the size of the claim, but the minimum cost is £30 for claims of up to £300 rising to £1,700 for a claim of over £300,000.

## Defending the claim

When the defendant receives the claim form he or she may admit the claim and pay the full amount to the claimant. If this occurs the case ends at this point, since the claimant has achieved what he or she wanted.

Where the defendant disputes the claim he or she should reply to the court within 14 days explaining that he or she wants to defend the action and file a document called a defence at the court setting out why he or she disputes the claim.

A copy of this is then sent to the claimant.

## The track system

Once a case is defended, both sides are asked to fill in a questionnaire so that a judge can decide which track the case should be allocated to. All cases are allocated to one of three tracks. These are:

• small claims for cases involving less than £5,000
• fast-track for cases between £5,000 and £25,000

**Claim Form**

In the

| | for court use only |
|---|---|
| Claim No. | |
| Issue date | |

Claimant

SEAL

Defendant(s)

Brief details of claim

Value

| | | £ |
|---|---|---|
| Amount claimed | | |
| Court fee | | |
| Solicitor's costs | | |
| Total amount | | |

Defendant's name and address

The court office at

is open between 10am and 4pm Monday to Friday. When corresponding with the court, please address forms or letters to the Court Manager and quote the claim number.

NI Claim form (CPR Part 7) (01.02)                                    *Printed on behalf of The Court Service*

**Figure 7.1** Claim form (N1)

Claim No.

Does, or will, your claim include any issues under the Human Rights Act 1998?    ☐ Yes    ☐ No

Particulars of Claim (attached)(to follow)

Statement of Truth
*(I believe)(The Claimant believes) that the facts stated in these particulars of claim are true.
*I am duly authorised by the claimant to sign this statement

Full name _____

Name of claimant's solicitor's firm _____

signed_____    position or office held _____
*(Claimant)(Litigation friend)(Claimant's solicitor)    (if signing on behalf of firm or company)

*delete as appropriate

Claimant's or claimant's solicitor's address to which documents or payments should be sent if different from overleaf including (if appropriate) details of DX, fax or e-mail.

| Amount of claim | Court | Track |
|---|---|---|
| Under £5,000 | County Court | small claims track |
| £5,000 to £25,000 | County Court | fast-track |
| £25,000 to £50,000 | Either the County Court or the High Court<br><br>Exception<br>personal injury claims up to £50,000 must be started in the County Court | multi-track |
| Over £50,000 | Normally High Court<br>County Court can deal with larger claims | multi-track |

**Figure 7.2** Where civil claims are usually dealt with

• multi-track for cases where the claim is for more than £25,000 or where the case is very complex.

Small claims track cases are always dealt with in the County Court. Claims between £5,000 and £25,000 are dealt with by the fast-track procedure of the County Court.

Both the County Court and the High Court can deal with multi-track cases. These are claims over £25,000 or cases that are very complicated and may involve important legal issues. Multi-track cases are dealt with by a more complicated procedure. They are likely to take a lot longer than fast-track cases.

## Small claims

Small claims are for amounts under £5,000. It is important that there should be a comparatively cheap and simple way of resolving them. The full County Court procedure is too expensive for many individuals to use.

The small claims court is often referred to as a do-it-yourself court. This is because people are encouraged to take action themselves and not use lawyers. To help people there are leaflets on how to sue and defend cases without a solicitor, which are available from County Court offices or Citizens Advice Bureaux.

Small claims cases are usually heard in private, but they can be heard in an ordinary court. They are usually heard by a District Judge. The judge will take an active part in the proceedings, asking questions and making sure that both parties explain all their important points. This is important when the parties do not have lawyers.

## Fast-track cases

Claims between £5,000 and £25,000 also need a fast and relatively cheap method of dealing with them. Otherwise the costs of the case could be a lot more than the amount claimed.

Fast-track means that the court will set down a very strict timetable for the pre-trial matters. This is aimed at preventing one or both sides from wasting time and running up unnecessary costs. Once a case is ready for hearing, the aim is to have the case heard within 30 weeks.

The actual trial will usually be heard by a Circuit Judge and take place in open court with a more formal procedure than for small claims. In order to speed up the trial itself, the hearing will be limited to a maximum of one day and the number of expert witnesses restricted, with usually only one expert being allowed.

## Multi-track cases

Claims for more than £25,000 are usually allocated to the multi-track. If the case was started in a County Court then it is likely to be tried there, though it can be sent to the High Court, especially for claims of over £50,000.

In the County Court the case will be heard by a Circuit Judge. In the High Court there will be a High Court Judge. The judge will be expected to 'manage' the case from the moment it is allocated to the multi-track route. The judge can set timetables. It is even possible to ask the parties to try an alternative method of dispute resolution in an effort to prevent waste of costs.

### ACTIVITY

#### Activity 2

Advise the people in the following situations:

1. Frank has bought a laptop computer, costing £600. The computer has never worked properly and he wants to claim back its cost. Advise him as to which type of court will hear this case and explain the likely court procedure to him.

2. Lester has been injured in a car accident. Lester claims that the accident was the fault of the other driver, Jason. Lester wants to claim £20,000 in damages. Advise Lester as to which court he should use to start the case and what track would be used.

3. Nadine has had an extension built at her home. Because some if the work was badly done, she has had to pay £12,000 to have the work put right. Advise Nadine as to which court she can use to start the case and what track would be used.

4. Ameeta has been seriously injured at work. She claims her employers were in breach of health and safety rules. She estimates that her total claim is over £250,000. Advise her as to which court she should use and under what track the case would be dealt with.

### Remedies

At the end of the case, when the claimant has won, the judge will award the claimant a remedy. The main remedy is damages. This is an award of a sum of money. There are other remedies, especially injunctions.

### Damages

The object of damages is to compensate the claimant for the defendant's actions. For example, if the defendant has not been paying rent which he should have paid to the claimant, the damages will be the amount of rent which is owed.

Another example is where you have had work done on your house, but it was done very badly, so that you had to have it redone by another firm. In this case the damages would be the reasonable cost of having it redone.

In personal injury cases, it is more difficult to calculate the amount which should be paid to the claimant. This is because a large amount of the damages will be money to compensate for the injuries the claimant suffered. It is difficult to set any sum which will adequately compensate for very serious injuries.

For example, if the claimant has been paralysed in a car crash caused by the defendant, then the damages will be intended to compensate for the disability and allow for the cost of future care. An amount may be added to allow the claimant to alter their home to make it suitable for a wheelchair.

### Injunctions

Another remedy is an injunction. This is an order to the defendant to do something or, more usually, not to do something.

In contract cases, an injunction may be awarded to prevent a breach of contract. However, injunctions are more usually used in tort cases, especially cases of nuisance. In these the injunction will order the defendant to stop the nuisance. It may be only at certain times, for example an order that the defendant does not operate noisy machinery at night.

An example of a case in which an injunction was granted is *Kennaway v Thompson* (1981).

### CASE EXAMPLE

**Kennaway v Thompson (1981)**

**Noise from frequent motor-boat racing by the defendant on a lake was found to be a nuisance. The claimant, who lived by the lake, was granted an injunction. The injunction limited the number of races that the defendant could hold.**

## Problems of using the courts

The courts have been set up to resolve disputes and there are advantages to using the courts to resolve a claim, but there can also be many problems.

### Advantages of using the civil courts

1. The judges who sit in the civil courts are trained lawyers who will have practised as lawyers for many years before becoming judges. They have a lot of experience of legal problems.
2. The courts have different remedies which can be enforced through the courts.
3. Public funding may be available to help a person bring a case or defend it.
4. The procedure under the Civil Procedure Rules is aimed at trying to get cases to settle and prevent delay.

### Disadvantages of using the civil courts

1. Cases going to court normally take longer than cases dealt with by alternative forms of dispute resolution (ADR). (See Chapter 8 for discussion of ADR.)
2. It is much more expensive to take a case to court than to have it resolved by another method. Court fees are high and lawyers' fees are also likely to be high. In some cases the costs have been over a million pounds.
3. In the court system each party will be trying to win the case. This can lead to bad feeling between the parties. This will cause problems in the future if the parties still have to deal with each other, for example in business or in family life after a divorce.
4. Although judges are experts on the law, some cases can involve technical points, for example on construction of buildings. A judge will not have any expert knowledge of this, so everything has to be explained in great detail adding to time and costs.
5. Courts proceedings are public. This is likely to make the experience even more stressful and can lead to the media reporting on the case in newspapers or on television.

## Appeals in civil cases

The court to which an appeal is made after a decision in a case depends on three points. The first point is which court was the original case heard in? The second point is whether the case was a small claims one, a fast-track case or a multi-track case. The third point, which only applies where the original trial was in the County Court, is what type of judge heard the case.

### Appeals from the County Court

For small claim cases, the appeal is to the Circuit Judge in the County Court where the case was tried.

For fast-track cases, it depends on what type of judge heard the original case. If the case was tried by a District Judge, the appeal goes to a Circuit Judge in the same court. If the case was tried by a Circuit Judge the appeal goes to a High Court Judge.

From an appeal to the High Court, there can be a second appeal to the Court of Appeal (Civil Division), but the Court of Appeal must give permission to appeal. This will normally only be given where an appeal would raise an important point of law or there is some other reason why the Court of Appeal should hear the case.

An appeal about the decision in a multi-track case originally heard in the County Court is always made to the Court of Appeal (Civil Division). Permission to appeal is needed. Figure 7.3 shows the County Court appeal routes.

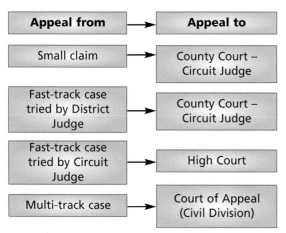

Figure 7.3 Appeal routes from the County Court

## Appeals from the High Court

These normally go to the Court of Appeal (Civil Division). Permission to appeal is needed.

There is also a special appeal route from the High Court to the Supreme Court, missing out the Court of Appeal. This type of appeal is known as a 'leapfrog' appeal. It can only be used in two circumstances. The first is where the Court of Appeal is bound by a previous decision of its own and there is reason to believe that the Supreme Court might change the law. The second is where the case involves interpreting the words of an Act of Parliament. There are only about four leapfrog appeals each year.

NB Up to 2009 the final Court of Appeal was the House of Lords. This was changed to the Supreme Court under the Constitutional Reform Act 2005. However, the actual change had to wait until a building was made ready for the new Supreme Court. The change was made so that the judges could be completely separate from Parliament.

## Further appeal

When the Court of Appeal (Civil Division) has made a decision on the appeal, it is possible for the losing party to the case to make a further appeal to the Supreme Court (see Figure 7.4).

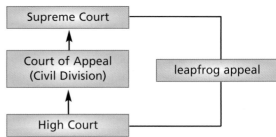

Figure 7.4 Appeal routes from the High Court

## BRIEF SUMMARY OF CHAPTER

**Where to get advice on civil problems**

- CABx
- Law centres
- Specialist organisations and charities
- Internet sites

**Funding a claim**

- private funding
- conditional fee agreement
- insurance – before the event
  - after the event
- public funding – Community Legal Service
- must be poor enough to qualify, AND
- case must have a realistic chance of success

**Bringing a civil claim**

- County Court OR High Court
- track system – small claims under £5,000
  - fast-track £5,000 to £25,000
  - multi-track – over £25,000 or complex

**Remedies**

- damages (money)
- injunction

**Appeals**

- small track – to Circuit Judge in County Court
- fast-track – to County Court OR High Court
- multi-track – to Court of Appeal (Civil Division)
- possible further appeal to Supreme Court

## EXAMINATION QUESTION

Note you will need to apply what you have learnt in Chapters 2 and 3 as well the information in this chapter.

Cases within the English legal system can be tried by different people. They include different judges such as District Judges, Circuit Judges, High Court Judges and Lords Justices of Appeal. Cases can also be decided by magistrates or juries sitting in different criminal courts.

In **each** of the following situations, identify **who** is most likely to be trying the case, and briefly explain **why**.

(a) Ivy, aged 16, has been charged with actual bodily harm (abh) and is due in court next week. (2 marks)

(b) Josef has been accused of a serious assault on a teacher. At an initial hearing, the magistrates decided that the offence was too serious to be tried by magistrates.

(2 marks)

(c) Keith bought a new fishing rod for £120 from *Anglers*, a shop which sells fishing equipment. Two weeks later, the rod snapped while Keith was using it. *Anglers* have refused to refund Keith's money.

(2 marks)

(d) Megan was seriously injured at work in an accident caused by the negligence of Nazir. Megan has been awarded £120,000 damages by the High Court, much less than she was hoping for. Megan is now planning to appeal. (2 marks)

*AQA GCSE Law, Specimen Paper, Unit 1*

# CHAPTER 8

# TRIBUNALS AND ADR

There are methods of resolving disputes outside the court structure and this chapter looks at these.

## Tribunals

Tribunals were set up to deal with specific types of claim. Most tribunals are there to help enforce individual rights, for example social or employment rights.

In order to protect these rights it is necessary to have either a court or another place to which one can apply if there are any problems. Since the courts were already very busy, the government set up separate tribunals to deal with specific types of rights.

### Types of tribunal

There are different types of tribunal. They include:

- employment tribunals
- social security tribunals
- immigration tribunals.

Employment tribunals only hear cases connected to employment. For instance they hear claims for payments for people who are made redundant from their job, or who have been discriminated against because of their sex, race or age, or who claim to have been unfairly dismissed from work.

Social security tribunals hear appeals from the refusal to grant certain state benefits. These include payments for people who are suffering from a disability.

Immigration tribunals hear claims from immigrants against a refusal to allow them to stay in this country.

These are only a few examples; there are many more tribunals.

### Composition

Since the various tribunals have been set up over a number of years they do not all operate in the same way. However, the majority will have a panel of three people sitting to decide the case. The chairman will usually be legally qualified. The other two members will have some experience or specialist knowledge in the particular subject matter of the tribunal.

For instance in any tribunal where there is a question involving health, the two lay (non-lawyer) members will be doctors; in employment tribunals one will be from an employers' organisation and the other from an employees' organisation, often a trade union.

### Procedure

The procedure for each tribunal varies, with many using no formal rules of evidence or procedure. Employment tribunals are the most formal and their procedure is very similar to that of a court. Social security appeals tribunals are less formal. In all tribunals individuals are encouraged to bring their own case and not to use lawyers.

Public funding is not available for most tribunals so that anyone wishing to be represented by a lawyer will have to pay his or her own legal fees.

Public funding is only available for a very small number of tribunals. These are mainly ones where the individual's liberty is an issue such as the Mental Health Review Tribunal which decides if a refusal to release a mental patient from hospital is justified and immigration tribunals where the immigrant is at risk of being deported from this country.

## Advantages of tribunals

There are many advantages to using this system of tribunals instead of the courts.

1. It is cheaper since there are no expensive lawyers' fees to pay as most applicants represent themselves. In employment tribunals people are more likely to be represented by a lawyer than at social security tribunals.
2. The proceedings are less formal than a court, making it easier for ordinary people to start proceedings and conduct their own case.
3. Each tribunal specialises in one type of case so that they become expert in that area. In addition the two lay members will have their own specialist knowledge of the subject.
4. Cases are dealt with more quickly than in the courts.

## Disadvantages of tribunals

Although there are advantages to using tribunals, the system also has some drawbacks.

1. Applicants who have no lawyer are less likely to win their case. One of the main problems in tribunals is that although the individual will not have a lawyer, the employer or government department on the other side is likely to have its own lawyer.
2. Government funding for legal representation is not available.
3. Although the procedure is comparatively informal, many people still find it confusing and intimidating. The fact that each tribunal is likely to have its own methods adds to this confusion.

4. The specialist knowledge of tribunals may make an applicant feel at a disadvantage since he or she will not share that knowledge.
5. Tribunals do not always operate quickly. It is normal for employment cases to take a year or more to be heard and if the case goes to appeal there will probably be another year to wait.

### ACTIVITY

**Activity 1**

1. Name two different types of tribunal.
2. Why were tribunals set up?
3. Who will usually make the decision in a tribunal?
4. Explain in your own words three advantages of using tribunals.
5. Explain in your own words three disadvantages of using tribunals.

## Alternative Dispute Resolution (ADR)

We will now look at methods of resolving disputes which are quite independent of the legal system. Remember that in civil cases it is the claimant who decides whether or not to start a court case. People do not want to start a case unnecessarily and will usually try to settle the problem in another way where possible.

Alternative Dispute Resolution (ADR) has become popular, especially with businesses, as a cheap and quick way of sorting out a dispute. ADR takes a number of different forms. The main ones are:

- negotiation
- mediation
- conciliation
- arbitration.

| Reasons for having tribunals | To protect individual rights<br>To stop the courts being over-loaded<br>To provide specialist tribunals dealing with one area of law |
|---|---|
| Types of tribunal | Employment tribunals<br>Social security tribunals<br>Immigration tribunals<br>Mental Health Review Tribunal and many more |
| Composition and procedure | Usually a panel of three (chairman and two lay members)<br>Some tribunals are quite formal, for example employment<br>Other tribunals are quite informal, for example social security |
| Advantages of using tribunals | Cheaper than the courts<br>Less formal than the courts<br>Specialise in one type of case<br>Quicker than using the courts |
| Disadvantages of using tribunals | Those without lawyers are less likely to win case<br>Public funding is not normally available for tribunal cases<br>People still find the procedure confusing and intimidating<br>Applicant may feel at a disadvantage as they do not share the specialist<br>    knowledge the panel have<br>There can be delays |

Figure 8.1 Summary of tribunals

In the first three the parties are encouraged to come to a settlement themselves, instead of allowing another person (a judge or arbitrator) to make a decision. Arbitration is different as this is where the parties get an independent arbitrator to decide the dispute.

## Negotiation

Anyone who has a dispute with another person can always try to resolve it by negotiating directly with them. This has the advantage of being completely private, and is also the quickest and cheapest method of settling a dispute. If the parties cannot come to an agreement, they may decide to take the step of instructing solicitors, and those solicitors will usually try to negotiate a settlement.

In fact, even when court proceedings have been commenced, the lawyers for the parties will often continue to negotiate on behalf of their clients, and this is reflected in the high number of cases which are settled out of court.

## Advantages of negotiation

1. Negotiation is much quicker than taking a case to court.
2. It is more convenient as the parties can conduct the negotiation in writing, by telephone or by email.
3. It is informal. People prefer this to the formality of court proceedings.
4. It also allows the parties flexibility in the terms of their settlement. The court can only award damages (money) but in negotiation the parties may agree other matters as well as or instead of a money settlement. These could include future business terms, or giving a consumer a voucher to use on future purchases.
5. Negotiation is much cheaper than taking a case to court. If the parties can come to an

agreement between themselves there are no lawyers' costs. The only costs will be postage on letters, or the cost of telephone calls. It is also the cheapest method of ADR as no other people are involved.

6. All negotiations are conducted in private. The agreement will not be made public. Court proceedings are open to the public and high-profile cases may even be featured in newspapers and on TV.

## Disadvantages of negotiation

1. There may be an imbalance of power. In particular, this will occur where one party is an individual and the other a big business.
2. The parties may not be able to come to an agreement. If they cannot, then they will have to try another method of resolving their dispute.
3. If the dispute involves a point of law, the parties will not have the necessary legal knowledge to deal with it. They will either have to use lawyers to negotiate or take the matter to court.

## Mediation

This is where a neutral mediator helps the parties to reach a compromise solution. The role of a mediator is to consult with each party and see how much common ground there is between them. The mediator will explore the position with each party, looking at their needs and carrying offers to and fro, while keeping confidentiality.

A mediator will not usually tell the parties his own views of the merits of the dispute. The role is to act as a 'facilitator', so that an agreement is reached by the parties. However, a mediator can be asked for an opinion of the merits, and in this case the mediation becomes more of an evaluation exercise, which again aims at ending the dispute.

## Advantages of mediation

1. Using mediation is quicker than taking a case to court.
2. It is also more convenient than using the courts, as the parties can agree where and when the mediation will take place.
3. It is less formal than a court case.
4. It allows the parties to continue with their business relationship. Court proceedings are about winning a case and leave bad feelings between the parties. Mediation is about the parties reaching an agreement with which both parties are happy.
5. Mediation is cheaper than a court case. There will be fees for the use of a professional mediator but these fees are not that expensive. In family cases, it is also possible to get public funding for mediation.
6. Mediators are trained in the art of mediation and are often expert in the area of the dispute.
7. Mediation takes place in private and is not publicised in the media.

## Disadvantages of mediation

1. One party may be intimidated by the mediator. This may lead to that party agreeing to a settlement which is not very favourable to them. This could not happen in a courtroom.
2. Mediators are not always legal experts, so they may not appreciate or be able to deal with it if there is a point of law in the case.
3. Mediation may not work. There is no guarantee that a settlement will be reached. If there is no settlement it will still be necessary to take court proceedings. The mediation will then have added to the costs and time of the case with no result. An example of a failure to reach a settlement happened in the divorce between Paul McCartney and Heather Mills.
4. A mediation settlement is not binding unless the parties agree that it shall be. If this is not

agreed then it cannot be enforced in the courts.

This is our latest form of mediation.

## Conciliation

This has similarities to mediation in that a neutral third party helps to resolve the dispute, but the main difference is that the conciliator will usually play a more active role. The conciliator will be expected to suggest grounds for compromise, and the possible basis for a settlement.

## Advantages of conciliation

The advantages of conciliation are similar to mediation. It is quicker and cheaper than going to court. It is also convenient as the parties and the conciliator can arrange where and when the conciliation will take place.

As with mediation, conciliation allows for parties to include terms about future business deals, and helps the parties continue in their business relationship. It is private and terms of any settlement will not be open to the media.

Conciliators are trained and are often expert in the particular type of dispute.

There is one point which may be an advantage over mediation.

- The conciliator has the power to suggest terms and advise parties on the offers made by the other side.

This means that a settlement is more likely to be achieved.

## Disadvantages of conciliation

Again the disadvantages are similar to the disadvantages of mediation. Conciliators are not always legal experts. The conciliation may not lead to a settlement, so that the case still has to go to court. Also the settlement is not binding unless the parties agree to this.

An additional disadvantage is that one of the parties may feel the conciliator's suggestions and advice are not truly neutral. The conciliator may appear to favour one party. If this occurs then the party feeling at a disadvantage is not likely to agree to any settlement.

## Arbitration

Going to arbitration means that the parties voluntarily agree to have their dispute judged by another person privately, not in court. They agree to accept the decision as final.

## The agreement to go to arbitration

The agreement to go to arbitration is often made in writing at the time the parties made their original contract. At this time, of course, there would have been no dispute, but the agreement would be aimed at any possible future disputes. This type of arbitration agreement is known as a *Scott v Avery* clause, being named after a case in 1855.

Many organisations automatically include arbitration clauses in any contracts made. In particular arbitration clauses are commonly found in car insurance contracts and contracts

| Method of ADR | Who makes decision |
|---|---|
| Negotiation | Parties themselves |
| Mediation | Parties with help of neutral third party |
| Conciliation | Parties with help of neutral third party who plays an active role in suggesting a solution |
| Arbitration | Parties agree to let third party make a binding decision |

**Figure 8.2** Methods of alternative dispute resolution

for package holidays. The example below is an extract from a holiday brochure.

**66** Disputes arising out of, or in connection with this contract which cannot be amicably settled may be referred to arbitration under a special scheme arranged by the Association of British Travel Agents and administered independently by the Chartered Institute of Arbitrators. The scheme provides for a simple and inexpensive method of arbitration on documents alone with restricted liability on the customer in respect of costs. **99**

## ACTIVITY

### Activity 2

Look at travel brochures to see if you can find an arbitration clause. Such a clause is usually in the booking conditions.

Apart from making an arbitration agreement at this early stage, it is also possible to agree to go to arbitration after a dispute arises.

When people agree to use arbitration the courts will normally refuse to allow them to take proceedings in court instead of going to arbitration.

## Using arbitration

Arbitration is popular with businesses and is used by many companies. International companies often use what is called the London Court of Arbitration to resolve their disputes. There is also the Institute of Arbitrators which provides arbitrators for major disputes.

Apart from these major disputes, arbitration is also used as a way of resolving disputes between businesses and customers in a variety of services and industries.

The difference between arbitration and other forms of ADR is that in arbitration a decision is made by the arbitrator and both parties are then bound by that decision, while in other forms of ADR the parties either negotiate directly to come to a settlement or are helped to come to an agreement by a neutral third party.

## The arbitrator

An arbitrator can be anyone whom the parties agree should decide their case. The arbitrator may be a lawyer who specialises in the type of law involved in the dispute or may be a non-lawyer who is a technical expert in the area involved.

This second type of arbitrator is often used where the dispute is over the quality of goods or work done. An example would be an engineer being asked to make a decision in a case about faulty machinery. The agreement to go to arbitration will generally name, or provide a method for choosing, the arbitrator.

## The award

The decision of the arbitrator is called an award. The award can be enforced in the same way as a judgment of the court. There is normally no appeal from a decision made by an arbitrator.

## Advantages of arbitration

There are many advantages to using arbitration instead of going to court:

- The parties can make their own rules as to how the arbitration should be conducted. This means they can choose either a formal hearing with witnesses giving evidence on oath in a similar way to a court hearing or they can agree to a more informal hearing. They may even agree that all the evidence will be put in as documents and have a 'paper' arbitration with no witnesses.
- The time and place of the hearing can be arranged to suit the parties. Where suitable the hearing may be in the evening or at a weekend so as not to interfere with business.
- The whole case will take place in private, so that business disputes are not made public. If a case goes to court the hearing is almost always open to the public.
- The case will be finished more quickly than in the courts.
- Questions of quality are decided by an expert, rather than a judge. This can also save time since the parties will not have to waste time explaining technical points.
- It is much cheaper than going to court. Some estimates suggest that a court case costs 10 times more than an arbitration hearing. This is particularly true if the parties agree that they will not use lawyers at the hearing.

## Disadvantages of arbitration

As with all schemes, however, there are some disadvantages:

- Arbitration is not always cheap. If the parties use a professional arbitrator from an organisation such as the London Institute of Arbitrators, the charge for such an arbitrator could be over £1,000 per day. In addition, if the parties use lawyers to present their cases at the hearing, the costs may well be the same as going to court.
- An individual with a dispute against a big business may feel at a disadvantage. Legal aid is not available for arbitration hearings, although it may be if the same dispute were heard in court, so the individual will either have to do without a lawyer or pay their own costs.
- The fact that there is no general right of appeal can be a disadvantage.
- Arbitration is being increasingly criticised as being almost as costly and time-consuming as going to court and many companies now prefer to use ADR.

### ACTIVITY

**Activity 3**

1. Explain how negotiation works.
2. Give two advantages of negotiation.
3. Give two disadvantages of negotiation.
4. What is the main difference in the role of a mediator and that of a conciliator?
5. Give two advantages which are common to mediation and conciliation.
6. Give two disadvantages which are common to mediation and conciliation.
7. Who makes the decision in arbitration?
8. Explain when the parties may make an agreement to arbitrate.
9. Give three advantages of arbitration.
10. Give three disadvantages of arbitration.

## BRIEF SUMMARY OF CHAPTER

It is not necessary for a dispute to go to court. It can be resolved by other methods.

**Tribunals**

- specialise in a particular area of law, for example employment
- panel of three
- informal procedure

**ADR**

- different methods: negotiation, mediation, conciliation, arbitration
- All are cheaper, quicker and less formal than going to court

**Arbitration**

- Decision made by arbitrator can be allowed for by original contract
- Procedure decided by the parties
- Award is binding

# CHAPTER 9

# JURIES

## Use of juries

The use of a jury in the courts to help decide cases goes back over a thousand years. Originally they were there to provide guidance on local customs, but gradually they became independent decision-makers in cases.

## Independence of juries

Juries have the right to come to the decision they wish. No one is allowed to interfere with their decision-making. The independence of the jury became firmly established in *Bushell's Case* (1670).

### CASE EXAMPLE

#### *Bushell's Case* (1670)

In *Bushell's Case* several jurors refused to convict Quaker activists of unlawful assembly. The trial judge would not accept the not guilty verdict, and ordered the jurors to continue to discuss the case, but would not allow them food or drink. When the jurors continued to refuse to convict, the judge fined them and sent them to prison until the fines were paid.

They appealed against the fines and a higher court ordered their release. It was held that jurors could not be punished for their verdict, even if the judge disagreed with it. This established that the jury were the deciders of fact and the judge could not challenge their decision.

## Juries in the Crown Court

Today the main use of juries is in trials in the Crown Court to try indictable and triable either way offences. (See Chapter 4 for more detail on this.) Here they decide whether the defendant is guilty or not guilty. A jury in the Crown Court consists of 12 people.

## Juries in the civil courts

Juries can also be used in a very small number of cases in the civil courts. In the High Court the jury will consist of 12 members. In the County Court the jury will consist of eight members. Parties have the right to jury trial only in the following types of civil case:

• defamation, ie cases of libel and slander
• false imprisonment
• malicious prosecution
• fraud.

These cases do not have to be tried by jury: if the parties prefer, they can have a judge to decide the case.

In civil cases juries are only used in about 10 or fewer cases a year in the High Court and about once a year in the County Court. So you can see that the use of juries in these cases is very rare indeed.

Where a civil jury is used, the jury decide whether the defendant is liable or not. If they find the defendant is liable, then the jury also has the role of deciding how much money the claimant should be awarded in damages.

## Juries in the Coroner's Courts

Juries are also used at the Coroner's Court. Here a jury of between 7 and 11 members may be used to inquire into deaths. A jury has to be used in four types of case; these are where there has been a death in:

● prison
● an industrial accident
● circumstances where the health and safety of the public is involved, such as deaths in a train crash
● police custody or resulting from an injury caused by a police officer in the execution of his or her duty.

### Jury qualifications

A jury consists of ordinary people. No educational qualifications are required, but there are some basic rules about who can serve on a jury.

## Basic requirements

To be eligible for jury service a person must:

● be aged between 18 and 70;
● be registered to vote on the electoral register; and
● have lived in the United Kingdom, Channel Islands or Isle of Man for at least five years since reaching the age of 13.

These qualifications are set out in the Juries Act 1974. However some people, who qualify under the criteria above, are still not allowed to serve on a jury, because they are disqualified.

## Disqualification

Some criminal convictions will disqualify you from serving on a jury. The length of time of the disqualification depends on the sentence given.

Disqualified for life from jury service are those who at any time have been sentenced to:

| Court | Number on jury | Role of jury |
|---|---|---|
| Crown Court | 12 | Tries indictable and triable either way offences<br>Makes decision on facts<br>Decides verdict of guilty or not guilty |
| High Court | 12 | Can be used only for<br>● defamation, ie cases of libel and slander |
| County Court | 8 | ● false imprisonment<br>● malicious prosecution<br>● fraud<br><br>Very rarely used, even for these types of case<br><br>If used decide liability and amount of damages |
| Coroner's Court | 7–11 | Inquire into deaths:<br>● in prison<br>● in an industrial accident<br>● where health and safety of the public is involved<br>● in police custody or resulting from an injury caused by a police officer |

Figure 9.1 Use of juries in different courts

- imprisonment for life, detention for life or custody for life;
- detention during Her Majesty's pleasure;
- imprisonment for public protection;
- an extended sentence;
- a term of imprisonment of five years or more.

Disqualified for ten years are those who in the last ten years:

- have served a sentence of imprisonment;
- have had a suspended sentence passed on them;
- have had a community sentence passed on them.

In addition, anyone who is currently on bail in criminal proceedings is disqualified from sitting as a juror.

If a disqualified person fails to disclose this fact and sits on a jury, they can be fined up to £5,000.

## Mentally disordered persons

People who are suffering from serious mental illness or mental handicap and are either resident in a hospital or institution or are receiving treatment for their condition are not allowed to sit on a jury.

## Lack of capacity

A person may be discharged from being a juror if they lack the capacity to cope with the trial. This could be because the person does not understand English adequately or because of some disability. The mere fact that a person is disabled does not prevent them from being a juror. It is only if their disability makes them unable to perform a juror's duties. For example, a blind person could not sit as a juror in a case where there was a lot of visual evidence. This is because they would be unable to see such things as plans and photographs produced in evidence.

In 1999 a deaf man was prevented from sitting as a juror. He challenged this. It was held that there was no practical reason why he should not sit, but the problem arose because he needed a sign-language interpreter to help him follow the case. This was not a problem in the courtroom, but it would have been a problem when the jury retired to consider their verdict. The law only allows the 12 jury members to be present in the jury room. It does not allow a 13th person – a sign-language interpreter – to be present. This made it impossible for the deaf man to be a juror.

## Right of excusal

Full-time serving members of the forces may be excused from jury service if their commanding officer certifies that their absence from duty (because of jury service) would be prejudicial to the efficiency of the service.

Also anyone who has served as a juror within the past two years has the right to be excused jury service.

## Discretionary excusals

There will also be other people who do not want to do jury service and they have to explain their reasons in writing to the court. This sort of excusal is called a discretionary excusal, since it is up to the court to decide whether that person should be excused or not.

In these situations the court is most likely to defer jury service (put it off to a future date) to when it is more convenient for the person to do jury service. They try not to excuse people completely. This could happen where a person already has a holiday booked.

However, there are some people who may be granted a discretionary excusal because of their work or their personal circumstances. For example, a doctor in a busy hospital might be excused from jury service; or a woman who is the only carer for a seriously disabled child. It may not be possible to find a suitable date for them to do jury service as their situation will not have changed.

If a person is not excused he or she must attend court on the date given on the summons or risk being fined for failing to do so. The maximum fine for non-attendance is £1,000.

## Police and lawyers on juries

Up to 2004, police and lawyers were not allowed to sit on juries. But since 2004 they have been allowed. In a few cases where there has been a lawyer or police officer on the jury, the defendant has appealed against the conviction on the basis that the police officer or the lawyer was biased.

In *R v Abdroikof, R v Green and R v Williamson* (2007) the House of Lords considered appeals where a police officer or prosecutor had been one of the jury members.

The judges held that the fact that one of the members of jury was a police officer did not of itself make a trial unfair. However, a majority of three of the five judges held that in the situation where a police officer on the jury had worked in the same station as a police officer giving evidence for the prosecution in the trial, then there was the risk of bias. The test to be applied in such cases was:

**66** whether the fair-minded and informed observer, having considered the facts, would conclude that there was a real possibility that the tribunal was biased. **99**

They also pointed out that justice must not only be done, but must be seen to be done. This meant that the presence of a juror who was a local Crown Prosecutor in the Crown Prosecutor Service meant that justice was clearly not being seen to be done.

**ACTIVITY**

### Activity 1

Explain whether or not the following people are qualified to do jury service, including whether they might be excused from service.

1. A 24-year-old woman who is a serving soldier.
2. A 19-year-old man who was born and lived in Australia until he was 16. He is now resident in the UK and registered as a voter.
3. A man, aged 35, who is suffering from severe depression and receiving treatment for this.
4. A doctor who is a surgeon at a local hospital.
5. A 23-year-old woman who was fined for shoplifting at the local Magistrates' Court a month ago.
6. A 71-year-old man who is working as a company director.
7. A man who was convicted of robbery 11 years ago and given a 4-year sentence of imprisonment. He was released from prison 8 years ago.
8. A 56-year-old woman who has been resident in the UK all her life, but forgot to register to vote.
9. A 17-year-old student at an FE college.
10. A 28-year-old deaf woman who is an excellent lip-reader and is sure she would be able to understand all the evidence.

## Selection of a jury

Jurors are selected at random from computerised lists of the electoral registers for each area. Once the names have been chosen, those people are sent a jury summons telling them to come to the Crown Court on a certain date.

| Basic qualifications | Aged between 18 and 70<br>Registered to vote<br>Have lived in the UK for at least five years |
|---|---|
| Disqualified | Disqualified for life if:<br>• imprisonment for life;<br>• detention during Her Majesty's pleasure;<br>• imprisonment for public protection;<br>• an extended sentence;<br>• a term of imprisonment of five years or more.<br><br>Disqualified for ten years if:<br>• have served a sentence of imprisonment;<br>• have had a suspended sentence;<br>• have had a community sentence.<br><br>While on bail |
| Mentally disordered | Cannot sit on a jury if:<br>• suffering from serious mental illness or mental handicap and are either resident in a hospital or institution or are receiving treatment. |
| Lack of capacity | • eg unable to understand English;<br>• disabled in a way which prevents the person from being an effective member of the jury.<br>NB Disability as such does not prevent a person from serving on a jury. |
| Right of excusal | • Full-time serving members of the forces (if commanding officer certifies that their absence from duty would be prejudicial to the efficiency of the service). |
| Discretionary excusals | • If person has a good reason they may be excused jury service<br>OR<br>• their jury service may be deferred to a later time. |

Figure 9.2 Summary of who can serve on a jury

The normal length of jury service is two weeks, though jurors are warned that some trials may last longer.

## At court

In most Crown Courts there will be several courtrooms, each with a different case going on. Where a defendant is pleading not guilty, then jurors who are waiting to be used will come to that courtroom. The court clerk will have cards with their names on and, if there are more than 12 waiting, the clerk will shuffle the cards and choose 12 at random to form the jury. This part of the selection process is done in public in the courtroom, with the clerk reading out the names of those chosen.

## Challenging

As the 12 jurors come into the jury box it is possible that some of them may be challenged by either the prosecution or the defence. This is only done if there is a reason why the juror should not sit on the jury, for example because they are disqualified or because they know the defendant.

If the judge agrees with the challenge, that person will be told they cannot sit on the jury.

Do you think I ought to challenge that juror on the end?

## Stand-by

The prosecution has one further right, the right to put a juror on stand-by. This means that the juror's name is put at the end of the list of available jurors and he or she will only become a juror in that particular trial if there are not 12 others.

## Role in criminal trials

The role of the jury in the Crown Court is to listen to the evidence and decide whether the accused is guilty or not guilty. During the trial jurors may make notes of any points they wish and will be given copies of any documentary evidence or photographs.

The judge decides any necessary points of law during the trial and at the end of the trial he or she explains any legal matters that the jury need to know to reach their verdict. If any member of the jury wishes to ask a question, he or she can write it down and a court official, called an usher, will hand the question to the judge.

All trials start with 12 jurors, but if the case is a long one it is possible that one or more members of the jury may become ill or even die.

When this happens the law allows the judge to let the trial continue with a reduced number of jurors, provided the number does not fall below nine.

## Verdict

In order to make their decision the jurors leave the court and go to a private room to discuss the case. No-one else is allowed to hear their discussions, nor are members of the jury allowed to tell anyone about these. If a juror does disclose what happened, he or she is guilty of contempt of court and may be fined or even sent to prison.

When the jury first retires to consider its verdict, the judge tells the jurors they must try to come to a decision on which they all agree. This is called a unanimous decision.

However, if after long discussion the jurors cannot agree, the judge will ask them to return to the courtroom and then tell them they may reach a majority decision. This will not happen until the jury has spent at least two hours trying to come to a unanimous decision.

## Majority verdict

When a majority verdict is allowed, at least 10 jurors must agree, so that the vote could be 11–1 or 10–2 for either guilty or not guilty. Where the jury has fallen below 11, then at least 9 jurors must agree.

## Announcing the verdict

Once the jury have decided, they return to court and the clerk asks what their verdict is. The spokesman for the jury, who is known as the foreman, must give the verdict and say whether it was a unanimous verdict or a majority one.

When it is a majority verdict of guilty, the foreman must also state how many jurors agreed. If the verdict is guilty, the judge then has to decide what sentence to give the defendant; if the verdict is not guilty the defendant is acquitted.

## Advantages of jury trial

### Lay participation

The most important advantage is that ordinary people are involved in the decision. The idea is that a defendant is tried by his peers (his equals). There should be a cross-section of society involved. It also means that the law has to be explained in simple terms to the jury. This keeps the law more open and accessible.

### Public confidence

Most people feel that the jury is an important element in the administration of justice. Juries are not biased; the fact that there are 12 jurors will help cancel out any individual biases. The jury has no direct interest in the case; they do not know any of those involved. The jury should not be pressurised by the judge. In *R v McKenna* (1960) the defendant's conviction was quashed on appeal because the judge at the trial threatened the jury that if they did not return a verdict within another 10 minutes, they would be locked up all night.

### Jury equity

The jury can acquit a defendant even though the judge disagrees with that verdict and even if the judge has told the jury that the defendant legally has no defence. As a result a jury can refuse to operate a law they feel is unjust. This happened in the case of Clive Ponting in 1985, when Ponting was charged with an offence against section 2 of the Official Secrets Act 1911 because he leaked information to an MP about the sinking of a ship, the *Belgrano*, in the Falklands War. Later, mainly as a result of Ponting's case, Parliament reformed the law.

The following is an example of a decision by a jury where they refused to convict the defendants even though they admitted causing damage.

## CLEARED

**Jury decides that threat of global warming justifies breaking the law**

The threat of global warming is so great that campaigners were justified in causing more that £35,000 of damage to a coal-fired power station, a jury decided yesterday. In a verdict that will have shocked ministers and energy companies the jury at Maidstone Crown Court cleared six Greenpeace activists of criminal damage.

Jurors accepted defence arguments that the six had a 'lawful excuse' to damage property at Kingsnorth power station in Kent to prevent even greater damage caused by climate change.

*(Source: taken from an article by Michael McCarthy, The Independent, 11 September 2008)*

It is examples like this that caused one famous judge, Lord Devlin, to say that the jury is 'the lamp that shows that freedom lives'.

### Impartiality

The members of the jury have no involvement in the case. They must not know the defendant or the prosecution witnesses. This means that they are not likely to be biased in any way.

## Disadvantages of jury trial

### No reason for decision

No reasons have to be given for the verdict. This means there is no way of knowing if the jury did understand the case and came to the decision for the right reasons. In some cases it has become known after the case was finished that the reasons were not based on the evidence given in the case.

In *R v Connor and Rollock* (2004) a juror wrote to the Crown Court stating that the jurors thought it was one or other of the two defendants who had committed the stabbing, but were not sure which one. They decided to convict both to 'teach them a lesson'. It was held that the court was not entitled to hear what had happened in the jury room. The convictions could not be appealed against.

In *R v Young (Stephen)* (1995) it was discovered that some of the jury had convicted the defendant because they held a séance using a ouija board. The jury had to stay overnight in a hotel as they had not reached a verdict by the end of the first day of discussion. During this stay at the hotel some of them had tried to contact the dead victims to ask them who had killed them.

In this case the conviction was quashed and the defendant was tried by a fresh jury. This was because the séance had not occurred during the discussions of the jury in the jury room.

## Perverse verdicts

Earlier in this chapter we looked at the idea of jury equity. That is the fact that the jury can ignore an unjust law. However, in some circumstances this type of decision can be seen as a perverse decision and one which was not justified.

Juries have refused to convict in clear cut cases such as *R v Randle and Pottle* (1991) where the defendants were charged with helping the spy George Blake to escape from prison. Their prosecution did not occur until 25 years after the escape, when they wrote about what they had done. The jury acquitted them, possibly as a protest over the time lapse between the offence and the prosecution.

## Lack of understanding

One of the main arguments against the use of juries is that some jurors find court procedure confusing and are unable to understand the evidence even in a straightforward case.

To help jurors a booklet is sent out with the jury summons explaining in simple language what is likely to happen at court and some courts show a short video to jurors when they first arrive at court, again explaining where the different people in the case will be sitting and the general procedure of the court.

Since it is illegal to interview jurors about their decision, it is not possible to know whether they did understand the case or not. To try to research this area, there have been studies using shadow juries. These are people chosen in exactly the same way as the real jury, who listen to the whole case, discuss it and come to a verdict, but because they are not the real jury their verdict does not count.

The important thing about shadow juries is that their discussions can be filmed and they can be questioned about their findings. This type of research shows that usually the jury gets the main facts right, but that they may miss some of the fine distinctions.

There have been proposals to stop using juries in long complicated fraud trials, since this type of trial is particularly difficult for an ordinary person to understand.

## Time and cost

The use of a jury makes a trial longer as everything has to be explained to the jury. This in turn means that it costs more to have a trial with a jury than without one.

## Media influence

High-profile cases, especially murder cases, are likely to have a lot of coverage in the newspapers and on television when the crime occurs. The police investigations may be followed in great detail. Media coverage can cause jurors to form a biased view of the case.

This definitely occurred in a murder case involving two sisters in 1993. Some newspapers published a still picture from a video sequence which gave a false impression of what was happening. After the jury convicted the defendants, the trial judge gave leave to appeal because of the possible influence the media coverage might have had on the decision and the Court of Appeal quashed the convictions.

## Other disadvantages

Some jurors dislike doing jury service or become bored and may rush the decision.

There is a risk that members of the jury will be bribed or threatened by the defendant's friends. Majority verdicts were introduced in order to make this more difficult, as at least three jurors will have to be 'nobbled' to affect the decision.

The lower age limit of 18 is too young; it could be said that a person of this age has not got enough experience of life to make such important decisions.

## Alternatives to jury trial

### Single judge

In Northern Ireland the decision used to be made by one judge without a jury. The courts were called Diplock Courts. This method of trial was used because of the extra risk of violence to jurors and possible bias during the IRA troubles.

Juries are now used in Northern Ireland.

Other countries also use this method. It is probably the cheapest and most efficient way of conducting a trial. However, it removes a long tradition of public participation and there has been strong opposition to it.

## A panel of judges

This is the method of trial in some continental countries. It is expensive and would mean that several hundred new judges would have to be found. There is also the same criticism that it does away with public participation.

## A judge and two lay assessors

This is probably the most acceptable alternative to jury trial, as it would eliminate the slowness and cost of using a jury, while retaining public involvement.

The two lay assessors could be chosen in much the same way as jurors. The decision would be made jointly by the judge and the lay assessors, thus avoiding problems of lack of understanding. The main objection is that there would not be such a wide cross-section of society as in the present system.

## A judge and a mini-jury

Another option is to reduce the size of the jury to six or seven jurors. This would only help by halving the number of jurors needed, so saving some cost, but most of the present disadvantages would remain.

### BRIEF SUMMARY OF CHAPTER

**Use of juries**
- Crown Court – indictable and triable either way offences – decide verdict
- High Court and County Court – in a very small number of civil cases, mostly for defamation
- Coroners' Courts to inquire into certain deaths

**Jury qualifications**
- 18–70, registered to vote, lived in UK for five years
- Must not be disqualified

- Some mentally disordered people are not allowed to sit on jury
- Members of armed forces can have a right to be excused jury service
- Cannot sit if lacks capacity, for example insufficient understanding of English
- May have a discretionary excusal

**Advantages of using juries**

- lay involvement, public confidence, jury equity, impartiality

**Disadvantages of using juries**

- Do not give reason for decision, perverse verdicts, lack of understanding, media influence, and other reasons

# CHAPTER 10

# LAY MAGISTRATES

Considering the amount and range of work that magistrates are required to deal with it is, perhaps, surprising to realise that apart from about 100 or so qualified magistrates, all the people who sit to hear cases in the Magistrates' Courts are ordinary, non-legally qualified people.

Non-qualified magistrates are called lay magistrates and they are not paid (except for expenses) and only sit part-time as magistrates.

The only requirements to become a lay magistrate are that one must:

- be between 18 and 65 when appointed; and
- live or work within or near to the local justice area to which they are allocated.

Lay magistrates sit part-time. They must do at least 26 half days per year and, if possible, 35 half days per year. The only payment they receive is for their travel expenses and meals.

Since they are not qualified they do not usually make decisions on their own, but sit as a bench. This means that there must be at least two magistrates sitting together and normally there will be a panel of three. A single lay magistrate has very limited powers but can do such things as issue warrants for arrest.

There are about 29,000 lay magistrates with about 1,800 to 2,000 being appointed each year.

## Applying to be a magistrate

Those who wish to be lay magistrates must apply to their local advisory committee.

## Key qualities

Although lay magistrates do not need any formal qualifications, there are six key qualities which lay magistrates should possess. These are:

- good character
- understanding and communication
- social awareness
- maturity and sound temperament
- sound judgement
- commitment and reliability.

## The interview process

The local committees will interview candidates. There is usually a two-stage interview process.

At the first interview the panel tries to find out more about the candidate's personal attributes, in particular looking to see if they have the six key qualities required. The interview panel will also explore the candidate's attitudes on various criminal justice issues such as youth crime or drink driving.

The second interview is aimed at testing candidates' potential judicial aptitude and this is done by a discussion of at least two case studies which are typical of those heard regularly in Magistrates' Courts. The discussion might, for example, focus on the type of sentence which should be imposed on specific case facts.

## Appointment

The committee will then recommend those they think are suitable for appointment to the Lord Chancellor. He will then appoint new magistrates from this list. Once appointed, magistrates may continue to sit until the age of 70.

**ACTIVITY**

**Activity 1**

1. Put the list of six key qualities above into order, with the one that you think is most important first and the least important last.
2. Compare your list with those of two other people.
3. Explain what other qualities you think magistrates need.

## Training

All new lay magistrates must undergo training. The first part of the training is carried out before they can start sitting as magistrates. New magistrates must attend training sessions. They must also sit as an observer in court to see how cases are dealt with.

Each new magistrate keeps a Personal Development Log of their progress and has a mentor (an experienced magistrate) to assist them. The framework of training is divided into three areas of competence. These are:

1. Managing yourself – this focuses on some of the basic aspects of self-management in relation to preparing for court, conduct in court and ongoing learning.
2. Working as a member of a team – this focuses on the team aspect of decision-making in the Magistrates' Court.
3. Making judicial decisions – this focuses on impartial and structured decision-making.

### Appraisal

During the first two years of the new magistrate sitting in court, between 8 and 11 of the sessions will be mentored. In the same period the magistrate is also expected to attend about

seven training sessions. After two years, or whenever it is felt that the magistrate is ready, there will be an appraisal of the magistrate to check if they have acquired the competencies.

Any magistrate who cannot show that they have achieved the competencies will be given extra training. If they still cannot achieve the competencies, then the matter is referred to the local Advisory Committee, who may recommend to the Lord Chancellor that the magistrate is removed from sitting.

The training scheme involves practical training 'on the job'. It also answers the criticisms of the previous system where there was no check made on whether magistrates had actually benefited from the training sessions they had attended.

## The role of magistrates

Magistrates have a very wide workload. Most of the work they do is connected to criminal cases. They also deal with some civil matters, especially family cases.

### Role in criminal cases

Magistrates try 97 per cent of all criminal cases. For these they deal with all stages of the case. If the case cannot be finished at the first hearing, the magistrates will hear bail applications and remand the defendant in custody or on bail to another date for the case to be fully dealt with.

At the full hearing they will find out if the defendant pleads guilty or not guilty. They will sentence anyone who pleads guilty and they will try the case of anyone who is pleading not guilty. If they find that person guilty, they will also deal with sentencing.

They have the power to fine individuals up to £5,000 (and companies up to £20,000). They can also send individuals to prison for up to six months for one offence or 6 + 6 months for two offences. They also have power to impose a community sentence on a guilty defendant.

As well as trying 97 per cent of all criminal cases, magistrates also deal with the first hearing in the remaining 3 per cent of criminal cases. The first hearing will deal with preliminary matters such as bail applications. The magistrates will then send the case to the Crown Court.

## Role in civil cases

They also deal with civil matters which include the enforcing of debts owed to the utilities (gas, electric and water), non-payment of the council tax and non-payment of television licences. In addition they hear appeals from the refusal of a local authority to grant licences for the sale of alcohol and licences for betting and gaming establishments.

## Youth Court

Specially nominated and trained justices form the Youth Court panel to hear criminal charges against young offenders aged 10–17 years old. These magistrates must be under 65 and a panel must usually include at least one man and one woman.

## Family Court

There is also a special panel for the Family Court to hear family cases including orders for protection against violence, affiliation cases, adoption orders and proceedings under the Children Act 1989.

## Appeals

Lay magistrates also sit at the Crown Court to hear appeals from the Magistrates' Court. In these cases two lay justices form a panel with a qualified judge.

## The magistrates' clerk

Every bench of lay magistrates is assisted by a clerk who is their legal adviser. The senior clerk in each court has to be a barrister or solicitor of at least five years' standing.

The duty of the clerk is to guide the magistrates on questions of law, practice and procedure. The clerk is not meant to assist in the decision-making and should not normally retire with the magistrates when they leave the court at the end of a case to consider their verdict.

### ACTIVITY

#### Activity 2

Look up the website of the Magistrates' Association at www.magistrates-association.org.uk and look at sentencing examples given on the site.

## Composition of the bench

Lay magistrates are often thought of as being middle-aged and middle class.

The report *The Judiciary in the Magistrates' Courts* (2002) showed that this was largely true. They found that lay magistrates:

- were drawn overwhelmingly from professional and managerial ranks; and
- 40 per cent of them were retired from full-time employment.

However, there are very positive facts about the composition of the panels of lay magistrates.

There are about the same number of men and women in the lay magistracy. In 2008, for the first time, there were actually slightly more women than men: 14,747 women and 14,747 men.

This is very much better than in the professional judiciary where only about 16 per cent of judges are women. In fact in the higher courts only about 10 per cent of judges are women.

There is also good representation of ethnic minorities in the lay bench. About 8.5 per cent of magistrates are from ethnic minorities. Again this compares very favourably with the professional judiciary where only 1 to 2 per cent of judges are from ethnic minorities.

## ACTIVITY

### Activity 3

Decide if the following statements are TRUE or FALSE.

1. Lay magistrates have to have a qualification in law.
2. To be appointed, lay magistrates must be over 25.
3. Lay magistrates are not paid.
4. Anyone wishing to become a lay magistrate must apply to their local Advisory Committee.
5. The Prime Minister appoints lay magistrates.
6. New lay magistrates must attend training sessions and sit as an observer in court.
7. Magistrates try indictable offences.
8. Magistrates try 97 per cent of all criminal cases.
9. Lay magistrates are assisted by a clerk.
10. There are many more male lay magistrates than there are female lay magistrates.

## Advantages of lay magistrates

There are many good points to the system of lay magistrates.

1. The system involves members of the community and provides a wider cross-section than would be possible if only professional judges were used. In particular

women and ethnic minorities are proportionately represented.
2. Lay magistrates have local knowledge because they live or work in or near the area in which they sit as magistrates.
3. Improved training, together with the availability of a legally trained clerk, means the system is not as amateur as it used to be.
4. It is cheaper to have magistrates than to have a hearing in the Crown Court, both for the defendant and for the Government.
5. Cases are dealt with more quickly in Magistrates' Courts than at the Crown Court, but even so there may be a delay of several months.
6. There are only a small number of appeals from magistrates' decisions. Usually about 12,000 to 13,000 appeals a year out of one million cases dealt with in the Magistrates' Courts. This suggests that the system is working satisfactorily.

## Disadvantages of lay magistrates

The system of using unqualified local people as magistrates has been criticised. The following is a list of possible criticisms:

1. Lay justices are middle-class, middle-aged and middle-minded.
2. There is inadequate compensation for loss of earnings, so 'workers' are discouraged from applying to become magistrates.
3. The training is inadequate, although this has improved.
4. Lay justices are prosecution minded, pro-police and more likely than a jury to believe police officers, partly due to their class background and partly because they are likely to see the same police officers giving evidence often. The conviction rate is higher than in the Crown Court.
5. Since lay magistrates are not qualified, they rely too heavily on their clerk.

6. There is inconsistency in sentencing and in granting bail. There are big variations from one court to another, even in the same area.

7. There is too wide and heavy a workload for amateurs. This is particularly so with the increasing crime rate, the increasing number of offences made summary only and the move to prevent some defendants electing jury trial. The Family Court's workload has also increased and become more complicated.

The advantages and disadvantages of lay magistrates can be compared with each other as shown in Figure 10.1.

| Fact | Advantage | Disadvantage |
|---|---|---|
| Ordinary members of society | Involves members of the community in the justice system<br><br>Women and ethnic minorities are well represented | Have no knowledge of law and may rely too heavily on their clerk<br><br>Not a good cross-section of society Tend to be over 40 and many are retired from full-time work |
| All lay magistrates are trained for their work | Training has improved<br><br>There are few appeals | Inconsistency in sentencing Inconsistency in granting bail |
| Lay magistrates are not paid | The system is cheaper than using the Crown Court | The workload is too wide and heavy for unpaid 'amateurs'. |

Figure 10.1 Comparison chart of advantages and disadvantages of lay magistrates

## BRIEF SUMMARY OF CHAPTER

**Selection and appointment**
- no formal qualifications needed
- should have the six 'key qualities'
- interviewed by local Advisory Committee
- appointed by Lord Chancellor

**Role**
- first hearing of all criminal cases
- try all summary offences and triable either way offences where defendant chooses Magistrates' Courts
- sentence all those who plead guilty or are found guilty
- some civil work
- Family Court, Youth Court
- sit with judge to hear appeals at Crown Court

**Clerk**
- legally qualified, advises magistrates on law, does not help with decision-making

**Advantages**
- involves community in legal system, women and ethnic minorities well represented, local knowledge, training, cheap, cases dealt with quickly, few appeals

**Disadvantages**
- not a true cross-section of society, often middle-aged and middle-class, may be prosecution-minded, may rely on clerk, inconsistency in sentencing and bail, workload too wide and heavy for 'amateurs'

Study the extract below and then answer **all** parts of the question which follows.

'Cases which are brought under English law can be heard either in the criminal or the civil court system.

Civil cases, which are disputes between individuals, are generally heard either in the County Court or the High Court, with most being tried locally in the County Court. Cases in the County Court will be heard either by the Circuit Judge or District Judge, sitting alone.

Alternatively, civil disputes can be resolved through the process of negotiation.

Criminal cases will be tried either in the Magistrates' Court or the Crown Court, depending on how serious the case is, how the accused decides to plead, and whether or not the magistrates feel they would have sufficient powers to sentence the accused.

Lay people play an important role in running the criminal justice system. Lay magistrates deal with most criminal cases which are tried by the criminal courts. In a trial in the Crown Court, the judge will sit with a jury of 12 ordinary members of the public. The jurors are chosen at random to try serious cases which have been committed or transferred from the Magistrates' Court.'

*(Source: adapted from John Wilman Brown, GCSE Law (9th edn, Sweet & Maxwell, 2005))*

(a)  Outline the important differences between **civil** and **criminal** courts.

(4 marks)

(b)  Outline any two different types of case heard by the County Court.

(4 marks)

(c)  The Civil Procedure Act 1997 introduced a system for dealing with civil cases based on each case being allocated to the appropriate track. Explain what is meant by:

(i) the small claims track;

(ii) the fast track.                (4 marks)

(d)

(i) Explain how, and in what circumstances, negotiation might be used as a method of dispute resolution.

(4 marks)

(ii) Comment on the advantages **and** disadvantages of a claim being settled by negotiation.              (5 marks)

(e)  Explain **three** differences between the Magistrates' Court and the Crown Court.

(6 marks)

(f)  Outline how lay magistrates are appointed.                (3 marks)

(g)  Describe how jurors qualify and are selected for jury service.       (5 marks)

(h)  Comment on how well each of the following carry out their role within the criminal justice system. **(Answer in continuous prose.)**

(i) Lay magistrates              (5 marks)

(ii) Jurors.              (5 marks)

*AQA Specimen Paper*

# CHAPTER 11

# THE LEGAL PROFESSION

In England and Wales there are two types of lawyers – solicitors and barristers. Most countries do not have such a definite division among lawyers; a person will qualify as a lawyer though it will be possible after qualifying to specialise in one particular area of law.

So in England and Wales you must decide quite early on in your training whether you want to be a solicitor or a barrister.

## Solicitors

There are about 100,000 solicitors practising in England and Wales and they are controlled by their own professional body called the Law Society.

## Training

To become a solicitor it is usual to have a law degree and then to take a one-year Legal Practice Course. This is followed by a two-year training contract where the trainee solicitor works in a firm of solicitors or for an organisation such as the Crown Prosecution Service or local or central government.

During this two-year period the trainee solicitor will be paid, though not at the same rate as a fully qualified solicitor, and will do his or her own work supervised by a qualified solicitor. The trainee will also have to complete a Professional Skills Course which gives training in interviewing clients and witnesses, negotiating, advocacy and business management including dealing with accounts.

Finally the trainee will be admitted as a solicitor by the Law Society and his or her name will be added to the list or roll of solicitors.

Those who have a degree in a subject other than law must take an extra year's course on law and pass the Graduate Diploma in Law (GDL).

There is also a possible entry route which does not involve taking a degree first, but this is only available to mature students and it takes longer to qualify by this route. The three routes to becoming a solicitor are shown in Figure 11.1.

The main criticisms of the training process are that: first, many people with good degrees cannot get a place on the Legal Practice Course (LPC); second, students have to pay the fees for this course and also support themselves during the year it lasts. Many students from lower- and middle-income backgrounds take out bank loans and by the time they qualify, they may owe thousands of pounds.

The third criticism is that even after passing the Legal Practice Course students are not qualified as solicitors but must find a training place with a firm of solicitors or other suitable organisation. Not all students will be able to find training places and may be prevented from qualifying as solicitors as a result.

## Solicitors' work

The majority of those qualifying as a solicitor work in private practice in a solicitor's firm. There are, however, other careers available and some newly qualified solicitors may go to work

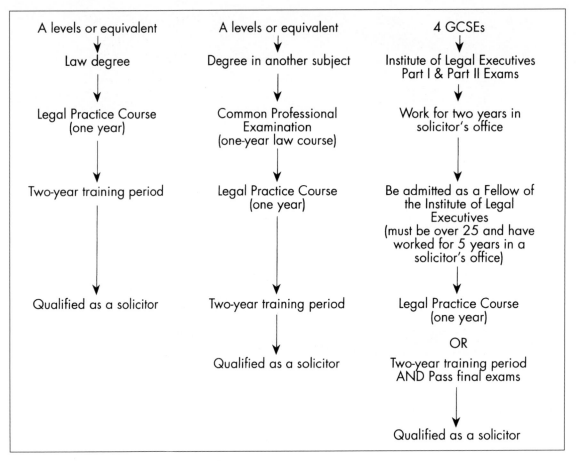

Figure 11.1 Training routes to become a solicitor

in the Crown Prosecution Service or become advisers in local government or 'in-house' solicitors for commercial or industrial businesses.

Private solicitors' firms vary enormously, from small 'high street' practices in towns throughout England and Wales to the very large firms in London. The number of solicitors working in each type of practice will also vary from the 'one-man band', known as a sole practitioner, to hundreds of solicitors. One of the largest firms has over 200 partners and over a thousand assistant solicitors. The work of these firms is equally varied.

A small high street firm will be a general practice advising clients on a wide variety of topics, such as consumer problems, housing problems, business matters and family problems. A solicitor working in such a practice will spend some of his or her time interviewing clients in the office and dealing with paperwork, possibly drafting a contract, drawing up a will, dealing with conveyancing (preparing documents for the sale of houses), or preparing papers for court.

Solicitors may also, if they wish, act for some of their clients in court. Standing up in court to put a client's case is known as advocacy and some solicitors will spend much of their time in court while others may prefer to concentrate on office work.

In most firms of solicitors there is an element of specialisation. The firm itself may only deal with a certain type of work; for example, some firms

A solicitor's office

will only deal with civil matters and not take any criminal cases. Within the firm solicitors are likely to specialise so that, for example, one solicitor may deal solely with property matters while another concentrates on family work. The bigger the firm of solicitors the more the individual solicitors will specialise. Some of the big city firms will deal mainly with company work and solicitors working for them are likely to do highly specialised work.

## Advocacy

All solicitors can do advocacy work in the Magistrates' Courts and in the County Courts but have very limited rights to appear in the Crown Court and High Court.

If a solicitor wishes to specialise in advocacy and have an unlimited right to appear as an advocate in all courts they must get a certificate in advocacy. Such a certificate will only be granted if the solicitor has already acted as an advocate in the Magistrates' Court and the

County Court, taken a short training course and passed examinations about court work.

Solicitors were given the right to apply for these certificates under the Courts and Legal Services Act 1990 and the first certificates were granted in 1994. By the beginning of 2009 only about 2,000 solicitors had applied for a certificate of advocacy.

## Barristers

There are about 12,000 barristers in independent practice in England and Wales and they are controlled by their own professional body called the General Council of the Bar.

## Training

To become a barrister it is usual to start by obtaining a law degree; those with a degree in another subject will have to do a one-year course on law and pass the Graduate Diploma in Law (GDL).

In order to go on to the next stage of training it is necessary to join an Inn of Court and be accepted on the Bar Vocational Course (BVC) which lasts one academic year. The Vocational Training Course concentrates on practical skills, particularly advocacy, and students learn to draft legal documents and present cases in court.

As with solicitors there is a financial problem for students doing the Vocational Course. Joining an Inn of Court and attending there to dine or for weekend courses is compulsory, but students may choose which of the four Inns – Lincoln's Inn, the Inner Temple, the Middle Temple and Gray's Inn – they wish to join.

## Pupillage

Once students have passed the Vocational Course and dined the correct number of times they will be called to the Bar by their Inn of Court. They are then barristers but will not be allowed to practise in court until they have completed the first six months of the next stage of their training, which is called pupillage.

Being a pupil barrister means studying under an experienced barrister, reading their work, practising writing advices and opinions on points of law, drafting other legal documents and going to court with the pupil master to observe cases. The total length of pupillage is one year and this can be served with the same pupil

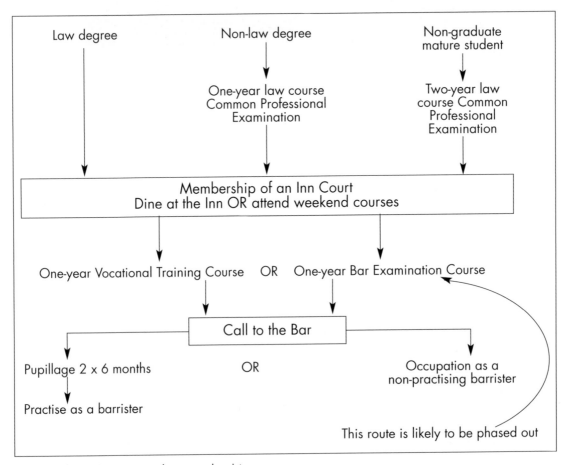

**Figure 11.2** Training routes to become a barrister

master or as two periods of six months with different pupil masters.

During this period the trainee barrister must also take part in a programme of continuing education organised by the Bar Council. In order to help people with this stage of training the Bar has introduced a scheme to provide a minimum level of funding for all pupils.

It is possible for mature non-graduates to read for the Bar, but they must first do a two-year Law Course before going on to take the Vocational Course. There is also an alternative one-year course to the Vocational Course for those who want to qualify as barristers but not practise at the Bar. The various training routes are shown in Figure 11.2.

## Barristers' work

Barristers practising at the Bar are self-employed, but usually join a set of chambers (offices) consisting of a small number of barristers (often about 20) and support staff of whom the most important is the clerk. The clerk is effectively the business manager and is in charge of administration and acts as an agent for their barristers.

Solicitors who want a barrister to act for them in a case will ring up the clerk to arrange it. When a solicitor sends work to a barrister it is known as briefing a barrister and the papers that the barrister receives are called a brief. It is now possible for clients to go directly to a barrister.

Appearing in court on behalf of clients is the main part of most barristers' work. Barristers have the right to appear in any court in England and Wales. When a barrister appears in court, the instructing solicitor or someone from the solicitor's firm will also be present at court, sitting behind the barrister to provide any necessary information and to take notes.

Barristers also do paperwork, mainly giving advice and opinions about the law or drafting

A barrister

documents for use in court. Indeed, some barristers who specialise in certain areas of law such as company law, tax law, planning and housing law will rarely, if ever, appear in court.

## Queen's Counsel

Some senior solicitors and barristers will become Queen's Counsel and be able to use the initials QC after their names. A solicitor or barrister must have been qualified for at least 10 years before applying to become a Queen's Counsel. Only those who are recognised as being the best barristers and solicitors are appointed.

There is criticism that not enough women or candidates from ethnic minority groups are chosen. Only about 10 per cent of Queen's Counsel are women. Also only a very small number of solicitors become Queen's Counsel.

The Lord Chancellor used to choose QCs. There were criticisms that this method was too secretive. The system was changed so they are now selected by a special selection panel. Selection is by interview and applicants can provide references (including references from clients).

Becoming a QC is also known as 'taking silk'. This is because QCs (or silks) wear a different gown in court from that worn by junior barristers (all barristers who are not QCs are junior barristers regardless of their age!) and this gown is traditionally made of silk. As a QC the barrister will be able to charge more and will undertake more complicated cases. Often a QC will have a junior barrister to work with them on cases.

## Organisation of the legal profession

Solicitors are governed by the Law Society. Barristers are governed by the General Council of the Bar, usually known as the Bar Council. Both these are overseen by the Legal Services Board. This was set up under the Legal Services Act 2007.

There used to be rules that meant that barristers and solicitors could not work together. Also lawyers and non-lawyers were not allowed to work together in legal businesses. The Legal Services Act 2007 changed this. Under the Act the following will be allowed:

• legal businesses with lawyers and non-lawyers
• legal businesses with barristers and solicitors.

These are known as Legal Disciplinary Practices (LPDs). Allowing LPDs will give the public access to a fuller service in one place – the one-stop-shop. It may be that a client wants to make a new will, but also needs advice on finance and taxation in connection with the will. If there are solicitors and accountants working together, the client will be able to get all the advice from the same firm.

The Act also allows in the future for:

• non-lawyers to own legal businesses
• legal businesses to operate as companies.

These are known as Alternative Business Structures. They will not be allowed until at least 2011.

## ACTIVITY

### Activity 1

Fill in the gaps in the following passage from the words and phrases given in the box below.

Solicitors and barristers must normally have a degree. This is usually a ................. degree. If it is in any other subject, it is necessary to do the ................... .

Next, would-be solicitors must take the ........................., then do a two-year ...................... . Would-be barristers must take the ...................... and then do a one-year ........................ .

Solicitors work in ........................... Barristers work in ...................... . Solicitors' work is usually more office-based, though they can take cases in court. Presenting a case in court is known as ................... . Barristers often specialise in presenting cases in court as they have full rights of .................... . However, some barristers, such as tax law specialists, may rarely go to court.

After practising for at least 10 years, solicitors and barristers can apply to become a ........................... .

Solicitors are governed by the ............................... . Barristers are governed by the ................................ .

| | |
|---|---|
| advocacy | Bar Council |
| chambers | firms |
| Bar Vocational Course | Law Society |
| law | Graduate Diploma in Law |
| pupillage | Legal Practice Course |
| Queen's Counsel | training contract |

# Legal executives

Apart from solicitors and barristers, there are also legal executives who work in solicitors' firms. To become a legal executive it is necessary to pass the Part I and Part II examinations of the Institute of Legal Executives and to have worked in a firm of solicitors or an organisation such as the Crown Prosecution Service for at least five years.

Legal executives will often deal with the more straightforward cases themselves, for example preparing simple wills or leases. They also have some limited rights to appear in court, mainly making applications in the County Court where the case is not defended. The partners in the firm of solicitors for whom the legal executive works are responsible for his or her work.

## BRIEF SUMMARY OF CHAPTER

The legal profession has two branches: solicitors and barristers.

**Solicitors**
- governed by the Law Society
- work is office based
- can present cases in court
- approached directly by the public

**Barristers**
- governed by the General Council of the Bar
- more likely to specialise in court work but also do paperwork
- clients can now go to them direct

**Training for both**
- law degree or GDL
- vocational course and exams (LPC or BVC)
- on-the-job training (training contract or pupillage)

**Organisation**
- The Law Society and the Bar Council are overseen by the Legal Services Board
- The Legal Services Act 2007 allows solicitors and barristers to work in the same firm: it also allows lawyers and non-lawyers to work in the same firm

# CHAPTER 12

# JUDGES

## Types of judge

Judges as a group are also called the judiciary. There are many different levels of judges who sit in different courts. There are the following:

- District Judges
- Recorders
- Circuit Judges
- High Court Judges
- Lords Justices of Appeal
- Law Lords.

### District Judges

This is lowest level of full-time judge. They sit in either the Magistrates' Courts or the County Courts.

### Recorders

These are part-time judges who sit mainly in the Crown Court. It is also possible for a Recorder to sit in a County Court.

### Circuit Judges

Circuit Judges sit in the Crown Court or the County Court. They do the majority of the work in these two courts.

### High Court Judges

These sit in the High Court to try civil cases. They also sit in the Crown Court to hear the most serious criminal cases, such as murder and manslaughter.

### Lords Justices of Appeal

These sit to hear appeals in the Court of Appeal. They will deal with cases in both the civil division of the Court of Appeal and the criminal division of the Court of Appeal.

### Supreme Court Judges

These sit in the Supreme Court. There are only 12 of them. They were known as Law Lords before the Supreme Court came into operation.

## Role of judges

### District Judges

District Judges sit in the County Court to deal with small claims cases (under £5,000) and can also hear other cases for larger amounts.

District Judges who are appointed to the Magistrates' Courts try criminal cases in the Magistrates' Courts. They sit on their own and decide facts and law. When a defendant pleads guilty or is found guilty, they also have to decide on the sentence.

They may also sit to hear family cases, but this will usually be with two lay magistrates.

### Recorders

Recorders are part-time judges who are appointed for a period of five years. They are used mainly in the Crown Court to try criminal cases, but some sit in the County Court to help with civil cases. They will only sit for about one month a year. The rest of the year they will work as a solicitor or barrister, or as a legal academic.

## Circuit Judges

Circuit Judges sit in the County Court to hear civil cases and also in the Crown Court to try criminal cases.

In civil cases they sit on their own (it is very rare to have a jury in a civil case in the County Court). They decide the law and the facts. They make the decision on who has won the case.

In criminal cases they sit with a jury. The jury decide the facts and the judge decides the law. Where a defendant pleads guilty or is found guilty by a jury, the judge then has to decide on the sentence.

## High Court Judges

Each judge in the High Court will be assigned to one of the Divisions. There are 72 judges in the Queen's Bench Division, 17 in the Chancery Division and 18 in the Family Division.

The main role of High Court Judges is to try cases. These are cases at first instance because it is the first time the case has been heard by a court. The judges will hear evidence from witnesses, decide what the law is and make the decision as to which side has won the case. If the claim is for damages (an amount of money) the judge decides how much should be awarded to the winning claimant.

High Court Judges also hear some appeals. These are mainly from civil cases tried in the County Court. The judges in the Queen's Bench Division also hear criminal appeals from the Magistrates' Courts by a special case stated method. These are appeals on law only. When sitting to hear appeals, there will be a panel of two or three judges.

## Role in criminal cases

Judges from the Queen's Bench Division also sit to hear criminal trials in the Crown Court. When they do this they sit with a jury. The jury decide the facts and the judge decides the law. Where a defendant pleads guilty or is found guilty by a jury, the judge then has to decide on the sentence.

## Lords Justices of Appeal

There are some 37 Lords Justices of Appeal. They sit in both the civil and criminal divisions of the Court of Appeal, so they deal with both civil and criminal cases.

On the criminal side they hear over 7,000 applications for leave to appeal against sentence or conviction each year. These are dealt with by one judge. Only about a quarter of these get leave to appeal, so the full court then has about 1,800 criminal appeals to hear.

In addition, they hear over 3,000 civil appeals each year. These may be appeals against the finding of liability or an appeal about the remedy awarded, for example the amount of money given as damages.

Court of Appeal Judges usually sit as a panel of three to hear cases. On rare occasions in important cases, there may be a panel of five. Decisions by the Court of Appeal on points of law become precedents which lower courts must follow.

## Supreme Court Judges

Supreme Court Judges hear only about 70 cases each year. These cases are always appeals. They can be in civil or criminal cases. However, there are always far more civil appeals each year. They usually sit as a panel of five judges to hear a case.

A case can only be appealed to the Supreme Court if there is a point of law involved. Often civil cases involve complicated and technical areas of law such as planning law or tax law.

Any decision the Supreme Court makes on a point of law becomes a precedent for all the other courts to follow.

## Qualifications

To become a judge at any level it is necessary to be qualified as either a barrister or a solicitor. The levels for judges are based on certificates of advocacy and rights of audience in the courts. A barrister or solicitor must have been qualified to be an advocate in the court to which he or she is appointed as a judge.

Once a lawyer has been appointed as a judge, there is the possibility of being promoted from a lower judicial office to the next one up on the ladder. However, most High Court Judges are appointed straight to that level without first being a judge at a lower level.

### District Judges

For this position the person must have been qualified for at least seven years as a barrister or a solicitor.

### Recorders

A Recorder must have been qualified as a barrister or a solicitor for at least 10 years. They are part-time judges, usually sitting for one month a year and continuing to work as a barrister or a solicitor for the rest of the time.

The appointment is for five years and their work is normally in the Crown Court, although they can also be asked to sit to hear cases in the County Court.

### Circuit Judges

To become a Circuit Judge it is necessary to have been qualified as a barrister for 10 years **or** to have held a certificate of advocacy in the Crown Court for 10 years **or** to have been a Recorder or District Judge for three years.

### High Court Judges

The qualification is 10 years' practice as a barrister. Now it is also possible for a Circuit Judge to be promoted to the High Court Bench after at least two years as a Circuit Judge.

### Lords Justices of Appeal

The qualifications for these judges are that they must have been qualified as a barrister or have held a High Court certificate in advocacy for at least 10 years **or** be an existing High Court Judge.

This last is the more usual route and almost all Lords Justices of Appeal will have previously been a High Court judge.

### Supreme Court Judge

To be a Supreme Court Judge it is necessary to have held high judicial office in England and Wales, Scotland or Northern Ireland for at least two years or been able to act as an advocate in the higher courts for at least 15 years.

### Selection

Virtually all judges are now selected by the Judicial Appointments Commission.

Positions are advertised widely in newspapers, legal journals and also online. To encourage a wide range of candidates to apply, the Commission runs road shows and other outreach events designed to communicate and explain the appointments system to potential applicants.

All candidates have to fill in an application form. Candidates are also asked to nominate between three and six referees. In addition, the Commission has published a list of people whom it may consult about candidates. These include existing judges.

For lower level posts, applicants will also be asked to write an essay or do a case study.

The Commission will then select the best candidates to be interviewed. The interview process may include role play or taking part in a formal, structured discussion. After the interviews, the final selections will be made and recommended to the Lord Chancellor for appointment.

The Lord Chancellor has limited powers in relation to each recommendation for appointment. He can reject a candidate once or ask the Commission to reconsider once but he must give reasons in writing for this.

## Appointment

Once a candidate has been selected and that selection accepted by the Lord Chancellor, then the appointment is made by the Queen for all judicial posts from District Judges up to the Supreme Court.

More information can be found on the Judicial Appointments Commission's website at www.judicialappointments.gov.uk.

## Criticisms of the judiciary

One of the main criticisms of the Bench is that it is dominated by elderly, white, upper-class males. There are very few women judges, and even fewer judges from ethnic minorities. So far as the age of judges is concerned, it is unusual for any judge to be appointed under the age of 40, with superior judges usually being well above this age.

## Women in the judiciary

The number of women in judicial posts is very small, although there has been an improvement in recent years. During the 1990s there was an increase in the number of women appointed to the High Court. The first woman judge in the Queen's Bench Division was appointed in 1992, and the first in the Chancery Division in 1993.

In 2009 the total number of women judges in the High Court was 16 out of over 100 judges, with only three women out of 39 judges in the Court of Appeal.

Lower down the judicial ladder, there are slightly more women being appointed than in the past. In 2009, 12 per cent of Circuit Judges and 17 per cent of Recorders were female. The highest percentages of women were for District Judges (23 per cent).

## Ethnic minorities

In 2004 the first ethnic minority judge was appointed to the High Court. Even at the lower levels, ethnic minorities are still poorly represented. In 2009 only 1.5 per cent of Circuit Judges and 4.5 per cent of Recorders were from an ethnic minority. These percentages have not changed much over the past five years.

## Educational and social background

At the higher levels judges tend to come from the upper levels of society, with many having been educated at public school and nearly all attending Oxford or Cambridge University.

| Court | Judges | Qualifications | Role |
|---|---|---|---|
| House of Lords | Lords of Appeal in Ordinary<br><br>Also known as Law Lords | 15 year Supreme Court qualification<br>*or*<br>have held high judicial office | Hear appeals on points of law<br>Civil and criminal cases |
| Court of Appeal | Lords Justices of Appeal | 10 year Supreme Court qualification<br>*or*<br>be an existing High Court Judge | Hear appeals<br>Criminal cases against conviction and/or sentence<br>Civil cases on the finding and/or the amount awarded |
| High Court | High Court Judges | 10 year Supreme Court qualification<br>*or*<br>be a Circuit Judge for 2 years | Sit in one of the 3 Divisions<br>Hear first instance cases and decide liability and remedy<br>Some appeal work |
| Crown Court | High Court Judges<br><br>Circuit Judges<br><br>Recorders | See above<br><br>10 year Crown Court or County Court qualification<br>*or*<br>be a Recorder or District Judge for 2 years<br><br>10 year Crown Court or County Court qualification | Try cases with a jury<br><br>Decide the law<br><br>Pass sentence on guilty defendants |
| County Court | Circuit Judges<br><br>District Judges | See above<br><br>7 year general qualification | Civil cases – decide liability and remedy<br>District Judges hear small claims |
| Magistrates' Courts | District Judges (Magistrates' Courts) | 7 year general qualification | Criminal cases – decide law and verdict<br>Pass sentence on guilty defendants<br>Some family work |

Figure 12.1 Key facts chart on judges

## BRIEF SUMMARY OF CHAPTER

### Different types of judges

- District Judges
- Recorders
- Circuit Judges
- High Court Judges
- Lords Justices of Appeal
- Law Lords

### Judges qualifications and selection

- To become a judge it is necessary to be either a barrister or a solicitor
- Qualifications are based on certificates of advocacy and rights of audience in the courts
- Judges are now selected by the Judicial Appointments Commission

### Criticisms of the judiciary

- having too few women judges
- having too few ethnic minority judges
- too upper-class

# CHAPTER 13

# ACTS OF PARLIAMENT

In today's world there is often the need for new laws to be made. Most of our laws are made by Parliament or government departments. Any law made by these is called, in general terms, legislation. Law passed by Parliament is also known as statute law or Acts of Parliament. Law made by government ministers and their departments is called delegated legislation.

This chapter looks at Acts of Parliament and Chapter 14 deals with delegated legislation.

## Parliament

Parliament consists of the House of Commons and the House of Lords.

## House of Commons

The House of Commons has 646 Members of Parliament (MPs), who are elected by the public. The country is divided into constituencies and each of these votes for one Member of Parliament.

There must be a general election at least once every five years, though such an election can be called sooner by the Prime Minister. In addition, there may be individual by-elections in constituencies where the MP has died or retired during the current session of Parliament.

The Government of the day is formed by the political party which has a majority in the House of Commons, and it is the Government which has the main say in formulating new Acts of Parliament.

## House of Lords

The House of Lords consists of about 750 members. The majority are life peers. This means that they have been created a peer so that they can sit in the House of Lords. Quite often former Prime Ministers and government ministers are given a life peerage.

There are also 92 hereditary peers in the House of Lords. They have an inherited title and have been chosen by other members of the House of Lords. There are also 26 bishops who have the right to sit in the House of Lords.

Up to 2009 the 12 judges of the Judicial Committee of the House of Lords also sat in the main House of Lords. However, the Supreme Court is replacing the Judicial Committee of the House of Lords. As a result the judges will be completely separate from Parliament and no longer able to sit in the main House of Lords.

It is intended that in the future some of the House of Lords will be chosen by the voting public, so that it will be at least a partly elected body.

## Green and White Papers

Each government minister has a department of civil servants and advisers. The particular ministry which is responsible for the area in which a change in the law is being considered will draft ideas for change.

These ideas may be published as a consultation paper. This will outline possible changes, often

The Houses of Parliament

with alternatives, and anyone can then send in comments on those ideas. All consultation papers are published on the website of the ministry issuing them.

## Green Paper

On major matters a Green Paper may be issued by the minister with responsibility for the matter involved. For example if it is thought there is a need to change the law on employment, the minister in charge of employment will issue the Green Paper.

A Green Paper is a consultative document on a topic in which the Government's view is put forward with ideas on how the law could be reformed. Interested parties are then invited to send comments to the relevant government department, so that a full consideration of all points can be made. After this, necessary changes are made by the Government to its proposals.

## White Paper

Once the issues have been fully considered, the Government will publish a White Paper with its firm proposals for new law. Quite often a White Paper will include a draft of the proposed new law.

Consultation before any new law is put before Parliament is valuable as it allows time for mature consideration. Governments have been criticised for sometimes responding in a 'knee-jerk' fashion to incidents and, as a result, rushing law through that has subsequently proved to be unworkable.

## Bills

Before an Act is passed by Parliament it is known as a *Bill*. There are different types of Bill:

1. *A public Bill*. This is a Bill involving matters of public policy which will affect either the whole country or a large section of it, for

example the Legal Services Act 2007. A public Bill is usually introduced into Parliament by the Government. It will normally have been drafted by lawyers in the civil service on instructions from the Prime Minister or another government minister. The majority of Bills are in this category.

2. *A private Bill*. This is a Bill designed to pass a law which will only affect or benefit individual people or corporations. A private Bill does not make law for the whole country.

3. *A private members' Bill*. This is a Bill introduced by an individual Member of Parliament. It may be a public Bill intended to affect the whole country or it may be a private Bill. Very few private members' Bills become law, but there have been some important laws passed as a result of such Bills. Some examples are the Abortion Act 1967 and the Household Waste Recycling Act 2003.

## The passage of a public Bill through Parliament

Most Bills start in the House of Commons, but it is possible for them to start in the House of Lords. The procedure normally requires both Houses to pass Bills before they become law. The exceptions to this are any Bills which involve taxation, which do not have to be passed by the House of Lords.

Whether the Bill starts in the Commons or the Lords it will have to go through the following stages.

### First Reading

This is a formal procedure in which the name of the Bill and its main aims are read out and there is usually no discussion or debate on the Bill.

### Second Reading

This is the main debate on the whole Bill. It is a debate on the main principles rather than the

details. The MPs who wish to speak in the debate will try to catch the Speaker's eye, since the Speaker controls all debates in the House. At the end of the debate there will be a vote. If at any stage there is a majority vote against the Bill, then it does not go any further.

### Committee Stage

At this stage the Bill is examined in detail by a committee of MPs. There are a number of committees called select committees, made up of between 20 and 50 MPs chosen so that the political parties in the House are proportionately represented. The committee's task is to go through each clause of the Bill and where it thinks necessary propose amendments or alterations. For money Bills the whole House sits as a committee instead of a select committee.

### Report Stage

The committee reports back to the House with its suggested amendments and each one is voted on. The amendment will only take place if a majority of the House are in favour of it.

### Third Reading

There is then a final vote on the Bill as a whole. There will be a further debate on the general principles of the Bill only if at least six MPs request it. If there is a vote in favour of the Bill it then passes to the other House where it will have to go through the same stages.

### House of Lords

The power of the House of Lords is limited. When the House of Lords makes amendments to the Bill those amendments will be considered by the House of Commons before the Bill goes through to its final stage. If the House of Lords refuses to pass a Bill, the House of Commons can introduce that same Bill in the next session of Parliament and if it is passed by the Commons for a second time it can then receive the Royal Assent and become law without the agreement of the House of Lords.

This procedure is set out in the Parliament Acts 1911 and 1949 and is based on the idea that the principal legislative function of the non-elected House of Lords is to revise and add to the law rather than oppose the will of the democratically elected House of Commons. There have been only four occasions when this procedure has been used to bypass the House of Lords after they voted against a Bill. The most recent Act passed by this method was the Hunting Act 2004.

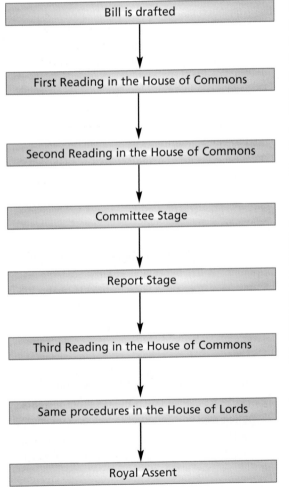

**Figure 13.1** Flow chart of the passing of an Act of Parliament starting in the House of Commons

## Royal Assent

The monarch has to approve the Bill and give Her Assent (agreement) to its becoming law. This stage is nowadays a formality. The last time the Royal Assent was refused was in 1707 when Queen Anne refused to consent to the Scottish Militia Bill.

## Commencement of an Act

Once the Royal Assent has been given the Bill becomes an Act of Parliament and normally it comes into force, that is, it becomes part of the law on the day it receives the Royal Assent. However, in some Acts there is a section which either states the date in the future when the Act is to become law, or gives a government minister the power to decide the date on which the Act is to become law. This can mean that some Acts passed by Parliament do not actually become law for some time. In fact, the Easter Act 1928, which was intended to fix the date for Easter, has never come into force.

Figure 13.2 summarises these different stages.

---

### ACTIVITY

**Activity 1**

Using the Internet

Look at the website of Parliament to see what Bills are currently going through Parliament. The website is www.parliament.uk.

Also look at www.opsi.gov.uk where you can find Acts of Parliament that have already been passed by Parliament. Look for the Legal Services Act 2007 and find out how many sections it has.

| First Reading | Formal |
|---|---|
| Second Reading | Main debate |
| Committee Stage | Each clause considered by a committee |
| Report Stage | Committee report back on proposed amendments to the Bill |
| Third Reading | Final vote, there may be a debate |
| House of Lords | Same stages repeated in the House of Lords.<br>The Bill may return to House of Commons if Lords make amendments |
| Royal Assent | Formality<br>The Bill now becomes an Act of Parliament |

**Figure 13.2** Passing an Act of Parliament when a Bill starts in the House of Commons

## ACTIVITY

### Activity 2

Fill in the gaps in the description of the court structure by selecting the appropriate word or phrase from the list in the box below the text.

Parliament consists of the House of ........................ and the House of ..................... .

When reform of the law is being considered, the Government may issue a ..................... Paper containing their ideas on how the law could be reformed. This is a consultative document. Interested parties may send their comments on the ideas to the Government. After this the Government may issue a ..................... Paper with its firm ideas of how the law will be reformed.

To become an Act of Parliament a Bill has to pass through several stages. There is the ..................... which is the formal introduction of the Bill into Parliament, then the ..................... which is the main debate on the Bill. After this there is the ..................... where each clause of the Bill is considered. Any amendments suggested at this stage are then put before Parliament at the ..................... . Next is the ..................... which is the final vote on the Bill in that House.

Now the Bill has to go through the same procedure in the other House. Finally, to become law, it must receive the ..................... .

| Committee Stage | Commons |
|---|---|
| First Reading | Green |
| Lords | Report Stage |
| Royal Assent | Second Reading |
| Third Reading | White |

## Looking at an Act of Parliament

On page 101 there is a reproduction of an Act of Parliament. The name of the Act is given at the top, in this case the Cheques Act 1992.

1992 Chapter 32 means that this was the 32nd Act to be passed in 1992. There is then a short statement about the purpose of the Act. Next follows a formal statement showing that the Act has been passed by both Houses of Parliament and received the Royal Assent; this is included in all Acts.

Then come the sections of the Act; this Act is unusually short as it has only four sections. Sections 1, 2 and 3 change the law on cheques by making alterations to other Acts of Parliament. The effect of these changes is to make sure that if two lines are drawn across a cheque and the person writing the cheque includes the words 'account payee' or 'a/c payee' that cheque cannot be paid into anybody else's account. This is aimed at preventing theft of cheques or fraud.

The last section, section 4, has two subsections. Section 4(2) says when the Act is to come into force and in this case it is three months after the Act has received the Royal Assent.

## ACTIVITY

### Activity 3

Look at a cheque book and see if all the cheques have the words mentioned in the Cheques Act 1992 printed on them.

## Parliamentary supremacy

Parliamentary supremacy means that:

1. Parliament can make law on any subject-matter.
2. No Parliament can be bound by any previous Parliament, nor can a Parliament pass any Act that will bind a later Parliament.
3. No other body has the right to override or set aside an Act of Parliament.

## The right to legislate on any subject-matter

There are no limits on what Parliament can make laws about. It can make any law it wants. For example, in the past Parliament changed the rule on who should succeed to the throne. This was in 1700 when Parliament passed the Act of Settlement which stated that the children of King James II (who were the direct line of the monarchy) could not succeed to the throne.

Parliament can also change its own powers. It did this with the Parliament Acts 1911 and 1949 which placed limits on the right of the House of Lords to block a Bill by voting against it (see Chapter 2).

## Parliament cannot bind any successor

Each new Parliament should be free to make or change what laws they wish. They cannot be bound by a law made by a previous Parliament. They can repeal any previous Act of Parliament.

There are, however, some laws that become such an important part of the British constitution that they cannot realistically be repealed. For example, the Act of Settlement in 1700 changed the line of succession to the throne. It affected who was entitled to become King or Queen. Realistically, after 300 years, this cannot now be repealed.

## An Act of Parliament cannot be overruled by others

This means that judges in the courts cannot ignore an Act of Parliament. They must enforce it, even if they do not agree with it.

This rule is kept to even where the Act of Parliament may have been made because of incorrect information. This was shown in the case of *British Railways Board v Pickin* (1974). The British Railways Act 1968, a private Act of Parliament, was passed by Parliament. *Pickin* challenged the Act on the basis that the British Railways Board had fraudulently concealed certain matters from Parliament.

Pickin's claim failed because no court is entitled to go behind an Act once it has been passed. A challenge cannot be made to an Act of Parliament even if there was fraud.

**ELIZABETH II**    c. **32**

# Cheques Act 1992

### 1992 CHAPTER 32

An Act to amend the law relating to cheques.

[16th March 1992]

**B**E IT ENACTED by the Queen's most Excellent Majesty, by and with the advice and consent of the Lords Spiritual and Temporal, and Commons, in this present Parliament assembled, and by the authority of the same, as follows:—

**1.** After section 81 of the Bills of Exchange Act 1882 there shall be inserted the following section—

"Non-transferable cheques.

   81A.—(1) Where a cheque is crossed and bears across its face the words "account payee" or "a/c payee", either with or without the word "only", the cheque shall not be transferable, but shall only be valid as between the parties thereto.

   (2) A banker is not to be treated for the purposes of section 80 above as having been negligent by reason only of his failure to concern himself with any purported indorsement of a cheque which under subsection (1) above or otherwise is not transferable.".

*Amendment of Bills of Exchange Act 1882: non-transferable cheques.*
*1882 c. 61.*

**2.** In section 80 of the Bills of Exchange Act 1882 (protection to banker and drawer where cheque is crossed) after "crossed cheque" there shall be inserted "(including a cheque which under section 81A below or otherwise is not transferable)".

*Amendment of Bills of Exchange Act 1882: protection to banker and drawer where cheque is crossed.*

**3.** In section 4(2)(a) of the Cheques Act 1957 (protection of bankers collecting payment of cheques, etc) there shall be inserted after the word "cheques" the words "(including cheques which under section 81A(1) of the Bills of Exchange Act 1882 or otherwise are not transferable)".

*Amendment of Cheques Act 1957.*
*1957 c. 36.*

**4.**—(1) This Act may be cited as the Cheques Act 1992.

*Citation and commencement.*

   (2) This Act shall come into force at the end of the period of three months beginning on the day on which this Act is passed.

PRINTED IN THE UNITED KINGDOM BY PAUL FREEMAN
Controller and Chief Executive of Her Majesty's Stationery Office
and Queen's Printer of Acts of Parliament

## Limitations on Parliamentary supremacy

There are now some limitations on Parliament's supremacy but all these limits have been self-imposed by previous Parliaments. The main limitation is because of the UK's membership of the European Union.

## Effect of membership of EU

The United Kingdom joined the European Union in 1973. In order to become a member, Parliament passed the European Communities Act 1972. Although, as Parliament passed that Act, it is theoretically possible for a later Parliament to pass an Act withdrawing from the European Union, political reality means that this is very unlikely. Membership of the EU affects much of our law and political system.

Membership of the EU means that EU laws take priority over English law even where the English law was passed after the relevant EU law.

This was shown by the Merchant Shipping Act 1988 which set down rules for who could own or manage fishing boats registered in Britain. The Act stated that 75 per cent of directors and shareholders had to be British. The European Court of Justice ruled that this was contrary to European Union law under which citizens of all Member States can work in other Member States. The Merchant Shipping Act 1988 could not be effective so far as other EU citizens were concerned.

## Human Rights

Each Act of Parliament passed is supposed to be compatible with the European Convention on Human Rights (see Chapter 38 for the rights given under this convention).

If there is a challenge about the compatibility of any Act, this will be heard in the courts. Where

the courts hold that an Act (or part of an Act) is not compatible they can make a declaration that it is incompatible.

The Human Rights Act 1998 gives this power to the courts. However, the Government does not have to change any Act which has been declared incompatible.

## BRIEF SUMMARY OF CHAPTER

**Parliament**

- is made up of the House of Commons and the House of Lords

**Pre legislation**

- Green Paper – a consultative document with ideas for reform of the law
- White Papers – firm proposals for a new Act of Parliament

**Bills**

- public Bill – affects whole country
- private Bill – affects individual people or corporations
- private members' Bill – introduced to Parliament by an individual MP

**Process in Parliament**

- First Reading, Second Reading, Committee Stage, Report Stage, Third Reading, other House, Royal Assent

**Parliamentary supremacy**

- can make any law; cannot bind successors; cannot be overruled by other bodies, for example judges
- limitations – membership of EU means that EU law takes priority over an Act of Parliament
- Acts should be compatible with the European Convention on Human Rights

# CHAPTER 14

# DELEGATED LEGISLATION

The verb 'to delegate' means to hand over the right to do something to others. So the phrase 'delegated legislation' means law made by some person or organisation other than Parliament, but with the authority of Parliament.

Generally, Parliament lays down the framework of the law in an Act but within that Act gives the right to make more detailed law to other people. An Act doing this is called an **enabling Act** or **parent Act**.

There are three different types of delegated legislation. These are:

- Orders in Council
- statutory instruments
- bylaws.

## Orders in Council

These are made by the Queen and Privy Council. Under the Emergency Powers Act 1920 the Queen and the Privy Council has the right to make laws which can affect the whole country. This right to make law is normally only used in times of emergency, when Parliament is not sitting.

## Statutory instruments

The term 'statutory instruments' refers to rules and regulations made by government ministers.

Ministers and government departments are given authority to make regulations for areas under their particular responsibility. This means that, for example, the Lord Chancellor has power regarding the legal aid schemes, while

the Minister for Transport is able to deal with necessary road traffic regulations.

The use of statutory instruments is a major method of law-making as there are about 3,000 statutory instruments brought into force each year.

## Bylaws

These can be made by local authorities to cover matters within their own area; for example, Essex County Council can pass laws affecting the whole county, while a District or Town council can only make bylaws for its district or town. Many local bylaws will involve traffic control, such as parking restrictions. In some areas there may be bylaws about not drinking alcohol in public.

Alcohol Free Zone

It is an offence to drink alcohol in this area

PENALTY £500

NORTH LINCOLNSHIRE HELP US PROTECT YOUR ENVIRONMENT

| Type of delegated legislation | Who it is made by | Comment |
|---|---|---|
| Orders in Council | Made by Queen and Privy Council | Usually for emergencies only when Parliament is not sitting |
| Statutory instruments | Made by government ministers | Major source of law with over 3,000 passed most years |
| Bylaws | Made by local authorities or public corporations | Regulations for local areas OR places such as an airport |

Figure 14.1 Types of delegated legislation

Bylaws can also be made by public corporations and certain companies for matters within their jurisdiction which involve the public. This means that bodies such as the British Airports Authority and the railways can enforce rules about public behaviour on their premises. An example of such a bylaw is the smoking ban on the London Underground system.

## Advantages of delegated legislation

1. Delegated legislation creates the detailed law that Parliament does not have time to deal with. As already noted there are about 3,000 statutory instruments passed each year and Parliament would not have the time to do all this work. Some of the work is very detailed; regulations on such topics as traffic law need precise details.
2. Delegated legislation can be passed quickly in an emergency. Parliament may not be able to deal with necessary laws quickly or may not even be sitting.
3. Some laws require technical knowledge. For example, building regulations may deal with different types of building materials and the safety requirements for each. The Members of Parliament are unlikely to be expert on these matters and so it is sensible that the government department responsible should make the necessary rules. The department will have experts available to make sure that any technicalities are correctly understood.

4. Local knowledge may be needed for some regulations, such as deciding where it is necessary to have double yellow lines banning parking. This type of law is much better decided by the local council in the area concerned.
5. Delegated legislation can be amended or revoked more easily than an Act of Parliament so that if the situation alters or the law is not working properly, changes can be made to keep it up to date.

## Disadvantages of delegated legislation

1. The main criticism is that it takes law making away from our democratically elected MPs and allows non-elected people to make law. This criticism is not true of bylaws made by local authorities as they are elected bodies.
2. In some areas there will be sub-delegation: this means that the power to make the law is passed on to yet another person, and so the law making is even further removed from Parliament. It is said that some of our law is made by civil servants who are not elected and who are not accountable to the public for their actions.
3. The large volume of delegated legislation makes it difficult to discover what the present law is. Since ignorance of the law is no excuse this could mean that someone could be guilty of an offence although he or she did not know about the law.

4. There is also a lack of publicity for delegated legislation. Most of it is made in private and some may even come into effect before being published. This is in sharp contrast with the public debates in Parliament.

## ACTIVITY

### Activity 1

As this is a short chapter, read it through again and then see if you can do the following from memory:

1. Name the three types of delegated legislation and explain who can make each type.

2. Give three advantages of delegated legislation.

3. Give three disadvantages of delegated legislation.

## BRIEF SUMMARY OF CHAPTER

**Delegated legislation**

- Parliament gives power for law to be made. There are three types:

1. Orders in Council made by Queen and Privy Council.

2. statutory instruments made by government ministers

3. bylaws made by local authorities or public corporations

**Advantages**

- detailed law, passed quickly, useful if technical or local knowledge is needed, can be amended easily

**Disadvantages**

- made by non-elected people, can be sub-delegated, large volume and lack of publicity

# CHAPTER 15

# JUDICIAL PRECEDENT

Judicial precedent refers to decisions by judges which create laws for later judges to follow. This source of law can also be called case law.

## Judgments

When a judge decides a case he or she makes a speech at the end of the case explaining what his or her decision is. This speech is called a judgment.

In the County Court or High Court each case is heard by a single judge and so there is just one judgment. In the appeal courts (the Divisional Courts, the Court of Appeal and the Supreme Court) there will be at least two judges and there can be up to seven judges in the Supreme Court; as a result there may be speeches (judgments) from more than one judge.

### Ratio decidendi

In each judgment the judge will give a summary of the facts of the case and explain the principle of law he or she is using to come to a decision. The judge may sometimes discuss what the law would have been if the facts had been different. These are called hypothetical situations.

The important part of each judgment is the principle of law the judge is using to come to a decision. This is known as the *ratio decidendi*. These words are Latin and mean 'the reason for deciding'. The *ratio decidendi* is the part of the judgment that creates law (or a precedent) for future judges to follow.

### Obiter dicta

All the rest of the judgment is called *obiter dicta*. This means 'other things said'. The *obiter dicta* does not create binding law, although judges in subsequent cases may look at it and use it if they wish.

## Stare decisis

Precedent is based on another Latin phrase, *stare decisis*. This literally means 'stand by the decision' and expresses the idea that once a decision has been made in one case on a point of law, it is fair and just to keep to that decision in later cases.

Most countries have the same basic rule about this, but the English legal system follows precedent more rigidly than other countries.

## Hierarchy of the courts

The system of courts in England and Wales has a clear order or hierarchy. The Supreme Court is at the top of the court structure. The position of a court in the court hierarchy is important in judicial precedent.

The more senior the court the more likely its decision will create a binding precedent, that is a precedent the other courts must follow. Figure 15.1 shows the hierarchy.

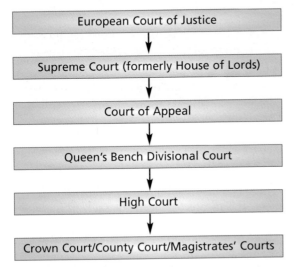

**Figure 15.1** Hierarchy of the courts

There are special rules about whether the appellate courts, that is courts which hear appeals, are bound by their own past decisions. It is therefore necessary to consider each appellate court in turn.

## European Court of Justice

On points of European law the decisions of the European Court of Justice are binding on all English courts. However, this court is not bound by its own past decisions.

## Supreme Court (formerly the House of Lords)

The Supreme Court is the most senior court in England and Wales. Any decisions by the Supreme Court must be followed by all other courts. The Supreme Court does not always have to follow its own previous decisions.

When the senior court was the House of Lords it originally used to follow its own previous decisions. This was because of a decision at the end of the nineteenth century in a case called *London Street Tramways Co Ltd v London County Council* (1898).

In this case the House of Lords decided that it would always follow its own past decisions. The reason for this was that the judges of the time felt that certainty in the law was very important. They argued that if they could decide cases in different ways it would be difficult for people to know what the law was and this could lead to more cases coming to court because the law was uncertain.

Although this rule created certainty, judges realised that it also meant the law could not change to meet changing social conditions. Decisions which had been made a hundred years ago would always have to be followed even though social conditions and ideas had changed. It was realised that this was not a good thing, so the system was changed by the Practice Statement.

## Practice Statement

In 1966 the Lord Chancellor issued a Practice Statement regarding the use of precedent in the House of Lords. This said:

**66** Their Lordships regard the use of precedent as an indispensable foundation upon which to decide what is the law and its application to individual cases. It provides at least some degree of certainty upon which individuals can rely in the conduct of their affairs, as well as a basis for orderly development of legal rules.

Their Lordships nevertheless recognise that too rigid adherence to precedent may lead to injustice in a particular case and also unduly restrict the proper development of the law. They propose, therefore, to modify their present practice and, while treating former decisions of this House as normally binding, to depart from a previous decision when it appears right to do so. **99**

This made it clear that the House of Lords would normally follow its own past decisions, but it gave the judges flexibility so that they could refuse to follow a previous decision when 'it appears right to do so'. However, the House of Lords initially was reluctant to use this flexibility.

## Use of the Practice Statement

The Practice Statement was used in *Herrington v British Railways Board* (1972) to change the law in respect of the duty of care owed by the occupier of land to children who trespassed on the land. The previous decision had been made in 1929 when it was held that the occupier would only be liable for injuries suffered by the child if the occupier had caused those injuries deliberately or recklessly. In *Herrington* the Law Lords held that social and physical conditions had changed since 1929 and an occupier had to take some care to protect child trespassers from coming to harm.

The House of Lords felt that it was especially important to have certainty in the criminal law but even here it has used the Practice Statement to overrule past decisions. The first criminal case in which this occurred was *R v Shivpuri* (1986) which involved the law of attempting to commit a crime.

Another criminal law case in which the House of Lords used the Practice Statement to overrule an earlier decision of their own is *R v Gemmell and Richards* (2003).

### CASE EXAMPLE

#### *R v Gemmell and Richards* (2003)

This case concerned the test for deciding if the defendant had been reckless in his behaviour and so guilty of the offence of criminal damage. In 1981, in *Metropolitan Police Commissioner v Caldwell*, the House of Lords had held that a defendant could be guilty if he was reckless if a sober and reasonable adult would have realised the risk.

Under this test, the defendant was guilty even if he, personally, had not realised there were any risks.

In *Gemmell and Richards* the defendants were two boys, aged 11 and 12 years, who set fire to some bundles of newspapers in a shop yard. They threw the newspapers under a large wheelie bin and left. They thought the fire would go out by itself. In fact, the bin caught fire and this spread to the shop and other buildings, causing about £1 million worth of damage.

At their trial the judge, following the decision in *Caldwell*, directed the jury that they had to decide whether ordinary adults would have realised the risk. The boys were convicted. On appeal the House of Lords overruled the decision in *Caldwell*. They held that a defendant could not be guilty unless he or she had realised the risk and decided to take it.

The Supreme Court has the same flexibility as the House of Lords had. It will usually follow its own past decisions but need not do so.

## Court of Appeal (Civil Division)

The Court of Appeal has to follow decisions by the European Court of Justice and the House of Lords. It is also bound to follow its own past decisions. This was decided by the Court of Appeal in *Young v Bristol Aeroplane Co Ltd* (1944)

## Court of Appeal (Criminal Division)

The Criminal Division of the Court of Appeal has a little more freedom than the Civil Division because criminal cases often involve the risk that the defendant will have to serve a lengthy prison sentence. This means that the Criminal Division will refuse to follow a previous decision where it feels that the law was misapplied or misunderstood.

Middlesex Guildhall, home to the new Supreme Court

## Queen's Bench Divisional Court

The Queen's Bench Divisional Court is bound by its own past decisions unless the case involves the liberty of the subject. The court must, of course, follow decisions of the European Court, Supreme Court and Court of Appeal.

## High Court

The High Court has to follow decisions made by all the courts above but it is not bound by its own past decisions.

## Lower courts

The lower courts, that is the Crown Court, County Court and Magistrates' Courts, do not make precedent. They are bound by decisions of all the courts above. They must follow all precedents.

Figure 15.2 shows which courts must follow which decisions of other courts.

## Precedent and human rights

The Human Rights Act 1998 states that all courts in England and Wales must take into account any judgment or decision given by the European Court of Human Rights.

This has the effect that courts should follow a decision by the European Court of Human Rights rather than a decision by a higher court in our legal system. So, for example, if there is a decision of the Supreme Court and decision by the European Court of Human Rights which are different, then the Court of Appeal should take into account the decision by the European Court.

## Precedent in operation

### Binding precedent

When a case involves a point of law, the lawyers for both parties will research past cases in the Law Reports to try and find decisions that will help their client win the case. If there is a previous case on similar facts, the judge will consider that case and if the decision is by a court above in the hierarchy, the judge must follow it. This is known as a *binding precedent*.

So a precedent or past decision is binding only if the court making the decision is at the right level in the hierarchy and the facts of the second case are sufficiently similar.

### Original precedent

If the point of law has never been decided before, the decision the judge comes to will form a new precedent for subsequent cases. This is known as an *original precedent* and again it will depend on the court's position in the hierarchy as to whether that precedent will be binding or not.

| Court | Courts bound by it | Courts it must follow |
|---|---|---|
| European Court of Justice | All courts | None |
| Supreme Court | All courts in England and Wales | European Court |
| Court of Appeal | Divisional Courts<br>High Court<br>Crown Court<br>County Court<br>Magistrates' Court | European Court<br>Supreme Court |
| Divisional Courts | High Court<br>Crown Court<br>County Court<br>Magistrates' Court | European Court<br>Supreme Court<br>Court of Appeal |
| High Court | Crown Court<br>County Court<br>Magistrates' Court | European Court<br>Supreme Court<br>Court of Appeal<br>Divisional Courts |
| Crown Court<br>County Court<br>Magistrates' Court | None | European Court<br>Supreme Court<br>Court of Appeal<br>Divisional Courts<br>High Court |

**Figure 15.2** The courts and precedent

An example of a new decision being made can be seen in *R v R* (1991), which was a case about whether in law a husband could be guilty of raping his wife. The case started at Leicester Crown Court where the judge was asked to make a ruling on this point. The judge, a High Court judge, ruled that if a wife did not consent to sexual intercourse, her husband could be guilty of rape.

Following this ruling the defendant appealed to the Court of Appeal (Criminal Division) on the ground that the judge had got the law wrong. The judges in the Court of Appeal agreed with the original judge and so their decision made an original precedent which would bind the Crown Court in any future cases but did not bind the House of Lords.

The defendant appealed again, this time to the House of Lords, which also agreed that the act

of 'marital rape' was a crime. This decision in the House of Lords made a binding precedent which all courts have to follow.

## Persuasive precedent

Sometimes there is a past decision on a point of law but it does not have to be followed in a later case. However, the judge may still consider it and if he thinks that it was a correct decision he can decide to follow it. In this instance he has been persuaded by the previous decision and so it is called a *persuasive precedent*.

A persuasive precedent can also be created where the judge makes a comment which is not the *ratio decidendi* of the case, only *obiter dicta* (other things said). A later court may consider this *obiter* statement and decide they are 'persuaded' to follow it.

An example of where a court followed an *obiter* statement is seen in the case of *R v Gotts* (1992) on the law of duress as a defence to a criminal charge.

## CASE EXAMPLE

### *R v Gotts* (1992)

In *R v Howe* (1987) the House of Lords ruled that duress could not be a defence to a charge of murder. In the judgment the Lords also commented, as an *obiter* statement, that duress would not be available as a defence to someone charged with attempted murder.

In *R v Gotts* the defendant was charged with attempted murder. He argued that he could use the defence of duress. The Court of Appeal considered the *obiter* statement from *Howe* and decided to follow it as persuasive precedent.

## Overruling

This is the term used where a court in a later case decides that the law in a previous case was wrongly decided. This occurred in the case of *Herrington*, which we have already looked at (see above and The Use of the Practice Statement). Here the House of Lords decided to overrule the old decision made in 1929.

Also, in *R v Gemmell and Richards* (2003), the House of Lords overruled their own previous decision in *Metropolitan Police Commissioner v Caldwell* (1981). (See above for case details.)

## Reversing

This occurs on an appeal when a higher court rules that the lower court made the wrong decision in the same case. So a decision by the Court of Appeal could be reversed if the losing party successfully appealed against the Court of Appeal's decision to the Supreme Court.

## Distinguishing

This is a method used by judges to avoid following what would otherwise be a binding precedent. The judge will point out some difference in the facts between the previous precedent and the present case he is trying. That is, the judge draws a distinction between the two cases. As a result the judge can say that he need not follow the previous decision because it was based on a different set of facts.

The following two cases show how distinguishing can work.

## CASE EXAMPLE

In *Balfour v Balfour* (1919) a husband agreed to pay his wife a monthly allowance as she was not well enough to go with him when he went abroad to work. The husband stopped paying the allowance and the wife claimed for it.

It was decided that the wife's claim could not succeed because there was no intention to create legal relations; there was merely a domestic arrangement between a husband and wife and so there was no legally binding contract.

In *Merritt v Merritt* (1971) a husband and wife, who had separated, agreed that the wife would pay the mortgage on the house and that it would become her house. They made a written record of this agreement. The court held that there was a legally binding contract.

In both cases the wife made a claim against her husband for breach of the contract. But the court found that the facts of *Merritt* were sufficiently different to *Balfour* so that they were justified in distinguishing between them.

The differences were (1) that the agreement in *Merritt* was made after they had separated and (2) the agreement was made in writing. This distinguished the case from *Balfour*. The agreement in *Merritt* was not just a domestic arrangement but meant as a legally enforceable contract.

## ACTIVITY

### Activity 1

Read the following passage and answer the questions below.

The Practice Statement is one of great importance, although it should not be supposed that there will frequently be cases in which the House thinks it right not to follow their own precedent. An example of a case in which the House might think it right to depart from a precedent is where they consider that the earlier decision was

influenced by the existence of conditions which no longer prevail, and that in modern conditions the law ought to be different.

*(Source: adapted from an explanatory note issued with the Practice Statement)*

1. To which 'House' does this passage refer?
2. Which court has now replaced that 'House' as the senior court in England and Wales?
3. Why is the Practice Statement of great importance?
4. Do you agree with the statement that 'in modern conditions the law ought to be different'? Give examples to support your answer.
5. How can the Practice Statement help to keep the law up to date?

| Term | Explanation |
|---|---|
| judgment | the speech by the judge at the end of a case in which he or she explains his or her decision and the reasons for it |
| *ratio decidendi* | the reason for deciding<br>this is the binding part of a judgment |
| *obiter dicta* | other things said<br>this part of the judgment is not binding |
| *stare decisis* | stand by the decision<br>this is the principle on which precedent works |
| hierarchy of the courts | the order of the courts<br>decisions of courts higher in the order bind all courts below them |
| binding precedent | this is a decision which must be followed |
| original precedent | this is a decision on a new point of law |
| persuasive precedent | a decision which does not have to be followed but may 'persuade' the judge(s) to follow it |
| overruling | where a court decides that the law in a previous case was wrongly decided |
| reversing | when a higher court rules that the lower court made the wrong decision in the same case |
| distinguishing | where a judge draws a distinction between the case he or she is trying and an earlier case, so that the previous case does not have to be followed |

Figure 15.3 The terms used in judicial precedent

## Advantages and disadvantages of judicial precedent

As with all systems there are both advantages and disadvantages to the system of precedent as it is operated in the courts of England and Wales.

## Advantages of judicial precedent

1. *Certainty*. The strict hierarchy of the courts means that it is often possible to state with certainty what the courts' decision will be on a given set of facts. In particular this makes it easier for people to organise their businesses and make contracts. They know what the effect of a particular term in a contract will be. It also makes it easier for lawyers to advise their clients on what to do and what the law is. As a result fewer cases will need to go to court for a decision.
2. *Flexibility*. Although there is certainty, there is also room for the law to grow and change with changing conditions. In this the Practice Statement is very important, since it allows this flexibility. Distinguishing gives flexibility too, as judges can use it to avoid following past decisions which they feel are not suitable to the present case.
3. *Precision*. Since there are about half a million reported cases, there is a vast amount of detail in the law. It would be difficult to write as much detail into a code of law.
4. *Examples*. All decisions are based on true facts and so the law is illustrated by real cases. Having real examples makes it easier to understand the law and to apply it to future cases.

## Disadvantages of judicial precedent

For each of the above advantages it is possible to argue that there is a corresponding disadvantage.

1. *Rigidity*. It is claimed that our system is too rigid. The law is not merely certain, it is too difficult to change. Critics argue that the House of Lords has been too unwilling to use its power in the Practice Statement to overrule old decisions even when judges in the House of Lords themselves agreed the old law was wrong.
2. *Illogical distinctions*. When distinguishing is used to avoid a previous decision, there is the risk that the judge may distinguish the two cases on a very small point that is difficult to justify.
3. *Bulk and complexity*. Having such a large number of cases to illustrate the law makes it too complex. Lawyers will have difficulty in finding all the relevant past cases, although computer databases have made this easier. Where there are several different decisions on the same point of law, the law may be very complicated.
4. *Slow to change*. Judges can only change the law when a suitable case comes before them. This may mean a long wait and so the law is slow to change.

Apart from these disadvantages there is another problem in the system of precedent. This is the problem of finding the *ratio decidendi* in a judgment. Some judgments are several pages long and the judges do not always separate the relevant and irrelevant points clearly.

The problem becomes worse if, in an appeal court, more than one judge gives a judgment in a case. In one instance the judges in the Court of Appeal said they were unable to discover the *ratio decidendi* in a previous case decided by the House of Lords!

Despite all the problems of precedent it is generally agreed that there must be some form of following past decisions. If there were no consistency in decision making, the law would become chaotic.

## Law reporting

For a system of judicial precedent to operate, there must be full and accurate written reports of cases and judgments. In England there has been some form of law reports since the thirteenth century. However the early reports were brief and not always accurate.

The earliest reports (from about 1275 to 1535) were called Year Books. These were short reports of medieval cases, usually written in French. They are rarely cited (referred to) in court today. From 1535 to 1865 cases were reported by individuals, who made a business out of selling the reports to lawyers. The detail and accuracy of the reports varied from reporter to reporter, but many of them are still used today.

In 1865 the Incorporated Council of Law Reporting was set up and reports made since then are recognised as being accurate with the judgments being word for word reports of what the judge said. Two of the main series of reports today are the All England Law Reports and the Weekly Law Reports. In addition some newspapers, especially *The Times*, give shortened reports of important cases.

## Internet law reports

Law reports are now also published on the Internet.

### ACTIVITY

### Activity 2

Look at reports on the Internet on the following free sites:

www.parliament.uk – this gives all House of Lords' judgments since 1996

www.bailii.org – this has main cases from the Court of Appeal and all other lower courts, again since 1996.

## BRIEF SUMMARY OF CHAPTER

**Supreme Court (formerly the House of Lords)**
- must follow decisions of the European Court of Justice
- normally follows its own past decisions but the Practice Statement allows it to depart from a previous decision 'when it is right to do so'

**Court of Appeal**
- must follow decisions of the European Court of Justice and the House of Lords
- must follow its own past decisions

**Precedent in operation**
- *binding precedent* **must** be followed
- *persuasive precedent* **may** be followed but need not be
- *distinguishing* means that there is a difference so that the previous case need not be followed

**Advantages**
- certainty, flexibility, precision, examples

**Disadvantages**
- rigidity, illogical distinctions, complex, slow to change

## EXAMINATION QUESTION

Note that you will need to understand the topics in Chapters 12 and 13 and the work of the courts as well as this chapter to answer all the parts of the question.

Study the extract below and then answer **all** parts of the question which follows.

'English law comes from a range of different sources. These include:

- legislation passed by Parliament
- case law based on the doctrine of judicial precedent
- European Union (EU) law.

Legislation is law made by Parliament under the authority of the Crown. A Parliamentary Bill must pass all the relevant stages in both Houses of Parliament before receiving the Royal Assent. The Bill, at that point, becomes an Act of Parliament. Case law has been developed by judges over hundreds of years. It depends on a system of law reporting and also on the doctrine of judicial precedent. Judicial precedent is based on the authority of decisions from different levels in the court hierarchy. This should ensure that like cases are treated alike. Within the hierarchy of courts, there are civil courts such as the County Court and the High Court, and criminal courts such as the Magistrates' Court and the Crown Court. There are also two different levels of appeal courts for dealing with civil and criminal cases.

European Union (EU) law has been in force in this country since 1 January 1973. EU law is made and enforced through a number of different EU institutions, such as the European Commission, the Council of Ministers and the European Court of Justice. EU law takes priority over English law when the two are in conflict.'

*(Source: adapted from John Wilman Brown, GCSE Law (9th edn, Sweet & Maxwell, 2005) and from Britain and the EU website, www.fco.gov.uk.)*

## Questions

(a) When considering passing an Act of Parliament, the Government will often issue both a **Green Paper** and a **White Paper**.

Briefly explain the purpose of **each** of these two documents. (3 marks)

(b) (i) Explain the role of the House of Commons in the passing of an Act of Parliament. (5 marks)

(ii) Explain the role of the House of Lords in the passing of an Act of Parliament. (3 marks)

(iii) Explain the role of the Crown in the passing of an Act of Parliament. (2 marks)

(c) Comment on the advantages **and** disadvantages of the system of law making by Parliament. **(Answer in continuous prose.)** (5 marks)

(d) Under English law, Parliament is said to be **supreme**.
(i) Briefly explain what this term means.
(ii) Discuss **one** way in which Parliamentary supremacy can be limited. (6 marks)

(e) Briefly explain the work of:
the Magistrates' Court
the Crown Court
the County Court. (6 marks)

(f) When referring to the system of case law and the doctrine of judicial precedent:
(i) explain what is meant by the 'hierarchy of the courts'; (5 marks)
(ii) explain, using examples, what is meant by a 'persuasive precedent'; (3 marks)
(iii) state the importance of law reports, giving an example of a law report. (2 marks)

# CHAPTER 16

# EUROPEAN UNION LAW

The United Kingdom joined the European Union (EU) on 1st January 1973 and since that date there has been another source of law in this country – European law. European law is mainly concerned with work and trade. This, however, affects many areas of law: agriculture, company law, consumer rights, employment rights and environmental law are just some of the aspects covered.

The original treaty setting up the EU is the Treaty of Rome. This is the most important treaty for

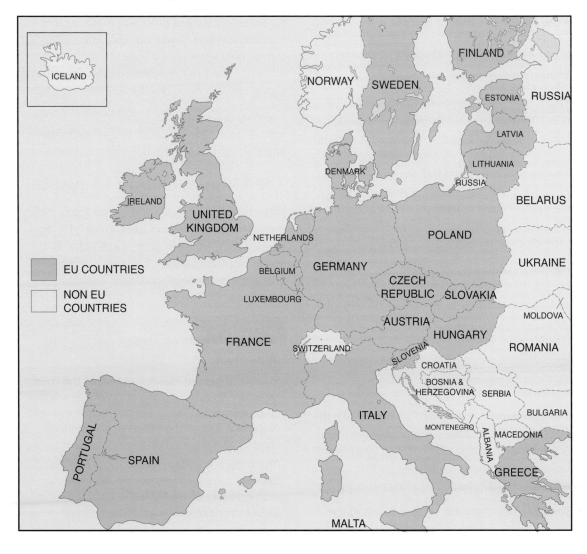

setting out the rights and obligations of the Member States. It has been added to from time to time and other treaties have also been made.

At the beginning of 2009, there were 27 Member States belonging to the EU.

## The institutions of the EU

There are four institutions involved in the running of the Union. These are:

- the Council of the European Union
- the Commission
- the European Parliament
- the European Court of Justice.

## The Council of the European Union

This is the Union's principal decision-making body. The government of each Member State has a seat on the Council. The foreign minister is usually a country's representative, but a government is free to send any of its ministers to Council meetings. Twice a year the heads of all member governments meet to discuss broad principles of policy, so our Prime Minister attends these meetings.

For some particularly important decisions all the ministers must be in agreement, but other decisions can be made by a qualified majority vote. For this each country has a 'weighted' vote roughly in proportion to the size of its population.

## The Commission

The Commission both proposes policies for the Council to discuss and is responsible for the administration of the Union. It has 27 Commissioners who are chosen by the agreement of all member governments.

The Commissioners are obliged to act in the

Union's interests and not in the interests of the country from which they come. Commissioners are appointed for a period of four years and can only be removed during this term of office by a vote of censure from the European Parliament.

Each Commissioner heads a department with special responsibilities for one area of Union policy, such as agriculture, environment or transport.

## The European Parliament

The members of the European Parliament are elected directly by the citizens of each Member State. There is an election every five years. The Parliament discusses proposals made by the Commission but, unlike our Parliament, it is not the primary law-making body. Its decision may influence the Council, although the Council can disregard such decisions if it wishes.

The only real power the Parliament has is the right to reject the Council's budget proposals and the right to dismiss the Commissioners.

## The European Court of Justice

This sits in Luxembourg and settles legal disputes involving Union laws. It has 27 judges, one for each Member State. Each judge is appointed for a period of six years. Judgments of the court are binding in each member country.

### ACTIVITY

**Activity 1**

Fill in the gaps in the description of the court structure by selecting the appropriate word or phrase from the list in the box below the text. Note that not all the words or phrases are used.

The United Kingdom joined the EU on 1st January .......... . The principle decision-making body of the EU is the ...................... Government ministers attend meetings.

Usually the ................. minister from each country goes, but at least twice a year the ................. will attend meetings.

The ............................ is responsible for the day-to-day running of the EU. It has 27 ........................... . People of each Member State vote for members of the European ................................... . This body has very little real power, but it can reject ..................... proposals made by the Commission.

| 1972 | 1973 | 1975 |
| --- | --- | --- |
| Commission | | budget |
| Council | | Commissioners |
| environment | | consultants |
| legal | | foreign |
| Prime Minister | | Councillors |
| Queen | | Parliament |

## Different types of EU law

The EU has the power to make different types of law. There are three main types of EU law. These are:

- treaties
- regulations
- directives.

## Treaties

The Treaty of Rome and any other treaty made by the EU are signed by all the heads of government. Such treaties are automatically law in every member country. In the United Kingdom such treaties are part of our law because of section 2(1) of the European Communities Act 1972, which says that 'all such rights, powers, liabilities, obligations and restrictions ... are

without further enactment to be given legal effect ...'.

This means that citizens can rely on the rights given under the Treaty of Rome even if British law does not give them that same right.

### CASE EXAMPLE

**Macarthys Ltd v Smith (1981)**

In this case Wendy Smith claimed that the company which employed her was in breach of the Treaty of Rome over equal pay for men and women. She was being paid less than the man who had previously done her job and this is discrimination under the Treaty of Rome. She had no rights under English statute law since the law at that time (the Equal Pay Act 1970) only applied when the man and woman are employed at the same time.

The European Court of Justice held that she could bring a claim against her employer as there was a breach of EU law.

## Regulations

Regulations are laws issued by the Commission and under Article 249 of the Treaty of Rome are 'binding in every respect and directly applicable in each Member State'. This means that once a regulation has been issued by the Commission it is automatically law in this country and all other Member States. This was shown in *Re Tachographs: EC Commission v United Kingdom* (1979).

### CASE EXAMPLE

**Re Tachographs: EC Commission v United Kingdom (1979)**

The case concerned a regulation which said that tachographs (mechanical recording equipment to record speed, etc) should be installed in all road vehicles used for the carriage of goods. The United Kingdom Government decided not to enforce the regulation but to allow lorry owners to choose whether they wished to install a tachograph or not.

The Commission referred the matter to the European Court of Justice which held that the United Kingdom had to apply the regulation. Article 249 of the Treaty of Rome made it quite clear that regulations were directly applicable.

## Directives

Directives are issued by the Commission, but merely direct each Member State on what the law should be, leaving each country to bring in its own law giving effect to the directive. Article 249 says, 'directives shall bind any Member State to which they are addressed as to the result to be achieved'. When a directive is issued the Commission will set a time limit within which it must be implemented.

An example is the directive on consumer liability which was issued in 1985 and required all Member States to implement it by July 1988. The United Kingdom met that requirement by passing the Consumer Protection Act 1987, which became law in March 1988.

Usually in this country directives are brought in to our law by the relevant minister making a statutory instrument (delegated legislation). Sometimes, as the Consumer Protection Act illustrates, directives can be implemented through an Act of Parliament.

### Vertical direct effect

Although a directive does not normally become part of our law automatically in the way that a regulation does, the European Court has decided that some directives are 'directly effective'. This means that they can be relied upon by citizens in claims against the State, even though the Government has not implemented them.

This happened in the case of *Marshall v Southampton and South West Hampshire Area Health Authority* (1986).

**CASE EXAMPLE**

### *Marshall v Southampton and South West Hampshire Area Health Authority* (1986)

Helen Marshall was dismissed from her job because she was 62 years old, but men doing the same work did not have to retire until they were 65. A European directive issued in 1976 said that men and women should be treated equally in employment and this included reasons for dismissal.

Helen Marshall started an action for unfair dismissal and the European Court held that, since the directive was clear, it had vertical direct effect. This was so even though the British Government had not brought it into effect over ages of retirement. Since Helen Marshall was employed by a State organisation she could rely on the directive in her claim against them and so win her case.

### Horizontal direct effect

When the Government has not implemented a directive, that directive does not create rights between private individuals or companies. If Helen Marshall had been working for a private company she would not have been able to rely on the Equal Treatment Directive and so would have lost her case.

This appears unfair but the European Court has created another way of claiming for any loss caused because the Government has not implemented a directive. Instead of claiming against the employer it is possible, in certain circumstances, to claim compensation from the Government. This is because the loss has been caused by the Government's failure to act. This was decided in an Italian case which was heard

Figure 16.1 The types of EU law

by the European Court of Justice, *Francovitch v Italian Republic* (1991).

These three types of EU law and their effect are summarised in Figure 16.1.

## Referring cases to the European Court of Justice

If a point of European law is involved in a case, the national court can refer that point to the European Court for a preliminary ruling. This is under Article 234 of the Treaty of Rome.

Where the case is being heard by a final Court of Appeal (usually in this country the Supreme Court) and a question of European law is raised, then that court has to send the point to the European Court for a decision.

Other courts have a discretion, that is they can choose whether to refer the case to the European Court or not. This is because their decision is not final but can be appealed against in the English courts.

Courts at all levels in our legal system have referred cases to the European Court, although most referrals have been by the higher courts; for example, the case of *Macarthys v Smith* was referred by the Court of Appeal.

## European law and the sovereignty of Parliament

As already discussed in Chapter 13, Parliament is seen as being the supreme law-maker in England and Wales. The law that Parliament makes can override any other English source of law. However, our entry into the European Union has affected Parliament's supremacy. European laws take priority over national laws.

This was decided even before the United Kingdom joined the EU in the Dutch case of *Van Gend en Loos* (1963). So far as this country is concerned it was also shown by the *Factortame case* (1991), where it was held that the Merchant Shipping Act 1988 was contrary to the Treaty of Rome in that it discriminated against ship owners on the ground of nationality.

However, Parliament can still be said to be supreme, since it is only through Parliament passing the European Communities Act 1972 that European law has direct effect in this country. Parliament also retains the final right to withdraw from the Union.

## EU law and judicial precedent

Since we joined the EU, the highest court in our legal system is the European Court of Justice. For all points of EU law a decision by the European Court of Justice is binding on all courts in England and Wales.

However, EU law does not affect all areas of our law. In particular, criminal law is rarely affected. For this law the highest court is the Supreme Court.

### BRIEF SUMMARY OF CHAPTER

UK joined the EU on 1st January 1973.

**EU law**

- **consists** of treaties, regulations and directives
- **Treaties and regulations** always apply in the UK
- **Directives** can be relied on as against the State, even if they have not been implemented
- Points of law are referred to the **European Court of Justice**
- **EU law has supremacy** over UK law

# CHAPTER 17

# LAW OF TORT: INTRODUCTION

The law of tort covers a wide range of actions. These include:

- a car passenger suing for injuries suffered in a car crash
- a visitor to premises claiming compensation for injuries suffered when part of a ceiling fell on them
- a claim for excessive noise and dust caused by building works next to your home
- a claim because your neighbour has built a wall between the two homes and part of this wall is on your land.

These are all examples of cases that could be brought.

## The nature of a tort

A tort is regarded as a civil wrong. The word 'tort' is actually the French word for 'wrong'.

Liability in tort comes from either a breach of duty owed by members of society to each other or the infringement of a right of another person. These rights and duties have been largely developed by the courts through case law, though there are some Acts of Parliament which create rights and duties, such as the Occupiers' Liability Act 1957 and the Torts (Interference with Goods) Act 1977.

The law of tort protects people, their property and their reputation. A claim in tort can be made if someone, through breach of duty or infringement of a right, injures you, your property or your reputation. There are several different torts recognised by English law and the next two chapters will consider some of the more common ones:

- negligence
- occupiers' liability
- trespass to the person
- trespass to land
- trespass to goods
- nuisance.

Look back at the examples of types of claim. Each of these is under a different tort.

- A claim for injuries in a car crash is under the tort of negligence.
- A claim for injuries caused by a fault in another person's premises is under the tort of occupiers' liability.
- A claim for excessive noise and dust is under the tort of nuisance.
- A claim for building a wall on your land is under the tort of trespass to land.

## Fault based liability

Liability in tort is based on the fact that the defendant is at fault in some way. The idea is that there can be no liability without fault.

Fault has quite a wide meaning as there are a number of ways in which a person can be at fault in the law of tort.

Of course, fault can be through an intention to do the wrongful act. This is seen where the defendant has deliberately assaulted the claimant. However, intention is not the usual type of fault which is concerned in the law of tort.

Each tort sets an expected standard of behaviour. A defendant who fails to meet that standard may be liable.

In the tort of negligence the defendant is liable if he or she wasn't sufficiently careful. A common example is where the claimant has been injured through the defendant's negligent driving. Perhaps the defendant drove too fast or failed to stop at a junction or failed to keep a proper lookout. In all these situations the defendant has not met the expected standard of behaviour and may be liable to compensate the claimant.

In the tort of trespass, whether the trespass is to the person, land or goods, the defendant is doing something which is regarded as an infringement of another's rights.

The main argument in favour of having fault based liability is its deterrent value. People know they may be liable to pay compensation and so will try not to commit a tort.

## Problems of fault based liability

The claimant may find it difficult to prove that the defendant was at fault. This is particularly so in negligence claims. If the claimant cannot prove fault, then they will not receive compensation even though they may have suffered very severe injuries through no fault of their own.

### No fault liability

As long ago as 1978 the Pearson Committee recommended that there should be a no fault system of compensation. Victims injured in accidents would not have to prove fault. The idea was that they would be entitled to a payment from a government funded scheme simply because of their injuries.

This recommendation has never been brought into effect in this country. However, New

Zealand has operated a no fault compensation scheme for over 30 years. This scheme has proved more expensive than expected and has had to be limited.

## Proving damage

For some torts the claimant must prove that damage was caused; for other torts, especially trespass, it is only necessary to show the infringement of a right. It is said that such torts are 'actionable per se' (of itself). This means the claimant can claim simply because their right has been infringed: the claimant does not need to prove that any damage has been caused.

## Differences between torts and crimes

It is important to realise the differences between torts and crimes as both can be considered 'wrongs'. A crime is an offence against society, even though it may only be directed against one individual. A tort is a wrong against an individual and does not affect society as a whole.

The main function of criminal law is to keep law and order and protect the public. The main function of the law of torts is to provide the individual who has suffered with a way of enforcing their rights.

A criminal case will take place in the criminal courts, while an action for tort will be in the civil courts. Finally, the purpose of the criminal case is to punish anybody found guilty of a crime; the purpose of an action for tort is to compensate the claimant or enforce their rights in some other way such as granting an injunction. These differences are shown in Figure 17.1.

In some cases the same action may be both a crime and a tort. Drunken driving both breaks the criminal law and, if it causes injury or damage to another person, can give rise to an

| Crimes | Torts |
|--------|-------|
| A wrong against the State | A wrong against an individual |
| Case will usually be started by the State | Case will be started by the individual affected |
| Defendant will be prosecuted in the criminal courts | Defendant will be sued in the civil courts |
| If guilty the defendant will be punished | If liable the defendant will have to compensate the claimant |

Figure 17.1 Differences between crimes and torts

action for the tort of negligence. This idea of double liability was considered in Chapter 1.

## ACTIVITY

### Activity 1

Explain whether the following situations could give rise to criminal liability or liability in tort or both.

1. Abigail lives very near a small factory. Recently the factory has been using a process which causes a lot of unpleasant smoke to be emitted from its chimneys. As a result Abigail has become ill and is suffering breathing problems.

2. Kieran is a drug dealer who sells illegal drugs to other people.

3. Zak took a car which did not belong to him from a cinema car park in order to drive to the next town to meet a friend at a pub. Zak decided to abandon the vehicle in the station car park near the pub. While parking, he hit and damaged another car belonging to Stefan.

4. Rena often takes a short cut across a neighbour's garden. Her neighbour objects to her doing this.

## BRIEF SUMMARY OF CHAPTER

**Nature of a tort**
- civil wrong, liable because of breach of duty or infringement of rights

**Fault based liability**
- defendant is liable because he or she is at fault by failing to reach expected standards of behaviour or by infringing another's rights

**Proving damage**
- claimant usually has to prove damage, but for some torts need only prove that the breach or infringement occurred

**Differences between torts and crimes**
- A crime is a wrong against the State, so the case is started by the State; the defendant is tried in a criminal court and will be punished if guilty
- A tort is a wrong against an individual, so the case will be started by the individual and heard in the civil courts; if the defendant is found liable he or she will have to compensate the claimant

# CHAPTER 18

# LAW OF TORT: NEGLIGENCE AND OCCUPIERS' LIABILITY

## Negligence

The tort of negligence is one of the most often-used torts because it covers such things as car crashes, medical negligence and defective workmanship which causes damage.

To prove negligence you need to prove **three** things:

1. The other person owes you a duty of care.
2. There was a breach of that duty of care.
3. As a result of that breach you have suffered damage to your person or property.

## Duty of care

The tort of negligence has developed this century, largely as a result of the judgment in the case of *Donoghue v Stevenson* (1932).

### CASE EXAMPLE

*Donoghue v Stevenson*

Mrs Donoghue went to a café with a friend. The friend bought her a bottle of ginger beer. She drank part of the ginger beer and then as she poured out the remainder from the bottle she found it contained a dead and decomposing snail. As a result she became ill.

She could not sue the shopkeeper under the law of contract since she had not bought the ginger beer. So she started a case against the manufacturers of the ginger beer. She claimed they were negligent in not making sure that bottles were properly cleaned and she won her case.

Lord Atkin giving the judgment of the House of Lords defined negligence by saying: 'You must take reasonable care to avoid acts or omissions which you can reasonably foresee would be likely to injure your neighbours'. He went on to say that your neighbour was anyone who would be so directly affected by your act that you ought reasonably to have them in contemplation.

Although the *Donoghue* case was about a manufacturer's duty of care to the consumer of their products, a duty of care has since been held to exist in numerous other situations:

(a) a lift repairer owes a duty of care to anyone using that lift
(b) an electricity company owes a duty of care to the public over the positioning of its electricity cables
(c) a solicitor owes a duty of care to anyone likely to suffer financially if he or she fails to make sure a will is properly witnessed
(d) a DIY enthusiast owes a duty of care to a fireman injured when he or she attended at a fire caused by the DIY enthusiast.

All the above examples come from cases where the courts held that a duty of care was owed; the claimant came into the category of being the defendant's 'neighbour' as set out in Lord Atkin's judgment.

## CASE EXAMPLES

*Haseldine v Daw* (1941) decided that a claimant who was injured when using a lift as a result of the negligent repair of that lift could sue the repairer of the lift.

In *Buckland v Guildford Gas Light and Coke Co* (1948) a 13-year-old girl was electrocuted when she climbed a tree and touched an overhead wire hidden in its branches. It was held that the electricity company should have foreseen this possibility and they owed a duty of care to the girl.

*Ross v Caunters* (1979) involved the situation of a solicitor owing a duty of care to check that a will was properly witnessed.

*Ogwu v Taylor* (1987) where a do-it-yourself enthusiast had negligently used a blow lamp to burn off paint and set fire to the roof timbers of his house. The fire brigade had to be called out and one of the firemen was injured in the fire. The House of Lords decided that a duty of care was owed to the fireman.

## The *Caparo* tests

The modern tests for deciding if there is a duty of care were explained in the case of *Caparo Industries v Dickman* (1990). They are wider than the neighbour test. It has to be shown that:

- damage was foreseeable
- there is a sufficiently 'proximate' relationship between the parties (this is really the same as the neighbour test)
- it is just and reasonable to impose a duty.

If damage is not foreseeable then there is no duty of care.

In some cases the courts have decided that there is no duty of care because the claimant does not come into the category of being the defendant's 'neighbour'. There is not a sufficiently proximate relationship between them. The defendant cannot reasonably be expected to have the

other person in mind since he or she is not likely to be directly affected by the defendant's acts or omissions. This is shown in *Bourhill v Young* (1943).

## CASE EXAMPLE

### *Bourhill v Young* (1943)

A motorcyclist crashed into a car and was killed. Mrs Bourhill, who was eight months pregnant, heard the crash but did not see it. She did, however, see blood from the accident on the road; she suffered shock and her baby was still-born. She sued the motorcyclist's estate, claiming that he had owed her a duty of care.

The court decided that she was not owed a duty of care; she was not his 'neighbour'; the motorcyclist could not reasonably anticipate that she would be affected by his negligent driving. He did, of course, owe a duty of care to the car driver with whom he collided.

## Breach of duty

Where a duty of care exists the claimant must still show that that duty had been broken if the claim of negligence is to be successful. The defendant must take reasonable care.

## Standard of care

The standard of care expected from the defendant will vary with the situation.

## CASE EXAMPLE

### *Paris v Stepney Borough Council* (1951)

The defendants knew that the claimant, an employee, was blind in one eye. They failed to provide him with protective goggles for his work and he was blinded when a chip of metal hit his good eye. The employers argued that it was not usual to provide goggles for

▶

the type of work the claimant was doing, but the court held that as the defendants knew their employee was blind in one eye, they had to take greater care for his safety than for that of normally sighted employees.

## Risk not known

If the risk is not known to anyone at the time of the injury, the defendant cannot be said to be in breach of his or her duty of care. This was seen in *Roe v Minister of Health* (1954).

### CASE EXAMPLE

#### Roe v Minister of Health (1954)

The claimant became paralysed because anaesthetic given to him during an operation was contaminated by disinfectant. The anaesthetic was kept in glass ampoules (small containers) which were stored in disinfectant. The disinfectant had got into the anaesthetic through invisible cracks in the glass. At the time of the operation in 1947, this risk was not known. It was held that the claimant had not proved that the hospital authorities had broken their duty of care and therefore he could not claim for negligence.

## Small risk

If the risk is very small then it may also be decided that the defendant is not in breach of the duty of care. This happened in *Bolton v Stone* (1951).

### CASE EXAMPLE

#### Bolton v Stone (1951)

The claimant was injured by a cricket ball hit into the street from a cricket ground. The evidence showed that the street was a

hundred yards from the wicket and there was a 17-foot-high fence between the ground and the road and balls had been hit out of the ground on only six other occasions in 35 years. The claimant was unable to claim that the defendant was negligent. The risk of a cricket ball landing in the street was so small that the defendant could not be expected to guard against it; the defendant was not in breach of the duty of care. The claimant was also unable to prove that there was a nuisance (see Chapter 19).

## Reasonable person

The standard of care is the level of care a reasonable person would use.

In cases where the defendant is an expert, for example a doctor, then the standard of care is the level of care to be expected from such an expert.

Where the situation involves everyday occurrences then the level is that of the ordinary person. In car accident cases the standard is that of normal drivers; the fact that the defendant is a learner driver does not mean that the standard expected is lower than that expected from other drivers. This was decided in *Nettleship v Weston* (1971) when it was said that a learner driver's 'incompetent best is not good enough'.

## Resulting damage

Assuming that the claimant has proved that the defendant owes a duty of care and has broken that duty of care, the claimant must still prove that the damage suffered was caused by the breach of duty. This is largely a matter of fact as was shown in *Barnett v Chelsea and Kensington Hospital Management Committee* (1968).

## CASE EXAMPLE

### Barnett v Chelsea and Kensington Hospital Management Committee (1968)

Three nightwatchmen (one of whom was the claimant's husband) called at a hospital complaining of sickness after drinking tea at work. The nurse in the casualty department telephoned the doctor on duty, who did not come to examine the men but recommended that they should go home and see their own doctors.

The claimant's husband went home and died a few hours later from arsenical poisoning. His widow sued the hospital alleging that the doctor was negligent in not examining her husband. She could easily show that the doctor owed her husband a duty of care and that by not examining him the doctor had broken that duty of care.

However, the evidence showed that by the time the husband called at the hospital it was too late to save his life; the arsenic was already in his system in such a quantity that he would have died anyway. There was nothing the doctor could have done to save him. This meant that the damage (the death) was not a result of the doctor's breach of his duty of care and the widow could not succeed in her claim.

The courts have called this the **'but for' test**. The claimant can only succeed if the harm would not have occurred 'but for' the defendant's negligence.

## Remoteness of damage

Even if the claimant can prove that the damage was caused by the defendant's breach of duty, the claimant will not win the case if it is shown that damage was too remote. This means that if the damage is too far removed from the defendant's negligence the claimant will not be able to claim for that damage. This rule comes from an Australian case called *The Wagon Mound* (1961).

## CASE EXAMPLE

### Overseas Tankship (UK) Ltd v Morts Dock and Engineering Co Ltd, The Wagon Mound (1961)

Fuel oil had negligently been spilled onto the water in a harbour. Two days later the oil caught fire because of welding work being done on another ship and the claimant's wharf was burnt down. The damage done to the wharf was a result of the negligent spilling of the oil, but it was held that such a result was not reasonably foreseeable.

This rule was followed in *Crossley v Rawlinson* (1981) where the claimant in running towards a burning vehicle with a fire extinguisher tripped and was injured. It was held that as the claimant was only on the way to the danger created by the defendant, the injury was too remote. The claimant could not claim for it.

## Foreseeable damage

However if it is foreseeable that a certain type of damage may result then the defendant is liable for it. This is so even if the extent of the injury was unexpected as shown by *Smith v Leech Brain & Co* (1962).

## CASE EXAMPLE

### Smith v Leech Brain & Co (1962)

The claimant's husband was burnt on the lip by hot metal because of the defendant's negligence. The burn caused cancer and the man died. Since a burn was a foreseeable injury, the defendant was liable for the death.

The defendant will also be liable if the type of injury was foreseeable, even though the exact way in which it happened was not. This happened in *Hughes v Lord Advocate* (1963).

**CASE EXAMPLE**

*Hughes v Lord Advocate* (1963)

Post Office workmen left a manhole unattended and covered only with a tent and with paraffin lamps by the hole. The claimant was a boy aged eight, who, with a friend, climbed into the hole. On their way out the boys knocked one of the paraffin lamps into the hole and caused an explosion in which the claimant was badly burned.

The boy was able to claim for his injuries since it was foreseeable that a child might explore the site and that a lamp might get broken and cause burns. The type of injury was foreseeable, even though it was not foreseeable that there would be an explosion, so the claimants were liable.

**CASE EXAMPLE**

*Jolley v Sutton Borough Council* (2000)

An old rotten boat was left on council land. The council accepted that children who used the area to play might be injured as the planking on the boat might give way if they tried to get into the boat. A 14-year-old boy tried to repair the boat and propped it up in order to get to the underside of it. The boat fell on to him and he suffered a severe injury to his back leaving him paralysed. The House of Lords held that as injury to children playing on the boat was foreseeable, the boy could claim for his injuries.

The same point was made in *Jolley v Sutton Borough Council* (2000).

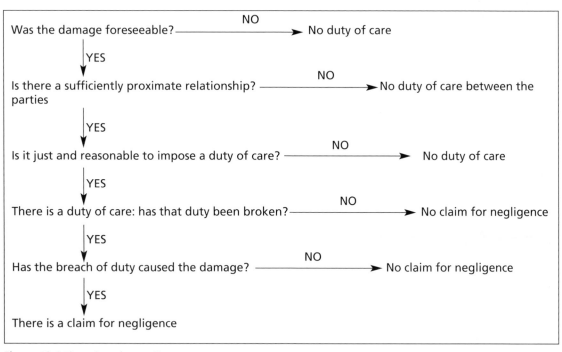

Figure 18.1 Flow chart for negligence

## ACTIVITY

### Activity 1

Fill in the empty boxes with appropriate cases connected to each of the three tests for negligence.

| Tests for negligence | Case where negligence was proved | Case where negligence was NOT proved |
|---|---|---|
| The defendant must owe a duty of care | | |
| The defendant must be in breach of the duty of care | | |
| The claimant must suffer damage as a result of the defendant's breach of the duty of care | | |

## ACTIVITY

### Activity 2

Answer the following questions.

1. What tests do the courts use to decide if there is a duty of care in negligence?

2. Give an example of a case where it was held there was a duty of care.

3. Give an example where it was held that there was *not* a duty of care.

4. What standard of care must be taken?

5. Give an example where greater care than usual had to be taken and explain why.

6. To be liable the defendant must be in breach of a duty of care. Give an example where the defendant owed a duty of care, but was held not to be in breach of that duty. Explain why the defendant was not in breach.

7. The claimant must show that he or she suffered damage as a result of the defendant's breach of a duty of care. Give an example where the claimant could not prove that the damage was a result of the breach.

8. Explain what is meant by 'remoteness of damage'.

9. Give an example where the damage was too remote for the claim to succeed.

10. The type of damage must be foreseeable. Give an example where the courts decided that the damage was foreseeable.

## Res ipsa loquitur

The general rule is that a claimant must prove all the three elements of negligence in order to win the case: that is, duty of care, breach of that duty and damage caused by that breach. In some cases the claimant is not able to say exactly what happened, but the facts clearly show that the defendant must have been negligent. If on the facts it is sufficiently obvious that there was negligence by the defendant, the claimant may rely on a rule of evidence called *res ipsa loquitur*, meaning 'the facts speak for themselves'.

The claimant has to show that:

(a) the defendant was in control of the situation which caused the claimant's injury; and

(b) the injury was more likely than not to have been caused by negligence.

If the claimant can show these, there is a *prima facie* case (case at first sight) of negligence and the burden of proof moves to the defendant who must now try to prove that he was not negligent.

Examples of cases where the rule has been used include *Scott v London & St Katherine Docks* (1865).

## CASE EXAMPLE

### *Scott v London & St Katherine Docks (1865)*

The claimant had been hit on the head by six bags of sugar which fell from the defendant's warehouse. The claimant could not say why the bags had fallen, but the court held that in those circumstances it was for the defendant to show that there had not been negligence. The defendant was unable to do so and the claimant won the case.

The rule was also used in *Mahon v Osborne* (1939) where swabs were left inside a patient during an operation. The claimant, the patient, could not prove exactly what had happened, but the facts spoke for themselves.

The rule does not mean that the defendant is automatically proved to have been negligent; the defendant may still be able to show that he was not negligent. This happened in *Pearson v NW Gas Board* (1968).

## CASE EXAMPLE

### *Pearson v NW Gas Board* (1968)

A gas explosion killed the claimant's husband and destroyed her home. The claimant could not prove how the explosion happened, but relied on *res ipsa loquitur* so that the defendants had to prove they were not negligent. The defendants were able to do this by showing that there had been an unusually severe frost which had damaged a gas pipe and caused the gas leak. The defendants had not been negligent and so the claimant lost her case.

# Contributory negligence

Contributory negligence means that the claimant has been partly to blame for the damage suffered. The claimant's acts or failure to act contributed to the damage they suffered.

The claimant may still make a claim against the defendant but any damages awarded to the claimant will be reduced by the amount the claimant was to blame. This rule comes from the Law Reform (Contributory Negligence) Act 1945. It is quite often used in cases arising from car crashes where both drivers may be partly to blame for the accident. The judge will decide how much each is at fault and then calculate the effect this has on the damages as in the example below:

**Claimant 25 per cent to blame**

| | |
|---|---|
| Damages would have been | £100,000 |
| Take away 25 per cent | £25,000 |
| Claimant awarded | £75,000 |

An example of contributory negligence happened in *Sayers v Harlow UDC* (1957).

**CASE EXAMPLE**

*Sayers v Harlow UDC* (1957)

The claimant was unable to get out of a public toilet because of a faulty lock on the door. She shouted and tried to attract attention for about 15 minutes, but when no-one came she tried to climb out. She stood on the toilet-roll holder which turned and caused her to fall and break her ankle. The defendants were held liable in negligence, but she was found to be 25 per cent to blame because she had stood on the toilet-roll holder. Her damages were reduced by 25 per cent.

In some cases the fact that the claimant has failed to take reasonable care for his own safety may make him contributorily negligent even though he did not cause the accident in any way. This is the position where a person working on a building site fails to wear his safety helmet and is hit on the head by a brick that has been negligently dropped by a workmate or where an adult passenger in a car fails to put the seat belt on.

**CASE EXAMPLE**

*Froom v Butcher* (1976)

The claimant was a front seat passenger in a car that was involved in an accident. As he was not the driver he obviously did not cause the accident, but he was held to be

contributorily negligent because he did not wear a seat-belt. He contributed to the injuries he suffered when in the accident he was thrown through the windscreen and his damages were reduced by 20 per cent.

In *Owens v Brimmell* (1976) it was also decided that a person contributes to his own injuries if he travels in a car with a driver he knows to be drunk.

**ACTIVITY**

Activity 3

Advise the people in the following situations.

Candy is given a box of chocolates by her boyfriend. When she eats one she is injured by a piece of glass inside the chocolate.

Advise Candy.

Denver has the electrical fittings in his house rewired by Arthur, an electrician. Arthur wrongly connects the wires in the TV socket so that when Denver next switches on the TV, he suffers an electric shock and burns to his arm. The TV set is ruined beyond repair.

Advise Denver.

Serena is walking down the street past some scaffolding when she is hit on the head by a spanner dropped by a worker on the scaffolding.

Advise Serena. What special rule might help Serena in proving her case?

Zena, a pillion passenger on a motorbike, suffers head injuries in an accident caused by the negligence of the motorbike driver. Zena was not wearing a crash helmet.

Advise Zena.

## Occupiers' liability

The law on the level of duty of care owed to anyone coming onto your land is set out in two Acts of Parliament.

## Lawful visitors

The first Act is the Occupiers' Liability Act 1957. This says that there are two categories of visitor: (a) lawful visitors and (b) persons who are not lawful visitors. This 1957 Act states that the occupier has:

**❝** a duty to take such care as in all the circumstances of the case is reasonable to see that the visitor will be reasonably safe in using the premises for the purposes for which he is invited to be there. **❞**

This duty is owed only to lawful visitors. A lawful visitor can be:

1. Someone invited to the premises by the occupier such as a friend invited to a party or to come round for coffee.
2. Someone who buys a ticket to come onto the land (eg to attend a football match or a concert).
3. Someone who has not been specifically invited but has implied permission to be there; this includes customers in a shop, a delivery person (eg delivering milk, papers or post to a house) and door-to-door salesmen.
4. Anyone who has the right in law to enter the premises (eg police officers with a search warrant or gas and electricity meter readers).

The duty is to take 'such care as is reasonable in all the circumstances' and so it will vary from case to case.

## Child visitors

The main rule is that an occupier must take greater care for child visitors, particularly young children, who are less careful and cannot always appreciate that something is dangerous. This is shown by *Glasgow Corporation v Taylor* (1922).

### CASE EXAMPLE

***Glasgow Corporation v Taylor* (1922)**

A seven-year-old boy died after eating poisonous berries he had picked in a park belonging to the corporation. There was no warning notice about the berries, nor was there any fence to prevent children reaching them so the court held that the corporation was liable. It had failed to take reasonable care of child visitors to the park.

## Adult visitors

Where the visitors are adults or older children, it may be enough if the occupier puts up warning notices about any dangers on the land. In the case of shops a coloured warning triangle is usually placed on any wet or slippery floors to warn visitors of the danger.

## Independent contractors

An occupier will not usually be liable if the danger has been created by a specialist independent contractor carrying out work on the occupier's land. In *O'Connor v Swan and Edgar* (1963), the defendant shop was not liable when some plaster fell from a ceiling and injured the claimant. The defendants had taken reasonable care in using independent specialist plasterers to do the work on the ceiling. In such a case the injured person should sue the independent contractor.

However, if the work done does not need any specialist knowledge to check on it, then the occupier will be liable. This happened in *Woodward v Mayor of Hastings* (1945) when the claimant slipped on ice on a step. Independent contractors had been used to clean the steps but as it did not need any expert knowledge to check whether the steps were safe to use the occupier was liable for the injury to the claimant.

# Non-visitors

The Occupiers' Liability Act 1957 only applies to lawful visitors. This means that it does not apply if the person on the land is a trespasser.

The old rule used to be that no matter how dangerous the land, nor how easy it was to get onto it, the occupier was never liable to any trespasser.

This rule was thought to be very harsh where young children were involved and eventually in *Herrington v British Railways Board* (1972) the House of Lords changed the law.

## CASE EXAMPLE

### *Herrington v British Railways Board* (1972)

Herrington was a six-year-old boy who was badly burned when playing on a railway track. The Railway Board knew that the fence alongside the railway line was damaged and that children had been seen playing on the track for some weeks before the boy was injured. The House of Lords ruled that where an occupier knew of a danger and had not taken reasonable steps to prevent trespassers from entering the premises, they could be liable for injuries to a trespasser.

The Occupiers' Liability Act 1984 was passed to make this area of the law clearer. It states that an occupier owes a duty of care to 'non-visitors' (eg trespassers) if:

(a) he is aware of the danger or has reasonable grounds to believe that it exists; and

(b) he knows or has reasonable grounds to believe that there are 'non-visitors' in the vicinity of the danger or that 'non-visitors' may come into the vicinity; and

(c) the risk is one against which, in all the circumstances, he may be reasonably expected to offer the 'non-visitor' some protection.

The Occupiers' Liability Act 1984 allows a 'non-visitor' to claim for injury but not for damage to property.

In order for a non-visitor to be able to make a claim, the risk of injury must be because of danger due to the state of the premises. It must also be a risk that is not obvious to the non-visitor. The case of *Tomlinson v Congleton Borough Council* (2003) is an example of where the risk was obvious.

## CASE EXAMPLE

### *Tomlinson v Congleton Borough Council* (2003)

The defendant council owned a park with a lake in it. There were warning signs saying 'Dangerous Water, No Swimming'. The council knew that people ignored these signs and they planned to put up a barrier to prevent people from reaching the lakeside. However, the council delayed this work, because of lack of funds.

The claimant, aged 18, ignored the warning signs, dived into the water and broke his neck. He tried to claim against the council but the House of Lords held that the council were not in breach of their duty to non-visitors. They held that there was no risk to the claimant from the state of the premises. They also held that, by diving into the lake, the claimant had chosen to run the risk of danger.

Even if the claimant had been a lawful visitor the council did not owe a duty to the claimant to prevent him from diving or warning him against dangers which were perfectly obvious.

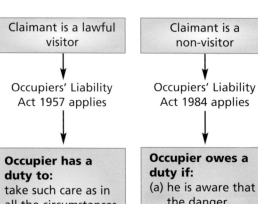

Figure 18.2 Flow chart on occupiers' liability

notices warning that the equipment should not be used without staff supervision. Barack falls from a climbing wall and is badly injured.

3. Caitlin goes shopping in her local supermarket. By one freezer cabinet there is a yellow triangle on the floor with the notice 'Wet floor'. Caitlin is in a hurry and rushes to the freezer to select the goods she wants. She slips on the wet floor and breaks her leg.

4. Daniel, aged 8, is injured when he trespasses on factory land and falls into a pit. The owners of the factory were aware that children frequently played on the land and that the fencing around the factory was broken in several places making it easy for children to get onto the land.

## Vicarious liability

Vicarious liability is the expression used when a person is liable for the torts of another. It means that one person who did not do the wrong act is automatically responsible for another's torts because the other is acting on his or her behalf. There must be a special relationship between the two people before one can be vicariously liable for the other's torts. The most common relationship is that of employer/employee, though it is possible for a partner in a business to be vicariously liable for acts done by another partner.

## Liability for employees' acts

### Acting in the course of employment

The employee must be acting in the course of his or her employment. It does not matter that an employee is using his employment to benefit himself: his employer will still be liable. This was shown in the case *Lloyd v Grace, Smith & Co* (1912).

**ACTIVITY**

### Activity 4

Explain whether each of the people in the following situations may be able to make a claim under the Occupiers' Liability Act 1957 or the Occupiers' Liability Act 1984.

1. Aziz, aged 5, is playing on a swing in the local playground. He is severely injured when the swing comes loose from the frame and he is thrown to the ground. The local council who own the playground knew that there was a fault with the swing.

2. Barack, aged 19, climbs over a wall to get into an outdoor activity centre. There are

## CASE EXAMPLE

### *Lloyd v Grace, Smith & Co* (1912)

A managing clerk in a firm of solicitors defrauded a client of some property, while advising her. It was held that the solicitors who employed him were liable for his actions since he was employed to advise clients and deal with property. The fact that he was the one to benefit from the fraud did not stop his employers from being liable.

## Negligence of employee

An employer will be liable even if the employee does his or her work particularly carelessly. This was the situation in *Century Insurance v Northern Ireland Road Transport Board* (1942).

## CASE EXAMPLE

### *Century Insurance v Northern Ireland Road Transport Board* (1942)

The defendant's employee was delivering petrol to a garage. While petrol was being piped from his lorry into a tank he lit a cigarette and threw down the match, causing an explosion. His employer was held liable for the damage caused.

## Doing work in a forbidden way

An employer may still be liable even if the employee does his work in a way in which he has been forbidden to. This was shown in the old case of *Limpus v London General Omnibus Co* (1862).

## CASE EXAMPLE

### *Limpus v London General Omnibus Co* (1862)

The driver of a horse-driven bus had been forbidden to race other drivers; he did so and caused an accident in which another bus

overturned. His employer was liable for the damage since the bus driver was acting in the course of his employment. The fact that the driver was doing his work in a forbidden way did not stop the employer from being liable.

This same rule was used over a hundred years later in *Rose v Plenty* (1976).

## CASE EXAMPLE

### *Rose v Plenty* (1976)

A milkman was forbidden to let children help him with his milk round. The milkman broke this rule and allowed the claimant, a boy of 13 years old, to help with deliveries. The boy was injured as a result of an accident caused by the milkman's negligence. He was able to claim against the milkman's employers as the milkman was acting in the course of his employment, even though he should not have let the boy help him.

## Not acting in the course of employment

Where an employee is not acting within the scope of his employment his employer is not liable for any tort he may commit. This means that where the employee is doing something that is not part of his work, then the employer is not liable even if the incident happens at the workplace. An example is the case of *Aldred v Nanconco* (1987).

## CASE EXAMPLE

### *Aldred v Nanconco* (1987)

The claimant, an employee, was in the washroom getting ready to leave work when another employee came in and pushed a washbasin that was loose against the claimant, causing an injury to the claimant's back. It was held that the employer was not vicariously liable since the second employee was not actually working at the time of the incident.

Another case illustrating that the employer is not vicariously liable if the employee is not acting within the scope of his employment is *Beard v London General Omnibus Co* (1900).

### CASE EXAMPLE

#### *Beard v London General Omnibus Co* (1900)

A bus conductor tried to drive the bus in order to turn it round at the end of the route. He was not employed to drive and so his employers were not liable for the accident he caused.

## Frolic of his own

If an employee is on a 'frolic of his own' then the employer is not liable. This usually happens where an employee uses his employer's vehicle for his own purpose. An example is *Hilton v Thomas Burton* (1961).

### CASE EXAMPLE

#### *Hilton v Thomas Burton* (1961)

Some demolition contractors used their employer's van to go to a café. On the return journey the driver crashed as a result of negligent driving and one of the other workmen was killed. They were allowed to drive the van, but on this occasion it was held that it was not part of their work as they were filling in time instead of working on the site. They were on a 'frolic of their own', so the claimant, the widow of the man killed, could not succeed in her claim against the employer.

## Travelling to work

Travelling to and from work is normally not part of the employment. So an employer will not be liable for any torts committed by employees during the journey. However, where the journey is made during working time for the employer's benefit, then the employer will be vicariously liable. This was the situation in *Smith v Stages* (1989).

### CASE EXAMPLE

#### *Smith v Stages* (1989)

Two employees were sent from Staffordshire to Pembroke in South Wales to do urgent work for their employer. As the distance was so long, they were paid for two extra days to cover travelling time. One of the employees drove and took the other employee as a passenger. On the return journey the driver crashed, injuring himself and the other employee. The House of Lords decided that the employer was vicariously liable to the passenger for his injuries since the journey was part of their employment. The driver was acting in the scope of his employment.

# Liability for torts of independent contractors

An employer is only liable for torts committed by employees. He is not normally liable for torts committed by an independent contractor. There are exceptions to this rule.

An employer is liable for the torts of independent contractors in the following situations:

**(a)** where the employer authorises the independent contractor to commit a tort;

**(b)** where the work involved is extra hazardous: that is, it involves an extra risk of damage being caused;

(c) where the work is being done on or over the highway, for example on a bridge crossing another road;

(d) where the law states that the employer is to remain liable, as where the employer has a duty to provide a safe system of work, he or she cannot avoid responsibility for torts committed by independent contractors.

## Distinguishing between employees and independent contractors

Sometimes it can be difficult to decide whether someone is an employee or an independent contractor. The courts will consider several points in trying to make this decision. One test is whether the employer has overall control of the work done. Can the employer tell the other not only what to do, but also how to do it? The greater the degree of control the more likely it is that the other is an employee.

However, there are other points to consider. These include:

1. How is the work to be paid for? An employee will receive regular wages, while an independent contractor will usually receive a lump sum.
2. How is income tax and National Insurance dealt with? An employer must deduct these from an employee's wages, but will not make deductions from any monies paid to an independent contractor; an independent contractor must pay his or her own tax and insurance.
3. Who supplies the tools and equipment used? Independent contractors will usually provide their own.
4. Is the work being done as an integral part of the employer's business? If so, that person is probably an employee; an independent contractor is more likely to be doing work that is an accessory to the employer's

business, but is not integrated into that business.

## Justifications for vicarious liability

At first sight it seems unfair to make one person responsible for a wrong done by another, particularly where the employer has expressly forbidden certain behaviour, as in *Limpus v London General Omnibus Co* above.

However there are a number of reasons for this principle.

1. The main reason is that the employer is usually in a better financial position that the employee. He will be more able to pay any compensation awarded to the injured person and will usually have insurance against the risk of accidents at work.
2. The employer is getting the profits from the work being done, so that he should also have to pay for losses.
3. The employer has control over choosing an employee and has the power to dismiss an incompetent employee. If he continues to employ someone who is known to create risks then it is fair that the employer should pay for any damage done by such an employee. This happened in *Hudson v Ridge Manufacturing Co* where an employee broke his wrist as a result of a practical joke played by another employee. The employer knew that the other employee was a practical joker and had, over a period of four years, often had to reprimand him for tripping up people and other similar behaviour. As such behaviour could be dangerous it was held that the employer was liable to compensate the claimant. The employer knew of the risk of injury.
4. An employer will be encouraged to provide a safe system of work and to improve standards of training and supervision.

## BRIEF SUMMARY OF CHAPTER

### Negligence

Three tests:

- must prove duty of care
- breach of duty, and
- damage which is not too remote

### Duty of care

- the damage must be foreseeable
- the parties must be sufficiently close, and
- it must be just fair and reasonable to impose a duty.

### Occupiers' liability

- duty of care to lawful visitors
- This is to take such care as is reasonable in all the circumstances (Occupiers' Liability Act 1957)
- duty owed to non-visitors
- The occupier must be aware of danger on his or her land and that non-visitors may be at risk from that danger (Occupiers' Liability Act 1984)

### Vicarious liability

- This is where one person is liable for the torts of another person
- An employer is liable for an employee's torts where the employee is acting in the course of employment

## EXAMINATION QUESTION

Read the following passage.

1. Negligence occurs when the defendant owes a duty of ..................... to the claimant and they breach this duty by an act or omission which falls below the ............................................... which is appropriate to the duty and where the defendant's breach of duty causes ............................. damage to the claimant.

Fill in the gaps choosing the most appropriate word from the list below.

- foreseeable
- behaviour
- severe
- standard
- protection
- care

*OCR Specimen Paper*

# CHAPTER 19

# LAW OF TORT: TRESPASS AND NUISANCE

All torts involving trespass are actionable *per se* (of itself). This means the claimant need only prove that the trespass occurred in order to succeed in a case. It is not necessary to show that the defendant caused any damage or injury. There are three different types of trespass. These are:

- trespass to the person;
- trespass to goods; and
- trespass to land.

We will look at each of these in turn.

## Trespass to the person

Trespass to the person can be committed in three different ways. These are:

- assault
- battery
- false imprisonment.

## Assault

In law the word 'assault' has a technical special meaning which is different from its everyday use. An assault in law is an act which causes another person to fear immediate and unlawful force will be used on them.

This definition covers a wide variety of acts including raising a fist, threatening with a stick or other weapon or throwing something at a person, but missing them. Even spitting in the direction of a person can be an assault.

There must be an act; words alone are not enough. If the defendant makes it clear from what he says that he will not use force, then there is no

assault even though he has used a threatening gesture. This is illustrated by a very old case, *Turbervell v Savadge* (1669).

### CASE EXAMPLE

*Turbervell v Savadge* (1669)

The defendant put his hand on his sword in a threatening way; it was not an assault because he said, 'If it were not assize-time, I would not take such language from you'. It was assize-time (the time when special courts were held in the town), and so the words made it clear that the claimant need not fear the use of force.

## Puts in fear

The claimant must reasonably fear that immediate force will be used against him. If the defendant is too far away to carry out his threat, then that is not an assault. So, if a person standing at a window on the fourth floor of a building raises his fist and threatens someone on the roadway outside the building that would not be an assault. But if someone at an open window on the ground floor raises his fist, then that might be an assault. The victim might reasonably fear that that person could carry out their threat.

There is no assault if the claimant did not know about the threatening gesture, for example if the defendant pointed a gun at his back unknown to him. As the victim did not know about it, he is not 'put in fear' of violence being used against him.

## Battery

Battery is the application of unlawful force to the body of another. The most obvious examples are slapping, punching or kicking another or hitting him with a stick or other weapon.

The attacker does not have to personally touch the other; an indirect use of force is also a battery. So it is a battery if water is thrown over another or a chair is pulled from under a person causing him to fall.

Although the word force is used in the definition, this does not have to be a violent act. Any touching to which the other does not agree can be a battery. Surgical treatment by a doctor could be a battery if the patient did not agree to it. Even kissing another person who does not wish to be kissed can be a battery.

Often the defendant will commit an assault and a battery. This can happen where the defendant raises his fist (assault) and then punches (battery) the claimant. However in some situations there will be a battery without an assault first. This will happen where the claimant is unaware that he is going to be hit, for example if he is hit from behind or if he is hit when asleep.

### Defences

There are some special defences to assault and battery. The main defences are:

1. *Self-defence*. A person may use reasonable force to defend himself or another. What is reasonable will depend on the facts in each case. Pushing away an attacker is probably reasonable in almost every case, but using a weapon will only be reasonable if it is necessary. There is a saying that 'fists may be met with fists but not with a deadly weapon'. This is generally true, but there could be circumstances where there is a particularly vicious attack without a weapon and the only

way the victim can protect him or herself adequately is by using a weapon.

2. *Lawful arrest*. Reasonable force may be used to make a lawful arrest. The law on arrests is set out in Chapter 6.

## False imprisonment

False imprisonment occurs where, without a lawful reason, the claimant is prevented from moving freely as he wishes. It is the deprivation of personal liberty.

False imprisonment, therefore, does not just cover situations where the claimant is wrongly put in prison or locked in a room. It also covers the following situations: handcuffing someone; refusing to allow a person to leave a house; refusing to stop a car and let a passenger get out.

The false imprisonment can even take place in the open air by preventing someone from leaving a field or other place.

The claimant need not know that he is unable to leave, the fact that he cannot leave is enough to prove this tort as happened in *Meering v Grahame-White Aviation Co* (1919).

### CASE EXAMPLE

**Meering v Grahame-White Aviation Co (1919)**

The claimant was being questioned in a room and, although he did not know it at the time, two men were standing outside the door to make sure that he did not leave. It was held he could still claim for false imprisonment.

### No reasonable way out

If the person has a reasonable way out, then it is not false imprisonment. This was the situation in *Bird v Jones* (1845).

**CASE EXAMPLE**

### *Bird v Jones* (1845)

The claimant insisted on trying to walk over a part of Hammersmith Bridge that was temporarily fenced off. The defendant stopped him going any further but told the claimant he could go back and then use the footpath on the other side of the bridge. Since the claimant had a reasonable alternative way out this was not false imprisonment.

## Length of time

In some situations detaining a person for a very short period of time is not false imprisonment as shown in *John Lewis & Co v Timms* (1952).

**CASE EXAMPLE**

### *John Lewis & Co v Timms* (1952)

The claimant and her daughter had been wrongly suspected of stealing. They were kept in an office against their will until the store manager had been informed. It was decided that the length of time they were held was not unreasonable and they could not claim for false imprisonment.

# Defences to false imprisonment

As with assault and battery there are some special defences to false imprisonment. These are:

- lawful arrest
- court order of imprisonment
- mental health order
- parental authority.

## Lawful arrest

Any person who has been lawfully arrested may be detained. The police can hold someone for up to 36 hours or longer if authorised by magistrates. The full rules are set out in Chapter 6.

## A court order of imprisonment

Any sentence passed by a court allows a prisoner to be lawfully detained.

## A mental health order

The Mental Health Acts allow a person to be held in a mental hospital under certain circumstances.

## Parental authority

Parents and guardians have the right to prevent a child from leaving home or school in reasonable circumstances.

**ACTIVITY**

### Activity 1

Explain whether the tort of trespass to the person has occurred in each of the following situations.

1. At an office party Amy throws her arms around Damien and kisses him. Damien is very annoyed as he has never liked Amy and has told her to leave him alone on previous occasions.

2. Barney aims a punch at Farouk. Farouk ducks out of the way so that Barney misses him and hits Julian on the back of the head instead.

3. Charlie refuses to let his girlfriend, Jane, leave her flat until she agrees to lend him £10.

# Trespass to goods

Trespass to goods consists of direct and unlawful damage to, or interference with, goods in the possession of another person. Goods are moveable items of property such as clothes, jewellery, furniture, books, cars, cash and cheques.

| Type of trespass to the person | Definition | Examples |
|---|---|---|
| Assault | An act which causes another person to fear immediate and unlawful force | Raising a fist<br>Threatening someone with a stick or other weapon<br>Throwing an object at a person<br>Spitting in direction of someone |
| Battery | The application of unlawful force to another | Punching<br>Kicking<br>Hitting with a stick<br>Indirect – throwing water over person or pulling a chair from under them |
| False imprisonment | Preventing another from moving freely without a lawful reason | Locking in a room<br>Putting on handcuffs<br>Refusing to allow someone out of a car |

Figure 19.1 The different types of trespass to the person

## Interference

As with trespass to the person and trespass to land, the claimant can claim damages just because there has been an interference with his goods. The slightest touching is enough; there is no need to prove that the defendant damaged the goods. Nor does the claimant need to show that the defendant was acting in a spiteful way. In *Kirk v Gregory* (1876) the defendant was doing his best to take care of the goods, but he was still liable for trespass to goods.

### CASE EXAMPLE

**Kirk v Gregory (1876)**

The defendant was genuinely worried that jewellery belonging to a man who had just died might be stolen and so decided to move it to a safer place in another room. Unfortunately the second room was not a good choice as the jewellery was then stolen from there by an unknown person. The defendant was held liable for trespass to the goods because she had interfered with the jewellery by moving it.

## In possession

It is not necessary to own the goods to be able to sue for this tort. The person in possession can bring an action as shown by the old case of *Armory v Delamirie* (1721).

### CASE EXAMPLE

**Armory v Delamirie (1721)**

A boy chimney sweep found a jewel and took it to a goldsmith for it to be valued. The goldsmith refused to return the jewel to the boy, so the boy sued him successfully.

A similar situation happened in a more modern setting in *Parker v British Airways Board* (1982).

### CASE EXAMPLE

**Parker v British Airways Board (1982)**

The claimant found a gold bracelet on the floor in the executive lounge at Heathrow Airport. He handed it in to an airline official and also left his name and address so that it could be returned to him if the true owner was not found. The owner was not found and British Airways sold the bracelet for £850. The claimant sued them successfully for the value of the bracelet.

Of course, in both the above examples, the real owner of the goods has the right to claim them from the finders or any other person. But the finders have a right against other people. They are in possession.

## Trespass to land

Trespass to land is any unlawful entry onto land or buildings in the possession of another person.

Remaining on land after the owner has withdrawn permission for you to be there is also a trespass; this could happen if a person decided to remain in a theatre after the end of a performance or in a football stadium after the match was finished. The original entry would not be a trespass, provided an entrance ticket had been bought, but the permission to be on the land only lasts while the play or game is going on.

There can also be a trespass through an unlawful physical interference with land or buildings in the possession of another, for example by digging a tunnel underneath someone's land. Like trespass to the person and trespass to goods, trespass to land is actionable *per se* (of itself), so that the claimant does not have to prove the trespasser caused any damage. The fact of the trespass is enough to prove the case.

An important point about trespass to land is that it is a direct interference with land. This is a major difference between trespass to land and nuisance (see Nuisance and Figure 19.4 below).

To be liable for trespass, the defendant must have entered the land voluntarily. Where someone is pushed onto land, that person is not liable for trespass, but the person who pushed him would be.

Trespass to land can be committed in a number of different ways; the most common are by walking, riding or driving across another person's land. Other ways of committing trespass include sitting on someone's fence or wall; throwing objects onto the land; allowing one's animals to go onto the land; or, as already mentioned, digging a tunnel under another person's land or buildings.

## The space above land

It is also possible for there to be a trespass in the air space immediately above land, even though the object is not touching the surface of the land in any way. This happened in *Kelson v Imperial Tobacco Co Ltd* (1957).

### CASE EXAMPLE

*Kelson v Imperial Tobacco Co Ltd (1957)*

An advertising sign projected over the claimant's land. The court granted the claimant an injunction ordering the defendant to remove the sign even though the sign only projected by 20 centimetres.

A crane swinging above another person's land was also held to be a trespass in *Woollerton and Wilson v Costain* (1970). There is a problem, however, in deciding how far above the land the claimant can claim the air space as seen in the case of *Lord Bernstein of Leigh v Skyviews and General Ltd* (1977).

## CASE EXAMPLE

### Lord Bernstein of Leigh v Skyviews and General Ltd (1977)

The defendant's aircraft flew a few hundred feet above the claimant's house for the purpose of taking photographs of the house. The judge ruled that an owner of land could only claim a right to the air space above it to such a height as was necessary for the ordinary enjoyment of land and buildings on the land. It was decided that the claimant could not claim a trespass as the aircraft was too high.

## In possession of the land

The claimant must be in possession of the land in order to have the right to sue for trespass. This means that the claimant has the right to exclude other people from the land; it does not only mean physical control. A person who is on holiday and not at home is still 'in possession' and could sue for trespass if anyone entered the house.

## Defences

The main defences to trespass are that:

• the defendant had authority in law to be there; this applies to (among others) police with a search warrant and court bailiffs with a court order to seize goods
• the defendant had a licence to be there; this is the position where the defendant has a valid ticket to watch a football match, but a licence can be withdrawn by the person in possession of the land (eg a football hooligan can be asked to leave)
• the defendant was on the land only to retake goods belonging to him and put on the land by the claimant
• the trespass was necessary to save life (eg to rescue a child from a burning house)
• the defendant was abating (ending) a nuisance – see below.

## Abatement

This is a 'self-help' remedy. A person affected by a nuisance has the right to abate (put an end to) the nuisance. There are no problems where this can be done without going onto the defendant's land, for example cutting off branches that overhang from a neighbour's land onto your own land. It must be noted, however, that the branches can only be cut off up to the boundary line and must be offered back to your neighbour. If the abatement involves going onto the defendant's land, then notice of the intention to do this must be given, unless it is an emergency.

## ACTIVITY

### Activity 2

Explain whether any tort of trespass is involved in the following situations.

1.  Nancy frequently takes her dog for a walk in a field belonging to a farmer. One day the farmer sees her, and without warning grabs hold of her, tearing the sleeve of her coat. He threatens to shoot her dog if he finds her on his land again.

    What types of trespass have been committed?

2.  Emily often throws rubbish from her garden into her neighbour, Sam's, garden. She also often walks across Sam's garden as a short cut when coming home from the shops.

    Advise Sam on what remedies he may have.

3.  Donald visits his friend Owen. While at Owen's house, he picks up an antique vase and carelessly drops it, smashing it.

    Advise Owen.

## Nuisance

The law recognises two different types of nuisance. These are private nuisance and public nuisance. The two types are quite different and must be considered separately.

| Definition | Unlawful entry onto land or buildings in possession of another |
|---|---|
| Voluntary trespass | The defendant must have gone onto the land voluntarily |
| Examples | Walking on land<br>Driving over land<br>Entering a building<br>Sitting on a wall<br>Throwing objects onto land<br>Digging a tunnel under the land<br>Interfering with the air space above the land BUT if it is too high it will not be trespass |
| Special defences to trespass to land | Authority in law to be there<br>A licence to be there<br>Defendant was on the land only to retake goods belonging to him or her and put on the land by the claimant<br>The trespass was necessary to save life<br>The defendant was abating (ending) a nuisance |

Figure 19.2 Trespass to land

# Private nuisance

Private nuisance is something which unreasonably interferes with the claimant's use or enjoyment of his land. A nuisance can be caused by a wide variety of things and behaviour. In *Butler v Standard Telephone and Cables Ltd* (1940) it was held that tree roots growing under a neighbour's land were in law a nuisance; while in *Lemmon v Webb* (1894) overhanging branches were also considered to amount to a nuisance.

Other types of nuisance may be less tangible but may equally affect the enjoyment of one's land. In *Bone v Seal* (1975) smells coming from a pig farm were held to be a nuisance. Noise, vibration, fumes, gas and heat have all been held to be capable of being a nuisance in law.

Other behaviour which could amount to a nuisance would be blocking a person's driveway so that he was unable to get any vehicles in or out of the property. Also, blocking light from entering through a window could be a nuisance as was shown in *Carr-Saunders v Dick McNeil* (1986) where a two-storey addition to a building

owned by the defendants blocked light from windows in the claimant's building.

To amount to a nuisance under the law several points will have to be considered: continuity, unreasonableness and what is or is not unreasonable.

## Continuity

The normal rule is that a 'one-off' happening is not a nuisance as shown by *SCM (UK) Ltd v Whittal* (1970).

> **CASE EXAMPLE**
>
> ### *SCM (UK) Ltd v Whittal* (1970)
>
> A workman cut a power cable and stopped production in the claimant's factory. It was held that this could not be nuisance, since it was a single isolated event.

However, if the single incident is caused by an ongoing state of affairs, there may be a nuisance. This happened in *Midwood v Mayor of Manchester* (1905) where there was a gas explosion.

**CASE EXAMPLE**

### *Midwood v Mayor of Manchester* (1905)

There was a gas explosion on the defendant's land. This was a single event. However, it had been caused by the build-up of gas on the defendant's land, which was an ongoing state of affairs, so the claimant was able to succeed with a claim for nuisance.

Even where the behaviour occurs more than once it will not always be a nuisance. This is illustrated by *Bolton v Stone* (1951).

**CASE EXAMPLE**

### *Bolton v Stone* (1951)

The claimant was injured by a cricket ball hit into the roadway outside a cricket field. The evidence was that a cricket ball had only been hit into the roadway six times in 35 years and this was held to be too infrequent for it to be a nuisance.

Where the happening occurs more often then it can be a nuisance as in *Castle v St Augustine's Links* (1922).

**CASE EXAMPLE**

### *Castle v St Augustine's Links* (1922)

Golf balls were regularly hit into the road running alongside the thirteenth hole; it was held this was a nuisance.

## Unreasonableness

To succeed with a claim for nuisance, the claimant must show not only that there was an interference with his use or enjoyment of his land, but also that such interference was unreasonable. The question of what is reasonable and what is unreasonable is one of fact. The court will consider:

• the time
• the place
• the degree and way

in which the act alleged to be a nuisance occurred.

## Time

The time of day may need to be considered; more noise will be allowed during the daytime than at night. The length of time could also be important since the longer the noise, fumes or other unpleasant interference lasts, the more likely that it is a nuisance.

## Place

Different standards may apply in different areas. More noise, vibration, etc would be expected in an industrial estate than in a quiet residential street. So some noise or vibration might not be a nuisance on an industrial estate, but the same level of noise or vibration could be a nuisance if it happened in a quiet residential area.

## Sensitivity of the claimant

The fact that the claimant or his property is extra-sensitive will not make reasonable behaviour a nuisance. This was the situation in *Robinson v Kilvert* (1889).

**CASE EXAMPLE**

### *Robinson v Kilvert* (1889)

The claimant stored some unusually sensitive brown paper in a room near the defendant's boiler. Heat from the boiler damaged the paper. It was held that this was not a nuisance since ordinary paper would not have been damaged.

## Defendant's malice

Normally in tort cases the defendant's motive for his actions is not relevant. However in nuisance cases the fact that the defendant acted maliciously out of spite to annoy the claimant may make his behaviour unreasonable so that it becomes a nuisance. An example of malice occurred in the case of *Christie v Davey* (1893).

### CASE EXAMPLE

#### *Christie v Davey* (1893)

The defendant disliked his neighbour giving music lessons and deliberately created a noise during any lessons. He did this by blowing whistles, shouting, hammering and banging on trays. Each one of these on its own and done for a good purpose would probably not be a nuisance, but as he was acting out of spite the court held that it was a nuisance.

## Who can sue for nuisance?

Since nuisance is interference with the use or enjoyment of land only someone with a legal right in the land can sue. This means the owner or tenant of the land can sue but a member of their family cannot. This was shown in *Malone v Laskey* (1907).

### CASE EXAMPLE

#### *Malone v Laskey* (1907)

Vibration from machinery belonging to the defendants caused a lavatory cistern to come loose and fall onto the tenant's wife. She could not make a claim for nuisance since she did not have any legal right in the land; she was not the tenant. Of course, if a lease is in joint names then both tenants could claim.

## Who can be sued for nuisance?

The person who created the nuisance can be sued. The occupier of the land from which the nuisance comes can also be sued. This is so even if another person created the nuisance, provided the occupier knows about it or reasonably should have known of it. This was the reason why the defendants were liable in *Sedleigh-Denfield v O'Callaghan* (1940).

### CASE EXAMPLE

#### *Sedleigh-Denfield v O'Callaghan* (1940)

A trespasser had laid a pipe in a ditch in such a way that the grating became choked with leaves and the next-door field was flooded. The defendants knew about the pipe and should have realised the possibility of a flood. They were therefore liable in nuisance even though they had not created the nuisance in the first place.

A similar situation happened in *Lippiatt v South Gloucester Council* (1999), where there were travellers staying illegally on the council's land.

### CASE EXAMPLE

#### *Lippiatt v South Gloucester Council* (1999)

Travellers repeatedly caused problems to the neighbouring land, creating a nuisance. The council knew the travellers were there and also that they were creating a nuisance, so the council was liable for the nuisance.

| Private nuisance | Public nuisance |
| --- | --- |
| Affects an individual | Affects a section of the community |
| Case started by the individual affected | Case started by the Attorney-General or the individual affected |
| Can never be a crime | Can be both a crime and a tort |

Figure 19.3 Differences between private and public nuisance

## ACTIVITY

### Activity 3

Explain whether the following situations would amount to a nuisance in law.

1. Robin, who lives in a quiet residential street, frequently gives noisy parties. The parties usually start at about 10 pm and go on until 3 or 4 o'clock in the morning.

2. Elliot and Mary are next-door neighbours. Elliot complains that the roots from one of Mary's trees are growing under his driveway and causing damage to the driveway. Because Mary refuses to do anything about this, Elliott starts having a bonfire every time Mary hangs her washing in the garden. Smoke and ash from the bonfire blow across Mary's garden, badly marking her washing.

| Nuisance | Trespass to land |
| --- | --- |
| Indirect interference to land, for example noise, smells etc | Direct interference to land, for example walking on land |
| Must be repetitive | One act enough |
| Must prove damage | No need to prove damage – actionable *per se* (of itself) |
| Can be a crime if it affects enough people | Normally not a crime |
| For both private nuisance and trespass to land only a person with an interest in the land can sue | |

Figure 19.4 Comparison of nuisance and trespass to land

## BRIEF SUMMARY OF CHAPTER

**Trespass to the person**

- There are three types: assault, battery and false imprisonment
- Assault is putting a person in fear of unlawful force
- Battery is the application of unlawful force
- False imprisonment is depriving a person of liberty

**Trespass to goods**

- is direct or indirect interference with goods in the possession of another

**Trespass to land**

- is unlawful entry onto the land of another or remaining there after permission has been withdrawn
- The trespass can be to the surface of the land or underneath it or in the air immediately above it

**Nuisance**

- There are two types: private nuisance and public nuisance
- **Private nuisance** is something which unreasonably interferes with the claimant's use or enjoyment of his land
- **Public nuisance** is something which materially affects the reasonable comfort and convenience of life for a class of people
- A public nuisance is both a tort and a crime

# CHAPTER 20

# LAW OF TORT: GENERAL DEFENCES AND REMEDIES

## General defences

There are some defences which can be used for most torts. If a defendant successfully shows that he has one of these defences, then he or she will not be liable for the tort.

These defences are:

- statutory authority
- consent
- inevitable accident
- necessity
- act of God
- intervening act.

## Statutory authority

If an Act of Parliament grants the defendant the right to do something, then the same Act may protect him from being sued for any damage done while exercising that right.

An example is that the Police and Criminal Evidence Act 1984 gives the police the right to enter and search premises in certain situations. Provided the police keep to the rules under that Act, they will not be liable for trespass to land (the building they are entering) or for trespass to goods.

Another example is the Environment Act 1995 which gives the right to enter land where there is an environmental issue. This covers situations such as where pollution is coming from a factory and causing damage to local rivers and wildlife. A member of the Environment Agency has the power to enter to investigate the cause of the pollution.

## Consent

If the claimant consented to the behaviour or event, then the defendant is not liable in tort.

For example, if a person consents to be kissed then this is not battery under the tort of battery.

Similarly if the person in possession of land allows you to come onto the land, then you are not trespassing.

If a person consents to the risk of injury then he cannot claim for any injury done. An extreme example is the case of *Morris v Murray* (1990).

### CASE EXAMPLE

**_Morris v Murray_ (1990)**

The claimant knew that Murray had drunk about 17 whiskies, but he still agreed to go for a joy ride in Murray's plane. The plane crashed, killing Murray and badly injuring the claimant. The claimant tried to sue Murray's estate but the Court of Appeal held that he had consented to the obvious risk of injury as he knew the pilot was drunk and he could not claim for his injuries.

### Sporting activities

One of the most common areas of where consent is a defence is in sporting activities. By implication players agree to risks which are normal in their chosen sport. A boxer cannot sue his opponent for trespass to the person even if he is badly injured in the course of the contest.

However in *Watson v British Boxing Board of Control* (2001) a boxer claimed against the organisers when they did not provide adequate medical cover.

### CASE EXAMPLE

**Watson v British Boxing Board of Control (2001)**

The claimant suffered severe head injuries after a blow to the head during a boxing match. His claim in negligence against the organisers was successful as the organisers had failed to provide suitable medical cover at the ringside. If immediate medical help had been available the claimant's injuries would not have been so severe.

Players in team games such as football, rugby and hockey know that they are likely to be tackled during the course of the match. Provided the tackle is within the rules of the game, an injured player cannot sue. However, where the tackle goes beyond what is acceptable, a player can sue since he does not consent to illegal tackles as shown by the case of *Condon v Basi* (1985).

### CASE EXAMPLE

**Condon v Basi (1985)**

The claimant's leg was broken during an amateur football match when a player on the other side tackled him in a reckless and dangerous manner. He succeeded in his claim as the tackle was an illegal one.

## Inevitable accident

It is a defence that the damage was caused by an inevitable accident. This is a happening which could not have been avoided by any reasonable care or precautions. It is different from Act of God (see below) in that a person will have started the chain of events in motion. An example of inevitable accident occurred in *Stanley v Powell* (1891).

### CASE EXAMPLE

**Stanley v Powell (1891)**

The claimant was injured when the defendant fired a shot at a pheasant. The pellet hit a tree and glanced off almost at right angles, hitting the claimant. The defendant was not liable for the injury as he had not been negligent; the accident was inevitable.

## Necessity

Where a defendant can show that the damage he caused was done to prevent a worse evil happening, he will have a defence. If a defendant had broken a window of the claimant's house in order to rescue the claimant's children from a fire, the defendant would have a defence to a claim of trespass to land. This, of course, is an extreme example.

A case illustrating where the defence could be used is *Cope v Sharpe* (1912).

### CASE EXAMPLE

**Cope v Sharpe (1912)**

The defendant was able to use the defence of necessity when a fire broke out on the claimant's land and he destroyed heather on another part of the claimant's land to prevent the original fire from spreading onto his employer's land, where there were pheasants.

A case where the defence of necessity was not allowed is *Monsanto plc v Tilly* (1999).

## CASE EXAMPLE

*Monsanto plc v Tilly* (1999)

Protesters who were against the use of artificially created crops pulled up some genetically modified crops. The Court of Appeal held that they could not use the defence of necessity. They were liable for trespass to goods (the crops) and trespass to land.

## Act of God

An Act of God is an act of nature which no-one could have foreseen. In other words, it is a natural happening which caused the damage; it was not caused by man. Further it was so unusual that no reasonable person would have thought of it happening. The hurricane which affected parts of southern England in October 1987 would come into this definition. Flash floods and extraordinary rainfall would also be within the definition as shown by the case of *Nichols v Marsland* (1876).

## CASE EXAMPLE

*Nichols v Marsland* (1876)

A rainstorm 'greater and more violent than any within the memory of witnesses' caused an ornamental lake to overflow and cause damage to the claimant's land. The defendant was not liable for the damage since it was due to an Act of God.

## Intervening act

Where the defendant has started a chain of events, but a new act by someone else has caused the final damage, then this may give the defendant a defence. A good example is seen in the case of *Topp v London Country Bus (South West) Ltd* (1993).

## CASE EXAMPLE

*Topp v London Country Bus (South West) Ltd* (1993)

A minibus was left unattended with the keys in the ignition. The bus was stolen and the thief knocked down and killed the claimant's wife. The claimant tried to sue the bus company for the accident, claiming it was the negligence of the company's driver in leaving the bus unattended that led to the accident. This claim failed as the court held the accident was caused by the new act of the thief's negligent driving. It was a situation where there was an intervening act.

However not all intervening acts will provide a defence. This was shown by the old case of *Scott v Sheppard* (1773).

## CASE EXAMPLE

*Scott v Sheppard* (1773)

The defendant threw a lighted squib onto a stall. Two other people in turn picked up the squib and threw it away from themselves in alarm for their own safety. After the second person had thrown the squib it exploded and injured the claimant. The defendant was held liable for the injury to the claimant, since the onward throwing of the squib was reasonably foreseeable and was only done in self-protection.

## ACTIVITY

### Activity 1

Fill in the empty boxes in the following chart with the appropriate defence or explanation.

| Defence | Explanation |
|---|---|
| Inevitable accident | |
| | An Act of Parliament gives the defendant the right to do something, such as enter premises. |
| Act of God | |
| | The defendant caused the damage or trespassed in order to prevent a worse evil happening. |
| Consent | |
| | Although the defendant committed a tort, a new act by someone else caused the final damage. |

## Remedies

The main remedy that courts award in tort cases is damages. But there are other remedies, in particular an injunction may be ordered by the court.

### Damages

When the claimant has been injured or his or her property damaged then the court will award damages, that is a sum of money, in order to compensate the claimant.

If the injury is to property, then the amount of damages can be worked out exactly. If a car is damaged in a crash then the damages would be the amount it cost the claimant to have it repaired. If the car was a 'write-off', the amount would be the cost of buying a similar car to replace it.

Where the claimant was unable to use the car while it was being repaired, the claimant may also be able to claim the cost of hiring another car during that period, provided he needed to use a car and had no other means of transport.

If the injury is to a person then it is more difficult to work out how much the claimant should receive as compensation. The courts award damages for pain and suffering and damages for loss of earnings, including future earnings.

The amount for pain and suffering is decided by looking at cases where there have been similar injuries and trying to keep to a similar scale. Any amount for loss of earnings will depend on what the claimant would have been likely to earn if he had not been disabled in some way.

Where a person has died as a result of negligence, that person's dependants can also claim for future financial loss.

The court can also award damages for trespass even though there was no injury or physical damage to property. In this case the amount of the damages will not be very large.

### Injunctions

Injunctions are often used in cases of trespass and nuisance.

Where a trespass has occurred more than once and there is reason to think it might occur again in the future, then the court can grant an injunction ordering the defendant not to repeat or continue his behaviour.

An example is seen in the case of *Kelson v Imperial Tobacco Co Ltd* (1957).

## CASE EXAMPLE

### Kelson v Imperial Tobacco Co Ltd (1957)

The defendant's advertising signboard overhung the claimant's land. It was held that this was trespass to land and the court made an injunction ordering the defendant to remove the sign.

Where the defendant has frequently trespassed, for example by riding a horse across the land, the injunction would order him not to do it in the future.

Injunctions can be used to prevent a nuisance continuing; an example is the case of *Kennaway v Thompson* (1981).

## CASE EXAMPLE

### Kennaway v Thompson (1981)

Noise from motor-boat racing on a lake was found to be a nuisance. The claimant who lived by the lake was granted an injunction restricting the number of races that could be held.

However, because an injunction is a discretionary remedy, the court may decide not to grant one even though the claimant has proved that there is a nuisance. This occurred in *Miller v Jackson* (1977).

## CASE EXAMPLE

### Miller v Jackson (1977)

The claimant successfully proved that cricket balls which were frequently hit into his garden were a nuisance. He tried to get an injunction stopping the cricket club from playing on the village ground. The court refused to grant an injunction since the club had played there for 70 years and public enjoyment of the sport had to be balanced against the danger and inconvenience to the claimant. The claimant was awarded damages instead.

## ACTIVITY

### Activity 2

Look at the situations in Activity 3 on page 154 in Chapter 19 and suggest what remedies would be appropriate.

## BRIEF SUMMARY OF CHAPTER

**General defences**

- statutory authority – power under an Act of Parliament
- consent – claimant consented to the risk of injury or the trespass
- inevitable accident – a happening that could not have been prevented by any reasonable care
- necessity – the defendant acted to prevent a worse evil
- Act of God – an act of nature that is so extreme it cannot be foreseen
- intervening act – another person does a new act which causes the final injury

**Remedies**

- damages – an award of money to compensate
- injunctions – court orders to the defendant to do something or to stop doing something

# CHAPTER 21

# CRIMINAL LAW: INTRODUCTION

## Elements of a crime

In order for a person to be found guilty of a crime it is necessary for the prosecution, in the majority of crimes, to prove two elements – the *actus reus* and the *mens rea*. '*Actus reus*' means the guilty act: it is the physical element of an offence. '*Mens rea*' means the guilty mind or intention: it is the mental element of an offence.

There are some exceptions, called crimes of strict liability, where the *actus reus* alone is enough to make a person guilty without proving any element of intention (see the section on strict liability crimes below).

Figure 21.1 The elements of an offence

Each crime has its own *actus reus* and *mens rea* and they are different for the different crimes. The elements of *actus reus* and *mens rea* are easier to understand if we look at actual situations.

If Jane deliberately and meaning to be dishonest takes a purse, containing £40, from another woman's shopping bag and spends the money, she has committed theft. The *actus reus* of theft is appropriation of property belonging to another and in Jane's case it is the physical taking of the purse. Intending to be dishonest and to 'permanently deprive' the other woman

of the purse is the *mens rea*. In this example both elements of the crime of theft are present.

However if, on leaving a friend's house, you pick up a jacket thinking it is your own and leave with it you have not committed theft. This is because only the *actus reus*, in this example the act of picking up the jacket, is present. There is no *mens rea* because you had no intention to be dishonest.

It is also possible for the defendant to have the *mens rea* for a crime but not do the *actus reus*. This would be the position if the defendant, intending to kill, stabbed what he thought was a sleeping victim, when, unknown to him, the victim was already dead from a heart attack. The attacker has the *mens rea* for murder; he intended to kill. However, the attacker has not killed the victim; the attacker has not done the *actus reus*; he has attempted to murder and can be charged with this, but he is not guilty of the completed crime of murder.

Although each offence has its own *actus reus* and *mens rea*, there are some general rules which apply to all offences. These are explained in the next two sections.

## *Actus reus*

*Actus reus* is usually an act, as in the example above of theft, but the *actus reus* can sometimes be an omission. Failure to stop at a red traffic light and failure to wear a seat belt when driving are examples where the *actus reus* is not an act but an omission. Most crimes of omission are minor crimes created by statute, but serious crimes can be committed by a failure to do something. For example if a mother deliberately stops feeding her child, knowing that it is too young to feed itself and will die without food, that failure to feed the child can be the *actus reus* for a charge of murder or manslaughter.

## Consequences

Sometimes it is necessary for a consequence to happen as a result of the defendant's act in order for the *actus reus* to be complete.

An example is the crime of an assault occasioning actual bodily harm, contrary to section 47 of the Offences Against the Person Act 1861 (see Chapter 23). The defendant must have committed an assault, but for the *actus reus* to be complete that assault must have 'occasioned' actual bodily harm. In other words the consequence of the assault must be an injury.

Another example is murder where the consequence of the defendant's act or omission has to be the death of the victim.

## Chain of causation

Where the act has to cause a consequence for the accused to be guilty, it is necessary to show the link between the defendant's act and the consequence. In most cases there is no problem over this. In an assault occasioning actual bodily harm, the act may be a punch to the face of the victim and the injury a broken nose. In this example there is a clear link or chain of causation between the two.

Problems arise where there is an intervening act contributing to that consequence. This can occur:

- where the victim takes avoiding action
- where another person intervenes.

## The victim takes avoiding action

This could be by the victim jumping into a river to escape an attack and drowning. This occurred in the old case of *R v Pitts* (1842) and the defendant was held responsible for the death.

A similar case was *R v Lewis* (1970).

> **CASE EXAMPLE**
>
> ### R v Lewis (1970)
>
> In this case a wife broke her legs when she jumped from a third floor flat because she feared violence from her husband who was shouting threats and trying to break down the door to her room. The husband was convicted of causing grievous bodily harm to her.

But the defendant is not guilty if the action taken by the victim was unreasonable or too far removed from the original attack, as where for example three months after an assault the victim, suffering from depression as a result of the assault, commits suicide.

## Another person intervenes

If the defendant starts off a chain of events which ends with the forbidden consequence, can he be guilty if a third person has intervened and done something which contributes to that consequence?

This type of problem can occur in cases where there is poor medical treatment which contributes to the death. In such cases the courts are very reluctant to conclude that the intervening medical treatment broke the chain of causation. This happened in *R v Smith* (1959).

## CASE EXAMPLE

### *R v Smith* (1959)

A soldier was stabbed in a barrack-room brawl. His medical treatment was described by the Court of Appeal as 'thoroughly bad'. The wound had penetrated a lung and on the way to the medical centre he was dropped twice and then given artificial respiration which aggravated the wound. There was evidence that the poor medical treatment had affected his chance of recovery by as much as 75 per cent. The Court of Appeal held the defendant's stabbing was still the cause of death and he was guilty of murder.

Also in *R v Cheshire* (1991) there was a problem with the medical treatment but the original attacker was found to be the cause of the death.

## CASE EXAMPLE

### *R v Cheshire* (1991)

The victim was shot twice and his treatment included the insertion of a tube to help him breathe. This tube caused a rare complication that led to the victim's death. Even though there was evidence that the original wounds were no longer life threatening and it was the failure of medical staff to recognise and deal with the complication that had directly led to the death, the Court of Appeal held that the defendant was guilty of murder. It was his act of shooting that had caused the victim to need the treatment. When the medical staff put the tube in, they were only trying to repair the harm done.

The court said that it would only be in the most extraordinary or unusual case that such treatment could be said to be so independent of the acts of the accused that it could in law be regarded as the cause of the victim's death to the exclusion of the accused's acts.

## CASE EXAMPLE

### *R v Malcherek* (1981)

In this case it was decided that switching off a life support machine did not break the chain of causation. The original injury was still an 'operating and substantial cause of death'.

It is only in exceptional circumstances that medical treatment will be held to have caused the death, so that the defendant is not guilty. This happened in *R v Jordan* (1956).

## CASE EXAMPLE

### *R v Jordan* (1956)

The victim had been stabbed in the stomach. He was treated in hospital and the wounds were healing well. He was given an antibiotic but suffered an allergic reaction to it. One doctor stopped the use of the antibiotic but the next day another doctor ordered that a large dose of it be given. The victim died from the allergic reaction to the drug. In this case the actions of the doctor were held to be an intervening act which caused the death. The defendant was not guilty of murder.

## Victim refuses treatment

In *R v Blaue* (1975) the defendant was guilty of murder, even though the victim refused treatment which could have saved her life.

## CASE EXAMPLE

### *R v Blaue* (1975)

The victim was a Jehovah's Witness. She had been stabbed, but, because of her religion, refused a blood transfusion which would have saved her life. Blaue, her attacker was found guilty of her murder since the wound he had caused was an 'operating and substantial cause' of her death.

## Mens rea

Although the phrase *mens rea* means guilty mind it does not mean that the defendant has to know that what he is doing is against the law. It means that the defendant must have the level of intention required for the particular offence with which he is charged. The criminal law recognises that there are different levels of intention.

## Specific intention

For most serious crimes it is necessary to show that the defendant had what the law calls specific intention or intention. This concept of intention is difficult to define. In *R v Mohan* (1976) the judges in the Court of Appeal said that intention was: 'a decision to bring about, in so far as it lies within the accused's power, [a particular consequence], no matter whether the accused desires that consequence of his act or not'. This makes it clear that the defendant's motive or reason for doing the act is not important.

### Foresight of consequences

The main difficulties with proving specific intention occur in cases where the crime with which the person is charged was not the defendant's main aim. However, in achieving his main aim he realised or foresaw that he would also cause or commit the crime with which he is charged. This idea is referred to as 'foresight of consequences'.

An example of this situation is where a person decides to set fire to his factory so that he can claim the insurance. His main aim is the claiming of the insurance. Unfortunately, he chooses to start the fire when there are people working in the factory and some of them die because they are unable to escape the flames. Does that person have the specific intention to kill or cause serious harm to the victims of the fire?

To answer this we must look at the law on foresight of consequences.

The first rule about foresight of consequences is that it is not the same as intention, but it can be evidence of intention.

The second rule is that to decide if there is evidence of intention the jury must be sure that death or serious bodily harm was a virtual certainty as a result of the defendant's action. They must also be sure that the defendant appreciated that this was the case.

If the jury decided that it was virtually certain that people would be killed or seriously injured and that the defendant realised this, there is evidence on which the jury can find that the defendant had the specific intention for murder.

Let's apply these rules to the example of the person setting fire to his factory to claim insurance. Is it virtually certain that people will be killed or seriously injured? As the man started the fire when there were people working in the factory, it does seem to be virtually certain that someone will be seriously injured.

Did the man realise that someone was virtually certain to be killed or seriously injured? This is for the jury to decide. However, as the man was the owner of the factory and knew there were people in the factory when he started the fire, it is likely that most juries would decide that he realised that someone was virtually certain to be killed or seriously injured.

## Recklessness

For other crimes it is not necessary to prove such a high degree of intention. The law only requires proof of basic intention or what is called recklessness or basic intention. Of course, if the prosecution can prove specific intent the defendant will be guilty, but the prosecution do not have to go as far as that.

Recklessness involves taking a risk. This is when the defendant realises that there is a risk involved, but still carries on with his conduct.

It is perhaps easier to think of the different levels of intention as the steps of a ladder. At the bottom of the ladder is strict liability where no *mens rea* is needed. For the crimes where recklessness is enough to prove the defendant guilty, the lowest rung on the ladder will do. Of course, the defendant is also guilty if the prosecution can prove specific intention, but there is no need to do this. For crimes of specific intention only the top rung will do. The different types of *mens rea* are illustrated in this way in Figure 21.2.

**Specific intention –** This level must be proved for most serious crimes including murder, theft, burglary, robbery

**Recklessness –** Deliberate risk taking. This level must be proved for assault, battery, s 47 assault and s 20 assault (see Chapter 23)

**Strict liability –** no need to prove any *mens rea*

Figure 21.2 The different types of *mens rea*

## Strict liability crimes

Strict liability crimes are those where the defendant will be guilty because he did the *actus reus*. There is no need to prove *mens rea*. An extreme example is *Winzar v Chief Constable for Kent* (1983).

### CASE EXAMPLE

*Winzar v Chief Constable for Kent* (1983)

The police were called to remove a drunken man from the casualty department of a hospital. The police took him to their car on the road outside and then charged him with being 'found' drunk on a highway. The court held that the offence did not require any *mens rea* and so the defendant was guilty. He had been drunk on a highway.

Another example is *Strowger v John* (1978).

### CASE EXAMPLE

*Strowger v John* (1978)

A car tax disc fell from the window onto the floor of the car after the owner had parked the car. The owner was guilty of the offence of failing to display a car tax disc. It was not necessary to show that he had deliberately left the tax disc off; he was guilty simply because it was not in the window.

## Justification for strict liability

One of the main reasons for having strict liability offences is that it helps to protect the public from harm. Many strict liability offences are aimed at preventing potential danger to public health and safety.

Examples include such matters as causing pollution, driving a vehicle with dangerous brakes, or selling contaminated food. All these are strict liability offences. Offenders do not have to intend to do any of these to be guilty; the act of doing them is enough. It is hoped that because such behaviour is a crime there is pressure on people to take extra care. Companies will be more careful not to cause pollution; drivers more careful in maintaining and checking their vehicles; and shops more careful about food handling and keeping to sell-by dates.

Another reason for having strict liability offences is that it would be too time consuming for the prosecutor to have to prove *mens rea* in every case. The case of *Strowger v John* (1978) – the tax disc case – comes into this category. It would be almost impossible to prove *mens rea* in many of the cases and the law would then not be enforced.

## Problems of strict liability offences

The defendant may be found guilty even though he took all possible care not to commit the offence. This happened in *Harrow London Borough Council v Shah and Shah* (1999).

### CASE EXAMPLE

#### *Harrow LBC v Shah and Shah* (1999)

The defendants owned a newsagents' business where lottery tickets were sold. They had told their staff not to sell tickets to anyone under 16 years old. They frequently reminded their staff that if there was any doubt about a customer's age, the staff should ask for proof of age, and if still in doubt should refer the matter to the defendants.

One of their staff sold a lottery ticket to a 13-year-old boy, without asking for proof of age. The salesman mistakenly believed the boy was over 16 years old. D1 was in a back room of the premises at the time: D2 was not on the premises. The defendants were charged with selling a lottery ticket to a person under 16. It was held that the offence was one of strict liability and so they were guilty, even though they had done their best to prevent this happening in their shop.

Another argument against strict liability is that a defendant may be at risk of a prison sentence even though he took all possible care.

Normally offences which can be punished by imprisonment are not strict liability offences, since it seems unfair to put people at the risk of going to prison when they had no intention of committing a crime. However, some crimes which do carry a possible penalty of imprisonment are strict liability offences. An example is *Pharmaceutical Society of Great Britain v Storkwain* (1986).

### CASE EXAMPLE

#### *Pharmaceutical Society of Great Britain v Storkwain* (1986)

A forged prescription had been handed in to a chemists. The pharmacist dispensed the drugs because he had no reason to suspect that the prescription was a forgery. In fact it was a forgery. He was therefore found guilty of supplying drugs without a prescription. This offence has a maximum penalty of three months' imprisonment. The fact that the pharmacist had made a genuine mistake about the prescription did not stop him from being guilty. The pharmacist was not sent to prison, but the fact remains that any pharmacist in this position could be at risk of going to prison.

### ACTIVITY

#### Activity 1

Fill in the gaps with the appropriate word or phrase from the list in the box below.

The *actus reus* of an offence is the .............................. element. The *mens rea* of an offence is the ............................... element.

The *actus reus* is usually an ................. , but it can be an ..................... or failure to act in some offences.

Where the *actus reus* requires a consequence, it is necessary to show the link between what the defendant did and the consequence. This is known as the chain of ........................... .

There are two main types of *mens rea*. These are ............................... and

............................... .

Strict ......................... offences are those where the prosecution only needs to prove that the defendant did the

............................... of the offence. It is not necessary to prove ............................... .

| | |
|---|---|
| act | *actus reus* |
| causation | events |
| guilty | physical |
| reason | liability |
| limits | *mens rea* |
| mental | omission |
| recklessness | specific intention |

## BRIEF SUMMARY OF CHAPTER

**There are two elements of a crime:**
- *actus reus* (the physical element) and
- *mens rea* (the mental element)

### Actus reus
- This can be an act or an omission; for some crimes a consequence may also be needed and there must be no break in the chain of causation

### Mens rea
- Different levels of *mens rea* are required for different crimes: the main levels are specific intention and recklessness

### Strict liability
- This is where it is not necessary to prove any *mens rea* for the offence. Such offences are usually regulatory, aimed at protecting public health and safety

# CHAPTER 22

# CRIMINAL LAW: FATAL OFFENCES

There are two main fatal offences. These are:

- murder
- manslaughter.

Both murder and manslaughter involve the killing of a human being. The most serious crime is murder and the difference between it and manslaughter is in the intention of the defendant.

## Murder

Murder is a common law crime. This means it is not defined by any Act of Parliament. It comes from the decisions of judges in cases dealing with murder. The definition at common law dates back to the seventeenth century. Murder is defined as:

> **❝ … where a person of sound mind unlawfully kills any reasonable creature in being and under the Queen's peace with malice aforethought, either express or implied. ❞**

The *actus reus* is the unlawful killing of a person. The *mens rea* of murder is 'malice aforethought, either express or implied'. It is this that distinguishes murder from manslaughter.

### *Actus reus* of murder

The important elements of the *actus reus* in both murder and manslaughter are as follows.

### The killing must be unlawful

This means there must not be any legal justification or excuse, such as killing in self-defence.

### Causation must be established

It must be established that the defendant's act caused the death. The killing can be by any means, shooting, stabbing, poisoning etc, but it must cause the death. Also there must not be a break in the chain of causation. The general rules on causation as set out in Chapter 21 apply.

### The victim must be a human being when attacked

This means that he or she must have been born; killing a foetus is not murder, though it may be another crime. However, injuring a child in the womb so that after it is born it dies of those injuries could be murder or manslaughter.

### The victim must die

The rule used to be that the victim had to die within a year and a day of the attack. If the death occurred after this period the attacker could not be charged with murder or manslaughter.

However, there were considerable criticisms of this rule as the developments in medical science, especially life support machines, meant that victims could be kept alive for longer than a year before eventually dying from their injuries. Parliament abolished this rule by passing the Law Reform (Year and a Day Rule) Act 1996. If the death occurs more than three years after the attack, then the Attorney-General must give consent for the proceedings.

## Under the Queen's peace

The killing of an enemy during the conduct of war is not considered as constituting the *actus reus* for murder.

# *Mens rea* of murder

*Malice aforethought* means that murder is a specific intent crime. *Express or implied* means that either of two intentions is sufficient:

• *express malice* is the intention to kill;
• *implied malice* is the intention to do grievous bodily harm.

It was decided in *R v Vickers* (1957) that the intention to cause grievous bodily harm is sufficient to make a defendant guilty of murder if his victim dies.

---

**CASE EXAMPLE**

### *R v Vickers* (1957)

Vickers in the course of stealing from a shop was found by an old lady. He struck her a number of blows which killed her. He did not use a weapon and there was no suggestion that he intended to kill her. The Court of Criminal Appeal held that there were two types of malice aforethought and either was sufficient to make the defendant guilty.

---

This decision was confirmed by the House of Lords in *R v Cunningham* (1982).

---

**CASE EXAMPLE**

### *R v Cunningham* (1982)

Cunningham attacked his victim in a public house in Margate, repeatedly hitting him with a chair, wrongly believing him to be associating with his, Cunningham's, girlfriend. The victim died as a result of his injuries. Lord Hailsham said '*R v Vickers* was a correct statement of the law'.

---

## Foresight of consequences

Foresight of consequence as evidence of the specific intention for murder has been considered in several cases. The most important cases are *R v Moloney* (1985) and *R v Hancock and Shankland* (1986) and *R v Woollin* (1998).

---

**CASE EXAMPLE**

### *R v Moloney* (1985)

A father and his stepson, who had both had a lot to drink, were having a friendly argument about the stepson's wish to leave the army. The father said the son was no good with guns and challenged him to see which one of them could load a gun the faster. The stepson won easily and his father then said that the boy would not have 'the guts' to pull the trigger. The stepson pulled the trigger and the shot killed the father. The stepson said he had not intended to kill his father. He just pulled the trigger without thinking of the consequences. His conviction for murder was quashed by the House of Lords and replaced with a conviction for manslaughter.

---

In *Moloney* the House of Lords held that foresight of consequences was not the same as intention but only evidence from which intention might be proved.

Another important case where the defendant claimed he did not realise that his actions could cause death or serious injury was *R v Woollin* (1998).

---

**CASE EXAMPLE**

### *R v Woollin* (1998)

The defendant threw his three-month-old son some four or five feet towards his pram. The child hit his head and suffered a fractured skull from which he died. At the trial the prosecution accepted that it had not been the defendant's aim or purpose to kill or seriously

▶

injure his son. It was a case where foresight of consequences had to be considered. However, the jury convicted Woollin of murder after the trial judge told them that the defendant could be guilty if he had seen a substantial risk that the child would be killed or seriously injured.

The House of Lords quashed the conviction for murder and substituted a conviction for manslaughter as the judge was wrong to use the test of a substantial risk.

The Law Lords said that the jury in *Woollin* should have been told that they were not entitled to find the necessary intention for murder unless they were sure that death or serious injury was a virtual certainty as a result of the defendant's action. The jury also had to be sure that the defendant appreciated that death or serious injury was a virtual certainty. Only if the jury were sure about both these points were they entitled to find that the defendant had the specific intention for murder.

So the tests for deciding if there is evidence of intention in foresight of consequences situations are:

• was death or serious injury a virtual certainty as a result of the defendant's acts?
• did the defendant appreciate that death or serious injury was a virtual certainty?

If the answer to these two questions is 'yes', then there is evidence on which the jury are entitled to find that the defendant had the necessary intention for murder.

## Special defences to murder

There are two special defences which are available only on a charge of murder and which have the effect of reducing the charge of murder to one of manslaughter. These are:

• diminished responsibility
• provocation.

Where the defendant has committed the *actus reus* for murder, that is unlawfully killed, and has the *mens rea*, that is the specific intention to kill or cause grievous bodily harm, the law allows these defences to reduce the charge to manslaughter.

This is important since a judge must send anyone found guilty of murder to prison for life; the judge has no discretion. For manslaughter, on the other hand, while the maximum penalty is life imprisonment, the judge can impose a lesser sentence if he thinks it suitable in the case. This means that it is possible for a defendant found guilty of manslaughter to be imprisoned for a shorter term or, in some cases, not to be sent to prison at all but instead put on probation or given any sentence the judge thinks suitable. In these cases the manslaughter is referred to as voluntary manslaughter.

## Diminished responsibility

The defence of diminished responsibility is set out in section 2 of the Homicide Act 1957. This section says:

**66** Where a person kills or is party to the killing of another, he shall not be convicted of murder if he was suffering from such abnormality of mind (whether arising from a condition of arrested or retarded development of mind or any inherent causes or induced by disease or injury) as substantially impaired his mental responsibility for his acts and omissions in doing or being a party to the killing. **99**

The important factors are:

• the defendant is suffering from an abnormality of mind;

- that abnormality must be caused by arrested or retarded development of mind or an inherent cause or disease or injury; and
- the abnormality of mind must substantially impair the defendant's mental responsibility for the killing.

## Abnormality of mind

The defendant must be suffering from an abnormality of mind. In *R v Byrne* (1960), where a sexual psychopath had killed a young woman, the Court of Appeal said that the phrase 'abnormality of mind' meant a 'state of mind so different from that of ordinary human beings that the reasonable man would term it abnormal'. In other words it is up to the jury to take a commonsense approach when deciding whether the defendant was suffering from an abnormality of mind.

## Cause of abnormality of mind

The abnormality must be caused by arrested or retarded development or an internal cause or disease or injury. This covers a very wide range of problems, including mental illnesses such as depression and physical illnesses that affect the mind such as brain tumours. However, external causes such as taking drugs or alcohol are not included unless there is a disease or injury to the brain. This was the situation in *R v Tandy* (1988).

---

### CASE EXAMPLE

**R v Tandy (1988)**

The defendant, who suffered from alcoholism, had killed her 11-year-old daughter. It was decided that if the alcoholism had reached a level at which the defendant's brain had been injured, the defendant could plead diminished responsibility.

---

## Substantially impair responsibility

The abnormality must 'substantially' affect the accused's mental responsibility for his acts or omissions. It has been held that 'substantially' means more than some trivial degree of impairment, but less than total impairment. It has also been said that a jury should approach the word in a commonsense way.

The defence of diminished responsibility is used successfully in about 70 to 80 cases each year.

Where the defence of diminished responsibility is successful the defendant is found guilty of manslaughter, not murder.

## Provocation

The defence of provocation is set out in section 3 of the Homicide Act 1957 which says:

> **66** Where on a charge of murder there is evidence on which a jury can find that the person charged was provoked (whether by things done or things said or by both together) to lose his self-control, the question whether the provocation was enough to make a reasonable man do as he did shall be left to be determined by the jury; and in determining that question the jury shall take into account everything both done and said according to the effect which, in their opinion, it would have on a reasonable man. **99**

The section does not define what type of behaviour can be considered as provocation apart from saying that it can be 'things done or said or both together' and that it must be enough to provoke a 'reasonable man'.

Provocation covers many different situations, including:

- physical assaults, both on the defendant or on his relatives
- the continual crying of a young baby

- supplying drugs to the defendant's son
- racist remarks.

It can be a single incident or a series of things; it need not be by the victim, nor need it be deliberately aimed at the accused.

## Loss of self-control

The most important point is that the provocation must cause a sudden and temporary loss of self-control. If there is evidence that the accused did not lose his temper but used the situation to carry out a deliberate killing, then the accused cannot use the defence of provocation.

### CASE EXAMPLE

#### R v Thornton (1995)

The defendant was a 'battered wife' who killed her husband. The evidence was that after threatening her, he had fallen asleep on the settee. She had then gone into the kitchen, got a knife, returned to the room where her husband was sleeping and stabbed him. She was convicted because of the time lapse between the husband's threats and her killing him.

However, at a second appeal, the Court of Appeal ordered a re-trial because the jury in the original case had not been allowed to consider the effect of 'battered woman syndrome' on her reaction to the final incident. At the second trial she was acquitted.

## Degree of self-control

Even if the jury are sure that the defendant did suffer a sudden loss of self-control, this may not be enough to prove the defence of provocation. The law expects people to exercise control over their emotions.

The jury must think that the circumstances were such that they made the loss of self-control

sufficiently excusable to reduce the gravity of the offence from murder to manslaughter. The jury decides what degree of self-control should have been expected from the defendant.

They can take into account any relevant matters such as the age and sex of the defendant as in *DPP v Camplin* (1978).

### CASE EXAMPLE

#### DPP v Camplin (1978)

The accused was a 15-year-old boy who had been sexually assaulted by an older man. When the man laughed at him the boy had hit him over the head with a heavy cooking pan and killed him. At his trial the judge had told the jury to consider how a reasonable adult would have reacted in the same circumstances, but the House of Lords held that this was the wrong test to use. The jury should have considered whether an ordinary 15-year-old boy would have been provoked and acted as the defendant did.

There was a lot of debate about whether any other characteristics of the defendant should be considered when deciding what level of self-control should be expected. The matter was finally settled in the case of *Attorney-General for Jersey v Holley* (2005).

### CASE EXAMPLE

#### Attorney-General for Jersey v Holley (2005)

The defendant was an alcoholic who had been drinking heavily. He claimed that his long-standing girlfriend told him she had had sex with another man and taunted him. He struck and killed her with an axe he was using to chop wood. He was convicted of murder and his conviction was upheld by the Privy Council by a majority of six judges to three. They held that when considering the level of

> self-control to be expected, the defendant
> should be judged as an ordinary person.

So, when identifying and applying the objective standard of self-control, the only special features of the defendant that can be considered are age and sex. Other characteristics of the defendant are not relevant. The defendant is to be judged by the standard of a person having ordinary powers of self-control. This has the merits of being a constant, objective standard in all cases.

## Seriousness of the provocation to the defendant

The judges in *Holley* pointed out that special characteristics of the defendant can be taken into account in assessing the gravity of the provocation to the defendant. For this purpose the jury must 'take the defendant as they find him' and consider any special features of his or hers that could make the provocation more serious to him or her than to another person.

Let's look at some examples. A defendant who has a scar on his face would find comments about his appearance more provoking than someone without a scar. Similarly, a person with a limp would be very upset at comments about that. The provocation would be more serious because of the defendants' disability.

The characteristic or special feature of the defendant does not have to be a permanent one. This is shown by the case of *Morhall* (1995).

### CASE EXAMPLE

#### Morhall (1995)

The defendant was a glue-sniffer. This was a relevant characteristic to be taken into account in deciding the gravity of the provocation to him. Morhall had been persistently criticised by the victim about this immediately before the killing.

Where the defence of provocation is successful the defendant is found guilty of manslaughter, not murder.

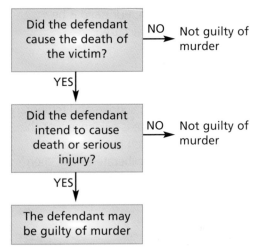

Now consider whether the defendant has a special defence to murder.

Figure 22.1 Flow chart for murder and the special defences

## Problems in the law of murder

There are several problems in the law of murder. A very important one is to do with the *mens rea* for murder. A defendant can be convicted of murder even though he did not intend to kill. He is guilty if he intended to cause serious harm.

There have been proposals that murder should be divided into different categories, so that someone who did not intend to kill is guilty of a lower level of murder.

Another problem is the mandatory life sentence. This means that a life sentence has to be given for every case of murder. Yet the level of blameworthiness may be very different. Should an elderly man who has killed his wife because she was in severe pain with no hope of recovery be given the same sentence as a man who has deliberately shot someone during a robbery?

This point is only partly covered by the fact that judges can state the minimum sentence a defendant should serve before being considered for parole. There are limits on what judges can recommend. The normal minimum recommendation is 15 years. Even this seems much longer than necessary for the example above of an elderly man killing his wife.

There are other problems in the law on provocation. The main ones are:

- It allows a defence for anger. Should a defendant be able to have his crime reduced from murder to manslaughter just because he lost his temper?
- Also, as it is necessary to prove that the defendant suffered a 'sudden loss' of self-control, it is often described as a male defence. Women are more likely to react slowly over a period of time.
- There is no limit to the conduct which is capable of 'provoking', so that completely innocent conduct may be regarded as provocation. An extreme example of this was seen in *R v Doughty* (1986) when the crying of a very young baby was held to be provocation.

The Government has suggested abolishing the defence of provocation. However, while there is still a mandatory life sentence for murder, it is more just to keep the defence, as it allows the judge discretion when sentencing the defendant.

## Involuntary manslaughter

Involuntary manslaughter is an unlawful killing where the accused did not have the specific intention for murder.

There are two possible ways in which a person may be guilty of involuntary manslaughter:

- by an act which is unlawful and dangerous
- by gross negligence.

## Unlawful act manslaughter

The elements of unlawful act manslaughter are:

- the defendant must do an unlawful act
- that act must be dangerous on an objective test
- the act must cause the death
- the defendant must have the required *mens rea* for the unlawful act.

### Unlawful act

The unlawful act can be any crime. Often, it is an assault of some kind. This is shown by the case of *R v Mitchell* (1983).

### CASE EXAMPLE

#### *R v Mitchell* (1983)

The defendant tried to push into a queue. A man in the queue objected and Mitchell punched him. This caused the man to fall against an 89-year-old woman. The woman's leg was broken as a result and she died from complications caused by the breaking of her leg. Mitchell was found guilty of manslaughter. The unlawful act was the punch to the man in the queue. The fact that the unlawful act was aimed at one person but killed another did not matter; Mitchell was still guilty.

The defendant can commit other types of offence and these will still be regarded as the unlawful act for the purposes of unlawful act manslaughter. An act of criminal damage was the unlawful act in *DPP v Newbury and Jones* (1976).

---

**CASE EXAMPLE**

### *DPP v Newbury and Jones* (1976)

Two 15-year-old boys pushed a paving stone from a bridge on to a railway line below as a train was passing. The stone killed a guard on the train. The unlawful act in this case was criminal damage.

---

## Dangerous act

The unlawful act must be dangerous on an objective test. This means that if a sober and reasonable person would realise that the unlawful act would put another person at the risk of some harm, then it is considered dangerous. The risk need only be of 'some harm'. The harm need not be serious.

In *R v Mitchell* a sober and reasonable person would realise that punching someone puts them at risk of 'some harm', even if it is only a bruise. In *DPP v Newbury and Jones* a sober and reasonable person would realise that pushing a paving stone so that it landed on a train would put people on the train at risk of being injured.

## Causing the death

The unlawful act must cause the death. It must be the factual cause of the death. In *R v Mitchell* the punch caused the man who was hit to fall against the woman, breaking her leg and causing her death.

## *Mens rea*

It must be proved that the defendant had the *mens rea* for the unlawful act, but it is not necessary for the defendant to realise that the

act is unlawful or dangerous. In *DPP v Newbury and Jones* (1976) the House of Lords held that it was not necessary to prove that the defendants foresaw any harm from their act. It was only necessary to prove that the defendants had the *mens rea* for the criminal damage.

# Gross negligence manslaughter

Where a person owes a duty of care then if he or she performs that duty so negligently that someone dies, he may be guilty of manslaughter.

The degree of negligence needed to make a person guilty has been described as negligence which *'went beyond a mere matter of compensation between subjects and showed such a disregard for life and safety of others as to amount to a crime against the state and conduct deserving of punishment'*.

The leading case on gross negligence manslaughter is *R v Adomako* (1994).

---

**CASE EXAMPLE**

### *R v Adomako* (1994)

The defendant was an anaesthetist who failed to notice that a tube giving the patient oxygen had become disconnected. As a result the patient died and Adomako was convicted of manslaughter. The House of Lords said that gross negligence in manslaughter cases was something for the jury to decide. The essential point was 'whether, having regard to the risk of death involved, the conduct of the defendant was so bad in all the circumstances as to amount in their judgment to a criminal act or omission'. If this was so then the defendant was guilty of manslaughter by gross negligence.

---

## Duty of care

In *R v Adomako* it was clear that a doctor owes a duty of care to his patient. However, for the purpose of gross negligence manslaughter, the courts have decided that a duty of care exists in very different situations. These include:

- a duty to manage and maintain property where a faulty gas-fire caused the deaths of tenants
- that the owner and master of a sailing ship owed a duty to the crew when he sailed knowing that the engines might fail because of contamination to the fuel. The ship was blown on to rocks and three crew members died.

A duty of care was also held to exist in the case of *R v Wacker* (2002).

## CASE EXAMPLE

### *R v Wacker* (2002)

The defendant was a lorry driver who agreed to bring 60 illegal immigrants into England. They were put in the back of his lorry for a cross-channel ferry crossing. The only air into the lorry was through a small vent and it was agreed that this vent should be closed at certain times to prevent the immigrants being discovered. The defendant closed the vent before boarding the ferry. The crossing took an hour longer than usual and at Dover the Customs officers found 58 of the 60 immigrants were dead.

## ACTIVITY

### Activity 1

Read the following newspaper article about a conviction for manslaughter and answer the questions below.

**Father admits manslaughter of girl, 7, in quad bike crash**

The father of a seven-year-old girl who was killed in a quad bike crash on Boxing Day was given a suspended sentence yesterday after admitting her manslaughter.

Gary Cooke, 46, pleaded guilty at Chelmsford Crown Court to causing the death of his daughter Elizabeth, who was hit by a Range Rover while riding the £1,200 petrol-engined Pro-Shark machine that he had given her for Christmas.

Elizabeth and her ten-year-old brother, Jack, were riding their bikes behind their father's car down an unlit country lane near their home when she was hit by an oncoming car.

It is illegal for anyone under 16 to ride a quad bike on a public road. Mr Harvey for the prosecution told the court that 'This tragic incident was a direct result of the defendant's gross negligence'.

*(Source: an article by Fran Yeoman, The Times, 21 October 2008)*

### Questions

1. What type of manslaughter was involved in this case?
2. Explain why the defendant was charged with this type of manslaughter.
3. Do you agree that the defendant should have been prosecuted? Explain your reasons for your answer.
4. What sentence did the defendant receive?
5. Do you think the sentence was an appropriate one? Give reasons for your answer.

## ACTIVITY

### Activity 2

In each of the following situations explain, giving reasons for your answer, whether the person involved is guilty of murder or manslaughter.

1. George, while driving at 60 mph through an area with a 30 mph speed limit, loses control of his car, mounts the pavement and knocks down and kills a pedestrian.

2. Patricia, who has a bad scar on her face, is teased by Andrew. Andrew keeps on calling her 'ugly mug'. In a temper Patricia seizes a knife and stabs Andrew, killing him.

3. Franklin, who is mentally retarded, hits Steven on the head with a hammer. Steven is taken to hospital and put on a life support machine. Three days later the doctors decide to switch off the life support machine and Steven dies.

## Problems in the law of manslaughter

A main problem with the law of manslaughter is that it covers a very wide range of conduct. It includes two very different types of conduct. These are a death caused through an unlawful act and a death caused through negligence in doing a lawful act.

Should a doctor who is doing his best to treat a patient, but does this in a grossly negligent way be liable for the same crime as a person who deliberately does an unlawful act?

Another problem is that death may be an unexpected result. If the same act had resulted in minor injury, the defendant would only be liable for the offence of assault occasioning actual bodily harm. Is it fair that a defendant where a relatively minor act results in death should be found guilty of the very serious crime of manslaughter?

It also seems unjust that a defendant who did not realise there was risk of any injury will still be guilty because of the objective nature of the test. In unlawful act manslaughter, the act is

considered dangerous if a sober and reasonable person would realise that the unlawful act would put another person at the risk of some harm. The fact that the defendant did not realise this is completely ignored.

### BRIEF SUMMARY OF CHAPTER

**Murder**

■ the unlawful killing of a person with 'malice aforethought', ie the intention to kill or cause grievous bodily harm

**Special defences to murder**

■ diminished responsibility – where the defendant is suffering from an abnormality of mind which substantially impaired his or her responsibility for the killing

■ provocation – where the defendant suffers a sudden loss of control due to provocation

**Manslaughter**

■ This can be **unlawful act manslaughter** where D does an unlawful act which is likely to cause some injury and it actually causes death

■ or it may be **gross negligence manslaughter** where D owes V a duty of care, breaches that duty so badly that it can be considered criminal and the breach causes death

# CHAPTER 23

# CRIMINAL LAW: NON-FATAL OFFENCES

There are many different types of non-fatal offences against the person. They include any assault, whether or not it causes an injury, sexual offences and even bigamy. There are too many to include them all in this book, so we shall concentrate on four main offences which involve assault. The word 'assault' has two meanings in law: the first is the general term for physical attacks on another person; the second is a very specific meaning which we consider in the first of the offences below.

## Common assault

This offence is not defined in any statute but is charged under section 39 of the Criminal Justice Act 1988. This section says that it is a summary offence and a person guilty of it shall be liable to be fined up to £5,000 or to be imprisoned for a term not exceeding six months, or to both.

There are two ways of committing the offence:

• assault
• battery.

## Assault

Assault is any act which intentionally or recklessly causes another to fear immediate and unlawful violence.

There is no need for contact, the *actus reus* is committed when the defendant does any act which causes the other person to believe that unlawful force is about to be used against him or her. Examples include:

• threatening with a fist or a cane or any weapon

• throwing a stone or other missile
• pointing a loaded gun at someone within range.

There is no assault if it is obvious to the victim that the defendant cannot carry out his threat of violence, for example where the defendant is in a passing train. However, if violence is possible then the fact that the defendant is on the other side of a window or door does not prevent his actions being an assault.

This was shown in *Smith v Chief Superintendent, Woking Police Station* (1983).

### CASE EXAMPLE

***Smith v Chief Superintendent, Woking Police Station* (1983)**

The defendant entered a private garden at night and looked through the bedroom window of the complainant. She was terrified and the Divisional Court upheld a conviction under section 4 of the Vagrancy Act 1824 which required proof that the defendant's purpose was to assault the victim.

## Words as an assault

It used to be thought that words on their own without any action were not enough to be an assault. However, in *R v Ireland* (1997) the House of Lords pointed out that a man saying to a woman in a dark alley 'Come with me or I will stab you' would cause her to fear immediate personal violence. So words can be an assault.

## CASE EXAMPLE

### R v Ireland (1997)

The defendant made several silent telephone calls to three women. He was found guilty of assault causing actual bodily harm even though he did not say anything. Making a silent call was intended to cause fear and the victim may fear that the caller is likely to come to her home immediately after the phone call. This means that the victim may fear the possibility of immediate personal violence and so it is an assault.

## Mens rea of assault

The mens rea for an assault is either an intention to cause another to fear immediate unlawful personal violence or recklessness as to whether such fear is caused.

If the prosecution are relying on recklessness, the test for recklessness is subjective. This means that the defendant must have realised there was a risk that his acts/words could cause another to fear unlawful personal violence.

## Battery

Battery is the application, intentionally or recklessly, of unlawful force to another person.

Force is a slightly misleading word as it can include the slightest touching, as shown by the case of Collins v Wilcock (1984).

## CASE EXAMPLE

### Collins v Wilcock (1984)

Two police officers saw two women apparently soliciting for the purposes of prostitution. They asked the appellant to get into the police car for questioning but she refused and walked away. As she was not known to the police, one of the officers walked after her to try to find out her identity. She refused to speak to the officer and again walked away. The officer then took hold of her by the arm to prevent her leaving. She became abusive and scratched the officer's arm. She was convicted of assaulting a police officer in the execution of his duty. She appealed against that conviction on the basis that the officer was not acting in the execution of his duty, but was acting unlawfully by holding her arm as the officer was not arresting her. The court held that the officer had committed a battery and the defendant was entitled to free herself.

Other examples of battery include:

• punching, slapping, kicking, pushing
• hitting someone with a stick
• hitting someone with a stone or other missile
• an indirect action, such as a booby trap which hits the victim.

For an offence to constitute a battery, the victim need not be aware that he is about to be struck. Many incidents include an assault and a battery. For example, the victim sees a knife drawn (assault) and is then stabbed (battery). But if the victim is hit from behind, so that the first he knows about it is when the blow lands, there is only a battery.

## Mens rea

The mens rea for battery is either an intention to apply unlawful physical force to another or recklessness as to whether unlawful force is applied.

As with assault the test for recklessness is subjective – what did the defendant realise? The prosecution must prove that the defendant realised there was a risk that his act (or omission) could cause unlawful force to be applied to another.

## Overlap of *actus reus* and *mens rea*

The *actus reus* and the *mens rea* must exist at the same time for the crime to be complete. This is shown by the case of *Fagan v Metropolitan Police Commissioner* (1969).

### CASE EXAMPLE

**Fagan v Metropolitan Police Commissioner (1969)**

The defendant drove his car onto a policeman's foot without realising it, but he then refused to move the car when the police officer told him the car was on his foot. It was held that there was sufficient overlap to make the completed crime. The judge pointed out:

**66** There was an act constituting a battery which at its inception was not criminal because there was no element of intention but which became criminal from the moment the intention was formed. **99**

### ACTIVITY

#### Activity 1

Explain whether there is an assault and/or battery in the following situations.

1.  Josh has always liked Kelly, but knows she has a boyfriend, Louis. At a party, a friend dares Josh to kiss Kelly. Josh immediately goes over to Kelly and kisses her.

    Louis sees what has happened and goes to Josh and says, 'If you ever do that again, I'll smash your face in'.

2.  Maninder turns round quickly without realising that Niel is standing behind him. Maninder bumps into Niel.

3.  Padma is angry that Roxanne has been using her make-up. Padma shouts at Roxanne, telling her never to do it again. Roxanne, who was combing her hair, waves the comb in front of Padma's face telling her to shut up.

## Assault occasioning actual bodily harm (abh)

Assault occasioning actual bodily harm is charged under section 47 of the Offences Against the Person Act 1861 and it must be an assault or battery which causes actual bodily harm.

### *Actus reus* of abh

The *actus reus* is that of assault or battery. This means that the prosecution can prove either an act which intentionally or recklessly caused another to fear immediate and unlawful violence (assault) OR the application, intentionally or recklessly, of unlawful force to another person (battery).

In addition there must be the consequence of actual bodily harm.

## Actual bodily harm

Actual bodily harm means any injury no matter how slight. A scratch or a bruise is enough. However, the Crown Prosecution Service standards suggest that if the injury is very trivial, then a charge of battery should be used.

The courts have accepted that a brief loss of consciousness is sufficient for actual bodily harm. It also includes psychiatric illness caused by the defendant's action.

## *Mens rea* of abh

The *mens rea* is the same as for an assault or battery. The defendant is guilty even if he or she did not intend to cause an injury as the *mens rea* does not include any intention to cause actual bodily harm or recklessness as to whether such harm is caused. *R v Savage* (1991) makes it quite clear that the mental element is the same as for a common assault. There is no further mental state which has to be established. The offence is proved by establishing an assault and showing that it did cause actual bodily harm.

### CASE EXAMPLE

#### *R v Savage* (1991)

The defendant, on seeing her husband's girlfriend in a pub, had deliberately thrown her drink over her. Savage said she did not mean to cause any injury, but in the course of the incident the glass had broken and caused a cut on the girlfriend's wrist. Savage was guilty because she had intentionally applied unlawful force in throwing the drink over the woman and a cut had been 'occasioned'.

## Section 20 offence

Section 20 of the Offences Against the Person Act 1861 says that:

**❝** Whosoever shall unlawfully and maliciously wound or inflict any grievous bodily harm upon another person, either with or without any weapon or instrument, shall be guilty of an offence triable either way and being convicted thereof shall be liable to imprisonment for five years. **❞**

This is known as malicious wounding.

## *Actus reus* of section 20

The *actus reus* of section 20 is that the defendant must 'wound or inflict grievous bodily harm'.

### Wound

A *wound* means a cutting of the whole skin. In *R v Wood* (1830) it was held that breaking a collar bone was not wounding. Similarly in *JJC v Eisenhower* (1983) it was decided that the rupturing of blood vessels internally was not a wound.

### CASE EXAMPLE

#### *JJC v Eisenhower* (1983)

The defendant fired an air pistol at the victim. A pellet struck the victim's eye, causing bleeding inside the eye but not puncturing it. He was found not guilty of an offence under s 20 as there was no 'wound'.

Note: The defendant was still guilty of an assault occasioning actual bodily harm.

A wound need not be a serious injury. A small cut is enough to be classed as a wound. A cut inside the mouth is classed as a wound, because it is a continuation of the external skin.

## Grievous bodily harm

*Grievous bodily harm* has the meaning of 'really serious' harm, but it is not necessary to show that the injuries are either permanent or life-threatening. Serious psychiatric illness can also be grievous bodily harm.

## Mens rea of section 20

The *mens rea* of section 20 has caused some problems since the section uses the word 'maliciously'. This does not have its everyday meaning. The legal meaning for cases of assault is that the word means intending to do some injury or foreseeing the risk that the act might cause injury and deciding to take that risk.

It is not necessary in section 20 cases for the defendant to have foreseen that the unlawful act might cause 'physical harm of the gravity described in the section'. So the defendant need only realise that some slight injury might be caused as a result of his act. That realisation makes him guilty under section 20. If he does not realise it, then he is not guilty as shown in *R v Parmenter* (1991).

### CASE EXAMPLE

#### *R v Parmenter* (1991)

The defendant threw a baby into the air and caught it, causing grievous bodily harm. The defendant said he had done this before with slightly older children and was unaware that his actions were likely to cause harm to a young baby. It was held that he was not guilty of an offence under section 20 as he did not intend to injure the child, nor did he realise there was a risk of injury to the child.

Intention to cause harm to property is not enough, unless the defendant is aware that his action may also cause harm to a person. So throwing a stone at a window intending to cause damage, but being unaware that any person was near enough to be hurt, would not be sufficient to make the defendant guilty under section 20 if the stone struck and seriously injured someone.

## Transferred malice

The rule about *transferred malice* applies to all crimes including assaults. Where a defendant intends to assault one person but actually hits another person, he will still be guilty because the intention is transferred from the intended victim to the actual victim. This is demonstrated by the case of *R v Latimer* (1886).

### CASE EXAMPLE

#### *R v Latimer* (1886)

The defendant aimed a blow with a belt at C with whom he had had words. In fact he struck R. The fact that he did not mean to strike R was no defence. He was held guilty of maliciously wounding R. The intention he had towards C was transferred to R.

## Section 18 offence

Section 18 of the Offences Against the Person Act 1861 creates the offence of wounding with intent. It is the most serious of the offences created by the Act.

## Actus reus of section 18

For the actus reus of section 18 the defendant must do something which causes a wound or grievous bodily harm. This is the same as for section 20, but the *mens rea* is the critical difference between the sections.

## Mens rea of section 18

Section 18 is a specific intention crime. The defendant must be proved to have the intention to wound or cause grievous bodily harm **or** to resist or prevent arrest. It is this intention which makes it a much more serious offence than a section 20 crime. It is also the reason why the maximum punishment is life imprisonment.

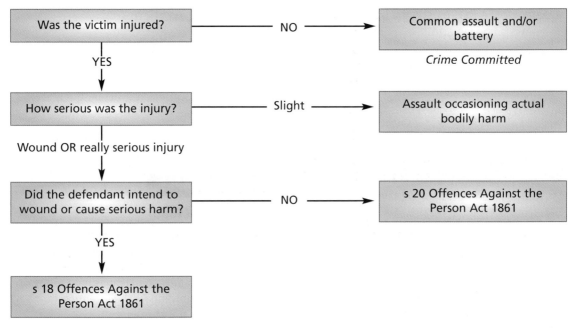

**Figure 23.1** Crimes involving assaults

Figure 23.1 shows a flow chart for these different assaults.

## ACTIVITY

### Activity 2

Explain in each of the following situations what offences, if any, have been committed.

1. Erica comes up behind Ibrahim and punches him hard in the back.

2. Leonard, in the course of an argument with Amy, pulls out a knife and threatens her with it.

3. Thomas kicks Steven, causing Steven severe bruising to his leg.

4. Marilyn jabs at Jane with a penknife and causes a small cut on Jane's arm.

5. Bruce, during a robbery, fires a gun at Anthea. The bullet hits Anthea in the chest causing injuries to her right lung.

## Problems in the law of assaults

The law on assaults is mostly set out in a very old Act, the Offences Against the Person Act 1861. This Act uses complicated, obscure and old-fashioned language, for example the words 'maliciously' and 'grievous'. It would be better if the law was re-written in modern language which would be more easily understood.

The Act also has inconsistencies between the different offences. An example is that section 47 has the same *mens rea* as for an assault or battery. It does not require the defendant to intend or even realise that there is a risk of any injury. This appears unjust. Why should a defendant be convicted of a more serious offence, when he or she did not realise that there was a risk of injury?

It is also unjust that a person who causes a small cut can be charged with the more serious offence of section 20 instead of the offence of 'occasioning actual bodily harm' under section 47. This is because section 20 refers to 'wound or grievous bodily harm'. Yet, clearly, there are different levels of wound and many of them are not nearly as serious as grievous bodily harm.

## BRIEF SUMMARY OF CHAPTER

**Assault**

- an act which intentionally or recklessly causes another to fear immediate and unlawful violence

**Battery**

- the application, intentionally or recklessly, of unlawful force to another person

**Assault occasioning actual bodily harm**

- an assault or battery which causes actual bodily harm

**Section 20 offence**

- unlawfully and maliciously wounding or inflicting grievous bodily harm upon another person

**Section 18 offence**

- wounding or causing grievous bodily harm with intent to do so

## EXAMINATION QUESTION

There is a range of non-fatal offences against the person. They include:

- common assault (consisting of assault and battery) which is charged under the Criminal Justice Act 1988
- assault occasioning actual bodily harm under the Offences Against the Person Act 1861
- grievous bodily harm and wounding, charged under two different sections of the 1861 Act.

Persons charged with such offences may be able to plead a number of possible defences, depending on the situation. These defences include mistake, self-defence, duress, automatism, insanity, intoxication and consent.

**The Problem**

Len, aged 28, has had a history of violence since he was involved in a car accident seven years ago. He needed a blood transfusion but was unfortunately given blood from an infected donor. Len has since been diagnosed as HIV positive and has been on tablets ever since. This has kept him, physically, reasonably healthy but has had the effect of producing alarming mood swings and periods of depression. Len makes his situation worse by often getting drunk and he is also heavily into illegal drugs.

Maggie, Len's ex-girlfriend, has just been diagnosed as HIV positive. She was not aware at the time that Len was HIV positive. As they had had unprotected sex, she is certain that Len must have infected her, and done so deliberately. When she confronted Len, who was drunk at the time, he became verbally aggressive and hit her, causing bruising and a split lip.

Maggie reported these incidents to the police who went round to Len's house to make an arrest. Len again became aggressive and attacked the two officers. DS Nixon suffered a fractured skull and PC Ogden was cut across the face when Len threw a glass at her.

Len was arrested and has since been charged with several offences.

(a)

(i) Discuss Len's criminal liability with respect to his aggressive behaviour and Maggie's injuries. (6 marks)

(ii) Discuss Len's criminal liability with respect to Maggie contracting HIV. (5 marks)

(iii) Len's solicitor has suggested that Len may be able to plead the defence of consent in respect of Maggie contracting HIV.

Discuss whether or not the solicitor's advice is correct. (4 marks)

(b) Identify and discuss the charge(s) that Len could face if Maggie dies from an HIV-related illness. (6 marks)

(c) Discuss what charges Len may face in respect of:

(i) DS Nixon's fractured skull;

(ii) the injury to PC Ogden's face.

(6 marks)

(d) Taking account of your answers to 2(c) above and the following factors:
● Len's mental state and the effect of his prescribed tablets
● Len's drunkenness and use of illegal drugs

identify which **defence(s)** may be appropriate and discuss the likely success of that defence/those defences. (8 marks)

(e) Choose **one** defence which can be pleaded in a criminal case. Identify and discuss advantages **and** disadvantages relating to that defence. (5 marks)

(f) Comment on whether or not the law in relation to non-fatal offences is in need of reform. **(Answer in continuous prose.)**

(5 marks)

*AQA Specimen Paper*

*Note that questions (d) and (e) are on defences which are covered in the next chapter.*

# CHAPTER 24

# CRIMINAL LAW: OFFENCES AGAINST PROPERTY

There are many offences against property and, as with assaults, it is impossible to discuss all of them in this book and only the following are included: theft, robbery, burglary, taking a car without consent and making off without payment.

## Theft

Theft is defined in section 1 of the Theft Act 1968 as follows:

> 66 a person is guilty of theft if he dishonestly appropriates property belonging to another with the intention of permanently depriving the other of it. 99

The *actus reus* of theft is the 'appropriation of property belonging to another'. The *mens rea* has two parts: the thief must both be dishonest and intend to 'permanently deprive' the other person of their property.

### *Actus reus* of theft

In order to establish the *actus reus* of theft there are three things that have to be proved:

- an appropriation
- of property
- belonging to another.

### Appropriation

Section 3 of the Theft Act 1968 says that this is 'any assumption of the rights of an owner'. This is very wide and covers a variety of different situations. Some of these are obvious, such as taking money from a handbag or a pickpocket taking a wallet from someone's pocket. Apart from these situations, there is also an appropriation where property is destroyed, because only the owner has the right to destroy any item.

Many of the cases on the meaning of appropriation involve stealing from a shop. Shoplifting is theft, but at what point can the thief be stopped and charged? All the following acts are an appropriation or 'an assumption of some of the rights of an owner'. In other words, the shoppers have treated the goods as their own.

(a) a shopper picks up a battery and puts it in his pocket;
(b) a shopper swaps price labels on two pairs of shoes, so that one pair will cost less, and takes those shoes to a sales assistant;
(c) a shopper puts several items in a supermarket trolley but does not pay for one item at the checkout.

Notice that in all these situations the shopper has not left the shop. This does not matter; the appropriation of the goods has already occurred. In (a) the appropriation is at the moment the shopper puts the battery into his pocket; in (b) it is when the shopper swapped the labels; in (c) it is at the checkout. At all these points the shoppers are acting as though they are the owners of the property. In fact it is possible to say that there is an appropriation at the moment the shopper takes the item from the shelf, since at that point the shopper is getting control of the article and preventing any other shopper from taking it.

## Property

The item taken must be property that can be stolen. This is obvious where the item is something like a watch or a car or any other moveable property. Coins and banknotes are also property. The main things that are not property for the purposes of the definition of theft are electricity (there is a separate offence of dishonestly using electricity) and knowledge. An interesting case on this is *Oxford v Moss* (1979).

### CASE EXAMPLE

#### *Oxford v Moss* (1979)

A student removed an examination paper, photocopied it and then replaced the original paper. This meant that no physical item had been permanently taken, only the knowledge of what was on the examination paper. It was decided that this was not theft, since knowledge was not 'property'.

## Land and plants

Section 4 of the Theft Act 1968 also places limits on when land and plants growing wild can be considered property that can be stolen. Land or items attached to the land can normally only be stolen by a tenant, for example by removing a sink from a rented flat.

Plants growing wild are another exception which cannot be stolen, unless the plant is completely dug up. When flowers, fruit or leaves are picked off the plant, there is theft only if the person doing the picking intends to sell them.

## Belonging to another

This again is very wide in its meaning, since it covers situations where someone else has possession or control of the item, as well as where someone else owns the property. So it is possible for the owner to be charged with

stealing his or her own property if it was in the control of another person who had a legal right to it. This happened in *R v Turner (No 2)* (1971).

### CASE EXAMPLE

#### *R v Turner (No 2)* (1971)

A car owner took his car from a garage where it had been repaired, without paying the repair bill. The garage had told him that he could not have the car back until he paid the bill and, under the civil law, the garage had the right to do this. So it was held that Turner was guilty of stealing his own car.

## *Mens rea* of theft

The *mens rea* of theft has two elements which must be proved:

• dishonesty
• intention to permanently deprive.

## Dishonesty

The Theft Act 1968 does not define dishonesty but it does give three situations where a person's act is not regarded as dishonest. These are set out in section 2 of the Theft Act 1968 and are:

• if he believes that he has in law the right to deprive the other person of the property;

• if he believes that the other person would consent to the appropriation if he knew of the circumstances;

• if he believes he cannot discover who the owner is by taking reasonable steps.

All these are easier to understand if we look at examples.

(a) An old lady keeps a football that has been kicked into her garden by a child. She believes she has a right in law to keep it. This would not be regarded as dishonest.

(b) A shop assistant cuts her hand at work. She

takes some money from the till to buy a bandage, believing that the shop owner would consent to this if he knew of the circumstances. Again this would not be regarded as being dishonest.

(c) A student finds a pound coin in the street. He keeps it since he believes that he cannot find out who the owner is by taking reasonable steps. Again this would not be regarded as being dishonest. The situation might be different if the student had found a purse with money in it and the owner's initials on it, since it is much easier to trace the owner, but it is the student's belief that is important.

On the other hand section 2 says that a person can be dishonest even if he or she is willing to pay for the property. This means that if a person takes a CD belonging to another person, but leaves money to cover the cost of the CD, this can still be dishonest behaviour if he or she knows that the other person does not want to sell the CD.

Since the Theft Act 1968 does not give a definition of dishonesty, the courts have had to consider it. In *R v Ghosh* (1982) the Court of Appeal said that in proving dishonesty there was a two-stage test. First, was what the defendant had done dishonest by the ordinary standards of reasonable people? Second, did the defendant realise that what he was doing was dishonest by those standards? The defendant is acting dishonestly if the answer to both those questions is 'yes'.

## Intention to permanently deprive

Theft is only proved if the person appropriating the property not only was being dishonest, but also intended to permanently deprive the other person of the property. This means that borrowing an item will not usually be considered theft as in *R v Lloyd* (1985).

### CASE EXAMPLE

#### *R v Lloyd* (1985)

A film was borrowed from a cinema without permission in order to make a copy of it. The original film was then returned. This meant that the defendant was not guilty of theft as he had not intended to permanently deprive the cinema of the film.

Borrowing can be considered theft if the property is kept until it has little or no value left. An example here would be 'borrowing' a week's season ticket for the train and using it for six days. The season ticket has very little value left and even if the taker then hands it back, he can be guilty of theft.

Theft can be tried either in the Magistrates' Court or in the Crown Court. It is a triable either way offence. The maximum penalty is seven years' imprisonment.

### ACTIVITY

#### Activity 1

Explain in each of the following situations whether a theft has occurred.

1. On leaving a friend's house Carol takes an umbrella from a stand in the hall, believing it is her own.

2. Frank, intending to steal, takes a packet of bacon from the shelf in a supermarket and puts it in his pocket. He then realises that he is being watched by a store detective and puts the bacon back on the shelf.

3. ET comes from a planet where shop keepers are obliged to let hungry people have two items to eat for free. ET is hungry and goes into Sainsway's supermarket, takes an apple and a packet of crisps and walks out without paying for them.

# Robbery

This is an offence under section 8 of the Theft Act 1968 which says that:

66 A person is guilty of robbery if he steals, and immediately before or at the time of doing so, and in order to do so, he uses force on any person or puts or seeks to put any person in fear of being then and there subjected to force. 99

So the elements which must be proved for robbery are:

- theft
- force or putting or seeking to put any person in fear of force.

So robbery is theft with force.

## Force

Any force will do. Pushing someone in order to snatch their handbag or tugging a bag from the victim's grip is enough. A threat of force is also sufficient, for example holding a knife in front of the victim and demanding that they hand over their mobile phone. Even putting one's fingers in a pocket and pointing them as though there is a gun there is a threat of force.

There are two conditions on the force and these are that it:

- must be immediately before or at the time of the theft; and
- must be in order to steal.

The first point about the theft being immediately before or at the time of the theft was important in the case of *R v Hale* (1979).

### CASE EXAMPLE

#### *R v Hale* (1979)

Two defendants knocked on the door of a house. When a woman opened the door they forced their way into the house and one

defendant put his hand over her mouth to stop her screaming while the other defendant went upstairs to see what he could find to take. He took a jewellery box. Before they left the house they tied up the householder. They were convicted of robbery.

They argued on appeal that the theft was complete as soon as the second defendant picked up the jewellery box, so the use of force in tying up the householder was not at the time of stealing. However, the Court of Appeal held that there was force immediately before the theft when one of the defendants put his hand over the householder's mouth. In addition, the Court of Appeal thought that the tying up of the householder could also be force for the purpose of robbery as they held the theft was still ongoing.

If a defendant attacks someone because of an argument, this is not force in order to steal. If, after the fight is over, the attacker then sees the victim's wallet on the ground and decides to take it, there is a separate theft. It cannot be robbery.

Another point to remember is that the force need not be used against the person whose property is stolen. In a bank robbery, the robber may point a gun at a customer in a bank in order to make the cashier hand over money. This is robbery. Robbery is an indictable offence and can only be tried at the Crown Court. The maximum penalty is life imprisonment.

### ACTIVITY

#### Activity 2

Explain whether or not a robbery has occurred in each of the following situations.

1. Anton walks into a small shop. He has one hand in his pocket making it look as if he has a gun there. In fact he has not got a gun. He tells the shopkeeper to hand over the money in the till or he will shoot him.

The shopkeeper hands over the money.

2. Caitlin snatches a handbag from Meesha. Meesha is so surprised that she lets go of the bag and Caitlin runs off with it.

3. Kian breaks into a car in a car park and takes a briefcase out of it. As he is walking away from the car, the owner arrives, realises what has happened and starts to chase after Kian. The owner eventually catches Kian after about 400 hundred metres, but Kian pushes him over and makes his escape.

## Burglary

This is an offence under section 9 of the Theft Act 1968. There are two subsections, s 9(1)(a) and s 9(1)(b), which set out different ways of committing burglary.

Figure 24.1 shows these different ways of committing burglary.

Although ss 9(1)(a) and 9(1)(b) set out different ways of committing burglary, they do have common elements. These are that there must be:

• entry
• of a building or part of a building
• as a trespasser.

## Entry

In order to have entered, it is only necessary for part of one's body to be in the building. This could occur where a thief puts his arm in through a window to steal. Even if the defendant is not successful, he may be held to have entered the building as in *R v Ryan* (1996).

### CASE EXAMPLE

*R v Ryan* (1996)

The defendant was trapped when trying to get through a window into a house at 2.30 am. His head and right arm were inside the house but the rest of his body was outside. The fire brigade had to be called to release him. This could scarcely be said to be an 'effective' entry. However, the Court of Appeal upheld his conviction for burglary saying that there was evidence on which the jury could find that the defendant had entered.

## Building or part of a building

The word building includes all buildings such as houses, shops and factories. It also includes sheds and garages and it includes caravans and houseboats if people live in them.

The words 'part of a building' are included because there are some instances where a

| Burglary | |
|---|---|
| s 9(1)(a) | s 9(1)(b) |
| Enters a building or part of a building as a trespasser. | Having entered a building or part of a building as a trespasser. |
| With intent to:<br>• steal<br>• inflict grievous bodily harm<br>• do unlawful damage. | • steals or attempts to steal, or<br>• inflicts or attempts to inflict grievous bodily harm. |

Figure 24.1 Different ways of committing burglary

person may have the right to be in one area of the building, but not in another part. For example, this happens in shops. Shoppers have the right to enter the main part of the shop, but they are not allowed into store rooms or any area marked 'private – staff only'. So, if a shopper steals an item off a shelf in the main part of the shop, the correct charge is usually theft, but if that same shopper goes into a store room and steals, he can then be charged with burglary.

## Trespasser

To be guilty of burglary the defendant must be a trespasser. This means he has not got permission to be there. The obvious example is where the defendant smashes a window of a house and then gets into the house through the window.

However, a person can be a trespasser even if they go into a building through an open door. This can apply to shops. If a person has been banned from entering a shop, then they will be a trespasser if they do enter the shop.

It has even been extended to include someone who enters with permission to do one thing, but goes beyond their permission. This was decided in *Smith and Jones* (1976).

### CASE EXAMPLE

#### *Smith and Jones* (1976)

Smith and his friend, Jones, went to Smith's father's house in the middle of the night and took two television sets without the father's knowledge or permission. The father stated that his son would not be a trespasser in the house; he had a general permission to enter. The Court of Appeal upheld their convictions for burglary. This was on the basis a person is a trespasser if he enters premises of another knowing that he is entering in excess of the permission that has been given to him to enter.

## Intention under section 9(1)(a)

Section 9(1)(a) makes it an offence to enter any building or part of a building as a trespasser with the intention of doing any one of three things. These are:

(a) stealing anything in the building
(b) inflicting grievous bodily harm on someone in the building, or
(c) doing unlawful damage to the building or anything in it.

Under section 9(1)(a) the burglar will be guilty the moment he enters the building if he has the intention of doing one of these three things. He does not have to actually do any of them. Intention when entering is enough.

A case example to demonstrate this is *Walkington* (1979). It is also an example of entering 'part of a building'.

### CASE EXAMPLE

#### *Walkington* (1979)

The defendant went into a counter area in a shop. This area was clearly marked by a three-sided counter. He intended stealing from the till. When he opened the till there was nothing in it. D's conviction for burglary under s 9(1)(a) was upheld as he had entered part of a building (the counter area) as a trespasser with the intention of stealing.

## Section 9(1)(b)

Section 9(1)(b) covers situations where the defendant does not have an intent when he enters as a trespasser. This section says that a person will also be guilty of burglary if, 'having entered any building or part of a building', he steals or attempts to steal anything in the building or he inflicts or attempts to inflict grievous bodily harm on any person in the building.

So to be guilty under section 9(1)(b) a defendant must do more than enter the building as a trespasser; he must steal or inflict grievous bodily harm or attempt to do one of these.

Burglary is a triable either way offence unless it involves the intention to inflict grievous bodily harm. If it involves this serious crime then the burglary charge must be tried at the Crown Court. The maximum penalty for burglary is 10 years' imprisonment or 14 years' for burglary of a dwelling-house.

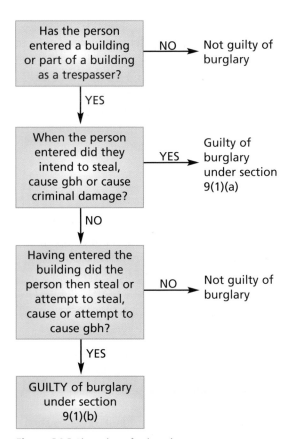

Figure 24.2 Flow chart for burglary

## ACTIVITY

### Activity 3

In each of the following, explain whether or not a burglary has occurred and, if so,

whether it would be an offence under s 9(1)(a) or s 9(1)(b).

1. Nic has been banned from his local supermarket because he has often shoplifted from it. One day he needs some shopping in a hurry, so he decides to go to the supermarket. He enters the shop and puts items into a basket. On the spur of the moment he takes a half bottle of vodka from a shelf and puts it in his pocket. At the checkout desk he pays for the items in the basket but does not pay for the vodka.

2. Tiffany has been sacked from her job in a hairdresser's. She is very annoyed about this and decides to damage the salon. She enters at night using a key she still has. When in the shop she decides to take some expensive bottles of cosmetics. She then leaves without doing any damage.

3. Wesley works as a shelf-filler in a DIY store. One day when he putting packs of batteries out onto a shelf, he slips one in his pocket. He does not intend to pay for it. Later in the day he sees the manager leave her office. Wesley goes in and takes money from the desk. The door to the office has a notice saying 'Private'.

## Making off without payment

After the Theft Act 1968 was passed it became clear that some dishonest behaviour was not covered by that Act and so in 1978 another Theft Act was passed.

Under section 3 of the Theft Act 1978 it is an offence, where the person knows that payment on the spot for goods or services is required, to dishonestly make off without having paid as required and with intent to avoid payment. This section covers situations such as running off without paying a taxi driver or leaving a restaurant without paying for a meal.

## *Actus reus* of making off

There are two points to prove. These are that:

- payment 'on the spot' must be required, and
- the defendant has made off without paying.

Payment 'on the spot' must be required. If payment is not expected 'on the spot' then the offence is not committed. This is shown by the case of *Vincent* (2001).

### CASE EXAMPLE

#### *Vincent* (2001)

The defendant stayed in two hotels and did not pay his bill. He said that he had arranged with the owners of the hotels to pay when he could. This meant that payment on the spot was not required. His conviction was quashed.

The defendant must 'make off' without paying. This means he must leave the scene where payment is expected. If he remains present then he has not made off and is not guilty as shown by *R v MacDavitt* (1981).

### CASE EXAMPLE

#### *R v MacDavitt* (1981)

The defendant had an argument with the manager of a restaurant and refused to pay his bill. He got up and started to go towards the exit, but then changed his mind and went into the toilets. He stayed there until the police arrived. It was held that he was not guilty of making off without payment as he had stayed in the premises.

## *Mens rea* of making off

The *mens rea* involves three points. These are:

- dishonesty
- knowledge that payment on the spot is required, and
- an intention to avoid paying.

## Problems in the law on property offences

## Theft

Generally the law on theft works well but there are some problems with it. For example, the phrase 'belonging to another' has a wide meaning. It was even decided that an owner can steal his own property in *Turner (No 2)* (1971) where the owner of a car took it from a garage without paying for repairs.

Another point is whether it should be necessary to prove that someone intended 'permanently to deprive'? If someone dishonestly takes property belonging to another does it matter whether they intend permanently to deprive that person of the property? This would make it possible to convict for theft in situations such as *Lloyd* (1985) where a film was copied and then returned.

## Robbery

The theft has to be completed otherwise there is no robbery. It can be argued that a completed theft should not be necessary. This would bring the law into line with burglary. In burglary a defendant is guilty under s 9(1)(a) where he intends to steal (or do various other offences) at the moment he enters as a trespasser.

Even a very low level of force will turn a theft into robbery. This means that a person who snatches a mobile phone is guilty of robbery. At the other end of the scale a person who threatens someone with a gun in order to steal thousands (or even millions) of pounds is guilty of the robbery. Should there be different offences for such very different levels of criminal behaviour?

# Burglary

An area of the law on burglary which can be criticised is where judges have decided that a person who is not a trespasser can become one when he goes beyond the permission given to him. In *Smith and Jones* (1976) the Court of Appeal ruled that the son of the householder was a trespasser where he had entered and stolen two television sets even though the father stated that his son would not be a trespasser in the house; he had a general permission to enter. This decision could mean that a guest at a dinner party in someone's house may become a trespasser if they go into another room, such as a bedroom, uninvited. If they then steal in that room then they could be guilty of burglary.

The concept of burglary originally was to protect people's homes and other buildings from trespassers who intended to (or did) steal, etc. There is no need to extend the law on burglary to include people who have permission to be in the house, even though they have gone beyond their permission. A thief, as in *Smith and Jones*, can still be charged with theft.

Also the defendant is guilty of the full offence of burglary if he intends to steal but does not actually take anything as in *Walkington* (1979) where the defendant would have stolen from the till in the shop if there had been anything in it to steal. This is in contrast to theft, where the defendant is only guilty of the full offence of theft if he actually takes something. He is only guilty of attempted theft if there is nothing there for him to steal.

## BRIEF SUMMARY OF CHAPTER

**Theft**

- dishonestly appropriating property belonging to another with the intention of permanently depriving the other of it

**Robbery**

- stealing and, immediately before or at the time of doing so, using force or putting someone in fear of being subjected to force

**Burglary**

- entering a building or part of a building as a trespasser and either:
  - intending to steal, inflict grievous bodily harm, or
  - do unlawful damage, or
  - having entered, steals or attempts to steal or inflicts or attempts to inflict grievous bodily harm

**Making off without payment**

- dishonestly making off without having paid, knowing that payment on the spot is required, and with intent to avoid payment

# CHAPTER 25

# CRIMINAL LAW: GENERAL DEFENCES

When a person is charged with a crime he may admit that he has done the act involved, but claim that he has a defence. If successful in showing one of these defences it will mean that he is not guilty of the crime. The general defences we will consider are:

- insanity
- automatism
- intoxication
- duress
- duress of circumstances/necessity
- self-defence
- consent.

Each of these is considered briefly below.

## Insanity

If a defendant is proved to be insane he or she cannot be guilty of any crime requiring *mens rea*. The verdict in such a case will be 'not guilty by reason of insanity'.

The legal definition of insanity comes from the M'Naghten rules, which date from 1843. These say that a person is insane if he or she:

**66** is suffering from a defect of reason due to disease of the mind so that either he does not know the nature and quality of his act or he does not know that he is doing wrong. **99**

It has to be stressed that this is a legal definition of insanity and not a medical one. The courts have held that a person acting in the course of an epileptic fit comes within this definition since he has a disease which affects the mind and during the fit does not know what he is doing. A defendant may therefore be considered as legally insane, even though his illness may be a physical one such as a brain tumour.

The courts have held that the effects of several physical illnesses can be considered as insanity. These include:

- epilepsy – where the defendant is having a fit
- diabetes – provided it is the illness that causes the automatic state – if the defendant has taken too much insulin (the drug used for controlling diabetes) then this is an external cause
- hardening of the arteries of the brain
- a sleep disorder which caused the defendant to sleep walk and cause injuries to another in his or her sleep.

Although the verdict is 'not guilty by reason of insanity', the judge has power to order that the defendant be:

- sent to an appropriate hospital
- given a community order with a treatment requirement
- given an absolute discharge.

In this way the judge can make sure that, where necessary, the public is protected from danger. However, where the defendant is not dangerous the judge has other suitable methods of dealing with the defendant.

## Automatism

This defence means that the defendant is not guilty of any crime since he acted like a robot because of some external cause. He was incapable of having the intention to commit any crime as he did not know what his body was doing.

This could happen where a blow to the head made the defendant semi-conscious. Another situation would be where a man was being attacked by a swarm of bees. Any movements made by him to protect himself from the bees would be reflex actions. If he hit another person as a result, he would be able to use the defence of automatism.

Another situation is where the defendant has taken a prescribed drug which has unexpectedly caused him to become dazed. An example of this is *R v Hardie* (1984).

### CASE EXAMPLE

#### *Hardie* (1984)

The defendant was depressed because his girlfriend had told him to move out of their flat. He took some Valium tablets which had been prescribed for his former girlfriend. She encouraged him to take the tablets, stating that it would calm him down. He then set fire to a wardrobe in the flat. He said he did not know what he was doing because of the Valium. His conviction for arson was quashed because he had taken the drug because he thought it would calm him down. This is the normal effect of Valium. So the defendant had not been reckless.

## Intoxication

This covers the effects of alcohol and drugs and is only a defence if it means that the defendant did not have the *mens rea* required for the crime.

If a defendant drinks so much that he does not know what he is doing, he has a defence to any crimes which involve specific intention such as murder or theft. However, he has no defence to any crimes where recklessness is sufficient for the *mens rea*, since getting drunk is a reckless course of conduct. This was decided in *DPP v Majewski* (1976).

### CASE EXAMPLE

#### *DPP v Majewski* (1976)

The defendant had taken both alcohol and drugs. In a very intoxicated state he then attacked people in a public house and also the police officers who tried to arrest him. He was convicted of three offences of assault occasioning actual bodily harm (section 47, Offences Against the Persons Act 1861) and three of assaulting a police officer in the execution of his duty. The House of Lords upheld all these convictions. His intoxicated state was not a defence as the House of Lords said:

66 It is a reckless course of conduct and recklessness is enough to constitute the necessary *mens rea*. 99

The situation is different if the defendant does not know that he is taking alcohol or drugs. This could occur where another person slips a drug into a cup of coffee the defendant is drinking. In this instance the defendant is not being reckless and so can plead the defence of involuntary intoxication. However, if a defendant has the intention to commit the crime anyway, he will be guilty as in *Kingston* (1994).

### CASE EXAMPLE

#### *Kingston* (1994)

The defendant's coffee was drugged by someone who wanted to blackmail him. He was then shown a 15-year-old boy who was asleep and invited to abuse him. The defendant did so and was photographed by the blackmailer. The House of Lords upheld his conviction for indecent assault. They held that if a defendant had formed the *mens rea* for an offence then the involuntary intoxication was not a defence.

## Duress

Duress occurs where another person forces the defendant to commit a crime by threatening him. The threat used to force the defendant to carry out the crime must be of death or serious injury to himself or his family.

An example would be where a bank robber seizes one of the customers in a bank as hostage and makes that hostage drive the getaway car by pointing a gun at his head. The hostage would have the defence of duress if he were charged with assisting the robber.

Another situation would be robbers holding the wife and children of a bank manager and threatening to kill them unless the bank manager opens the bank's safe and brings the money to the robbers. The bank manager would not be guilty of theft or robbery since he acted under duress.

Duress can be used as a defence to all crimes except murder and attempted murder.

## Duress of circumstances/ necessity

A defendant may be forced to act to protect himself or others because of events that are happening. This is known as duress of circumstances. An example is the case of *Willer* (1986).

### CASE EXAMPLE

#### *Willer* (1986)

The defendant and a passenger were driving down a narrow alley when the car was surrounded by a gang of youths who threatened them. The defendant realised that the only way to get away from the gang was by driving on the pavement. He did this quite slowly (about 10 mph) and having made his escape he drove to the police station to report the gang. His conviction for reckless driving was quashed.

Circumstances can also force a person to act in order to prevent a worse evil from occurring. This is sometimes referred to as necessity. The defence is very similar to the defence of duress of circumstances, yet the courts have been reluctant to recognise necessity as a defence in its own right. The leading case is *Dudley and Stephens* (1884).

### CASE EXAMPLE

#### *Dudley and Stephens* (1884)

The two defendants were shipwrecked with another man and the victim, a 17-year-old cabin boy, in a small boat about 1,600 miles from land. After drifting for 20 days and having been 9 days without food and 7 days without water, the two defendants killed and ate the cabin boy. Four days later they were picked up by a passing ship and on their return to England were convicted of murder. Their claim of necessity to save themselves from dying was rejected.

The defence of necessity has been recognised in some modern cases. In particular, in *Re A (Conjoined twins)* (2000), it was said that the defence of necessity could be available as a defence even to a potential charge of murder.

## CASE EXAMPLE

### Re A (Conjoined twins) (2000)

Conjoined twins were born with one of them having no proper heart or lungs. She was being kept alive by the other twin, whose heart circulated blood for both of them. Their parents refused to consent to an operation to separate them. Doctors applied for a declaration that it was lawful to operate to separate the twins, even though the weaker twin would certainly die. The Court of Appeal gave the declaration. The three judges gave very different reasons for why the operation would be lawful, but one of them said that the defence of necessity would be available to the doctors were they to be charged with murder of the weaker twin.

## Self-defence

If a person acts in self-defence or defence of another then he may have a defence to a charge of assault or even to a charge of murder or manslaughter and will be found not guilty. The fact that self-defence is a defence to murder is shown by the following extract from a newspaper article.

### Shopkeeper who fought for his takings killed knife-wielding robber in struggle

A shopkeeper told an inquest that he fought off and killed an armed robber who came at him like a 'mad dog' trying to steal the day's takings. Tony Singh, 34, was ambushed by Liam Kilroe, 25, a wanted criminal as he tried to get into his car after work.

The robber threw a brick through the shopkeeper's car window before announcing that he was armed with a knife and was going to stab him. Instead of handing over the £2,000 takings, Mr Singh fought back. Mr Singh was slashed across the face and stabbed in the back in the ensuing struggle.

By the time the police arrived Mr Singh had subdued Kilroe, who was either dead or dying. Officers arrested Mr Singh on suspicion of murder and, although he was released on bail, he feared he could face a murder charge before the Crown Prosecution Service declared that he had acted in self-defence.

*(Source: taken from an article by Russell Jenkins, The Times, 11 November 2008)*

The important point is that the person defending himself must use no more force than is reasonably necessary in the circumstances.

The amount of force which can be used in self-defence is explained in the Criminal Justice and Immigration Act 2008. This states that, in deciding whether the force used is reasonable in the circumstances, it must be considered:

**66** **(a) that a person acting for a legitimate purpose may not be able to weigh to a nicety the exact measure of any necessary action; and**

**(b) that evidence of a person's having only done what the person honestly and instinctively thought was necessary for a legitimate purpose constitutes strong evidence that only reasonable action was taken by that person for that purpose. 99**

So, if a person is attacked by someone with a gun then it will be reasonable to fire a gun back in self-defence. But if an attacker kicks another person in the ankle, it is unreasonable to stab that attacker. The amount of force has to be in proportion to the attack as the victim of the attack believes it to be.

The Act makes it clear that a defendant cannot rely on any mistaken belief, if that mistake is made due to the defendant being voluntarily intoxicated.

## Retaliation

If the attacker has stopped attacking and is walking away, then it is not self-defence if the victim runs after him and hits him. It is no longer necessary for the victim to defend himself as the attack has finished.

## Consent

Consent may be a defence to battery and other offences against the person. However, it is never a defence to murder or to situations where serious injury is caused.

Consent can be a defence to battery or where a minor injury is caused. The consent means that the 'force' is lawful. So, if your boyfriend or girlfriend hugs and kisses you, this is not a battery because you consent to them doing this. But if a stranger hugs and kisses you, this could be a battery.

Consent can also be a defence to an offence of causing actual bodily harm, but only if the injury caused is minor. Consent cannot be a defence where a serious injury is caused.

## Real consent

The victim must know the facts of the situation. If they do not then they are not consenting to the assault. This was decided in *R v Dica* (2004) where consent was given to sexual intercourse without knowledge of the fact that the defendant was HIV positive. The Court of Appeal held that there was no consent to the risk of infection.

### CASE EXAMPLE

#### *R v Dica* (2004)

The defendant who knew he was HIV positive, had relationships with two women. They had unprotected sex with him and both became infected. They claimed that they did not know

he was HIV positive and that if they had they would not have agreed to unprotected sex. D was charged with an offence under s 20 of the Offences Against the Person Act 1861. The fact that the women did not know he was HIV positive meant that they did not truly consent to run the risk of infection.

The following newspaper article shows a conviction for passing on hepatitis B.

#### Man jailed for passing on hepatitis B

Gloucester: A man who had unprotected sex and knowingly gave a woman potentially life-threatening hepatitis B was jailed for two years. Ercan Yasar, 29, a Turkish restaurant worker from Cheltenham, knew that he had the disease and had been warned that he should always practise safe sex. The woman fell ill a week after a one-night stand with him. Detective Constable Paul Day, of Gloucestershire police, said the use of DNA to prove the source of the infection made it the first case of its kind in Britain

*(Source: taken from The Times, 19 November 2008)*

## Sports

In some sports, such as boxing and judo, the whole object is to hit or throw your opponent. In these sports competitors consent to the assaults that are part of the sport. Even if a boxer is seriously injured, his opponent will not be guilty of any offence.

Sports such as football, rugby and hockey can also involve contact with other players. In these it is assumed that players consent to legal tackles. Even if a tackle is a bit late, it is still something which is likely to happen in a game. This means that it will not be an offence as the victim will be assumed to have consented to the contact. This happened in *R v Barnes* (2004).

## CASE EXAMPLE

### *R v Barnes* (2004)

The defendant made a late tackle on V during an amateur football match. V suffered a serious leg injury. The defendant's conviction of an offence under s 20 of the Offences against the Person Act 1861 was quashed.

However, where one player deliberately hits or kicks an opponent in a match, then this will be a criminal offence. By playing in the match, the opponent does not consent to deliberate assaults on him. If it is outside the rules of the game there is no consent.

## BRIEF SUMMARY OF CHAPTER

**Insanity**

■ The defendant is suffering from a defect of reason due to disease of the mind so that either he does not know the nature and quality of his act or he does not know that he or she is doing wrong

**Automatism**

■ The defendant acts like a robot because of some external cause

**Intoxication**

■ is only a defence if it means that the defendant did not have the *mens rea* required for the crime

**Duress**

■ The defendant commits the crime because of threats of death or serious injury

**Duress of circumstances/necessity**

■ The defendant commits the crime because of surrounding circumstances or to prevent a greater evil

**Self-defence**

■ Reasonable force can be used in self-defence

**Consent**

■ Consent can be a defence to minor assaults; the consent must be real to provide a defence

# CHAPTER 26

# FAMILY LAW: MARRIAGE

## Marriage

A marriage is 'the voluntary union for life of one man and one woman to the exclusion of all others'.

## Requirements of a valid marriage

When a couple decide to marry formally there are several factors needed to make such a union into a valid marriage. These are that they must:

- both be aged 16 or over
- not have a close blood relationship
- be single (not already married)
- be one man and one woman (not a same-sex couple).

## Age

The parties must be at least 16 years old. Anyone below that age who goes through a ceremony of marriage is not legally married. The age limit of 16 was set by the Age of Marriage Act 1929.

## No close blood relationship

The law forbids people who are too closely related from marrying each other.

This means that a man may not marry such close relatives as his mother, grandmother, daughter, granddaughter, sister or aunt, while a woman may not marry her father, grandfather, son, grandson, brother or uncle. The full list of prohibited degrees of relationship is set out in the Marriage Act 1949 (as amended by the Marriage (Prohibited Degrees of Relationship) Act 1986).

The main reason for this prohibition is a medical one. There is a great risk of genetic malformation in a child born to a close relative.

## Single

The parties must be single, that is, not already married to someone else at the time of the ceremony of marriage.

If a person goes through a second ceremony of marriage while already married, the second marriage is called a bigamous marriage and the person involved might be prosecuted for the crime of bigamy. The second marriage is not valid; the parties are not legally married.

Where a party has been married but has legally been divorced then he or she is able to re-marry legally.

## One man and one woman

As seen in the definition at the beginning of this chapter, the parties must be one man and one woman.

If two people of the same sex go through a ceremony of marriage the law will not recognise that as a marriage. However, they can now enter into a civil partnership (see below).

The sex registered on the birth certificate is regarded as the person's sex, even if a person has had a sex change operation in later life. This was shown by the case of *Corbett v Corbett* (1970).

**CASE EXAMPLE**

### Corbett v Corbett (1970)

The 'wife' had been registered at birth as a male. In adult life he had a sex change operation. 'She' then went through a ceremony of marriage with another male. Even though the 'wife' had had a sex change operation, the court ruled that 'she' could not legally marry another male.

## Void marriage

If any one of the four requirements above is absent, then the 'marriage' is not a valid marriage. It is a void marriage. This means it never existed, even though there was a ceremony of marriage.

This also means that any children born during the marriage are illegitimate, unless at the time of conception of the child or at the time of the ceremony of marriage (if later) one or both of the parties believed they were legally married.

## Formalities of marriage ceremonies

In order for the marriage ceremony to be valid there are also certain formalities which must be observed.

The most important of these are that:

• the marriage is conducted by an authorised person (usually a priest or registrar)
• the ceremony must take place in an authorised building (this may be a church or other religious building, a register office or another building licensed for marriages)
• the wedding is held at the correct times (there are some exceptions – see below)
• preliminary procedures are correctly followed. These will be different depending on where the marriage is going to take place and are set out in more detail below.

The formalities of marriage ceremonies vary according to where the ceremony is to be held. Ceremonies may be Church of England weddings or marriages authorised by a superintendent registrar's certificate, which can take place in a register office or other authorised building. This will be a building used for religious worship or a place licensed to hold weddings.

## Church of England ceremonies

Before a Church of England wedding service can take place the couple must arrange for one of the following:

1. *Banns to be published*. Banns are an announcement that the marriage is going to take place and this announcement must be read out in the church of both of the parties on three Sundays in the three months immediately before the wedding is to take place.
2. *A common licence*. This licence is granted by a bishop and is an alternative to having the banns read. In order to get such a licence the parties must swear that there is no impediment to their marriage (reason which would prevent their marrying) and one of the parties must live in the parish of the church to be used for at least 15 days before the wedding.
3. *A special licence*. This can only be granted by the Archbishop of Canterbury and it allows the couple to get married anywhere and at any time. All other methods mean there is at least a 15-day wait before the ceremony can take place.
4. *A superintendent registrar's certificate*. Any couple can give notice of their intended marriage to a register office. This notice is recorded in a book which is open to public inspection and after 21 days the couple will receive a certificate authorising their marriage.

Once one of these formalities has been observed, the wedding service can take place in a Church of England church. The service must be conducted by a qualified priest and should take place between 8 am and 6 pm (unless the couple are being married by special licence). As well as the priest and the couple there must also be two witnesses present.

## Other religious weddings

Where a couple wish to have a religious ceremony other than a Church of England ceremony, they need a superintendent registrar's certificate. This allows the ceremony to take place in a registered building (eg a chapel or synagogue).

The ceremony must be conducted by an authorised person, usually a priest or minister of the couple's chosen religion. Alternatively, the registrar may be present.

The ceremony must be held between 8 am and 6 pm; there must be two witnesses; and the building must be open to the public. The only exceptions are for Jewish marriages and Quaker marriages, which can take place at any time, without witnesses and behind closed doors.

## Civil marriage ceremonies

Where a couple do not wish to have a religious ceremony they may get married at a register office or other licensed building.

In order to do this they need a superintendent registrar's certificate, obtained as described above. Such a certificate can also authorise a marriage to take place in hospital or at home if one of the parties is too ill or disabled to get to another building.

Couples can marry in any register office or in any building with a licence to hold marriage ceremonies. Thousands of locations have a licence to hold weddings. Most of these are hotels or country houses, but places such as some football stadiums or zoos also have licences.

The ceremony must be conducted by a registrar and held between 8 am and 6 pm; there must be two witnesses; and the building must be open to the public.

## Marriage of those aged 16 and 17

Where one of the parties to a marriage is over the age of 16, but under the age of 18, it is necessary for that person to obtain the consent of a parent or guardian before he or she can get married.

If consent is refused then it is possible to apply to the local Magistrates' Court for permission to marry. The County Court and the High Court (Family Division) can also give consent, but it is more usual to go to the Magistrates' Court as the procedure will be quicker and cheaper.

However where a person aged 16 or 17 gets married without obtaining consent, it must be noted that the marriage is valid. The parties concerned may be prosecuted for giving false information (either about their age or the consent) but the law still recognises the marriage as a valid one.

## Formalities not observed

If the formalities are not observed the marriage will be declared void if **both** parties knew that the formalities had not been observed.

If one of the parties thought it was a genuine ceremony of marriage and believed that all the necessary formalities had been kept to, then the law will accept that it was a valid marriage.

### Activity 1

In the following situations explain whether there is a valid marriage.

1. Gregory marries his niece, Rosalind, aged 17, in a ceremony at a register office. Rosalind lies about her age, but the other formalities are complied with.

2. Because Terry and Susan want a quiet wedding Harold, a vicar, conducts the marriage at the vicarage at 7 pm with his wife and himself as witnesses.

3. A registrar conducts a marriage ceremony for Brian and Celine in a local hotel which has a licence for marriage ceremonies. Celine was born a male, but has had a sex change operation. The registrar does not know this.

## Voidable marriages

There are also factors which will make a marriage voidable.

A voidable marriage is one which is valid at the time of the ceremony of marriage, but because of one of the factors below, one or both of the parties may apply to the court for the marriage to be annulled (that is, declared invalid).

So when the ceremony of marriage has been completed the couple are legally regarded as married and will go on being legally married until a court annuls the marriage. An annulment of the marriage is not a divorce. The reasons for applying for an annulment are:

- non consummation
- no consent
- mental disorder making the person unfit for marriage
- one party was suffering from a sexual disease and the other party did not know this
- the bride was pregnant at the time of the marriage by another man.

## Non consummation

The marriage has not been consummated because of incapacity or wilful refusal. In other words, the parties have never had sexual intercourse after the marriage because one of them was unable to do so or because one of them refused to.

## Lack of consent

One of the parties did not validly consent to the marriage because his or her consent was obtained by duress or mistake or because he or she was suffering from unsoundness of mind or otherwise. This means that if one of the parties did not genuinely consent to the marriage that party can ask for an annulment.

Duress is something which forces the person to go through the marriage ceremony, but they do not really consent to the marriage. Duress can be threats of death or injury to the person if they refuse to marry. But it can be anything which 'overbears the will of the person' so they do not genuinely consent. This was seen in *Hirani v Hirani* (1982).

### *Hirani v Hirani* (1982)

A 19-year-old Hindu girl was forced by her parents into an arranged marriage. She did not want to marry. It was held that the test for duress was whether the 'force' experienced by the person was such as to overbear his or her will and destroy the reality of consent.

Mistake is illustrated by the case of *Valier v Valier* (1925).

CASE EXAMPLE

## CASE EXAMPLE

### *Valier v Valier* (1925)

An Italian who understood very little English thought that the ceremony was only an engagement ceremony and not the actual marriage. It was held that he had not consented to the marriage.

## Mental disorder

This is where one of the parties, though capable of giving a valid consent, was suffering from mental disorder within the meaning of the Mental Health Acts of such a kind as to be unfit for marriage.

## Sexually transmitted disease

If, at the time of the marriage, one of the parties, unknown to the other party, was suffering from a sexually transmitted disease and could infect his or her partner, then the other partner can apply for the marriage to be annulled.

## Pregnancy

If, at the time of the marriage, the bride was pregnant by some other man and the bridegroom did not know this, then the groom can apply for the marriage to be annulled.

## Time limits

A petition for an annulment can be made immediately after the marriage.

However, for reasons above the proceedings for annulment must be made within three years of the marriage ceremony. This limit can be extended if the petitioner (the person starting the proceedings) has been suffering from a mental disorder.

Where the petitioner is seeking an annulment on the grounds of their partner's venereal disease or pregnancy, the petitioner must have been unaware of the fact at the time of the marriage ceremony.

## Court's discretion

The court has discretion in deciding whether to grant an annulment. The court can always refuse to grant annulment if it is shown that the petitioner, knowing that he or she could get an annulment, behaved in such a way as to lead their partner to believe that they would not apply for an annulment.

An example of this was a case where the husband, who knew his wife was incapable of having sexual intercourse and that he could get an annulment on this ground, had jointly with his wife adopted a child. The court refused to annul the marriage. The court can also refuse to annul the marriage if it feels that to do so would be unjust to the respondent.

Children of a voidable marriage are always regarded as legitimate, even after the marriage has been annulled.

## Civil partnerships

Since 2005 same-sex couples can register a civil partnership. This gives the couple the same rights and responsibilities as a marriage but it is not a marriage.

Both parties must have resided in England and Wales for at least seven days before giving notice of their intention to form a civil partnership. After giving notice they must wait 15 days before the registration takes place.

The registration is at a civil ceremony conducted by a registrar. The partnership is formed when the both partners have signed the registration document.

| | |
|---|---|
| Under 16 | VOID MARRIAGE |
| Too close blood relationship | |
| Already married | |
| Same-sex couple | |
| Non consummation of marriage | VOIDABLE MARRIAGE |
| One party not consenting | |
| One party suffering from a mental disorder making them unfit for marriage | |
| One party was suffering from a sexual disease and the other party did not know this | |
| Bride, unknown to groom, was pregnant at the time of the marriage by another man | |

**Figure 26.1** Reasons for void and voidable marriages

## ACTIVITY

### Activity 2

State whether the following statements are TRUE or FALSE.

1. A 17-year-old can get married without their parents' consent.

2. A marriage ceremony can take place at any time of day.

3. If one of the parties does not consent to the marriage, then the marriage is void.

4. If the bride, unknown to the groom, is pregnant at the time of the marriage, then the marriage is void.

5. If the marriage is not consummated, then the marriage is voidable.

## BRIEF SUMMARY OF CHAPTER

### Marriage

■ is the voluntary union of one man and one woman to the exclusion of all others; the parties must be:
  • 16 or over
  • not too closely related
  • single status
  • of the opposite sexes

■ A **void** marriage is where one of these requirements is absent

■ A **voidable** marriage is valid at the time of marriage but can be declared invalid later for one of the following reasons:
  • non-consummation
  • no valid consent
  • suffering from mental disorder
  • suffering from a sexually transmitted disease (unknown to other party)
  • bride pregnant by another man (unknown to bridegroom)

### Formalities

■ If formalities of time, place, authorised person conducting ceremony and witnesses are not complied with **and** the parties know this, then the marriage will be void

### Civil partnership

■ Same-sex couples can register a civil partnership

# CHAPTER 27

# FAMILY LAW: DIVORCE

Although the definition of marriage given in the opening sentence of the previous chapter says it is the 'voluntary union for life', marriages do not always continue for life. The law allows couples to divorce. A divorce is a legal ending of the marriage and means that both partners are then free to marry another person.

## Applying for a divorce

To apply for a divorce one of the spouses must put in a document called a petition to the County Court or to the High Court. The spouse applying for a divorce is called the 'petitioner' and the other spouse is called the 'respondent'.

The vast majority of divorce cases are undefended: this means that the respondent does not dispute the case. In such cases there is a simple procedure which means that neither party nor their lawyers need personally go to court. The petitioner sets out the facts in a sworn document called an affidavit.

Everything (except the arrangements for dependent children) can be dealt with by posting documents to the court and so this is known as a 'postal divorce'.

### Defended divorce

If the respondent wants to defend he or she must answer the petition and there will be a hearing at court to decide the case. A defended case is likely to be dealt with in the High Court.

### Time limit

The Matrimonial and Family Proceedings Act 1984 states that no-one can apply for a divorce within a year of getting married. This rule is to try and encourage couples to work through any early difficulties in the marriage.

## Irretrievable breakdown of marriage

Under the Matrimonial Causes Act 1973 the only ground on which the court will grant a divorce is that the marriage has broken down irretrievably.

In order to prove that the marriage has broken down irretrievably, the petitioner must establish one of five facts. These are:

(a) adultery by the other spouse and that the petitioner finds it intolerable to live with the other spouse;
(b) unreasonable behaviour by the other spouse;
(c) desertion for at least two years;
(d) that the parties have lived apart for a period of at least two years and the other party consents to a divorce;
(e) that the parties have lived apart for at least five years.

Let's look at what is meant by each of these five facts.

### Adultery

Adultery is when a married person has voluntary sexual intercourse with a person of the opposite sex. If the petitioner can prove this fact and also show that he or she finds it intolerable to live with the respondent, then it is held that the marriage has irretrievably broken down and a divorce will be granted.

## Unreasonable behaviour

The behaviour must be such that the petitioner cannot reasonably be expected to live with the respondent.

This covers a wide range of behaviour including violence, child abuse, drunkenness, refusing to speak to the other spouse for long periods or being obsessively jealous.

The court will take into account the whole of the circumstances in deciding whether the behaviour is such that the petitioner cannot reasonably be expected to live with the respondent.

## Desertion

This is where one of the parties has left against the wishes of the other.

Usually it will mean that the parties are living at different addresses, but the courts recognise that desertion is possible where the couple continue to live under the same roof but lead completely separate lives. This means they do not sleep in the same room nor do they eat together nor even sit in the same room watching TV together.

The desertion must be for a minimum period of two years. The courts will ignore a period of up to six months living together during the desertion, provided the actual period of desertion lasts at least two years.

Let's explain this with an example. Liam left his wife Megan on 1st May 2007 but returned on 1st September 2007 and they then lived together until 1st December 2007 when Liam finally left. In this situation that two-month period (1st September 2007 to 1st December 2007) will be ignored.

Megan can apply for a divorce after 1st July 2009 because Liam will then have deserted her for a total of two years (1st May 2007 to 1st July 2009 less the two months they lived together during that period.)

## Living apart for two years

Both partners must agree to a divorce in this case. In working out the length of time the same rules apply as for desertion, that is, any period of six months will be ignored. Also as for desertion, the parties may be living in the same house provided they are living completely separate lives.

## Living apart for five years

For this there is no need for the other spouse to agree to a divorce; the fact that the couple have lived apart for five years is enough proof that the marriage has broken down irretrievably.

The respondent can oppose the granting of a divorce if it would cause grave financial or other hardship, for example that a respondent wife would lose rights to a pension from her husband's work.

However, wherever possible the court prefers to grant a divorce and protect the respondent's financial position by making suitable financial orders. Clearly if the couple have been living apart for five years the marriage has irretrievably broken down.

## Divorce decrees

### *Decree nisi*

When the court is satisfied that one of the five facts above is proved and that the marriage has irretrievably broken down, the court will grant a *decree nisi* of divorce. This does not end the marriage; it is only a stage on the way to the final divorce.

## Decree absolute

Six weeks after a *decree nisi* is granted the petitioner can apply for the decree to be made absolute; this *decree absolute* ends the marriage. A *decree absolute* will only be given if the court is satisfied about the arrangements for the welfare of any children under the age of 16.

## Financial orders

When there are divorce proceedings, either spouse can apply for various financial orders to be made by the court.

The courts have the power to award:

**(a)** maintenance (regular payments of money) by one spouse to the other

**(b)** maintenance payments for any dependent child

**(c)** a lump-sum payment to a spouse or to a child

**(d)** a transfer of property order (this will usually be the family home).

## Maintenance payments to a spouse

In deciding the amount of a payment to a spouse the court considers a number of things. These include the income, earning capacity and financial resources of both parties, the financial needs and obligations of both parties, their age and any disabilities (physical or mental) they have.

In addition the court will look at the length of time they were married, the standard of living enjoyed by the family before the breakdown of the marriage and the contribution made by each party to the welfare of the family.

A 'clean break' is encouraged wherever possible, so that the financial obligations of each party to each other end as soon as is just and reasonable after the decree of divorce.

This is more likely to apply where the couple are young, there are no children of the marriage and both parties are capable of earning their own living.

| | |
|---|---|
| Divorce is only available if a marriage has broken down irretrievably | One of the following facts must be proved:<br>• adultery by the other spouse and that the petitioner finds it intolerable to live with the other spouse<br>• unreasonable behaviour by the other spouse<br>• desertion for at least two years<br>• that the parties have lived apart for a period of at least two years and the other party consents to a divorce<br>• that the parties have lived apart for at least five years. |
| Petition to County Court or High Court for divorce | Cannot petition for divorce within the first year of marriage |
| The court will first grant a *decree nisi* of divorce | A *decree nisi* does not end the marriage |
| Then, after six weeks, the court will grant a *decree absolute* | A *decree absolute* ends the marriage; it will only be given when the court is satisfied about the arrangements for children under 16 |

**Figure 27.1** Divorce

## 'One-third rule'

Where an order for maintenance payments is made to a spouse, this amount may be worked out by what is called the 'one-third rule'.

This means the income of both parties is added up and then divided by three; if the income of the spouse applying for maintenance (usually the wife) is less than that one-third, the other spouse will be ordered to pay an amount to make up the difference.

This rule was first suggested in the case of *Wachtel v Wachtel* (1973) and the working of the rule is shown below by using the income of the parties in that case, although obviously the earnings were very much lower over 30 years ago.

### EXAMPLE

| | |
|---|---:|
| Husband's annual income | £6,000 |
| Wife's annual income | £750 |
| Total | £6,750 |

Divide that total of £6,750 by 3 = £2,250

The wife was already earning £750 so take that away from £2,250 and the amount required to make the wife's income up to £2,250 is £1,500. So, under the one-third rule, the husband was ordered to pay maintenance of £1,500 per year to his wife.

This is not a rule which will be used in every case, but it is a flexible starting point for the courts to consider. Once an order has been made by the court either party can ask for it to be varied at a later date if circumstances change.

## Child maintenance

Child maintenance is described as 'regular, reliable financial support that helps towards a child's everyday living costs'. The parent without the main day-to-day care of the child pays child maintenance to the other parent.

Maintenance payments for children can be arranged privately between the parents or the parents can use the Child Support Agency to decide the amount of maintenance.

There have been complaints about the Child Support Agency. The main complaints are the delay in working out how much child maintenance should be paid and delays in enforcing payments. These delays have meant that the parent with day-to-day care of the children has not received maintenance for them. Usually it is the mother who has day-to-day care, and she may have considerable financial difficulties if no maintenance is paid for the children.

## Child Maintenance and Enforcement Commission

In October 2008 the Child Maintenance and Enforcement Commission was set up. It is intended to provide an efficient statutory child maintenance service with improved assessment, collection and enforcement processes. The new enforcement powers will be introduced from 2009/10.

The Commission already runs an organisation, Child Maintenance Options, which is an impartial information and support service. The Commission offers this service to help parents gain a clear understanding of the options available for arranging child maintenance. The aim is that parents feel informed enough to make a decision about child maintenance and act on it.

Child Maintenance Options provides impartial information through a national telephone helpline, a website and a face-to-face service for those in most need of more personalised help and support.

## Lump-sum orders

A lump-sum payment is a single payment of an amount of money. The court can order that a lump sum be paid to a spouse or to a child of the family. Such an order will only be made where one of the spouses has capital assets such as shares or building society savings or owns a business. A lump-sum payment can be ordered as well as or instead of maintenance.

## Property-adjustment orders

In most marriages the only asset is the family home and the court can make orders about the transfer of ownership of the home. Usually it will be sold and the proceeds of the sale divided between the parties. Where the home was jointly owned by husband and wife during the marriage the court will normally order that it be divided evenly between them.

In *White v White* (2000) the House of Lords said that equality of division of the assets should be used as a yardstick. However, this does not mean that the wife will automatically get half of the assets. The judge should have regard to all the facts of the case and the overall requirements of fairness when deciding how much she should be given.

As with maintenance, the court will consider all the needs and obligations of both parties and the contributions made by both during the marriage. Where there is a child under the age of 18, the court can order that the parent with care of that child should be allowed to remain living in the home until that child becomes 18.

## Children

Where the parents cannot agree on what should happen to their dependent children the courts have wide-ranging powers. All the law on welfare of children is now in the Children Act 1989.

The key principle of this Act is that the welfare of the child is the most important consideration. The Act stresses that wherever possible children should be brought up and cared for within the family, but where there is a dispute the court will look at:

**(a)** the child's own wishes
**(b)** the child's physical, emotional and educational needs
**(c)** the child's age, sex, background and other relevant considerations
**(d)** any harm which the child has suffered or might suffer in the future
**(e)** how able the child's parents are to meet his or her needs
**(f)** how the child might be affected by any change in circumstance.

The court can make a number of different orders, but will only make an order if it thinks that doing so would be in the best interests of the child. The available orders are:

• residence order
• contact order
• prohibition order
• specific issue order.

### A residence order

This says where and with whom the child should live. Usually it will be one of the parents but it is possible to order that the child live with another relative if that is in the child's best interests.

### A contact order

This requires the person with whom the child is living to allow the child to have contact with the person named in the order. The type of contact might be a weekly or fortnightly visit or a weekend stay but can include other matters such as telephone calls. The order is normally in favour of the parent with whom the child is not living, but the court can also make contact orders with other people such as grandparents.

## ACTIVITY

### Activity 1

Fill in the gaps in the description of the court structure by selecting the appropriate word or phrase from the list in the box below the text.

A divorce will be granted if one party can show that the marriage has ..................... broken down. The person starting the divorce proceedings is called the ......................... .

To show that the marriage has broken down it is necessary to prove one of five facts. These are adultery, ...............................
behaviour, ......................... for two years, living apart for two years and the other party consenting to the divorce or living apart for ................... .

When the divorce is first given the court grants a decree ......................... . After six weeks the parties can then apply for this decree to be made .......................... .

Divorce proceedings cannot be started within .............................. of the marriage.

The husband or wife can claim financial payments from the other. These can be a .............................. order, which is regular payments or a one-off payment in the form of a .............................. .

abusive    absolute    claimant

desertion    five years

irretrievably    irrevocably

lump sum    maintenance

nisi    one year    two years

unreasonable    three years

## A prohibition order

This will stop a parent from taking some action, such as taking the child abroad, without first getting the permission of the court.

## A specific issue order

Where the parents cannot agree on a specific issue, for example which school the child should attend, the court can be asked to make an order about that specific issue.

## The role of the courts

A divorce decree can only be granted by a court. However, for all other matters connected to the divorce, such as maintenance orders, child maintenance, property orders, and where the children should live, the parties are encouraged to make their own agreements.

It is only if the parties cannot come to a private arrangement that the court will be asked to make orders about these matters.

## Mediation in family cases

In order to help married couples resolve their difficulties there are a number of counselling and mediation services. One of the most important is Relate which is an organisation that tries to help partners work through the difficulties in their marriage and, hopefully, keep the marriage going.

If the marriage cannot be saved, then there are mediation services to help the couple come to amicable agreements about finance, property and the children.

Mediation is felt to be important for married couples who are divorcing as it avoids the conflict of going to court to decide matters. The parties come to an arrangement on which they are both agreed. This is particularly important where there are young children and the parties will have to remain in contact for several years.

It is possible to get government-funded legal help to use mediation services in family disputes.

## Problems with divorce law

Much of the law on the grounds for divorce is based on fault. There has to be proof of irretrievable breakdown on one of the five facts. The first three – adultery, unreasonable behaviour and desertion – are all fault based.

This fact may cause antagonism between the parties and, as a result, problems for the future relationship of the couple. If the parties have to continue making arrangements about young children, this is a particular problem.

Even where the parties use mediation to try and resolve differences, there can be problems. A main problem is that if the mediation is unsuccessful, then there is more delay before a final resolution of the case is achieved. Also, mediation may be inappropriate in domestic violence situations. A battered wife may be too frightened to oppose any suggestions made by her husband.

There are often financial issues post-divorce. A major problem is that the couple's incomes will not stretch to two households.

Where parties have used the Child Support Agency there have been disputes over the amount set by the Agency, resulting in fathers refusing to pay anything.

Another major problem can be with access to children. A protest group, Fathers 4 Justice, has used high-profile demonstrations to highlight the fact that many fathers do not get access to their children. One such protest is set out in the following newspaper article.

### FATHERS IN PROTEST AT HARMAN HOME

Two Fathers 4 Justice protesters dressed as Spider-Man and Batman have scaled the roof of deputy Labour leader Harriet Harman's home.

The two men said they will not come down until the Government 'takes them seriously'. The men said their names were Nigel Ace, 40, who was dressed as Spider-Man, and Tony Ashby, 42, in the Batman costume.

They said they had enough food supplies to last for a week. Mr Ace, who described himself as a sales manager from Bristol, said the stunt was provoked by Ms Harman's recent pledge to ensure equality in the workforce.

He said: 'What about dads? We haven't got equality. The Government is ignoring us and has a feminist agenda. We want Harriet Harman to come back here and engage in a debate with us and, if not, then Gordon Brown should come. I am trained in survival, so I don't care how long we are up here.'

Mr Ashby, who described himself as a painter and decorator from Leicester, said he had not seen his children for seven years. He said: 'We have been up here since 6 am and we are in for the long haul. We don't want to cause trouble, we just want to get our message across.'

*(Source: taken from an article in the Daily Express, 9 July 2008)*

### BRIEF SUMMARY OF CHAPTER

**Divorce**

- This can only be because of the irretrievable breakdown of the marriage; this can be shown by one of the following facts:
  - adultery
  - unreasonable behaviour
  - desertion
  - living apart for two years and agreeing to a divorce
  - living apart for five years

### Financial orders

- Either spouse can apply for a maintenance payment for themselves and/or for the children, a lump-sum payment and a property-adjustment order

### Children

- The welfare of the child is the most important factor; the court can make a residence order, a contact order, a prohibition order or a specific issue order

### Role of court

- Divorce must be granted by a court; the parties may also get court orders on other issues, but only if they are unable to come to an agreement

### Mediation

- Couples are encouraged to use mediation to come to amicable resolution of their differences

## EXAMINATION QUESTION

Legislation lays down basic requirements for entering into a valid marriage. These requirements include minimum ages, minimum number of witnesses and permitted times of marriage. In addition, one party must be male and the other female.

The law on divorce is based upon proof that the marriage has broken down irretrievably. This proof must be based on one of five 'facts'. In consequence, a court will eventually grant the petitioner a divorce and possibly also an order for maintenance and/or child maintenance, though generally a process of mediation must first be undertaken.

Recent legislation has made provision for the registration of same-sex relationships from which certain legal benefits flow.

### The Problem

Trudy has recently started a job at the local register office and has only completed an initial training course. One day, because of an outbreak of flu, all the experienced staff are off sick and only Trudy and you, a work experience pupil from the local school, are in the office. However, Trudy knows that you are studying law and comes to you for advice about the following.

- Una, a local girl, and Vikram are in the reception area asking for a marriage licence. Vikram's passport indicates that he only entered the country two days ago.

- Warren and Yvette are also in reception asking for a marriage licence. Trudy is worried because Yvette looks very young and is wearing school uniform.

- Trudy has received a telephone call from Zoë asking about the law in relation to witnesses, permitted times of marriage and possible marriage venues. She has asked you to ring her back with the proper advice.

- At lunchtime, Trudy tells you that she and her husband, Andy, are having marital problems and that she needs some advice about a divorce. Trudy has a leaflet from the Citizens Advice Bureau, but clearly does not understand some of the terms in the leaflet.

- In the afternoon, two men, Bruno and Clive, come into reception saying that they want to 'get married'.

(a) Identify and discuss the legal issue(s) relating to the intended marriage of Una and Vikram. **(5 marks)**

(b) Explain to Trudy the legal requirements relating to age and marriage, and the potential consequences for Warren and Yvette if these requirements are not met. **(5 marks)**

(c) Describe the relevant law on marriage relating to witnesses, permitted times and legal venues that you will need to explain to Zoë when you return her call. **(5 marks)**

(d) In relation to the law on divorce, explain to Trudy the legal meaning of the following terms which she has read in her leaflet.

(i) 'Irretrievable breakdown' and how it can be proved; (4 marks)

(ii) *'Decree nisi'* and *'decree absolute'*; (4 marks)

(iii) 'Maintenance' and 'child maintenance'; (4 marks)

(iv) 'Mediation'. (3 marks)

(e)

(i) Identify the courts which can be used in divorce proceedings. (2 marks)

(ii) Comment on whether or not the law on divorce is suitable to meet the needs of a modern society. (5 marks)

(f)

(i) Outline the relevant law which applies to civil partnerships (the registration of same-sex relationships). (3 marks)

(ii) Identify and comment on the **legal benefits of registration. (Answer in continuous prose.)** (5 marks)

*AQA Specimen Paper*

# CHAPTER 28

# FAMILY LAW: INHERITANCE

## Making a valid will

A will is a formal declaration by a person of what he wants to happen to his property after he dies. Of course the will does not take effect until the person dies. This means that it is possible for that person to change his mind (perhaps several times!) about who should inherit his property and make another will (or wills) before he dies. If this happens it is the last will that counts when the person eventually dies.

The law provides several rules about making a will, though a will need not be complicated. In one case a will simply said 'All to mother'. It is possible to buy a standard form for a will from a stationers, but no particular words are needed, provided the will is clear. However, unless the situation is very straightforward, it is probably sensible to get legal advice on the wording of the will.

Another name for a will is a testament and the person making a will is called a testator (male) or testatrix (female). The law lays down several rules which must be satisfied for a will to be valid. These rules are about the capacity of the testator, in other words whether that person is legally able to make a will, his intention to make a will and about the formalities that are needed to make a legal will.

The testator must be:

(a) at least 18 years of age; the only exception is that those in the forces on active service and sailors at sea may make a will from the age of 14

(b) of sound mind; this means that the testator must be able to understand that he is making a will and what effect it will have; where someone suffering from a mental illness has periods when he can understand, then a will made during such a period would be valid

(c) acting of his own free will; if someone makes a will because of threats or fraud that will is not valid.

The formalities of making a will are set out in the Wills Act 1837 as amended by the Administration of Justice Act 1982 and are that the will must be:

• written and
• signed by the testator in the presence of two witnesses.

## In writing

The will must be written; again there is an exception for those in the forces on active service and seamen at sea (see below). It does not matter what the will is written on; in one case a will written on an egg shell was accepted as a valid will. But video wills are not legally valid since they are not written.

## Signed by the testator

The will must be signed by the testator or another person in the presence of the testator and at his direction. If the testator cannot write, then he may make his mark instead of signing; this could be a cross, a rubber stamp or by the testator's thumb print.

If the testator is physically unable to write, perhaps because of paralysis, the testator may tell someone else to sign the will for him.

The signature can be anywhere on the will, provided that it is intended to give effect to the will. Originally it had to be signed at the 'foot or end thereof', but this is no longer the rule. This is shown by the case of *Wood v Smith* (1993).

### CASE EXAMPLE

#### *Wood v Smith* (1993)

The testator wrote a will two days before he died. He did not sign it at the bottom and when one of the witnesses pointed this out, the testator said 'I have signed it at the top. It can be signed anywhere.' In fact the testator had started the document by writing 'My Will by Percy Winterbone' and the Court of Appeal held that in writing his name at the top the testator had meant that to be his signature and the will was valid.

## Witnesses

The signature or mark must be made or acknowledged in the presence of at least two witnesses who are present at the same time

(wills made by soldiers etc again have special rules – see below).

The witnesses must see the signature or mark, but do not need to see it being made; it is enough if the testator acknowledges the signature as his. Nor do witnesses need to see the whole of the will; they do not need to know what is in it.

Those witnesses must be competent; that is, they must be able to understand that they are witnessing a signature, but there is no set age limit. A witness can be under the age of 18 provided he is old enough to understand. It has been held that a blind person could not be a witness, since he could not see the signature of the testator.

At least two witnesses must sign (or make their marks on) the will. The witnesses must sign in the presence of the testator. It is not necessary, however, for the witnesses to sign in each other's presence, but, where they do so, a will drawn up by a lawyer will probably have an 'attestation clause' which says that both were present together. At the end of the draft will shown below, just before the witnesses' signatures, there is an attestation clause.

The witnesses cannot benefit from the will; nor can the spouse of a witness. This was shown in *Ross v Caunters* (1979).

### CASE EXAMPLE

#### *Ross v Caunters* (1979)

The wife of one of the witnesses had been left £5,000 in the will and was not allowed to inherit that money. She sued the solicitor who had drawn up the will and had not checked that it had been witnessed properly.

The fact that a witness has been left property in the will does not make the will invalid. Only the gift to the witness is affected; the rest of the will stands.

THIS IS THE LAST WILL AND TESTAMENT

of me ...... Henry Horner .....................................................

of ...... 10, High Street, Anytown, Blankshire .......................

I hereby revoke all previous wills and codicils I have made. This is my last Will.

As executor(s) of this my will, I appoint: my wife Margaret Horner and my brother Jack Horner of 21 Station Road Anytown, Blankshire

I direct that all my debts and funeral and testamentary expenses be paid as soon as is convenient after my death.

I leave all my estate to my wife Margaret Horner of 10, High Street, Anytown, Blankshire, as long as she survives me by 28 days.

If she does not survive me by 28 days I leave all my estate to my son Thomas Horner of Honey Cottage, Beesfield, Mayshire.

H. Horner

Dated this 25th day of October 19 94

Signed by the
testator/testatrix
in our presence and
by us in his/hers

...... Jack Spratt ...... (1st witness)

of 12 High Street, Anytown, Blankshire

...... John Smith ...... (2nd witness)

of 47. New Road. Anytown

The other point to note is that if there are more than two witnesses then it is possible for some of the witnesses to inherit under the will, provided there are at least two other competent witnesses who do not benefit by the will.

This rule was made by the Wills Act 1968 in order to change the law after the case of *Re Bravda* (1968) in which a father left property to his two daughters but they could not inherit it because they had witnessed the will. There were two other independent witnesses, but the father wanted the two daughters to sign as well so that they would know about the will. The change in the law did not help the two daughters but it made sure that anyone in the same position in future could inherit.

## Privileged wills

While all the formalities set out above have to be followed for the great majority of wills, there are clearly some situations in which it is impracticable to make a formal will. A soldier in the middle of a battle, for example, or a sailor on a sinking ship cannot be expected to organise witnesses and follow the rules on signing.

The law recognises this by allowing soldiers and airmen who are on 'actual military service' and sailors who are at sea to make informal wills.

For these the age limit for making a will is lowered to 14 years. If the will is written then there is no need for witnesses or the will can be unwritten provided two witnesses hear what the testator says. This happened in the case of *Re Jones* (1981).

### CASE EXAMPLE

**Re Jones (1981)**

The testator was a soldier on duty in Northern Ireland. He was shot and taken to hospital. On the way to hospital he said in front of two officers, 'If I don't make it, make sure that Anne gets all my stuff'. Anne was his fiancée and they were due to be married the following week. Jones died the day after he was shot and it was decided that his oral statement was a valid will and that his fiancée was entitled to inherit all his property.

The important point is that the soldier or airman must be on 'actual military service' when making the will. This depends on the facts of each case. In *Jones* there was not a state of war, but clearly he was on actual military service. For sailors the rule is that the sailor must be at sea when making the will as shown by *Rapley v Rapley* (1983).

### CASE EXAMPLE

**Rapley v Rapley (1983)**

A 19-year-old seaman made a written will and signed it while at home on leave, but the will was not witnessed. If he had been at sea when he made this will it would have come under the rules for privileged wills and been valid. Since he was at home when he made the will, it was not valid as it needed to be witnessed by two witnesses in the normal way. This was so even though he actually died at sea as a result of a ship sinking some 20 years later.

### ACTIVITY

**Activity 1**

In each of the following situations explain with reasons whether there is a valid will.

1. Olive writes her will on the back of an old cheque book. She signs it at the top of the will. The will is then correctly witnessed by two people.

2. Maurice, who cannot write because of a physical disability, asks a friend, Trevor, to

write out a will for him and to sign it on his behalf. The will is then witnessed by Jane, aged 17 and Bill, aged 21.

3. Dennis, who is a sailor, writes his will out on a will form he has bought from a stationers. He signs it at the bottom but does not get it witnessed.

## Changing a will

If a testator has made a will he or she can change or vary it or revoke (cancel) it. Any alteration to a will must be signed by the testator and witnessed in the same way as the original will. The rule on this is very strict, probably to make sure that there is no fraud by someone other than the testator altering the will. The strictness of the rule can be seen in *Re White* (1990) where amendments to the will were written onto the original will and at the end of the will the testator wrote 'Alterations to will dated 14.12.84. Witnessed.' and two witnesses signed below this. The court would still not accept these alterations as changing the original will since the actual alterations were not signed or initialled by the testator or the witnesses.

## Codicils

A change can be made by making a codicil. This is a document which is used to add to, amend or partially revoke an existing will. A codicil must be written, witnessed and signed in the same way as a will. It then changes part of the will. For example, if the testator has made a will leaving all his property to his wife, he could later make a codicil in which he left £1,000 to his sister. The original will is then partly changed as the sister will now inherit £1,000 and the wife will inherit the remainder of the property.

## Revoking a will

A testator can revoke a will at any time during his or her lifetime, provided he is still of sound mind, by any of the following methods:

- making another will
- making a formal revocation
- deliberately destroying the will
- by marriage
- by divorce.

## Making another will

In the new will the testator must declare that all previous wills are revoked. If a new will does not expressly say that all previous wills are revoked then only the parts of the old will that conflict with the new will are revoked.

This is more easily understood by looking at an example. If a testator in his first will has left his house to his wife, all the money in his bank account to his daughter and his car to his son, then in a second will he leaves all the money in his bank account and the car to his brother, the second will does not mention the house so the wife still inherits the house, although the son and daughter do not inherit anything as the second will takes priority.

## Making a formal revocation

This will revoke the will even though the testator has not made another will. The formal revocation must be signed, witnessed etc in the same manner as a will. It will then cancel the will.

## Destroying the will

If a testator intentionally destroys his will or orders another person to destroy it in his presence then that will is revoked. The will can be destroyed by any means. The Wills Act 1837 says that a will is revoked by 'burning, tearing or otherwise destroying the same by the testator'.

Where the testator intended to revoke the will, it need not be completely destroyed as shown in *Re Adams* (1990).

### CASE EXAMPLE

#### *Re Adams* (1990)

The testatrix telephoned her solicitor and told him to destroy her will. The solicitor sent the will to her and wrote that it would be better if she destroyed the will herself. After her death the will was found, but the testatrix had scribbled over parts of the will, in particular the signatures were heavily scored out. The court decided that, even though parts of the will could still be read, the testator had clearly intended to destroy the will and heavily scoring out the signatures was sufficient to revoke it.

Of course if the destruction is accidental then the will is not revoked and evidence of what it contained (possibly from a copy held by a solicitor) can be used to decide who should inherit.

## By marriage

If a testator makes a will and later gets married, that marriage will automatically revoke the will. The only exception to this rule is where the will was made 'in contemplation of marriage'. In other words, the testator stated in the will that he intended marrying and also named the person he was going to marry, then when he married that named person the will would not be revoked.

## By divorce

Where the testator makes a will and then later is divorced, any gift to the former spouse will fail but the rest of the will remains in effect.

If the whole of the testator's property was left to the former spouse then the will does not take effect but the testator's property will be inherited by his nearest relations under the rules on intestacy (see below). If the former spouse was named as executor (see below), then that part of the will is also omitted and the spouse cannot be the executor.

## Gifts of property

The law has different terms for gifts of property in a will. The first distinction is between leaving real property (land or a house) and personal property (any other property including money, cars, furniture, jewellery etc). Where real property is left the technical term is a devise; where personal property is left it is called a legacy or a bequest.

There are also different types of legacy. These are:

- a specific legacy
- a general legacy
- a residuary legacy.

## A specific legacy

This is when the testator leaves a clearly identified thing to someone. The item or money that the legatee (person inheriting) is to get is a specific item or a specific sum of money, for example leaving 'my car, registration number ...'. If the item no longer exists then the legatee will not be able to inherit it.

## A general legacy

This is where the testator does not identify a specific thing but says (for example), 'I leave a painting from my collection to ...'. The exact painting is not specified; the legatee has the right to choose one.

## A residuary legacy

Quite often in a will the testator leaves specific things to a few people and then states, 'I leave all the rest of my property to ...'. This means that the person named gets what, if anything, is left over. This is called the residue of the estate and the person inheriting is called the residuary legatee.

Sometimes a legatee who has been left a specific or a general legacy has died before the testator and in this case the legacy lapses and becomes part of the residue.

The only exception to this is where the legacy was to a son or daughter of the testator and, although that son or daughter has died, they have left a child or children of their own. The legacy will then go to the child or, where there is more than one child, be divided equally between them, unless the testator has made it clear in the will that he or she does not wish this to happen.

If the residuary legatee has died before the testator, then any residuary property is treated as though there was no will and distributed according to the rules of intestacy. The same exception applies where the legacy was to a son or daughter: the legacy goes to their children.

## The rules of intestacy

Not everyone makes a will; only about one-third of those who could make a will do so. Anyone who dies without making a valid will is said to have died intestate and his or her property will be distributed according to the rules of intestacy. These rules are laid down by the Administration of Estates Act 1925 (as amended). The same rules apply whether it is a man or woman who has died and are as follows.

## Where there is a surviving spouse or civil partner

Where a person dies leaving a surviving spouse, the spouse or civil partner will be entitled to inherit part or all of the estate depending on what other relatives there are:

1. *Surviving spouse or civil partner and children (grandchildren or greatgrandchildren).* The spouse will receive the first £125,000 of the estate and all the personal goods such as furniture, clothing, jewellery and car (personal goods do not include money or shares or other investments). Where there is more than £125,000 in the estate the remainder is divided into two parts and the spouse or civil partner gets a life interest in one half (that means the spouse or civil partner is entitled to the income from that half but when he or she dies it will belong to the children) while the other half goes to the children. If any child has died before its parent, then the issue of that child (grandchildren) would take that share. Illegitimate children have equal rights of inheritance to legitimate children.
Since this sounds complicated let's put it into practice with an example (see Figure 28.1).

2. *Surviving spouse or civil partner*, no children, but *surviving parent/s*. The spouse or civil partner will receive the first £200,000 of the estate and all the personal goods. The remainder, if any, will be divided into two parts and the spouse or civil partner will get one half outright, while the parent gets the other half. If both parents are still living they share this half between them. Step-parents are not counted as parents for this rule and do not inherit.

3. *Surviving spouse or civil partner*, no children or parents, but *surviving brother/s, sister/s or nephew/s and niece/s*. The spouse or civil partner will get the first £200,000 of the estate and all the personal goods. The remainder, if any, is divided into two parts and the spouse or civil partner gets one half outright, while the brothers and sisters share the other half. If any brothers or sisters have already died their share goes to their children.

4. *Surviving spouse or civil partner* but no children, grandchildren, parents, brother/s, sister/s, nephew/s or niece/s. The spouse or civil partner will inherit the whole estate.

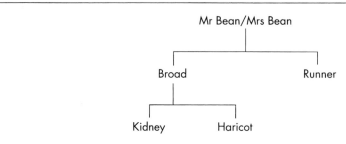

## Situation 1

Mr Bean dies without making a will. He has a wife and two children alive. He also has two grandchildren. He leaves an estate worth £225,000.
• Mrs Bean will inherit the first £125,000 plus the personal items.
• This leaves £100,000 which will be divided into two (£50,000 + £50,000). Mrs Bean will get a life interest in one half (£50,000) (although this will go to the children when she dies), as well as inheriting £125,000.
• The other £50,000 will be divided equally between the two children.
• This gives the following picture:

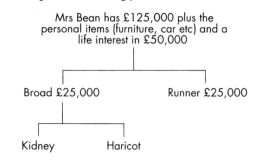

## Situation 2

Mr Bean dies without making a will. He has a wife, one child, Runner, and two grandchildren alive. His other child, Broad, has already died.
• Mrs Bean gets exactly the same as in Situation 1.
• The remaining £50,000 is still divided into two and Runner gets one half.
• The other half is divided between Broad's two children.
• This gives the following picture:

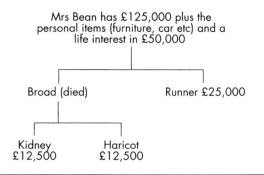

Figure 28.1 The Bean family tree

# Where there is no surviving spouse or civil partner

Where a person dies without leaving a surviving spouse, the nearest relatives inherit and the order is:

1. *Children*. If a child has already died then his or her children take that share.
2. *Parents*. If both parents are still alive they share the estate equally; if only one parent survives that parent inherits the whole estate. (As before step-parents are not counted as parents for the rules of inheritance.)
3. *Brothers or sisters*. These divide the estate between them so: if there are two each will get a half; if there are three each will get a third; and so on. If any brother or sister has already died then their share goes to their children.
4. *Half-brothers and sisters*. The rules are the same as for brothers and sisters. Step-brothers and sisters do not inherit.
5. *Grandparents*.
6. *Aunts and uncles of the whole blood*. That is, aunts and uncles who had the same parents as your father or mother.

**7.** *Aunts and uncles of the half blood.* That is, aunts and uncles who had one parent in common with your father or mother. In other words your parents' half-brothers and sisters. (Again step-relatives do not inherit.)

## Bona vacantia

If there are no surviving close relatives the estate is known as *bona vacantia* (goods without an owner) and the whole estate will go to the Crown. This means all the property will be sold and the proceeds paid into the Exchequer.

Figure 28.2 shows, by means of a flow chart, who inherits when there is no will.

---

### ACTIVITY

#### Activity 2

Assuming there is no will, explain who will inherit in the following situations.

1. Anthony dies leaving an ex-wife (he was divorced three years ago) and two sons. One of the sons is illegitimate. Anthony's estate is worth £150,000.

2. Brenda dies leaving a husband from whom she is separated, but not divorced. She also has one surviving son. Her daughter died two years ago but there are two grandchildren. Brenda's estate is worth £175,000.

3. Candice, who is not married and has no children, dies. Her mother is still alive and Candice has two brothers. Candice's estate is worth £60,000.

---

## Personal representatives

When someone dies whether having made a will or not, someone has to deal with the estate and sort out all the property. The people who do this are called the deceased's *personal representatives*. If there is a will, the will may name the person or persons the deceased wanted to act as his personal representative (PR). In this case the PRs are known as executors.

If there is no-one named in the will to act as executor or if there is no will, then the PRs are called administrators. The nearest relative has the right to apply to administer the estate. (Technically the female for executor is executrix and the female for administrator is administratrix.)

## Applying for probate

The first thing a PR has to do is obtain the right to act. An executor has the right to act under the will but still has to apply for *probate*, that is, prove the will and his right to act. An administrator has to apply for *letters of administration* before he has the right to act.

If the estate is small and only involves personal effects, cash or money in certain saving schemes such as building societies, and there is no dispute about who should inherit, then it is not necessary to apply for probate or letters of administration.

However if the deceased owned a house or such items as shares, then it will be necessary to make an application. A solicitor can help the PR to make the application or the person can make it themselves. The Government publishes a booklet called 'How to Obtain Probate' which explains the necessary procedure and helps PRs to act without a solicitor.

The Probate Registry will only issue probate or letters of administration once it is satisfied that full details of the deceased's estate have been given. The PRs must list all the debts that were owed at the time the deceased died; these could include mortgage payments or other household bills, credit card accounts or hire purchase payments. Expenses caused by the death are also listed; these will include the cost of the funeral as well as fees for the grant of probate and, where a solicitor is used, that bill.

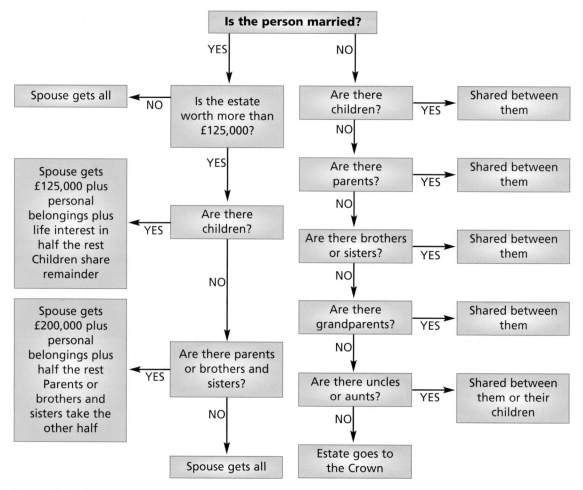

**Figure 28.2** Who inherits when there is no will?

The PRs must also list all the deceased's assets, that is all the property owned by the deceased at the time of death. This could include money in a bank account or savings account, premium bonds, stocks and shares, as well as any house owned by the deceased and personal property, that is items such as clothing, furniture, jewellery and cars.

Once the PRs are sure that they have details of all debts and assets, then the PRs must:

**(a)** fill in a probate application form
**(b)** fill in a form giving details of the estate
**(c)** send or take those forms, together with the death certificate and the original will (if there is a will), to the local Probate Registry.

Where PRs are acting without a solicitor the Probate Registry will ask the PRs to attend for an interview and then to swear an oath that the information given is true to the best of their knowledge. Where a solicitor is instructed, then that solicitor will draw up the necessary forms, including the Executor's Oath and an Inland Revenue Affidavit for the PRs to swear on oath that the information is true to the best of their knowledge.

## Caveats

Where there is an objection to probate or letters of administration being granted, the person who objects must inform the Probate Registry of the objection. This is called filing a caveat. A caveat might be filed because there is a challenge to the will; there might be a dispute as to whether the will is the last will made by the deceased or as to whether the will is valid. Any objection must be heard and decided upon before a grant of probate can be made.

## Distributing the estate

Once probate or letters of administration have been granted the PRs can collect in all the deceased's assets. The PRs must first pay the debts, starting with the funeral expenses. If there is money left after all the debts, including any inheritance tax, have been paid, then the PRs distribute it to the people who are entitled to inherit.

## Provision for family and dependants

Technically a person making a will can leave his property to anybody he wishes. This means that relatives could be disinherited and all the money could be left to a charity or someone else. A wife might have to move out of the family home and end up with no home and no money. Young children might have no provision made for them.

It was felt that in some cases this was not right and so the Inheritance (Provision for Family and Dependants) Act 1975 gives the courts powers to make an award from the estate in cases where family, dependants or co-habitees have not been reasonably provided for by the will or intestacy.

The following people have the right to apply:

(a) the wife or husband of the deceased
(b) a former wife or former husband of the deceased, but only if the former spouse has not remarried
(c) a child of the deceased

(d) anyone who was treated as a child of the family by the deceased (this could include step-children)
(e) any other person who was being maintained immediately before the death, partly or wholly, by the deceased (this could include elderly relatives or younger brothers and sisters)
(f) and the Law Reform (Succession) Act 1995 also allows someone who, though not married, has cohabited with the deceased as husband or wife for at least two years immediately prior to the death.

## Reasonable financial provision

If the applicant is the husband or wife of the deceased, the court decides whether the financial provision under the will or intestacy is reasonable in all the circumstances, so that where the estate is large, a spouse may be given more money out of an estate, even though that spouse already has enough to live on.

Other applicants must show that they have not been left sufficient financial provision as is reasonable in all the circumstances for their maintenance.

The court will take into consideration:

(a) the size of the estate
(b) the needs of the applicant
(c) the needs of those who do benefit under the will or intestacy
(d) the reasons why the deceased failed to leave money to the applicant
(e) the way in which the applicant had behaved towards the deceased during his or her life.

An application must be made within six months of probate or letters of administration being granted. The application is heard by the County Court or the Family Division of the High Court, depending on the amount of money involved.

# The forfeiture rule

Normally the law rules that people cannot benefit from crimes they have committed. Where one person kills another, the killer should not inherit money or other property from his victim. This is called the forfeiture rule. The killer forfeits the right to inherit. Where the killing is deliberate murder then this rule is obviously sensible, but in other situations the rule may appear unfair. For this reason the Forfeiture Act 1982 was passed. This Act allows people convicted of unlawful killing, other than murder, to claim for financial provision from the estate of the victim. It also allows such people to receive pensions and benefits such as a widow's allowance.

A claim must be made within three months of the conviction for the unlawful killing (this could be manslaughter or causing death by dangerous driving etc). The court will only 'modify' the forfeiture rule and allow the claim if it is just in all the circumstances.

The first claim, *Re K* (1985), made under the Act illustrates this. In this case a battered wife killed her husband during a quarrel. She pleaded guilty to manslaughter and was placed on probation for two years. The court decided that it would be just to allow her to receive part of his estate.

## BRIEF SUMMARY OF CHAPTER

**The will**

■ A will is a formal declaration by a person of what he or she wants to happen to his or her property when he or she dies

**The testator**

■ must be 18 or over (unless in the forces on active service or a sailor at sea – when the age is 14+), of sound mind and acting of his or her own free will

**Making a will**

■ The will must be written, signed or acknowledged by the testator in the presence of at least two competent witnesses; the witnesses must also sign the will in the presence of the testator and each other

**Revoking a will**

■ This can be by making another will, by making a formal revocation, by destroying it, by marrying or by divorce

**Intestacy**

■ is where a person dies without having made a will

**Inheritance**

■ Where there is no will inheritance is as follows:
  • the spouse takes all the property if there are no children or parents or brothers or sisters
  • if there are children or parents or brothers or sisters then the spouse gets the first part of the estate and the rest is divided
  • if there is no spouse then the nearest relatives inherit in the following order:
    • children
    • parents
    • brothers or sisters
    • half-brothers or sisters
    • grandparents
    • aunts and uncles
■ If there are no relatives the estate goes to the Crown

**Personal representatives**

■ Personal representatives have the responsibility for applying for probate (where there is a will) or letters of administration (where there is no will) and distributing the estate

**Provision for family and dependants**

■ Provision can be applied for if no provision was made by the deceased

# CHAPTER 29

# RIGHTS AND RESPONSIBILITIES: INTRODUCTION

## Rights

The law gives rights to individuals. Everyone wants their rights to be protected by the law. The law achieves this through various sets of rules.

In some situations the rights of one individual and the rights of another individual may conflict. This means that quite often the law is involved in a balancing act. It is trying to ensure that one person's rights do not affect another person's rights. In order to keep the balance the law also imposes duties on people.

It easier to understand this idea of rights and duties if we look at examples from different areas of law.

## Rights and corresponding duties

### Contract law

In contract law, it is quite easy to see the corresponding rights and duties. Generally this is because both are set out in the terms of the contract when it is made. For example, if a person buys a digital television from a shop, both parties will have rights and duties under the contract. The shop has the right to be paid the agreed price for the TV and the buyer is under a duty to pay the agreed price, while the buyer has the right to have a TV which is working properly and the shop has a duty to provide a TV which is in working order.

### Law of tort

Rights and duties also exist in tort, even though there is no agreement between the parties. Negligence is a tort based on proving a duty of care, so our rights are interfered with when the defendant fails to prevent his negligent acts or omissions which he should contemplate will lead to foreseeable harm (see Chapter 18).

Rights and duties can also be seen where people have the right to use land. Remember land has wide meaning – it includes anything built on land as well as the land itself. So it could be a house or a flat or a field or a factory. The law recognises that people have the right to use their land as they wish. However, this right is balanced by a duty to other land users. Other land users have the right to enjoy the use of their property.

So if one person creates too much noise or smoke from their property, the tort of nuisance allows users of nearby land who are affected by the noise or smoke to make a claim (see Chapter 19).

### Employment law

The idea of rights and duties can be clearly seen in employment law. An employee has the right to be paid wages and the employer has a duty to pay the wages. If the wages are not paid the employee can claim for them.

An employer has a right to expect that an employee will obey reasonable lawful orders and the employee has a duty to do so. If the employee breaches this right in a serious way or persistently then the employer has the right to dismiss him or her.

An employer has a duty to provide a safe system of work and the employee has a right to be protected from dangerous working practices. If this right is breached the employee can claim compensation from the employer.

## Human rights

The European Convention on Human Rights sets out the basic human rights of the individual. But each individual's rights have to be balanced against other people's rights.

One important right is the right to freedom of expression. People have the right to say what they want. However, this right is balanced by the right of other people not to have statements made about them which are untrue and could damage their reputation. If such a statement is made then they have a right to claim compensation under the law of defamation.

Another very important human right is the right to liberty. However, other people have the right not be attacked or robbed. So, if someone attacks or robs another then the State can impose a prison sentence on the attacker. This removes their right to liberty for a set time which is considered suitable or necessary for their criminal behaviour. In some cases, especially of multiple murder, it may be decided that the murderer will never be released. They lose their right to liberty because of their disregard for the lives of others.

## Restrictions on rights

## Restrictions in law

### Contract law

Although the parties to a contract normally have a right to agree the terms they wish, the law does place some restrictions on this, especially in contracts where one party is a business and the other a consumer.

In contracts for the sale of goods the law sets out certain terms that must be included. These are called implied terms. They are terms about the seller having the legal right to sell the goods, terms that the goods must match any description given to them by the seller and that they must be fit for the purpose for which they are sold.

Businesses selling goods cannot exclude these terms when selling to a consumer. They are automatically part of every consumer contract. These terms are explained more fully in Chapter 32.

### Law of tort

It is possible to limit one's liability in tort. For example, most car parks have a notice saying that the owner of the car park does not accept any liability for damage to cars parked there, no matter how the damage was caused.

| Employer | Employee |
|---|---|
| Duty to pay wages | Right to be paid |
| Right to expect employee will obey orders | Duty to obey lawful orders |
| Duty to provide safe system of work | Right to have safe system of work |

Figure 29.1 Corresponding rights and duties in employment law

Example of a notice limiting liability

However, it is not possible to limit liability for causing death or serious injury which results from negligence. Even if there is a notice saying that the company does not accept liability for death or serious injury, the company will be liable if it was caused by negligence of its staff.

## Employment law

Employees are protected in various ways. For example, employees are protected from being discriminated against, from being unfairly dismissed and through health and safety legislation. An employer cannot ignore these laws.

## Human rights

Although the European Convention on Human Rights sets out rights of the individual, it also recognises that there must be restrictions on those rights. For example, an individual has the right to freedom of expression, but it is restricted by our laws on defamation which allow a person to claim for untrue defamatory statements made about them.

Similarly we have already seen that the right to liberty can be restricted where the individual is convicted of a criminal offence. The more serious the offence and the greater the danger the offender poses to other people, then the longer the restriction on liberty (the prison sentence) can last. Human rights are dealt with in more detail in Chapters 38, 39 and 40.

### BRIEF SUMMARY OF CHAPTER

**Rights**

■ The law gives rights to individuals

**Duties**

■ The law imposes duties on people

**Restrictions on rights**

■ The law may place restrictions on rights to protect the rights of other people

# CHAPTER 30

# RIGHTS AND RESPONSIBILITIES: CONTRACT LAW

## Contracts

Contracts are very important, both in the business world and in everyday life. Businesses make multi-million pound deals, buy and sell factories and shops or lease buildings. All these arrangements would be recognised as contracts. However, ordinary people are just as likely to make contracts even if the amounts involved are smaller. Buying a car, renting a flat, hiring a DVD: all these situations involve contracts.

Even everyday occurrences involve making contracts. How do you travel to school or college or work? If it is by train, then you make a contract when you buy the ticket. If it is by car, then you make a contract when you buy fuel. And what about all the other small items one buys? Even buying a packet of crisps creates a contract.

Since contracts play such a large part in daily life, it is not surprising that the law has several rules about them.

First, **what is a contract?** It is an agreement that is legally binding: a promise that can be enforced in the courts. This means that where there is a dispute over an agreement the courts are prepared to hear the case and give a judgment on it.

The important point in deciding if the parties have made a contract is whether there is an offer and an acceptance.

## Offers

The courts will only recognise an offer as being a valid offer and capable of being accepted if it is intended as an offer. The law distinguishes between an offer and what it calls 'an invitation to treat'. An invitation to treat is where the other person is inviting you to make an offer, so that he or she can consider it and accept or reject it.

## Invitation to treat

This is inviting the other person to make an offer. An invitation to treat can be seen in the case of *Fisher v Bell* (1961).

### CASE EXAMPLE

*Fisher v Bell* (1961)

A shopkeeper had a display of flick knives in his shop window. He was charged with a criminal offence of 'offering' the knives for sale. The court held he was not offering them for sale. The display was an invitation to treat.

In all shops where there are goods on display, the customer who goes into the shop and asks to buy them is making the offer. The salesperson in the shop can accept that offer and sell the customer the item or refuse the offer and not sell the item to the customer.

Two important situations which are *always* invitations to treat and *not* offers are:

- articles for sale on display in a shop window or on a shelf in a store, and
- advertisements of items for sale in newspapers, magazines or catalogues.

## Shops

Another case where the courts held that goods on display in a shop were an invitation to treat and not an offer to sell is *Pharmaceutical Society of Great Britain v Boots Chemists* (1953).

### CASE EXAMPLE

**Pharmaceutical Society of Great Britain v Boots Chemists (1953)**

Having items on a shelf in a self-service store was only inviting customers to offer to buy them. There was an invitation to treat and not an offer. The offer was made by the customer at the checkout and could be accepted or refused by the cashier.

This decision was important for self-service stores as it meant that they could include items on their shelves which have by law to be supervised at the moment the contract of sale is made.

This covers items such as bottles of wine and spirits. If the display of a bottle on a shelf was an offer this would mean that the customer would accept the offer when he or she picked the bottle off the shelf. The contract for sale would be complete at that moment. So, in order to comply with the law and supervise the sale, the store would need to have a member of staff standing by every customer when he or she picked up a bottle.

As the law stands, the contract for sale is made at the checkout, making it easier for stores and supermarkets to supervise the sale.

## Magazine advertising

A case showing that an advertisement in a magazine was an invitation to treat is *Partridge v Crittenden* (1968).

### CASE EXAMPLE

**Partridge v Crittenden (1968)**

There was an advert in a magazine saying that the advertiser had wild birds for sale. This advert was held to be invitation to treat and not an offer.

This decision avoids any problems that could arise if demand exceeded supply.

Imagine an advertisement of 'six adorable puppies for sale at £20 each'. If this was an offer, then people writing in to buy the puppies would all be accepting the offer. So if 10 people wrote on the same day it would lead to an impossible situation of 10 contracts but only 6 puppies.

This illustration makes it easier to see why the courts have held that the original advertisement is not an offer. The person who responds to the advertisement is making the offer and the advertiser chooses whether to accept that offer or not. So if there is a situation of 6 puppies for sale and 10 people offering to buy them the advertiser can decide which, if any, of those 10 offers he will accept.

## Reward posters

Reward posters are, however, considered offers. They are different from advertising an item for sale. This was decided in *Carlill v Carbolic Smoke Ball Co* (1893).

## CASE EXAMPLE

### *Carlill v Carbolic Smoke Ball Co* (1893)

A company manufactured smoke balls which they claimed could prevent or cure a number of diseases. They published an advertisement which included the words '£100 reward' and offered this sum to anyone who bought one of their smoke balls, used it in the correct manner but still caught influenza.

Mrs Carlill bought a smoke ball, used it as directed, but unfortunately became ill with flu. She claimed the reward from the company and when they refused to pay she sued them. The court held that the advertisement was an offer and Mrs Carlill had accepted that offer when she bought and used the smoke ball. This meant that there was a contract and Mrs Carlill could get her £100.

More common reward posters are ones which offer a sum of money to anyone finding and returning a lost pet. As with Mrs Carlill's case these posters are considered in law to be offers so that if you see such a poster, find and return the missing animal, you have a right to the amount offered.

## Further rules about offers

There are other rules about offers. These are that an offer:

- must be certain
- may be by any method
- can be to anyone
- must be communicated before it is accepted
- must be still in existence at the time the acceptance is made.

1. **The offer must be certain**

   This means it must be definite enough in its terms so that, if it is accepted, both parties know exactly what they have agreed to. In other words they know what the terms of the contract are. An offer to employ a secretary and 'to pay a London salary' is not certain. The salary is not definite enough. If the parties have written several letters before coming to an agreement, then all the letters are looked at to see if the terms are certain. If the final letter offered to employ a secretary 'at the rate already mentioned' and an earlier letter had mentioned an actual figure, then that offer would be definite.

2. **The offer may be by any method**

   An offer can be in writing, spoken, made on the Internet or even made by conduct. Writing is not necessary. Just think of everyday contractual situations. A person buying a train ticket usually requests it verbally. Unless it is a season ticket it is very unlikely that the offer will be in writing. It is even less likely that anyone will write down their offer to buy an item in a shop.

   In fact in a self-service shop it is possible that the contract may be completed without either party saying anything. The customer takes the item he wants to buy to the checkout and, without speaking, places it on the counter, thus making an offer to buy it by conduct. The cashier rings up the price of the item on the till, accepting the offer. Neither person has said anything but there is already a completed contract.

A more common example of making an offer by conduct is at an auction, where the person making the bid (the offer) does so by nodding his or her head, raising his or her hand or making another signal to show that he or she is bidding.

3. **The offer can be to anyone**

An offer can be to an individual, or to a group of people or to the whole world. The person making the offer can decide whether he wants to make it to one person only or make it available to several persons, any one of whom can accept it.

If the offer is only to one person, then it cannot be accepted by anyone else. If Mr Jones offers to sell his car to Mr Robinson for £2,000, then Mr Brown who happens to hear what is said cannot accept that offer. It has not been made to him.

However, if Mr Jones had said to a group of friends, which included Mr Brown, that he was willing to sell his car to any of them, Mr Brown can accept that offer. He is one of the group to which the offer was made.

It is also possible to make an offer to the world at large so that anyone who wishes can accept the offer. This was the position in *Carlill v Carbolic Smoke Ball Co* (1893), which we have already met (see above). The offer was in such a form that anyone could accept it.

4. **The offer must be communicated before it is effective**

In other words, the person who accepts must know about the offer when he or she does the conduct needed to accept it. For example if Mrs Carlill had not seen the advertisement saying '£100 reward' before she bought the smoke ball, the offer would not have been communicated to her and she could not have accepted it.

Another situation is where someone advertises a reward for the return of a lost cat (remember that reward posters are offers) and a neighbour finds and returns the cat without having seen the reward poster. The neighbour is doing the action required to accept, but the offer is not effective as it has not been communicated to him. This is important because it means there is no contract and so the neighbour cannot claim the reward even if he later sees the poster. Where an offer is sent by post, it is communicated when it arrives.

5. **The offer must still be in existence when it is accepted**

If there is a time limit, the offer ceases when the time limit runs out. It cannot be accepted after that. Where no time limit has been set, the courts will assume that the offer exists for a reasonable length of time, but not indefinitely. This was shown by *Ramsgate Victoria Hotel v Montefiore* (1866).

## CASE EXAMPLE

### *Ramsgate Victoria Hotel v Montefiore* (1866)

An offer to buy shares was made on 8th June. The offeree (the person to whom the offer was made) tried to accept it on 25th November. The court decided that the offer no longer existed and so it could not be accepted. The delay between 8th June and 25th November was too great. What is considered a reasonable length of time for one case could be different in another. Where the offer is connected with buying and selling perishable goods, for example fruit, two days might be a reasonable time, whereas with electrical equipment, two weeks or even two months would be reasonable.

## Ending an offer

An offer may also cease if the person making it withdraws it before it is accepted. It is said in this case that the offer is ended or revoked.

However the offeree must know that the offer has been revoked. If the offeree did not know at the time he or she accepted an offer then the contract would exist. This is what happened in the case of *Byrne v Van Tienhoven* (1880).

### *Byrne v Van Tienhoven* (1880)

The defendants had offered to sell 1,000 boxes of tinplate to the claimants, who were in New York. The defendants then changed their mind and wrote on 8th October revoking their offer. This letter arrived at the claimants' office on 25th October. In the meantime the claimants telegraphed an acceptance on 11th October and confirmed this in a letter which they posted on 20th October.

It was, therefore, important to decide on which date the offer ceased to exist. Did it cease on the 8th, the day the letter of revocation was posted or did it cease on the 25th, the day it arrived and was communicated to the claimants? The court decided that the revocation of the offer occurred on 25th October, and therefore there was a contract between the parties, as the offer was in existence when the claimants accepted it.

This sort of complicated date sequence is sometimes easier to understand if it is shown in a diagram form, as in Figure 30.1.

The person who made the offer need not be the person to tell the offeree that it is revoked. Revocation can be effectively and reliably communicated in other ways. For example if the offeree is told by a reliable third person that the offer has been revoked, then the revocation has been communicated to him. He knows the offer no longer exists and cannot then try to accept it.

## Revoking a reward poster

If the offer was in the form of a reward poster, it can be revoked by taking the same steps to advertise the revocation as were taken to advertise the original offer. This means that if the reward poster offering £50 for the return of a lost pet was placed in a local shop window, then that offer can be revoked by placing a notice to that effect in the same shop window.

This has to be done before the offer has been accepted by someone starting to perform the act required in the original offer. So if someone, who knows about the offer, has already found the pet before the withdrawal notice is placed in the window, the revocation is not effective. The reward can be claimed.

As well as deliberately revoking an offer, it can be ended by other means. These are by:

• rejection of the offer
• making a counter-offer
• the death of the offeree.

## Rejecting an offer

An offer also ceases when it is rejected. Where Andrew offers to buy Bob's car for £2,000 but Bob says no he does not want to sell, the offer

Figure 30.1 *Byrne v Van Tienhoven:* date sequence

ceases at the moment he says no. If Bob changes his mind and writes the next day to Andrew saying he agrees to sell, there is no offer for Bob to accept and so there is no contract. What has happened is that Bob is now making an offer of his own to Andrew that Andrew can accept or reject.

Again a diagram (Figure 30.2) can show this clearly.

## Making a counter-offer

An offer also ceases to exist if the offeree makes a counter-offer. In the above example if Bob, instead of saying no, had said 'I'll sell for £2,100', this is a counter-offer. Its effect is the same as a rejection; it puts an end to the offer. A situation like this occurred in *Hyde v Wrench* (1840).

Figure 30.3 shows this sequence in diagram form.

### CASE EXAMPLE

**Hyde v Wrench (1840)**

The defendant offered to sell his farm for £1,000. The claimant initially counter-offered to buy it for £950. The defendant refused this counter-offer. The claimant then said he would buy the farm for the original asking price of £1,000. The claimant claimed that there was now a contract; the defendant had made an offer to sell for £1,000 and he, the claimant, had accepted that offer. The court decided that the counter-offer of £950 terminated the offer, so there was no offer in existence when the claimant agreed to pay the original price and therefore no contract.

## Death of the offeror

The death of the offeror will normally bring any offer to an end.

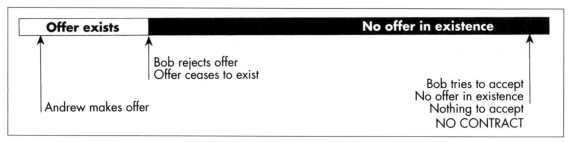

Figure 30.2 Rejection of offer: time sequence

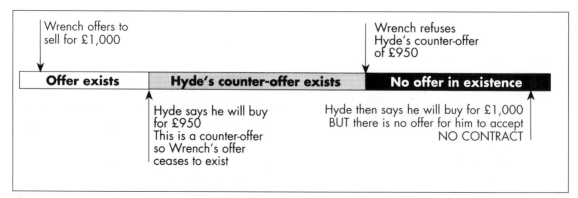

Figure 30.3 *Hyde v Wrench*: time sequence

## ACTIVITY

### Activity 1

Explain whether there is an offer which can be accepted in the following situations.

1. Anya sees a laptop computer in the window of a local shop with a price label of £69 on it. She is delighted to see the low price and goes in and says she will buy it. The shop assistant gets it out of the window and tells her that the price is £369. The number 3 had fallen to the floor and not been visible. Anya insists that she has a right to buy it for £69.

2. Brendan finds a dog running loose in the street about five miles from his home. When he looks at the name tag on the dog's collar, he realises it is his neighbour Cassie's dog that has been missing for two days. He takes the dog back to Cassie. As Brendan is leaving Cassie's house he sees a notice in her window saying that she will pay £100 for the safe return of the dog. Brendan immediately goes back to Cassie and demands the £100. Cassie refuses to pay.

3. Darvinder offers to sell a painting to Emily for £600. Emily says she likes the painting but can only afford to pay £500. Darvinder says he will not accept £500. Emily then agrees to pay the full price of £600. Darvinder refuses to sell the painting to her.

## Acceptance

As we have already said an acceptance is an agreement to the offer. The main rule about an acceptance is that it must agree to all the terms of the offer. It has to be absolute and unqualified. If the acceptance does not agree to the terms of the offer it is not an acceptance but a counter-offer. We have already seen this in *Hyde v Wrench*.

The difficulty sometimes is to distinguish between a request for information and a counter-offer. This is shown by *Stevenson v McLean* (1880).

## CASE EXAMPLE

### *Stevenson v McLean* (1880)

The defendant offered to sell iron to the claimant, the offer to be open until Monday. The claimant replied by asking if he might buy the goods on credit. No reply was received from the defendant, so on Monday he telegraphed a full acceptance. The court held that asking if he could buy on credit was a mere request for information, so the offer remained open and was accepted by the telegram.

It is suggested that the test for distinguishing between enquiries and counter-offers is: could the 'enquiry' be accepted? If not it cannot be a counter-offer. In *Hyde v Wrench* the counter-offer to buy for £950 could have been accepted by Wrench if he had wished to do so; it was quite clear and certain. In *Stevenson v McLean* the request could not form a counter-offer; it was not specific enough. It did not state in detail what credit terms the claimant was suggesting.

An acceptance must be by the person to whom the offer was made, unless it is open to the whole world as in *Carlill v Carbolic Smoke Ball Co* (see above).

## Communication of the acceptance

There are several rules about communicating acceptance to the person who made the offer. The normal rule is that it must be *communicated to the offeror*. This means that staying silent is not an acceptance, a situation that is illustrated in *Felthouse v Bindley* (1862).

## CASE EXAMPLE

### *Felthouse v Bindley* (1862)

The claimant wrote to his nephew offering to buy a horse for £30.15s. (£30.75), following a discussion as to whether he should pay £30 or 30 guineas (one guinea being equal to £1.05). He said, 'If I hear no more about it I will consider the horse to be mine.'

The nephew did not reply but ordered the auctioneer to withdraw the horse from open sale. By error the horse was auctioned and Felthouse sued for his loss, claiming that he had a contract with his nephew to buy the horse. It was held that as the nephew had not communicated his acceptance of the offer no contract existed.

## Exceptions to the normal rule

It is possible to imply acceptance from conduct or for the need for it to be waived by the person who has made the offer. This was the position in the smoke ball case. The buying of the smoke ball indicated acceptance; it was not necessary for Mrs Carlill to do anything else to communicate her acceptance.

In reward cases it is not only impractical to expect everyone seeing such a poster to communicate acceptance, but it is unlikely that the person offering the reward would want hundreds of people to write or telephone just to say that they had seen the poster and were intending to look for the lost item.

## Offeror sets method of acceptance

The person who makes the offer can lay down a *specific way for the offeree to accept*. If there is a prescribed way of communicating the acceptance then only that method or, possibly, one which places the offeror in a more advantageous position by arriving more quickly than the specified method will do. This is shown in *Eliason v Henshaw* (1819).

## CASE EXAMPLE

### *Eliason v Henshaw* (1819)

The claimant offered to buy flour from Henshaw. The offer said that acceptance had to be given to the waggoner who delivered the offer. Instead of doing this Henshaw sent his acceptance by post and it arrived after the return of the waggoner. Because Henshaw had not communicated by the specified method there was no contract.

If there is no prescribed way of communicating then *any effective method will do*. The important point here is that the method must be *effective*. So, for example, if A shouts an offer across a river but cannot hear B's reply because of noise from a passing aircraft, the reply is not

Speak up, I can't hear you!

communicated. Similarly, if a telephone line goes dead as B is accepting so that A does not hear the acceptance it is not effective.

## Postal acceptance

*Postal acceptance* is an exception to the rule that the acceptance must be effectively communicated. If the use of post is a reasonable method of accepting then the acceptance is assumed to have been made the moment it is posted. This is a very old rule and its operation can be seen in the case of *Adams v Lindsell* (1818).

### CASE EXAMPLE

#### *Adams v Lindsell* (1818)

On 2nd September 1817 the defendants wrote to the claimant offering to sell some wool and requiring an answer in the course of post. Because the letter was incorrectly addressed, it did not arrive until 5th September and that same evening the claimant posted a letter of acceptance. This arrived on 9th September whereas in the normal course a reply would have been expected on 7th September. On 8th September the defendants sold the wool to someone else. It was held that a contract came into being on 5th September when the claimant posted the letter so the defendants were in breach of contract by selling on 8th September.

Let's use a diagram (Figure 30.4) to make this sequence of events in *Adams v Lindsell* clearer.

### Letter lost in post

A problem arises where the letter of acceptance becomes lost in the post. The courts have decided that the postal rule of acceptance will still be used, provided the post was a reasonable way of accepting the offer.

So there is an effective acceptance, even if the letter is lost in the post. However, posting means placing the letter in a post box or into the hands of a Post Office employee authorised to receive letters. Handing a letter to a postman authorised to deliver letters is not 'posting' it and so does not count as a valid acceptance until the letter is delivered.

## Modern communication methods

*Telex* (and presumably texts or any other electronic mail system) are treated as being virtually instantaneous and therefore the normal rules of acceptance apply. The courts have decided that a telex is only communicated effectively when it arrives. However, if a telex (or email or text or voicemail message) arrives out of working hours, it will normally be effectively communicated at the beginning of the next working day.

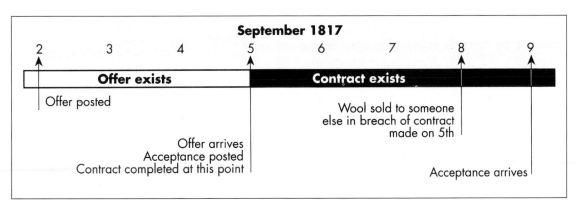

Figure 30.4 *Adams v Lindsell*: date sequence

# Comments on the postal rule

The normal rule that acceptance must be effectively communicated is common sense, but the rule that a letter of acceptance takes effect the moment it is placed in a post box does at first sight seem rather strange. How is the person who made the offer to know at what time a letter gets put in a post box, possibly hundreds or even thousands of miles away?

Would it not be more sensible to say that the contract comes into being when he receives the acceptance? But this creates problems for the offeree: how does he know at what moment his letter arrives? So the courts have had to balance the needs of the two parties. This they have done by limiting the rule to situations where use of the post is reasonable.

Also, since the offeror can specify how an acceptance should be made he can always exclude the use of post as a means of acceptance.

Two other points in support of the rule are that it is easier to prove postage than to prove receipt and it is argued that if an offer is sent by post then the offeror is using the postal service as his agent, so that when the person accepting puts his letter into a post box, he has given his acceptance to the offeror's agent.

The main argument against the rule is that it was created at a time when there was no other method of communicating directly with a person some miles away. Telephones had not been invented, let alone fax machines or email or text messaging. In a world of modern methods of communication, should the rule still apply?

## ACTIVITY

### Activity 2

Advise in the following situations:

1. Simon offers to sell his cricket bat to Anwar for £20. Anwar says he will buy it for £15, but Simon does not agree to this. Anwar then says he will pay the £20, but Simon now refuses to sell the bat.

   Advise Anwar whether he has a contract to purchase the bat.

2. Angelica receives a mail-order catalogue from Smart Homes Ltd, advertising microwave ovens. Angelica orders a 'Smart Special' microwave oven, costing £175. Two weeks later she receives a letter from the company saying that they are unable to supply the model she ordered and returning her cheque. Angelica believes that Smart Homes are in breach of contract.

   Advise Angelica.

3. Brian buys 'Take-off', a new brand of stain remover, having first seen an advertisement which included the words 'Take-off will remove all ink stains. £25 will be paid if it fails to work for you'. Brian uses the stain remover according to instructions but it does not remove ink stains from his shirt.

   Advise Brian whether he has a legal right to the £25.

4. On Wednesday Giles writes to Charles, offering to sell him an antique ring for £400. Charles receives the letter on Friday and immediately writes and posts a letter agreeing to buy the ring. On Sunday, while at an antique fair, Giles is offered £500 for the ring by Pandit. On Monday morning Giles telephones Charles and leaves a message on his answerphone, withdrawing his offer to him. Charles listens to the message that evening. His letter to Giles arrives at his home on Tuesday morning.

   Advise Giles as to his contractual liability.

## BRIEF SUMMARY OF CHAPTER

**For a contract to exist there must be:**

- an offer and an acceptance
- consideration, and
- the parties must intend to create legal relations

**Offer**

- An invitation to treat (eg goods in a shop window) is NOT an offer
- An offer must be certain; it can be made by any method; it can be to anyone; it must be communicated to be effective; it must be in existence when it is accepted

**An offer ceases**

- when the time limit runs out
- when it is withdrawn before it is accepted
- when it is rejected
- when a counter-offer is made
- when the offeror dies

**An acceptance**

- must be a full acceptance of all the terms of the offer
- It must be communicated to the offeror – silence is not acceptance
- The postal rule states that an acceptance is effective the moment it is posted, if the post is a reasonable method to use

# CHAPTER 31

# CONTRACT: CONSIDERATION AND INTENTION

## Consideration

Consideration means that both parties must put something into the contract. Consideration can also be thought of as the price in a bargain. The 'price' does not have to be money, but it must have some value. The important thing is that both sides must show that they have given something in return for the other's promise.

In fact, the consideration in a contract is really the whole point of the contract.

Look at an example of Marie agreeing to buy Joanna's car. Obviously Marie is only going to agree to it because she wants the car and is prepared to pay £1,500 for it, while Joanna is only entering into the contract because she wants to sell her car and get money in exchange.

## Rules about consideration

1. **Both sides must contribute something to the bargain**
   If one person gives another something but the person receiving it does not give anything in return, then this is a gift. A promise to give a gift is not legally enforceable. For example if Uncle Tom promises to give Andrew £100, Andrew is not contributing anything so the law will not enforce this promise (unless it is contained in a special deed).
2. **The consideration has to be real**
   It must have some value, but it need not be adequate. This means that the consideration given on each side need not match in value

so long as something is given. So, for example, Uncle Tom promises to pay Andrew £100 if Andrew will give him a packet of cigarettes. In this situation both are putting something into the contract even though the values are not equal. It does not matter that the packet of cigarettes does not cost £100. This point was considered in *Chappell & Co Ltd v Nestlé Ltd* (1960).

### CASE EXAMPLE

*Chappell & Co Ltd v Nestlé Ltd* **(1960)**
There was a special offer where customers were told they could send in three chocolate bar wrappers, together with a small amount of money, in return for a record. The House of Lords held that three chocolate bar wrappers could be valuable consideration.

In this case the Law Lords pointed out that:

> ❝ A contracting party can stipulate what consideration he chooses. A peppercorn does not cease to be good consideration if it is established that the promisee does not like pepper and will throw away the corn. ❞

In other words, if the parties are happy with the agreement, it does not matter what the value is, provided there is some value.

3. **The consideration must be tangible and real**
   This means that there must be something real put into the bargain by each party. In *White v*

*Bluett* (1853) the courts held that a promise not to complain was not tangible and real and could not be consideration.

## CASE EXAMPLE

### *White v Bluett* (1853)

A son owed his father money. When the father died his executors tried to recover the debt. The son claimed that he did not have to pay the debt as he had had an agreement with his father that the debt would be forgotten in return for the son's promise not to complain about the distribution of the father's assets in his will. The court held that the son's promise was too intangible to be consideration, so he had to pay the debt to the executors.

However, in the case of *Ward v Bytham* (1956) it was held that a promise to keep a child well looked after and happy was good consideration.

## CASE EXAMPLE

### *Ward v Bytham* (1956)

The child's father had promised the mother money towards the upkeep of the child if she would keep the child '... well looked after and happy ...'. When the father stopped paying the mother sued him for the money. The father argued that the mother was doing no more than she was already obliged to do in looking after her child. The court was prepared to enforce the agreement since there is no obligation in law to keep a child happy. The promise to do this was good consideration.

From these two cases it can be seen that it is difficult to know what will be held to be 'real' for consideration and what will not.

## Past consideration

Where the thing that you are offering to put into the contract has already occurred before the contract is made, it cannot be counted as consideration for the contract you are now making. This is shown by the case of *Re McArdle* (1951).

## CASE EXAMPLE

### *Re McArdle* (1951)

In this case a widow had been left a house for her to live in during her lifetime. She repaired and decorated the property. After she had done this her children, who were the ultimate beneficiaries, that is, the house was going to be theirs after the widow died, promised to pay towards the improvements. However, they did not keep their promise to pay. It was decided that they could not be sued because the widow had already finished the work when the children made the promise. Her consideration was in the past.

There is an exception to this. This is when one party asks the other to act and payment is implied. When the other party later promises payment, the courts will enforce that promise. This idea comes from a very old case, *Lampleigh v Braithwaite* (1615).

## CASE EXAMPLE

### *Lampleigh v Braithwaite* (1615)

Braithwaite, who had been tried and sentenced to death, asked Lampleigh to travel to the King and seek a reprieve from hanging for him (a king's pardon). Lampleigh did this successfully. Braithwaite was so delighted that he then promised to pay Lampleigh £100, but failed to do so. It was decided that Lampleigh could claim the money as he had acted at Braithwaite's request.

## ACTIVITY

### Activity 1

1. Louise rents a flat belonging to Caroline. Louise repaints all the rooms and repairs a broken window. Caroline is delighted when she sees the improvements that Louise has made and promises to pay Louise the cost of the paint. Two months later Caroline has still not paid this cost.

   Can Louise claim the money?

2. Toby, who has just won a new car in a competition, promises to give Kevin his old car. A week later Kevin sees Toby's old car advertised for sale in the local garage.

   Advise Kevin.

## Intention to create legal relations

There are some agreements where, even though there is a valid offer and acceptance and both sides have put in good consideration, the courts may still decide that they will not enforce the agreement. This is because, at the time the parties made their agreement, they did not intend it to be legally binding. In order to decide whether an agreement was meant to be legally binding the courts treat domestic and social agreements in a different way from business agreements.

## Social and domestic agreements

Social and domestic agreements are agreements made within the family or on social matters between friends. Examples are a parent's agreement to pay a son money for cutting the lawn or an agreement that everyone coming to a party will bring a bottle of wine. The courts normally assume that if the agreement is a domestic or social one then the parties do not intend to be legally bound. This happened in the case of *Balfour v Balfour* (1919).

## CASE EXAMPLE

### *Balfour v Balfour* (1919)

A husband agreed to pay his wife £31 a month when she was unable, through ill health, to return with him to Sri Lanka where he worked. The husband stopped paying the money and the wife made a claim in the courts for the money. It was decided that it was a domestic arrangement and not a legally binding contract.

Another case where the courts held there was only a domestic arrangement was *Jones v Padavatton* (1969).

## CASE EXAMPLE

### *Jones v Padavatton* (1969)

A daughter agreed with her mother that she would give up her highly paid job in New York and study to become a barrister in England. The mother promised to give the daughter an allowance during her studies. The daughter found it difficult to manage on the allowance, so the mother bought a house for her to live in part of it and let the other part for extra income. When the mother and daughter later quarrelled, the mother sought to re-possess the house. The daughter's case was that the agreement over the house was legally binding; the courts held that it was not: there was no intent to create legal relations.

There are several reasons why the courts are reluctant to make such agreements legally binding. One is that many will involve trivial matters and would be a waste of court time. Another is that family problems are best sorted out amicably and a court case will not help family relationships.

However, the courts may be persuaded by all the circumstances of the agreement that, even though it was between family or friends, it was meant as a legally binding contract. Clear examples are where a marriage is breaking up and the husband and wife come to a financial agreement. The surrounding circumstances of the marriage break-up make the situation different. This was seen in *Merritt v Merritt* (1970).

### CASE EXAMPLE

#### *Merritt v Merritt* (1970)

The husband left his wife for another woman. He and the wife met to discuss finances. The husband said that he would transfer the family home to his wife if she paid the remaining mortgage payments. They also wrote this agreement down. The court held that this was a legally binding contract.

Another example is *Simpkins v Pays* (1955).

### CASE EXAMPLE

#### *Simpkins v Pays* (1955)

The defendant, her granddaughter and the claimant, who was a lodger in the house, jointly entered a competition. The entry, which was sent in under the defendant's name, won £750, but the defendant refused to give the claimant any of the prize money. He sued for one-third of the money and the court decided that the arrangement had been intended as a legally binding contract, so he could get his share.

### ACTIVITY

#### Activity 2

Read the following extract from a newspaper article and explain with reasons whether there was a legally binding agreement or not. ▶

---

**Ex-partners reach deal on splitting £3m lottery jackpot**

A former couple battling in the courts over a £3 million National Lottery jackpot-win have agreed to settle their case.

High Court Judge Mr Justice Kitchin adjourned the hearing until this afternoon when he is expected to approve the terms of the settlement.

Maureen Todd, 55, took 53-year-old Desmond Congdon to court after he ran out on her 15 months after winning the lottery.

Before the win in 2004 he had moved into her home in Melksham, Wiltshire and promised to marry her.

They signed an agreement that the win would be shared between them but she claimed he took most of the money on what she said was a worldwide gambling spree …

After discussions outside court today, Bernard Weatherill QC, representing Mrs Todd, told the judge: 'The parties have been able to discuss terms to prevent the case from continuing'.

*(Source: taken from an article in the Daily Mail, 17 May 2007)*

## Business agreements

For business agreements the courts start with the presumption that such agreements are legally binding. This means the court assumes that the parties meant to enter into a contract that could be enforced through the courts if one of them did not carry out the contract. This was seen in *McGowan v Radio Buxton* (2001).

## CASE EXAMPLE

### *McGowan v Radio Buxton* (2001)

The claimant entered a radio competition for which the prize had been stated to be a Renault Clio car. The claimant was told she had won the competition but was given a four-inch scale model of a Clio. The defendants argued that there was no legally binding contract. The judge held that there was intention to create legal relations. The claimant had entered the competition as a member of the public and that 'looking at the transcript of the broadcast, there was not even a hint that the car would be a toy'.

However, if one of the parties can show that the parties did not intend the agreement to be a legally binding contract, then the courts may decide that there is no legally binding contract. This happened in *Rose & Frank Co v Crompton* (1925).

## CASE EXAMPLE

### *Rose & Frank Co v Crompton* (1925)

The parties had included in their written agreement the words 'this agreement is not entered into ... as a formal or legal agreement and shall not be subject to legal jurisdiction in the law courts'. It was held that these words made it quite clear that the parties did not mean to be legally bound.

# Binding in honour only

The courts have also held that the phrase 'binding in honour only' means there is no intention to be legally bound. These words appear on football pools coupons, so that when a person enters the football pools competition, he is agreeing that there is no legally binding contract between him and the pools company. This, of course, means that even if he correctly forecasts the results, he cannot sue the company for any winnings if they refuse to pay.

## ACTIVITY

### Activity 3

1. Sarah promises to pay her daughter, Kylie, £20 per week if she will do the household cleaning. Kylie keeps her side of the bargain, but after five weeks Sarah has only paid Kylie £10.

   Advise Kylie as to whether she can claim the money owed.

2. John, a haulage contractor, signs an agreement with Quick Move Ltd under which he is to provide lorries for carrying office furniture. The agreement contains the words: 'This agreement is binding in honour only'.

   Advise John as to the effect of this clause.

Figure 31.1 summarises the way in which courts approach decisions on domestic and business contracts.

| Domestic or Social Agreement | Business Agreement |
|---|---|
| Court starts by presuming that the parties DO NOT intend to be legally bound | Court starts by presuming that the parties DO intend to be legally bound |
| BUT | BUT |
| If there is evidence that the parties DID intend to be legally bound, the court will enforce the contract | If there is evidence that the parties DID NOT intend to be legally bound, the court will not enforce the contract |

**Figure 31.1** Intention to create legal relations

# Misleading statements

In some situations one of the parties may make a statement, which does not become a term of the contract, but which has persuaded the other party to enter into the contract.

Such statements are known as representations. If such a statement is not correct then it is a misrepresentation and the party persuaded by it to make the contract may lose out as a result.

An example of a statement which could persuade a person to make a contract can be seen in the case of *Esso Petroleum Co Ltd v Marden* (1976).

## CASE EXAMPLE

### *Esso Petroleum Co Ltd v Marden* (1976)

Esso were building a new petrol station near a busy road. Marden was interested in leasing it from Esso. During the negotiations for the lease, the representative for Esso stated that the amount of petrol which was likely to be sold in the course of a year was 200,000 gallons. Marden queried this figure, but eventually entered into the lease contract relying on the experience of the ESSO representative about the amount likely to be sold.

In fact the amount sold was never more than 86,502 gallon a year. This made the petrol station uneconomic and Marden lost a lot of money. When Esso sued Marden for rent he owed, he was able to counterclaim for the money he had lost because of the statement about the amount of petrol likely to be sold.

A misleading statement can be made by conduct as shown in the case of *Spice Girls Ltd v Aprilia World* (2000).

## CASE EXAMPLE

### *Spice Girls Ltd v Aprilia World* (2000)

A famous girl group was offered a contract with a scooter manufacturer to promote its products. Before the contract was signed the group filmed a commercial, knowing that one of the group was about to leave. The court held that by doing the commercial, the group

was representing that none of them intended leaving the group and that none of them were aware that one member was gong to leave. Their conduct in attending was a misrepresentation.

The misleading statement or representation must be about a fact and not merely an opinion. It also must be more than an advertising 'puff'. For example if a car salesman claims that a particular make is 'one of the best cars on the market', this is just an advertising 'puff'. However, if he states that the car has a particular type of brake fitted to it, then this is a representation which can be relied on.

## Different types of misrepresentation

The law recognises three different types of misrepresentation. These are:

• false misrepresentation
• negligent misrepresentation, and
• innocent misrepresentation.

The state of mind of the person making the statement is the essential feature in deciding which type of representation a statement is.

### False misrepresentation

This is where the person making the misrepresentation knows that it is not true or does not believe in its truth or is reckless as to whether it is true or not. Being reckless about the truth of a statement is more than just being careless. Essentially a false misrepresentation is one where the person making it is being dishonest.

### Negligent misrepresentation

This is where the maker of the statement is careless about the facts. Perhaps they do not check properly. A negligent misrepresentation can only be made where the person making it has specialist knowledge that the other person has not got. There was a negligent misrepresentation in *Esso Petroleum Co Ltd v Marden* as Esso had vast experience and knowledge of sales patterns which Marden did not.

## Innocent misrepresentation

This is where the maker of the statement honestly believes it is true.

# Remedies for misrepresentation

Where a misrepresentation has been made, the other person usually has a choice of whether or not to stop the contract. This is known as rescinding the contract. The parties are put back in the position they would have been if the contract had never happened.

It may also be possible to claim damages for any loss caused through entering into the contract.

The exact type of remedy available for a misleading statement depends on which type of misrepresentation is involved.

## False misrepresentation

For false representation the innocent party can choose whether to rescind the contract or not and can also claim damages.

## Negligent misrepresentation

The innocent party can choose whether to rescind the contract or whether to go ahead with the contract but claim damages for any loss caused by the contract.

## Innocent misrepresentation

The innocent party can ask for rescission of the contract but the court will decide if this is just in the circumstances. The court may decide to

award damages instead of rescinding the contract.

### Activity 4

Explain with reasons what type of misrepresentation is involved in the following situations.

1. Josh buys a painting from Piers who owns an art gallery. Piers tells Josh that the painting is by a well-known artist. Josh takes the picture to be restored and is told that it is a modern copy and that any experienced art dealer should be able to tell this.

2. Kativa is buying a car from Lee. She asks Lee what the engine capacity is. Lee looks at the registration document of the car and tells her that it is a 2 litre engine. Unknown to Lee the registration document is wrong.

3. Mia, who has only an A level in business studies, tells Naveem at a job interview that she has a degree in business studies.

## BRIEF SUMMARY OF CHAPTER

**Consideration**

■ Both sides must contribute something to the bargain

■ Consideration must be real but need not be adequate

■ Past consideration is NOT good consideration

**Intention to create legal relations**

■ This is presumed in business contracts, but if the parties agree that the contract should not have legal effect, then it will not

■ Social and domestic situations are presumed not be intended to create legal relations but the court will look at all the circumstances

**Misleading statements**

- An incorrect statement which persuades the other person to enter the contract is a misrepresentation
- The law recognises three types of misrepresentation:
  - false misrepresentation
  - negligent misrepresentation, and
  - innocent misrepresentation
- Remedies for misrepresentation are rescission of the contract and/or damages

## EXAMINATION QUESTION

Any contract is only formed when there has been an agreement between two parties. Both parties are bound to give something in exchange. Both parties must also understand that the agreement creates legal obligations which they can enforce against each other.

Place a tick next to the **three** statements below which are accurate descriptions of these rules on the formation of contracts.

(i) A contract is only formed when the agreement is written down.

(ii) An agreement only occurs when one party makes an offer which the other party accepts unconditionally.

(iii) A person offering to sell something to another person can withdraw the offer at any time.

(iv) An agreement to sell a car worth £10,000 for £20 could not be enforced in the courts.

(v) The courts will usually consider that promises made in a business agreement are intended to be enforceable.

(vi) The courts would not usually consider that a promise by a father to pay pocket money to his ten-year-old son is enforceable.

*Part question from OCR Specimen Paper, B144*

# CHAPTER 32

# CONSUMER LAW

Many contracts involve the ordinary person buying goods for personal or family use from shops or other businesses. These are known as consumer contracts. There are also other types of consumer contracts, in particular hire-purchase contracts, contracts to hire goods and contracts for services such as repairing a car or rewiring a house.

The normal rules of contract about offer, acceptance, consideration and capacity apply. At the same time the law recognises that it is necessary to make sure that the consumer is not at a disadvantage when dealing with a business and so there are a number of Acts of Parliament which imply terms into such contracts.

This idea of consumer protection is not new. One of the first Acts passed by Parliament was the Sale of Goods Act 1893. Since then there have been a number of Acts all designed to protect the consumer and in this chapter we are going to look at the main provisions in three of these: the Sale of Goods Act 1979, the Supply of Goods and Services Act 1982 and the Consumer Protection Act 1987.

## Sale of Goods Act 1979

This Act defines a contract of sale of goods as:

**66** a contract by which the seller transfers or agrees to transfer the property in goods to the buyer for a money consideration called the price (s 2). **99**

The word 'goods' means physical items which are moveable, for example furniture, food, cars, clothes, machinery and tools. In order to be covered by the Act it must be intended that the ownership of the item is to be given to the buyer for a sum of money.

It does not matter whether the contract is carried out straightaway, as in the case of buying food in a supermarket, or whether the transfer of the goods is to be carried out in the future, as might happen when furniture is ordered from a shop to be delivered and paid for in two weeks' time. Both these situations are sales of goods covered by the Sale of Goods Act.

The most important sections are sections 12, 13, 14 and 15. These four sections imply certain terms into contracts of sale of goods. An implied term automatically becomes part of the contract even though the parties do not mention it. The terms in these four sections are therefore automatically part of any consumer contract for the sale of goods. Figure 32.1 on page 261 summarises the implied conditions in these four sections.

## Section 12(1) – the right to sell

This section implies a condition that the seller has a right to sell the goods, in other words that the seller can transfer the ownership in the goods to the buyer. This is clearly very important as no-one wants to buy goods only to be told that the goods do not belong to them. This happened in *Rowland v Divall* (1923).

## CASE EXAMPLE

### *Rowland v Divall* (1923)

The claimant bought a car from the defendant. The claimant then discovered that the car had been stolen and so the defendant was not the owner of the car and had no right to sell it. The true owner reclaimed his car and the claimant sued the defendant for a breach of section 12. It was held that the claimant was entitled to get the purchase price back from the defendant.

Section 12 applies to all sales of goods, even where the seller is not acting in the course of business, but is a private person selling just one item.

## Section 13 – goods must match description

Where there is a contract for the sale of goods by description, there is an implied condition that the goods will correspond with (match) the description. This section covers situations where the buyer does not see the goods before he buys them but relies on what is said in an advertisement. It also covers situations where the buyer does see the goods but still relies to some extent on the description.

This happened in *Beale v Taylor* (1967).

## CASE EXAMPLE

### *Beale v Taylor* (1967)

A car was described in an advertisement as 'Herald, convertible white 1961'. The buyer went to see the car and agreed to buy it. The car was later discovered to be the back half of a 1961 model welded to the front half of an older car. Even though the claimant had looked at the car before he bought it, the court held that it was a sale by description and, since only half the car was a 1961 model,

section 13 had been broken. The buyer was able to treat the contract as at an end and claim damages.

Section 13(3) adds that a sale can be a sale by description even in situations where the buyer selects the goods. This covers sales in supermarkets or other shops where the buyer picks the item off the shelf but still relies on the description on the label or the packaging. If a can of drink is labelled 'lemonade' the buyer is relying on that description. There is no other way the buyer can discover what is in the can and so if that can then turns out to contain an orange flavoured drink there is a breach of section 13.

Section 13 applies to all sales by description, private sales as well as those in the course of a business.

## Section 14 – goods must be of satisfactory quality

Where goods are sold in the course of a business there is an implied condition that those goods will be of satisfactory quality.

### Satisfactory quality

Goods are of satisfactory quality if they meet the standard that a reasonable person would regard as satisfactory, taking account of any description of the goods, the price and any other relevant circumstances.

So where jackets, for example, are marked 'seconds' and sold cheaply, they will be of satisfactory quality even if there is a minor fault in the weave of the material. However, they would not be satisfactory if there was a major fault, such as one of the sleeves being missing! The test is an objective test because it is what a reasonable person would regard as satisfactory.

## Fit for purpose

The Act goes on to say that in considering quality an important point is whether the goods are fit for all the purposes for which goods of the kind in question are commonly supplied. A good example is *Priest v Last* (1903).

### CASE EXAMPLE

#### *Priest v Last* (1903)

The item bought was a hot water bottle; the court held that the bottle had to be fit for its obvious purpose of warming a bed. Since the bottle burst when used it was not fit for its normal purpose.

Similarly in *Godley v Perry* (1960) when a boy aged six bought a catapult which broke when he used it, causing an injury to his eye, it was not fit for its normal purpose.

The Sale and Supply of Goods Act 1994 now also includes a list of other points which are covered by the word quality; these are appearance and finish, freedom from minor defects, safety and durability.

## Particular purpose

Section 14(3) says that if the buyer makes known to the seller a particular purpose for which the goods are being bought, then the goods must be fit for that purpose unless the buyer did not rely on the seller's skill and judgement or it is unreasonable for the buyer to rely on the seller's skill and judgement. In buying computer software from a specialist firm, if the buyer asks for a package that is suitable for a particular type of computer, then he has made the purpose of the goods known to the seller and it would be reasonable for him to rely on the seller's skill and judgement.

But it was marked seconds, madam

## Known defects

Section 14 does not apply to any defects to which the seller has specifically drawn the buyer's attention before the contract was made. So, where a second-hand car is for sale and the seller tells the buyer that the clutch is worn and will soon need replacing, the buyer cannot claim that the car is not of satisfactory quality if the clutch goes wrong a few days after the sale.

Section 14 also does not apply where the buyer examines the goods and the defects are ones which that examination ought to reveal. If a shopper before buying a new washing machine examines the outside of it, but fails to notice that there is a bad dent on the front panel, that shopper cannot claim that the dent is a breach of the condition of satisfactory quality. However, if the spin cycle will not work, the shopper can claim there is a breach of section 14 as a visual examination in the shop could not show the fault with the spinner.

## Private sales

Since section 14 only applies to sales in the course of a business, it does not apply to private sales. For example it would not apply where a private individual advertises his or her car for sale. In this case the law has a rule, *caveat emptor*, which means let the buyer beware.

## Rejection of goods

Although section 14 implies a condition, the courts do not always hold that a breach of the condition means that the buyer can treat the contract as ended and reject the goods.

In some cases the courts have held that by using an item for a few weeks the buyer has accepted the goods and lost his right to reject them. Of course the buyer can still claim damages for putting any fault right. The right to reject the goods occurred in *Bernstein v Pamson Motors* (1987).

### CASE EXAMPLE

*Bernstein v Pamson Motors* **(1987)**

The claimant bought a brand new Nissan car. He used it for three weeks, but had only driven 143 miles when a piece of loose sealant caused the engine to seize up. The court held that the defect meant that the car was not of merchantable quality and there was a breach of section 14, but, because the claimant had had the car for three weeks he had accepted it and lost his right to treat the contract as at an end.

In *Rogers v Parish (Scarborough) Ltd* (1987) the buyer was held to have the right to reject the goods.

### CASE EXAMPLE

*Rogers v Parish (Scarborough) Ltd* **(1987)**

The claimant bought a new Range Rover. He found it had a number of faults, but was still driveable. He complained about the faults quickly and the court held he was entitled to treat the contract as at an end and reject the car.

These two cases are difficult to reconcile. A delay of three weeks was enough to lose the right to reject the goods in *Bernstein v Pamson Motors*. Yet the loose sealant caused a major problem with the car and could not have been discovered easily. Also the car had only done 143 miles.

The Sale and Supply of Goods Act 1994 has tried to improve this area for purchasers. Buyers do not lose the right to reject goods just because they sign a delivery note. Nor do they lose the right to reject if they agree to let the seller try to repair them and that repair does not work.

## Section 15 – sale by sample

Where having examined a sample the buyer then orders goods, there are implied conditions that:

(a) the goods must correspond with the sample
(b) the buyer will have a reasonable opportunity to compare the goods with the sample
(c) the goods will not have a hidden defect which would make their quality unsatisfactory.

This section will apply where a shopper chooses a carpet from seeing sample squares. It will also apply where a shop buys in bulk from a supplier after examining a sample. This occurred in *Godley v Perry* (1960).

**CASE EXAMPLE**

### *Godley v Perry* (1960)

A six-year-old boy bought a catapult which broke causing him injury to one eye. The shop which had sold him the catapult claimed against the wholesaler because the shopkeeper had bought the catapults after looking at a sample. He successfully claimed that there was a breach of section 15 since the fault was a hidden defect.

## Excluding sections 12–15

Before 1977 shops and wholesalers often added exclusion clauses to contracts which said that sections 12–15 of the Sale of Goods Act did not apply. (At this time an earlier Act from 1893 was in force, but the sections were basically the same.) By excluding these sections from a contract the whole purpose of consumer protection in the Sale of Goods Act was lost.

In order to make sure that consumers were protected Parliament passed the Unfair Contract Terms Act 1977. This Act, often called UCTA, says that section 12 of the Sale of Goods Act cannot be excluded from any contract for the sale of goods. UCTA also says that sections 13–15 of the Sale of Goods Act cannot be excluded from a consumer sale.

A consumer sale is defined as a sale where the goods are of a type ordinarily supplied for private use or consumption and the seller is selling in the course of a business and the buyer is not buying in the course of business.

So whenever a private individual buys goods which would normally be used for private use, such as a dining table and chairs, or for consumption, such as any food or drink, then this will be a consumer sale, provided the seller is selling in the course of business. However, if someone buys a second-hand car from his neighbour and not from a business, then this is not a consumer sale.

**ACTIVITY**

### Activity 1

Explain whether there is a breach of the Sale of Goods Act in each of the following situations and what remedy, if any, the buyer has.

1. Andrew reads an advertisement, in a newspaper, of a car for sale. It says, 'Ford Fiesta 2006 model, low mileage'. Andrew telephones the seller and agrees to buy the car without seeing it for £4,000. When he takes delivery he finds that the car is an older model than stated in the advert.

2. Banaz agrees to buy some material from a shop after being assured by the sales assistant that the material will not shrink. In fact the material does shrink and is completely unsuitable for the purpose Banaz intended.

3. Charlie buys an umbrella, but when he tries to use it he finds that the catch will not work so that the umbrella will not stay open.

| Section | Implied condition | Comment |
|---------|-------------------|---------|
| 12 | The seller has the right to sell the goods | Cannot be excluded from **any** contract |
| 13 | The goods match their description | Cannot be excluded from consumer sales<br>Can be excluded from private sales |
| 14 | The goods are of satisfactory quality | Cannot be excluded from consumer sales |
| 15 | The goods match sample | Cannot be excluded from consumer sales<br>Can be excluded from private sales |

Figure 32.1 Summary of the implied conditions in the Sale of Goods Act 1979

4. Della buys a brand new car. After 235 miles the car breaks down because a piece of loose sealing compound in the engine cuts off the oil flow causing severe damage to the engine. The dealer offers to repair it free of charge. Della says she wants her money back.

## Supply of services

Contracts for the supply of services cover a very wide range of services. Some examples are repairs to a car by a garage, work done by a plumber or an electrician, painting and decorating, hairdressing, cleaning clothes or providing a hotel room.

The Supply of Goods and Services Act 1982 implies three conditions into any contract for services where the supplier is acting in the course of a business. These are:

1. The supplier will carry out the service with reasonable care and skill.
2. Where the time for the service to be carried out is not fixed, the service will be carried out within a reasonable time.
3. Where the charge for the service has not been agreed, the supplier will be paid a reasonable charge.

These conditions apply whether or not any goods are supplied with the service. However, if goods are supplied then those goods are covered by the implied terms in the Sale of Goods Act 1979.

## 'Reasonable'

All three conditions use the word 'reasonable' and what is reasonable is a question of fact that may vary from one situation to another. Ruining a leather jacket which was sent for cleaning would hardly be 'carrying out the service with reasonable care and skill'; nor would rewiring a socket so badly that the wires shorted and caused a fire.

What is a reasonable time will depend on the amount and difficulty of the work to be done and the length of time normally taken for such work. This is seen in *Charnock v Liverpool Corporation* (1968).

### CASE EXAMPLE

**Charnock v Liverpool Corporation (1968)**

A garage took eight weeks to repair a car when a 'normally competent' repairer would have taken five weeks. It was held that the extra three weeks was an unreasonable delay and the claimant could claim damages from the repairer.

A reasonable charge is again a question of fact. If there is an estimate given before the work is done, then it is almost certainly unreasonable if the supplier tries to charge double the estimate. However, if the supplier at the finish of the work charges 5 per cent more than the original estimate because of rising costs then that is probably reasonable.

If there is no estimate given before the work starts then what is reasonable may be judged by what other reputable firms charge for the same service.

### ACTIVITY

**Activity 2**

Explain which implied condition is relevant in the following situations.

1. Eduin has made a contract with a firm of decorators to paint the outside of his house and repair some of the window frames. The firm gives Eduin an estimate of £1,750 for the work. When the work is finished the firm sends Eduin a bill for £2,800.

2. Freya sends an expensive silk dress to be cleaned by specialist cleaners. When the dress is returned to her she finds that the colour has become faded in patches.

3. Grant has had an accident with his car in which the side panels were badly dented. He agrees with a car body work shop that they will beat out the panels and re-spray the car. He takes the car to them on 5th May. He is told the repairs should be completed in ten days' time. In fact the car is not repaired and ready to be returned to Grant until 7th June.

## Consumer Protection Act 1987

The Consumer Protection Act 1987 gives consumers wider protection in relation to faulty goods than the Sales of Goods Act 1979.

The Act is important because it allows claims by any consumer, not just by the buyer. This means that someone who has been given a present may be able to claim for damage caused by defects in the present, whereas under the Sale of Goods Act that person has no rights as he is not the buyer.

It also allows for a claim against a wider range of defendants. So, if the manufacturer has gone out of business, it is possible to claim against the supplier.

A claim can be brought under the Act where *'any damage is caused wholly or partly by a defect in a product'*.

So what products are covered and what is meant by defect?

## Products

A product is defined in the Act as *'any goods or electricity'*. It includes any product which is part of another. For example, the engine of a car is considered a product in its own right even though it is part of the car.

The important point is that the goods must have been manufactured or won or abstracted (eg coal from a mine).

Products which are not included are:

• fresh food which has not been processed in any way
• buildings
• nuclear power.

## Defect

A product has a defect if *'the safety of the product is not such as persons generally are entitled to expect'*.

The defect can be:

• in design
• in processing or manufacturing
• in instructions or a lack of warning that means the product may be used, installed or assembled in an unsafe way.

In deciding whether the safety of the product is not such as persons generally are entitled to expect, the court can take into account the manner in which and the purposes for which a product has been marketed and also any labels, instructions or warnings attached to the product.

For example, many toys have the notice 'Not suitable for children aged under three' written on them. So the product should be safe for use by older children.

The court can also consider what might reasonably be done with a product. For example, a microwave can be reasonably used for cooking any food, but it is not reasonable to use it to dry a pet.

## 'Producer'

Where there is a defect, the consumer has a right to sue the 'producer'.

Under the Consumer Protection Act producer includes:

- the actual manufacturer
- those abstracting the product
- those applying an industrial or other process to the goods
- own-branders, that is any company which labels goods under its own brand name, even if the goods were made for it by another company
- any person who imports goods into the European Union countries when the goods were manufactured outside the European Union.

The supplier of a product, that is the seller, can also be sued. However, this can only be done where the consumer has asked the supplier to identify either a 'producer' or an importer and the supplier has not done so. The supplier becomes liable because the consumer cannot identify the producer or importer.

Let's look at examples of these categories.

## Manufacturer

The actual manufacturer obviously includes the business that makes the product. It also includes any business that assembles the product, even if they do not make any of the parts for it. Finally it includes businesses which produce the raw materials from which the product is made.

## Abstracter

Those abstracting the product refers to those mining for coal or extracting other minerals from the ground.

## Applying an industrial process

Those applying an industrial or other process to the goods are only within the Act if what they are doing is adding to the essential characteristic of the product. An obvious example is freezing vegetables.

## Own-branders

Own-branders are businesses which put their own brand name on a product. This happens a lot with supermarkets. If you go into your local Tesco's, Sainsbury's, Waitrose or Marks and Spencer and look at food products, you will find items on the shelves with the supermarkets' own name.

Quite often these products are made for the big supermarkets by smaller manufacturing companies. Under the Consumer Protection Act the own-brander is liable for defective products as well as the company that manufactured the product.

## Importers

The importer of products from outside the EU into the EU is also liable. This is because it would be impossible to sue a business on the other side of the world. The importer is getting the profits from selling the imported goods and so must bear liability for any defective products.

## Damage

In order to claim the consumer must show that the product caused damage.

Damage includes:

- death
- any injury caused by the defective product
- loss of property or damage to property but only if that loss or damage amounts to at least £275.

It does NOT include:

- damage to property under £275
- damage to business property
- damage to the product itself.

# Defences

The Consumer Protection Act lists defences which are available to the supplier. The defences available are:

- that the product complies with statutory or EU standards
- the defect did not exist at the time it was supplied by the defendant
- the product was not supplied in the course of business
- the defendant did not supply the product to anyone
- the state of scientific and technical knowledge at the time of production meant the defendant could not be expected to have discovered the defect.

# Comment on the Consumer Protection Act

The Act has given greater rights to consumers who are injured or whose property is damaged. They have a wider range of potential defendants to choose from. So, if a manufacturer has gone out of business, then the supplier can be sued.

This is also important where goods have been imported from a non-EU country. It would be very difficult to make a claim against the manufacturers in another country, but the Act gives the right to claim against the importer.

The Act has also made producers more careful. They have stricter checking and quality controls. They are also likely to recall products if any defect is discovered.

The main criticism of the Act is that it allows so many defences. This can make it difficult for the claimant to succeed. The Act is meant to create what is known as strict liability, but the number of defences mean this has not happened.

It is also difficult for the claimant to show that the defect was in the product when it came into their possession.

A comparison of the rights under the consumer protection laws is set out in Figure 32.2

## ACTIVITY

### Activity 3

Explain whether or not a claim could be brought under the Consumer Protection Act 1987 in the following situations.

| | Sale of Goods | Supply of Goods and Services | Consumer Protection |
|---|---|---|---|
| A buys a faulty iron, which causes a fire | Right against seller (s 14) | – | Right against producer if damage more than £275 |
| B's car is serviced badly and a defective brake pad is fitted causing a crash in which B is injured | Right against garage (s 14) for brake pad | Right against garage for bad workmanship | Right against producer |
| C buys a doll for her child, D, who is injured by the wire used for attaching the arms of the doll | C has right against seller | – | D has right against producer |

Figure 32.2 Comparing the rights under the consumer protection laws

1. Sidra's mother buys a new pushchair to give to Sidra to use for her one-year-old daughter. The second time that Sidra uses the pushchair, one of the metal bars comes loose and her daughter is thrown out of the chair and injured.

2. Tristan buys a box of fireworks which has a notice on it saying 'Not suitable for indoor use'. Tristan and his friend, Wyn, decide to light one of the smaller fireworks indoors. Wyn is badly burned as a result.

3. Zoë buys a new desk which needs to be put together from a kit. The desk comes with instructions on how to assemble it. Zoë follows these carefully and the desk appears to be alright. The next day when she is using her computer on the desk, one side of the desk collapses and the computer is thrown to the floor and damaged beyond repair. There was a mistake in the assembly instructions.

## BRIEF SUMMARY OF CHAPTER

**Sale of Goods Act 1979**

■ implies terms into contracts:
- s 12 right to sell
- s 13 must match description
- s 14 must be of satisfactory quality and fit for their purpose
- s 15 must match sample
- s 12 cannot be excluded from any contract for the sale of goods
- ss 13–15 cannot be excluded from consumer contracts

**Supply of Goods and Services Act 1982**

■ implies terms into contracts for supply of goods (other than when sold) and into contracts for services

■ Supply of goods has the same terms as for sale of goods

■ For supply of services there are three terms:
- reasonable care and skill
- reasonable time where no time is fixed
- reasonable price where no price is fixed

**Consumer Protection Act 1987**

■ gives rights to buyers and users when goods are defective

**A defect can be:**

■ a defect in design

■ a defect in processing or manufacturing

■ a defect in instruction or a lack of warning about possible dangers

**Making a claim**

■ To make a successful claim the product must have caused personal injury or financial damage of at least £275

■ **Can claim against:**
- the actual manufacturer
- those abstracting the product
- those applying an industrial process to the goods
- own-branders
- importers

## EXAMINATION QUESTION

1. Read each of the following three situations and complete activity **a)** and activity **b)** which follow them.

   (i) Danielle bought a new pair of trainers from a shoe shop. Danielle told the assistant that she would use the trainers to train for, and to run in, cross-country races. The assistant assured Danielle that the trainers were suitable for such use. The trainers fell apart the first time that Danielle wore them for training but the shoe shop is refusing to give Danielle her money back.

   (ii) Enrique contracted with a building firm to build a small extension on the back of his kitchen. The contract made no mention of the price of the building work but the building firm has now presented Enrique with a bill for £50,000. The usual price for this type and size of extension is £15,000.

(iii) Francoise bought a car from a motor dealer which was described as 'mechanically perfect'. The first time Francoise drove the car it broke down and she has now discovered that the engine in fact needed replacing when she bought the car.

(a) Identify which statutory implied term is involved in each of the above situations.
  (i)   Danielle
  (ii)  Enrique
  (iii) Francoise                    (3 marks)

(b) Explain how the implied term has been breached in each situation **(i)**, **(ii)** and **(iii)** and say what right(s) each person now has.
  (i)   Danielle
  (ii)  Enrique
  (iii) Francoise                    (9 marks)

*Part question from OCR Specimen Paper, B144*

2.  The Consumer Protection Act 1987 concerns product safety. People can use the Act to recover compensation for damage caused by unsafe products but certain types of damage or loss are not covered by the Act.

Identify **three** types of damage or loss which **are not** covered by the Act.    (3 marks)

The Consumer Protection Act 1987 classes defendants as **'producers'**, **'importers'**, and **'own branders'** which covers virtually everyone in the chain of manufacture or distribution of the defective goods. A variety of people can be classed as 'producers' under the Act.

Write either **'producer'**, **'importer'**, or **'own brander'** for each description below.

A person who manufactures the defective goods

A person who claims the defective goods to be their own product and gives no indication that they are made by someone else

A person who extracts minerals from the ground

A person who brings the defective goods into the country from a country outside the European Union

A person who carries out an industrial process on the defective goods eg freezing vegetables

A person who assembles component parts into the finished defective product   (6 marks)

*Part question from OCR Specimen Paper, B144*

# CHAPTER 33

# EXCLUSION CLAUSES

It is possible to include a term in a contract so that one party can avoid liability in the event of certain things happening.

Most car parks have notices saying, 'Cars parked at owners' risk'. This is an exclusion clause in the contract the car driver made with the parking firm when the owner paid to park his or her car. If the car is damaged while in the car park, the owner will not be able to make a claim against the car park firm.

Neither the courts nor Parliament like the use of exclusion clauses and both have developed strict rules about their use.

## Unfair Contract Terms Act 1977

Parliament has passed the Unfair Contract Terms Act 1977 which limits the use of exclusion clauses. The most important limitations are that:

- an exclusion clause cannot restrict liability for death or serious injury resulting from negligence
- liability for other loss or damage can only be restricted if the exclusion clause is reasonable
- in consumer contracts (see Chapter 32) an exclusion clause cannot prevent liability for a breach where the contractual performance is substantially different from that which was reasonably expected.

The fact that liability for death or serious injury cannot be excluded means that a car park firm could be liable if a car driver was seriously injured in their car park.

This would be the case even though there was a notice saying, 'Cars parked at owners' risk'. Such a notice can exclude liability for damage to property, so the car park firm would not be liable for any damage to a car.

To avoid liability for other loss or damage the exclusion clause must be reasonable. An example of a clause being held to be unreasonable occurred in *Woodman v Photo Trade Processing* (1981).

### CASE EXAMPLE

**Woodman v Photo Trade Processing (1981)**

Wedding photographs were ruined and the processing company tried to rely on a clause in the contract which said that their liability was limited to replacing the film. The court held that this clause was unreasonable and the claimant could recover damages for disappointment as well as the cost of the film.

The idea of contractual performance being substantially different from that which was reasonably expected can be illustrated by an example of a contract with a garage to re-spray the whole of your car. If the garage re-sprays all of the car but paints the roof a different colour to the rest of the car, this would be substantially different from what you expected them to do. The garage could not rely on any exclusion clause to avoid liability.

The exclusion clause must be clear. If it is too vague or if a claimant asks what it means and is told it only covers certain things, then it cannot be relied on to exclude liability. This happened in *Curtis v Chemical Cleaning and Dyeing Co Ltd* (1951).

## CASE EXAMPLE

### *Curtis v Chemical Cleaning and Dyeing Co Ltd* (1951)

The claimant took a wedding dress to be cleaned. She was asked to sign a document that said the company has no liability for any damage 'howsoever caused'. She asked what this meant and was told that the company did not accept liability damage to beads or sequins attached to the dress.

When the dress was returned to her, it had a chemical stain on it. She claimed for this damage. The defendants tried to rely on the exemption clause, but the court held they could not because of what has been said to the claimant about the only exempt damage being to beads or sequins.

## ACTIVITY

### Activity 1

Look at the two pictures below. Both are of notices excluding liability in car parks. Answer the following questions.

1. What is the important difference in the wording of the two notices?
2. Does the Unfair Contracts Terms Act 1977 limit either or both of these exclusion notices? Give reasons for your answer.

## Consumer sales

Another way in which Parliament has prevented the use of exclusion clauses is in section 6 of the Unfair Contract Terms Act 1977. This section stops sellers in consumer sales from excluding liability for breach of any of the implied terms in sections 12–15 of the Sale of Goods Act 1979.

In fact the implied condition as to title in s 12 cannot be excluded from any contract for sale, whether it is a business or consumer sale.

## Notice of the clause

Where the exclusion clause is not forbidden by Parliament, the courts have developed rules to try and control their use. The main rule is that the clause must be brought to the other party's notice before they enter into the contract. This was shown by *Olley v Marlborough Court Hotel* (1949).

## CASE EXAMPLE

### *Olley v Marlborough Court Hotel* (1949)

A couple booked into a hotel. The contract with the hotel was formed at that point. After they had booked in, they went to their room and in the room was a notice saying, 'The proprietors will not hold themselves responsible for articles lost or stolen unless handed to the manageress for safe custody'. The woman's furs were stolen from her hotel room. She claimed their value from the hotel and the hotel had to pay her. They could not rely on the exclusion notice since it had not been communicated to the couple before they made the contract.

The clause must be sufficiently brought to the claimant's notice before or at the time of the contract being made. If the contract is made through a machine where the claimant puts money in and a ticket is issued, then it is not sufficient to have the exclusion clause on the ticket issued by the machine.

The contract is made by then and, as it was through a machine, there is no way the claimant can negotiate about the clause with the machine or demand his or her money back. This was decided in *Thornton v Shoe Lane Parking Ltd* (1971).

## CASE EXAMPLE

### *Thornton v Shoe Lane Parking Ltd* (1971)

The claimant drove into a car park. He had to stop at a barrier, pay money into a machine and take a ticket from the machine. The barrier then opened to let him drive in. On the ticket was printed the words: 'This ticket is issued subject to the conditions of issue as displayed on the premises'. Notices inside the car park listed the conditions which included an exclusion clause covering both damage and personal injury.

The claimant was injured and claimed against the defendant. The defendant tried to rely on the exclusion clause, but the clause was held not to be effective. This was because the claimant could not know what the conditions were until after he had paid to park.

To make sure that exclusion clauses are effective, most car parks have the clause clearly printed on a board by the ticket machine or on the machine itself. In this way a person paying to

park their car will see the clause before they pay. This makes the clause effective for excluding damage to property.

Where the claimant has paid an employee of the defendant, then the clause may be printed on a receipt, but it must be properly brought to the claimant's attention. If the receipt is only a very small ticket then the clause may not be effective unless it is pointed out. This was decided in *Chapelton v Barry Urban District Council* (1940).

## CASE EXAMPLE

### *Chapelton v Barry Urban District Council* (1940)

The claimant hired two deckchairs and received two small tickets for this from the beach attendant. The claimant thought these tickets were just receipts. He did not look at the back of them on which was printed 'The council will not be liable for any accident or damage arising from the hire of the chair'.

The canvas on one of the chairs was defective and the chair collapsed injuring the claimant. The claimant sued the council. The council tried to rely in the exclusion clause on the back of the ticket. They could not rely on it as it had not been effectively brought to the attention of the claimant.

Note that both *Thornton v Shoe Lane Parking Ltd* (1971) and *Chapelton v Barry Urban District Council* (1940) were cases decided before the Unfair Contract Terms Act 1977 prevented exclusion clauses from excluding liability for injury. The defendants would be liable now even if the clause had been drawn to the claimant's notice.

## Previous dealings

Where the parties have dealt with each other before, the courts sometimes decide that the claimant has knowledge of the exclusion clause from the previous contracts.

The more previous contracts the parties have had the more likely the court is to decide that the claimant has knowledge of the exclusion clause. In one case the parties had had about 100 similar contracts over the previous three years.

Where the exclusion clause is one normally used in a certain trade, the court may decide that the claimant has knowledge of the exclusion clause even though there have only been two or three previous contracts between them. This only applies where both parties are businesses as they know the normal trade custom.

If one party is a business and the claimant is an individual consumer, then the courts are much more unwilling to enforce any exclusion clause, even though the consumer has had previous dealings with that business. This happened in *Hollier v Rambler Motors (AMC) Ltd* (1972).

### CASE EXAMPLE

#### *Hollier v Rambler Motors (AMC) Ltd* (1972)

The claimant left his car with a garage as he had done on four or five previous occasions. He did not sign any contract, although he had done on previous occasions. The contract contained an exclusion clause for damage to customers' cars while on the premises. Hollier's car was damaged by a fire caused by the defendants' negligence.

The garage tried to rely on the exclusion clause on the basis that Hollier knew of the exclusion clause from previous dealings. The court held that the term had not become a part of the contract.

### Signed contracts

Where a party signs a written contract he or she agrees to all the terms that are written down. This is so even if he or she does not read those terms. This happened in *L'Estrange v Graucob* (1934).

### CASE EXAMPLE

#### *L'Estrange v Graucob* (1934)

The claimant bought a vending machine from the defendant. The parties had a written contract which the claimant signed without reading it. The contract contained a clause excluding all implied terms (this included terms implied under the Sale of Goods Act 1893).

The machine was unsatisfactory and the claimant sued the defendant. It was held that the exclusion clause was effective even though the claimant had not read it. The defendants could rely on the clause and were not liable to the claimant.

This means that if there is an exclusion clause printed in the contract, then, unless it is one of those forbidden by Parliament, that exclusion clause will be valid. Sometimes this is referred to as the 'small print', since often the terms are printed in tiny letters. This does not matter. If you sign a contract you are assumed to be agreeing to all the terms written in it and will be bound by them.

The exception to this is where a term is unfair under the Unfair Terms in Consumer Contracts Regulations 1999. These regulations apply only to consumer contracts.

### Unfair Terms in Consumer Contracts Regulations 1999

These Regulations prevent businesses unfairly excluding liability in what are known as standard form contracts. These are contracts in which the business sets out all the terms which it always uses in that type of situation and the customer has to agree to those terms or not make a contract with that business.

The Regulations state that a term is unfair if:

- it is not in plain language
- the consumer's obligations are much heavier than those of the business
- the consumer does not have a real chance of seeing the goods before making the contract, for example where goods are ordered by telephone.

The Regulations only apply to contracts between businesses and consumers.

## The importance of restricting exclusion clauses

Where there is a contract between a business and an individual consumer it is important that the consumer is protected. If businesses could exclude liability as they liked, then consumers would have no rights.

Businesses would be able to exclude liability for causing death or injury. A consumer who was injured through the fault of the business would not be able to claim. If a consumer were killed as a result of negligence, the family of the consumer would not be able to make any claim.

Businesses could also exclude all liability for shoddy and defective goods or poor service, so consumers would have no rights.

Consumers would be unable to enforce rights given in other statutes. For example, if it was possible to exclude liability for not owning the goods, then consumers would have no guarantee that the business owned the goods and had a right to sell them. The rights given in section 12 of the Sale of Goods Act 1979 would be lost.

Businesses would be able to avoid liability for breaching the contract.

## BRIEF SUMMARY OF CHAPTER

**An exclusion clause**

- is a term excluding liability; certain terms cannot be excluded in consumer contracts

**The Unfair Contract Terms Act 1977**

- places limits on exclusion clauses:
  - cannot restrict liability for death or serious injury resulting from negligence
  - liability for other loss or damage can only be restricted if the exclusion clause is reasonable
  - cannot exclude liability in consumer contracts for substantially different performance of the contract
- If the other party does not have notice of the exclusion clause before or at the time of making the contact then the clause is not effective
- Notice of the clause can be through previous dealings
- Where a party has signed the contract the exclusion clause will be effective, even if they did not read it

**Unfair Terms in Consumer Contracts Regulations 1999**

- prevent businesses from unfairly excluding liability in standard form contracts
- A term is unfair if:
  - it is not in plain language
  - the consumer's obligations are much heavier than those of the business
  - the consumer does not have a real chance of seeing the goods before making the contract

## EXAMINATION QUESTION

Read the following passage and complete the activities **(a)** and **(b)**:

Exemption clauses are included in contracts, usually by sellers of goods or providers of services, with the purpose of avoiding or limiting their liability for their breaches of contract or sometimes for their negligence. Judges have tried to prevent the unfair consequences of this type of term by insisting that the clause cannot stand unless it was fully incorporated into the contract. This means that the other party must be fully aware of the clause when the contract is formed.

(a) Place a tick next to the **three** clauses listed below which will **not** be considered to be part of the contract.

A   A clause exempting liability for breach of contract which is contained in a document to be signed by both parties.

B   A clause exempting liability for damage to goods in a delivery note (which is not the contract) where the parties have always contracted on the same terms for many years.

C   A clause exempting liability for loss or damage to clients' goods in a hotel. Clients sign in at the desk but the clause is on a notice inside their hotel room.

D   A clause exempting liability for damage to cars in a multi-storey car park. The clause is displayed on the back of the ticket which comes out of the machine which lifts the barrier for entry to the car park.

E   A clause exempting liability for injury on the back of a cinema ticket.

F   A clause exempting liability for negligent work contained in a receipt for payment for decorating work. It is the practice of the decorating firm to ask all customers to read the receipt before paying their bills.

(3 marks)

(b) Terry took his suit to the dry cleaners. The assistant gave him a small ticket to produce when he returned to collect the suit. When he did return the suit was ruined. It had chemical stains down the front of the jacket; the trouser zip was broken; and the cloth around the zip was badly torn. The assistant said that the cleaners were not liable and showed him small writing on the back of the ticket which read 'See conditions'. She then pointed to a sign on the back wall of the shop listing the conditions which included 'the management accept no liability for clothes damaged during the dry cleaning process'.

Briefly explain why Terry will **not** be bound by this condition. (3 marks)

(c) Parliament protected consumers in the Unfair Contract Terms Act 1977 by making certain clauses in consumer contracts invalid and unenforceable.

Identify **three** types of exemption clause which will be unenforceable under the Act. (3 marks)

(d) Both the courts and Parliament have introduced controls on exemption clauses. Consumers are particularly protected because they contract on unequal terms with businesses.

Explain some of the possible consequences for consumers if they did not have these protections when it comes to exemption clauses.

*OCR Specimen Paper*

# CHAPTER 34

# EMPLOYMENT LAW: CONTRACTS OF EMPLOYMENT

## Distinguishing between employed and self-employed

The first important point to decide is whether someone is employed or whether they are self-employed. Most situations are obvious. For example sales assistant in shops, bus and train drivers, teachers in a school or a college are all in employment. In each case there is an employer:

| Employee | Employer |
|---|---|
| Sales assistant | Business or person owning the shop |
| Bus driver | Business or person running the bus service |
| Train driver | Rail company running the train |
| Teacher | School or college in which they teach |

Figure 34.1

In other situations, it may be obvious that the person is self-employed, for example a private tutor who gives tuition to several individual people, each for an hour or two each week, or a lorry driver who owns his own lorry, transports a variety of products for different people and arranges the loads he will carry.

However, there are some situations where it is more difficult to decide whether a person is employed or self-employed. There are many points to be considered. Some of these are:

1. How is the work to be paid for? An employee will receive regular wages, while a self-employed person will usually receive a lump sum.
2. How is income tax and National Insurance dealt with? An employer must deduct these from an employee's wages, but will not make deductions from any monies paid to an independent contractor; a self-employed person must pay his or her own tax and insurance.
3. Who supplies the tools and equipment used? Self-employed people will usually provide their own.
4. Is the work being done as an integral part of the employer's business? If so, that person is probably an employee; a self-employed person is more likely to be doing work that is an accessory to the employer's business, but is not integrated into that business.

## Tests of employment

As we have seen the courts will consider several points in trying to decide if a person is employed or not and through this they have developed different tests. The main tests are the:

• control test
• organisation or integration test
• economic reality test (or multiple test)
• self-description test.

### Control test

This looks at whether the employer has overall control of the work done. Can the employer tell the person what to do, how to do it or when to do it? The greater the degree of control the more likely it is that the other is an employee. If the individual worker decides what to do, how to do it and when to do it, then this is probably a self-employed situation.

## Organisation or integration test

Under this the key test is: is the person part and parcel of the organisation? This test is important where the employee is highly-skilled and makes decisions about what and how to do the work.

Under the control test it is possible that such a person could be regarded as self-employed. But under the organisational test, the person will be considered employed if what they are doing is part and parcel of the organisation.

## Economic reality test (or multiple test)

Under this test several points are looked at. These are:

- has the person agreed to provide work and skill for wages?
- is there an express or implied submission by the person to control?
- is there anything inconsistent with an employed situation?

This test takes all factors into account.

- What degree of control is there?
- Is there an obligation to do work?
- Who provides the tools or other equipment for work?
- How are the tax and National Insurance payments made?
- Is the person free to do other work?
- Are there any rules about holiday entitlement?

The court will make a decision after considering all these points.

## Self-description test

Is the person performing services in business on his or her own account? Or in simpler words – 'Are you your own boss?' If so, then under this test, there is strong evidence that it is a self-employed situation.

## Differences between employees and self-employed

It is important to establish whether a person is employed or whether they are self-employed. Employed people have wider rights than the self-employed.

Employees enjoy protection from redundancy and unfair dismissal. They also have maternity or paternity rights. Self-employed do not have these.

Employers owe employees a high level of care under health and safety laws. Self-employed are considered to have the expertise to guard their own safety, so there is a lower duty of care.

There are also administrative differences. Employed people have their tax deducted from their pay by the employer. Self-employed have to make their own payments, though this does mean that they can set off certain business expenses against tax.

Employers deduct the employee's National Insurance from pay and send these in. They also pay an employer's contribution to National Insurance. This has the effect that employed people will usually receive greater benefits and pension.

Whether someone is an employee or self-employed can also be important to other people. It becomes important when someone's negligence in the course of their work injures another person. If the negligence is by an employee, then the injured person can claim against the employer under the principle of vicarious liability (see Chapter 18). If the negligence is by a self-employed person, then the only claim is against that person.

This is important because an employer is more likely to be fully insured against claims and/or to have the financial means to pay the claim. Whereas, if you sue an individual, they may have no means of paying any claim. So you may not be able to get any compensation.

Figure 34.2 shows these points.

## ACTIVITY

### Activity 1

State with reasons whether the people in the following scenarios are employed or self-employed.

1. Fatima is at college and works on Saturdays at a local shop. She is paid £7.50 an hour. She does not earn enough to pay tax or National Insurance.

2. Greg is a painter and decorator. He gets most of his work through High Quality Decorators Ltd, a company. He is told what work they want him to do. Greg has his own van, ladder and paint brushes, but High Quality Decorators Ltd provide the paint for each job. They pay him a lump sum for each job and do not deduct tax or National Insurance from the money they pay him.

3. Jodie is a hairdresser. She goes to people's homes to cut or style their hair. Each person pays her separately.

## Contracts of employment

Where a person is employed, they will have a contract of employment.

The main rules of contract set out in Chapters 30 and 31 apply to contracts of employment. They are formed in the same way as any other contract: there must be an offer and an acceptance. The contract can be in writing or made verbally or even by conduct.

The difference between contracts of employment and other contracts is that the parties do not have the same freedom to include any terms they wish. In particular there are

| | EMPLOYEES | SELF-EMPLOYED |
|---|---|---|
| Statutory employment rights | Are protected in many ways, eg<br>• unfair dismissal<br>• redundancy<br>• maternity rights | Have very few protections |
| Health and safety | High level of care owed to employees | Low level of care<br>Are considered to have expertise to safeguard their own health and safety |
| Taxation | Deducted from pay by employer | Submit annual accounts and pay tax themselves |
| National Insurance | Deducted from pay by employer<br>Employer also pays NI contribution | Pay own<br>Usually only entitled to lower welfare benefits and pension |
| Vicarious liability | An employer is liable for negligence by an employee and can be sued by the person injured | Person injured will have to sue the self-employed person<br><br>Less likely to get claim fully paid |

Figure 34.2 Differences between employed and self-employed

several rules about employees' rights and also when and how a contract of employment can be ended.

Parliament has passed many laws affecting employment and most of these laws are designed to protect the employee. This chapter and Chapters 35, 36 and 37 will consider some of these laws about employment.

## Written particulars of employment

Although the contract does not have to be in writing, the employer must provide the employee with written particulars of employment. These have to be given to all employees who work for at least one month for the employer. They must also be given within two months of the employment starting.

The main points that have to be included in the written particulars of employment are:

- the names of the employer and employee
- the date when the employment started
- the job title **or** a brief description of the work
- the place of work **or** a statement that the employee is expected to work at various places
- hours of work
- the scale or rate of pay
- the intervals at which the pay is paid (ie weekly, monthly etc)
- holiday entitlement
- sick pay provision, if any
- pension and pension schemes, if any
- the length of notice which the employee is obliged to give and receive to end the contract of employment
- if the contract is for a fixed term, the date on which it ends
- details of disciplinary rules and procedure
- grievance procedure.

These particulars are NOT the contract of employment. The contract for employment may have been made verbally, but the particulars contain evidence of the terms of the contract. The parties can, of course, make additional terms about other matters.

If the employer refuses to provide an employee with written particulars, the employee has the right to apply to an Employment Tribunal for an order that the employer do so. Alternatively the employee can ask the Tribunal to decide the terms of employment.

## Terms of the contract

The parties will agree the main terms of the contract of employment. However, other terms will be imposed by the courts in order to protect employees. For example, there is an implied term that the employer must provide a safe system of work (see Chapter 36).

There are also statutory terms which affect contracts of employment. For example, there are minimum lengths of the notice which is given to end the employment. These are that the employer must give:

- at least one week's notice to anyone who has been employed between four weeks and two years
- an extra week for every year over two years that the employee has worked up to a maximum of 12 weeks.

The parties can agree longer periods and it is not unusual for a contract of employment with a skilled person to have a notice period of three or even six months.

The written particulars of the contract should also have the length of notice the employee must give the employer when terminating the contract of employment. If there is no period given then the law states that an employee will have to give one week's notice. Of course, where the parties have agreed a longer term, for example one month, then that is the length of notice.

## BRIEF SUMMARY OF CHAPTER

**Tests of employment**

- control test
- organisation or integration test
- economic reality test (or multiple test)
- self-description test

**Rights and responsibilities of employment**

- Employees have wider rights than self-employed and are protected from unfair dismissal
- Employers owe a duty of care to their employees
- Employers are vicariously liable for the acts of their employees

**Contract of employment**

- agreed by parties
- some terms imposed by law

**Written particulars of employment**

- must be given by the employer to the employee

## EXAMINATION QUESTION

In written contracts of employment basic information such as the name of the employer, the name of the employee and the start date must be included.

Identify **three** other pieces of information which an employer **must** include in an employee's written contract of employment.

(3 marks)

*Part question, OCR Specimen Question B143*

# CHAPTER 35

# EMPLOYMENT LAW: DISCRIMINATION

The law makes various different types of discrimination at work unlawful. Employers are not allowed to discriminate against employees or applicants for jobs on the grounds of:

- sex
- race
- disability
- sexual orientation
- age
- religion.

## Equal pay

The Equal Pay Act 1970 makes it unlawful to discriminate between men and women in any area of their pay. This includes overtime or bonuses as well as the basic pay.

The basic test under the Act is that there must be equal pay for:

- the same work
- like work
- work rated as equivalent
- work of equal value.

## Comparators

Where men and women are doing the same work for a business, then they should receive equal pay. If they do not, the woman can make a complaint that she is not receiving equal pay as a man doing the same work.

In order to decide if the complaint is justified, the work the woman is doing will be compared to that of a man working for the same or an associated employer. The person her pay is being compared with is known as the 'comparator'.

If her pay is lower than the comparator's pay then the complaint will be upheld and the business ordered to pay her equal wages and to compensate her for the period she was receiving lower wages.

This is easy to apply where the same work is being done. But it can also apply even though the people were not employed at the same time. This is clearly illustrated by the case of *Diocese of Hallam Trustees v Connaughten* (1996).

### CASE EXAMPLE

**Diocese of Hallam Trustees v Connaughten (1996)**

Josephine Connaughten was employed as director of music by the Diocese of Hallam from 1990 to September 1994, at which time her salary was £11,138. When she left the position, the post was advertised at a salary of £13,434, but the successful applicant, a man, was actually appointed at a salary of £20,000. It was held that the there could be a comparison of the two, even though they were not employed at the same time.

Nowadays we would expect people doing the same work to be paid the same. The only differences might be for experience or additional qualifications. However, at one time it was common for women to be paid less than men even though they were just as well qualified as the men they worked alongside.

The following newspaper article shows how attitudes have changed.

**Woman found her way to equal pay in a torpedo tube**

Being 4ft 11in paid off for Edith Kent. Her diminutive stature meant that she could crawl inside torpedo tubes – and helped her to become the first woman in Britain to earn the same wage as her male colleagues while working as a welder during the Second World War.

Mrs Kent began working at Devonport dockyard in Plymouth in 1941 but was so good that she received wage parity in 1943 – which was unheard of at the time.

Starting on five pounds and six shillings (£5.30) a week as a skilled female worker, she was soon given a rise to £6.30. A male manual worker in 1943 would have been on a weekly wage of only £5.42½.

Mrs Kent, who still lives near the dockyard, said she was extremely proud of her achievement but she was embarrassed at the time.

She said: 'I got the job because my brothers worked at the dockyard and they thought I would be good at it. I was the first woman to work as a welder there. It made me a bit uncomfortable that I was the first woman to earn the same as the men – and in some cases I was earning more than them.'

*(Source: taken from an article in The Times, 27 November 2008)*

## ACTIVITY

### Activity 1

Read the extract above and answer the following questions:

1. What work did Mrs Kent do in the Second World War?

2. What wage did she get at the start and what was this increased to?

3. What was the normal wage for a male manual worker in 1943?

4. What points in this article show the attitudes of people to women's wages in 1943?

## Like work

This is where there is no male employee doing exactly the same job, but there are men doing work of the same or broadly similar nature. As there is no man doing exactly the same job, there cannot be a real comparator. In this case the tribunals and courts are allowed to use a hypothetical comparator. This means they imagine one and work out what that imaginary male comparator would be earning in the job in order to have a comparison to use for the woman.

## Work rated as equivalent

This can only be used where the employer has had a job evaluation study carried out. If the job evaluation has found that the work should be rated as the same value, then women doing that work should be paid the same as men doing the work it was evaluated against.

This allows a comparison to be made in situations where the work is quite different. For example the work done by women as cooks in a canteen can be evaluated against work done by men operating certain machinery.

## Work of equal value

This where the work done by women is of the same value to the employer as work done by men.

As there are no other ways of comparing whether there should be equal pay, this allows the tribunal to assess whether the work is of equal value to the employer. An ACAS expert can be appointed to help decide this. A successful claim will be based on study of the work carried out by men and women and grading of those jobs.

## Comment on equal pay

Today we expect that women will receive equal pay for equal work, and in most areas this does happen. For example, men and women working on the same jobs in a supermarket are paid the same wage. Doctors in the health service receive the salary due for their level of job and experience. There is no difference between men and women in pay.

However, even though the Equal Pay Act was passed in 1970, women on average still earn less than men. Women are also less likely to be found in the high ranks of business and the professions. This is partly because women take career breaks to have children, but it suggests that there is still lack of equality.

Even in the legal profession, it has been found that there is not true equality in pay. This was shown by a survey conducted by the Law Society's Strategic Research Unit in 2007.

This found that the average yearly salary for male solicitors in 2007 was £60,000 but for women it was £41,000. When factors such as grade, firm size, region, post-qualification experience, hours worked, plus work breaks and area of law were taken into account, the pay gap was not as marked. However, even where all factors were taken into account, women were still found on average to be earning 7.6 per cent less than men.

## Sex discrimination

The Sex Discrimination Act 1975 makes it unlawful to discriminate in all areas of employment: This includes:

- recruitment and selection of staff
- access to training
- access to opportunities for promotion

- benefits such as pension schemes
- selection for redundancy
- termination of a contract of employment.

This Act applies equally to both men and women. For example, a male nursery nurse who was refused a job at a 'Tots' nursery because he was male was able to sue for discrimination. Similarly a teenage girl who was turned down for an apprenticeship as a motor mechanic because of her sex was also able to claim for discrimination.

The Sex Discrimination Act 1975 makes direct and indirect discrimination unlawful and also makes victimisation unlawful.

## Direct discrimination

This is where a person is treated differently in employment because of their sex. We saw that with the examples of the male nursery nurse who was refused a job and also the girl who wanted to be a motor mechanic.

Another example would be if a man was offered training to increase chances of promotion, but a woman working in the same place on the same level job was refused such training.

The following article shows a successful claim for direct racial discrimination.

---

**Asian bank worker gets record £2.8m race discrimination payout**

An Asian bank worker has won a record £2.8m in compensation for racial discrimination after losing his job.

Balbinder Chagger, 40, who is of Indian origin, won the payout after convincing a tribunal that during a round of cutbacks Abbey dumped him rather than a similarly performing woman due to his race.

The tribunal initially awarded Mr Chagger £50,000 but he went back for more after deciding he had underestimated his potential losses.

In his subsequent claim for £4.3m, he told how he was forced to retrain as a maths teacher after being made redundant from his £100,000-a-year job as a trading risk controller in 2006.

Mr Chagger, of Hayes, Middlesex, said he was turned down for more than 100 jobs before he quit the City entirely.

*(Source: Daily Mail, 24th October 2008)*

## Indirect discrimination

Indirect discrimination occurs where there is a provision or requirement applying equally to men and women but which:

- is such that it would be to the detriment of a considerably larger proportion of one sex than the other
- cannot be shown to be justified
- is to the complainant's detriment.

This means that the provision is likely to exclude one sex more than the other. For example, restricting applications for a job to those between 17 and 28 was held to be indirect discrimination against women. This was because many women are unavailable for work at this age due to child-bearing and child-rearing commitments.

Similarly, if a job is advertised with a restriction on the height of job applicants, this may be indirect discrimination, as women are on average shorter than men.

However, if the restriction is needed because of the work involved, then it will not be indirect discrimination. For example, to be allowed to train as a pilot in the Royal Air Force the applicant must be below a certain height. This is because the small size of the cockpit together with the need to be able to use an ejector seat in an emergency mean that a very tall person

would not be safe to be a pilot. So, although this might be indirect discrimination against men, it is lawful because it is necessary.

## Victimisation

This is aimed at preventing employers from discriminating against employees who complain about discriminatory practices at their work place.

It is unlawful to discriminate because a person has:

- brought proceedings under the Sex Discrimination Act
- given evidence or information in proceedings
- made allegations that there has been discrimination.

This means that a man who makes an allegation that his employers are discriminating against women is protected from victimisation for making the allegation. So, if the employer unjustifiably refuses to promote him or to pay a bonus, then that man can bring proceedings for victimisation.

## Harassment

This is not defined in the Sex Equality Act 1975 or any other British legislation. However, the tribunals and courts in this country have used the European Commission Codes of Practice definition. This is that harassment is:

**❝ unwanted conduct of a sexual nature, or other conduct based on sex affecting the dignity of men and women. ❞**

It includes any unpleasant treatment based on the employee's sex. The first case in which this was accepted by the courts as a ground for complaint was *Porcelli v Strathclyde Regional Council* (1986).

*Porcelli v Strathclyde Regional Council* (1986)

Mrs Porcelli was harassed by male employees working with her. They rubbed against her and made unpleasant remarks. Mrs Porcelli complained to her employers but they did nothing about it. Eventually she was so unhappy at work that she felt she had to resign.

Unwanted conduct includes anything which is unwelcome and offensive. This can be making remarks about a person's looks or touching them in an unwanted way such as patting someone's bottom or any other unpleasant treatment based on the person's sex.

## Genuine occupational qualification

The only time discrimination is allowed in appointing someone to a job is when the sex of the person is a 'genuine occupational qualification'.

Genuine occupational qualification includes:

- for authenticity of physiology
- to preserve decency or privacy
- where the job involves personal or welfare services.

### Authenticity of physiology

This is for such jobs as modelling and acting. For example, for a production of Romeo and Juliet, the director can insist that Romeo is played by a male actor and Juliet by a female actress.

Also for modelling men's or women's clothing, the employer is allowed to choose men for men's clothing and women for women's clothing.

## To preserve decency or privacy

There are situations where sex of the worker is important for privacy or decency of other people. For example, the job may involve physical contact which could be objectionable. It is also a factor where toilet facilities are staffed. An employer can decide only to employ same sex operatives for checking and cleaning toilets.

Another situation where it may be necessary to preserve decency is where the job involves contact between people in a state of undress.

It is also important where the employee will be living and working in a private home. A crippled woman who needs a live-in companion to help her get up and dress and go to the toilet is entitled to decide that she prefers to have a woman to do this. It is a genuine occupational qualification.

## Personal or welfare services

Other types of work where the sex of the employee may be a genuine occupational qualification is in the provision of certain types of personal services or some welfare work.

An example is that a female counsellor may be better for helping rape victims.

## Racial discrimination

The Race Relations Act 1976 makes it unlawful to discriminate against someone because of their colour, race, ethnic or national origin.

As with sex discrimination, the Race Relations Act makes direct and indirect discrimination unlawful and it outlaws victimisation.

## Direct and indirect discrimination

Direct discrimination occurs where a person is treated less favourably on racial grounds. An obvious example of direct discrimination is where an employer refuses to employ an applicant because of their race.

However, it can apply to someone who is not of an ethnic minority if he or she has been discriminated against for standing up for a person from an ethnic minority.

Indirect discrimination is where an employer applies a requirement or condition which has the effect that the proportion of one racial group that comply with it is significantly smaller than for another racial group.

In addition, it must be shown that the requirement is not justified and that the complainant suffers a detriment because of it.

## Victimisation

Victimisation is the same concept as for sex discrimination cases. It is unlawful to discriminate because a person has:

- brought proceedings under the Race Relations Act
- given evidence or information in proceedings
- made allegations of unlawful discrimination.

For example, if a person who has made an allegation of discrimination is refused a reference, then this is victimisation.

## Harassment

This is now unlawful under section 3A of the Race Relations Act 1976. This section was added to the Act comparatively recently.

It defines harassment as anything which violates a person's dignity or creates intimidating, hostile, degrading, humiliating or offensive treatment.

## Genuine occupational qualification

There are fewer situations than in sex discrimination law in which a genuine occupational qualification can be claimed as a

reason for discrimination on the basis of race. The only situations in which it is allowed are:

- authenticity in entertainment and for modelling
- to preserve the ambience of places selling food and drink; for example a Chinese restaurant is allowed to insist that all waiter/waitresses are of Chinese origin
- provision of personal and welfare services to a particular racial group.

## Disability discrimination

An employer is under a duty to take reasonable steps to accommodate a person's disability so as not to treat them less favourably than an able bodied person.

## Definition of disability

Disability is defined in the Disability Discrimination Act 1995 as:

**66** physical or mental impairment which has a substantial long-term effect on the ability to carry out normal day-to-day activities. **99**

The disability must already have lasted at least 12 months or be something which can reasonably be expected to last at least that long.

The disability (impairment) must affect normal activities. This includes anything which affects such matters as:

- mobility
- manual dexterity
- coordination
- speech
- hearing
- eyesight
- ability to lift or carry
- memory
- ability to concentrate, learn or understand.

If the claimant is relying on mental impairment, they have to prove that this is caused by a clinically recognised illness.

## Duties of employer

The employer is required, where reasonably practical, to take steps to remove arrangements that might discriminate against a disabled person.

So, the employer may be required to adapt the workplace to accommodate the disabled person. This would include providing ramps for easy access to wheelchair users. It also includes adapting equipment so that the person can use it.

Alternatively, the employer can be required to consider assigning the disabled person to a different work area. For example if the same work can be carried out in two different areas, one of which has difficult access and one of which has access suitable for the disabled person, the employer must assign the disabled person to the area where there is suitable access.

The employer may also be required to provide specialist facilities, for example providing a sign language interpreter.

However, the extent to which the employer is required to make adjustments to the working area or provide specialist facilities is considered against the practicality and cost of doing so.

If it would be very expensive for an employer to alter the premises, then it is probably not reasonable to expect him or her to do this. This would be more likely to be so where the employer had a very small business and the cost of alterations would be far more than the annual profits.

## Success of disability discrimination law

The law on disability discrimination is less satisfactory than for other types of discrimination. This is for a number of reasons including:

- the Act does not cover indirect discrimination
- it allows justifications for discrimination
- there is no real provision for people with a progressive illness, so the employer may discriminate against them while they are in the early stage of their illness and before they come under the definition of disability.

## Discrimination because of sexual orientation

Originally anyone complaining of discrimination because of their sexual orientation or gender reassignment had to rely on European law to bring a successful claim. This was seen in *P v S and Cornwall County Council* (1996).

### CASE EXAMPLE

#### *P v S and Cornwall County Council* (1996)

P was a manager in a college operated by Cornwall County Council. In April 1992 P informed S, the director of studies in the college, that he intended to undergo gender reassignment. In September 1992, when P was part way through the procedure, he was dismissed.

At that time UK law did not prohibit discrimination for this because he could not show that he was treated differently from any woman who was undergoing gender reassignment. However, the European Court of Justice found that it was a breach of European law.

In 2003, UK law specifically gave people the right not to be discriminated against because of gender reassignment or because of their sexual orientation.

It is now unlawful to discriminate directly or indirectly or to harass or victimise a person because of gender reassignment or sexual orientation.

## Religious discrimination

Since 2003, it has been unlawful to discriminate against a person because of their religion.

Religion is defined as:

**❝** any religion, religious belief or other philosophical belief. **❞**

Many of the cases since 2003 have been about employers' dress codes which prohibit the wearing of clothing or jewellery with a religious significance. One such case was *Azmi v Kirkless Metropolitan Council* (2007).

### CASE EXAMPLE

#### *Azmi v Kirkless Metropolitan Council* (2007)

The complainant was a classroom assistant who was asked to remove her face veil while teaching. The Employment Appeal Tribunal found that this was potentially indirect discrimination. However, they held that in this case such a request was justified. This was because the complainant was helping children to speak English and it was important that they could see her lips.

A case in which the complainant made a successful claim was *Noah v Sarah Desrosiers* (2007).

### CASE EXAMPLE

#### *Noah v Sarah Desrosiers* (2007)

The complainant applied for a job as a hair stylist. She was not considered for it as she wore a headscarf because of her religion. The employment tribunal held that requiring her to work bare-headed was indirect discrimination.

Religious discrimination is allowed if it is a *'genuine and determining occupational requirement'*.

## Age discrimination

Age discrimination is the most recent law to be brought in to protect workers from discrimination.

The Employment Equality (Age) Regulations 2006 prohibit age discrimination in employment and vocational training. They apply to all individuals in work or seeking work or access to training and to all employers.

However, the regulations do include a number of exemptions. For example there can be differences in relation to retirement and service related benefits. This allows employers to pay a higher pension to someone who is older.

Other differences of treatment will be allowed if they can be objectively justified. The regulations state that discrimination on the ground of age is allowed when it is *'a proportionate means of achieving a legitimate aim'*. This wording is very difficult to understand and is likely to lead to cases in the future about its meaning.

| Type of discrimination | Explanation |
|---|---|
| No equal pay | Women and men should be paid the same. This is for:<br>• the same work<br>• like work<br>• work rated as equivalent<br>• work of equal value |
| Sex discrimination | This is where a person is treated unfavourably because of their sex<br>Direct and indirect discrimination, harassment and victimisation are illegal |
| Racial discrimination | This is where a person is treated unfavourably because of their colour, race, ethnic or national origin<br>Direct and indirect discrimination, harassment and victimisation are illegal |
| Disability discrimination | An employer is under a duty to take reasonable steps to accommodate a person's disability so as not to treat them less favourably than an able bodied person |
| Discrimination because of sexual orientation or gender reassignment | It is now unlawful to discriminate directly or indirectly or to harass or victimise a person because of gender reassignment or sexual orientation |
| Religious discrimination | It is unlawful to discriminate because of any religion, religious belief or other philosophical belief<br>This includes discrimination because of religious dress |
| Age discrimination | The law prohibits age discrimination in employment and vocational training |

Figure 35.1 Different types of discrimination

## Making a claim for discrimination

Where a person believes they have been discriminated against in any employment area, they can make a claim to an employment tribunal.

The claim should be brought within three months of the act complained of. The burden of proof is on the employer to show that there was no discrimination.

## Remedies for discrimination

If the tribunal finds that there was discrimination, then it can award compensation. This is for the injury to the person's feelings and also for possible loss of wages, especially where the employee has been forced to leave their job because of the discrimination.

The tribunal can also:

- make a declaration that there has been an infringement of the employee's rights
- make recommendations for ending the discrimination. If the employer does not comply with this, extra compensation can be awarded to the employee.

## Reasons for having anti-discrimination laws

The most important reason for having anti-discrimination laws is to ensure fairness and justice in the workplace. It makes sure that people get appointed and promoted on merit.

It is also important to avoid prejudice and to prevent bullying and harassment in the workplace from employers or fellow employees. For this reason employers are liable for the acts of other employees in the course of their employment. This was seen in *Jones v Tower Boot Co Ltd* (1997).

## CASE EXAMPLE

### *Jones v Tower Boot Co Ltd* (1997)

The complainant was a young trainee motor mechanic of mixed race. The men he worked with insulted him because of his race and physically abused him. Because of this he left the work after one month. He brought a complaint against his employer. It was held that the employer was liable for the racial abuse by the other employees as it happened in the workplace.

Another reason for preventing discrimination is that it ensures a productive working environment. It allows full use of all people's talents regardless of their sex, race, disability, sexual orientation, religion or age. If all these groups of people were discriminated against then the world of work would lose their talents.

Finally it is also important to uphold a key feature of our legal system: that is that everyone is equal under the law.

## BRIEF SUMMARY OF CHAPTER

### Discrimination in employment

- Discrimination in employment is not allowed on the basis of:
  - sex
  - race
  - disability
  - sexual orientation
  - age
  - religion

### Equal pay

- is required for the same work, 'like work', 'work rated as equivalent' and 'work of equal value'

### Sex or race discrimination

- Direct and indirect discrimination, harassment or victimisation on the ground of sex or sexual orientation or race is unlawful

### Occupational qualification

- There are a few occupations where it can be claimed that there is a genuine occupational qualification

### Disability discrimination

- is where a person is discriminated against because of a physical or mental impairment which has a substantial long-term effect on their ability to carry out normal day-to-day activities

### Religious discrimination

- prevents discrimination through dress codes as well as direct discrimination

### Age discrimination

- prevents discrimination on the basis of a person's age

### Claim of discrimination

- A claim of discrimination is made to an **employment tribunal**

## EXAMINATION QUESTION

1. Read each of the following three situations and complete activity **a)** and activity **b)** which follow them.

   (i) Ann, a woman, and Brian, a man, are employed in the same restaurant by the same employer. Ann is a waitress and Brian is a waiter. They both work exactly the same hours and do exactly the same work but Ann is paid only half the wage that Brian is paid.

   (ii) Claude is employed by Derek who hates all gay people. Recently Claude has been dismissed by Derek who has found out that Claude is gay.

(iii) Fatima, a clerical worker, has developed severe arthritis in her knees and now has to use a wheelchair. Fatima used to work on the second floor and has requested an office on the ground floor as the controls in the only lift in the building are too high for Fatima to reach from her wheelchair. Her employers have refused.

(a) Identify which area of discrimination law is involved in each situation.
Situation (i)
Situation (ii)
Situation (iii)
(3 marks)

(b) Give reasons why the party in each situation **(i)**, **(ii)** and **(iii)** will be able to show that they have in fact been discriminated against.
Situation (i)
Situation (ii)
Situation (iii)
(9 marks)

(c) Without anti-discrimination laws in (b)(i) Ann would be doing the same job as a man for half the pay, in (b)(ii) Claude would lose his job just because he is gay, and in (b)(iii) Fatima would not be able to carry on with her job.

Discuss **three other reasons** why it is important to have laws preventing discrimination at work.        (6 marks)

*OCR Specimen question B143*

# CHAPTER 36

# EMPLOYMENT LAW: HEALTH AND SAFETY AT WORK

Both the common law and legislation provides protection for the health and safety of employees.

## Common law duty

At common law an employer is under a duty to take reasonable care of the safety of his employees.

This duty includes providing:

- safe competent working colleagues
- safe plant and equipment
- safe premises to work in
- safe system of work.

If the employee suffers injury through any of these being breached, he or she has the right to take an action under the tort of negligence (see Chapter 18).

## Safe competent working colleagues

An unusual case on the employer being in breach of his duty to provide competent staff is *Hudson v Ridge Manufacturing Co* (1957).

### CASE EXAMPLE

**Hudson v Ridge Manufacturing Co (1957)**

The claimant broke his wrist as a result of a practical joke played by another employee. The employer knew that this other employee was a persistent practical joker. Over the previous four years the employer had often reprimanded him for tripping up people and other similar behaviour. The employer knew that the behaviour was dangerous and as a result it was held that the employer was liable to compensate for the injury caused by the practical joke.

## Safe plant and equipment

An employer should make sure that machinery is safe. For example, there must be safety guards where there are sharp blades. The employer must also provide the necessary safety equipment for employees, such as safety goggles or protective clothing. An example of a breach of this occurred in *Paris v Stepney Borough Council* (1951).

### CASE EXAMPLE

**Paris v Stepney Borough Council (1951)**

The employer did not provide safety goggles for a motor mechanic who only had one good eye. He had to chip rust from under a bus. When he was doing this, a piece of metal hit his good eye, blinding him.

The court held that the employers should have provided him with safety goggles as they knew that he had only one good eye and any accident to that would have extra serious consequences.

## Safe premises to work

The place where the employee works must be reasonably safe. This includes entrances and exits from the premises. However, if the employer takes all reasonable steps to make the workplace safe, then he or she will not be liable. This was seen in *Latimer v AEC* (1953).

### CASE EXAMPLE

**Latimer v AEC (1953)**

There was a greasy patch on the factory floor. The employer did everything that was practicable. When an employee slipped and was injured it was held that the employer was not liable.

## A safe system of work

This has two parts to it. The employer must:
- create a safe system, and
- make sure that the safe system is implemented.

This includes, for example, making sure that staff are trained in the use of equipment.

This duty of care to employees has also been extended to include protection from work-related stress causing psychiatric injury. An example of this is *Johnstone v Bloomsbury Health Authority* (1991).

### CASE EXAMPLE

**Johnstone v Bloomsbury Health Authority (1991)**

A junior doctor was expected to work up to 48 hours' overtime a week and was on call. This damaged his general mental health. The court held there was a breach of the duty to provide a safe working system.

If the employer knows that an employee is at risk of suffering mental illness because of his working conditions, then they will liable even if they might not have been aware there was no known risk. This was decided in *Walker v Northumberland County Council* (1995).

### CASE EXAMPLE

**Walker v Northumberland County Council (1995)**

The employee was a senior social worker. He suffered a nervous breakdown as a result of work-related stress. When arranging to return to work, he was promised that his workload would be reduced.

In fact when he returned he found that there was a huge backlog of work from his absence and the council had done nothing about the understaffing. He suffered another breakdown and had to retire from work. The council was held liable as they knew that he had already suffered stress but had done nothing to improve his working conditions.

Safe working conditions also include protecting employees from bullying and harassment. This was shown by *Ratcliffe v Dyfed County Council* (1998).

## CASE EXAMPLE

### *Ratcliffe v Dyfed County Council* (1998)

A junior teacher was bullied by the head teacher. He suffered a stress-related illness as a result. The council was liable as they were in breach of the general duty to protect the health, safety and welfare of the employee.

## Health and Safety at Work Act 1974

As well as the common law duty, there are also many Acts of Parliament which place duties on employers to provide safe systems of work. The most important is the Health and Safety at Work Act 1974.

This gives all employees in any place of work the right to claim for injuries suffered as a result of a breach of the Act.

It also creates criminal liability for failure to maintain a safe system of work so that the employer can be prosecuted in the criminal courts for a serious breach of the Act.

The following newspaper article shows such a case.

### Rolls-Royce fined over health and safety

Rolls-Royce was fined £120,000 today after health and safety failures left five agency workers exposed to hazardous fumes.

The manufacturer admitted a number of breaches in the decommissioning of a light alloy foundry at its plant in Osmaston Road, Derby, in 2005, including failures to properly assess the risk of the work and to provide adequate protective clothing.

The men were exposed to potassium fluorosilicate during hot metal cutting and oxides of sulphur, resulting in all suffering from skin rashes and two of them developing respiratory problems.

One of the men, Jason Hall, 27, from Chesterfield, remains off work with blurred vision and dizziness, Derby Crown Court was told.

*(Source: taken from an article by Tim Walsh in The Independent, 18 July 2008)*

## General duty

Under section 2 of the Health and Safety at Work Act an employer is under a general duty to ensure, as far as is practicable, the health, safety and welfare at work of all his or her employees.

The Act also says that, so far as is reasonably practical, an employer must:

**(a)** provide and maintain a safe plant, systems of work and workplace

**(b)** ensure safety in the handling, storage and transport of articles and substances

**(c)** provide such information, instruction, training and supervision as is necessary to ensure health and safety at work

**(d)** provide a safe working environment.

## Enforcement of the Act

The Health and Safety at Work Act set up:

1. the Health and Safety Commission to administer the law
2. the Health and Safety Executive to enforce the law.

Examples of safety equipment

## The Health and Safety Commission

The Commission reviews the law on health and safety at work. It will make recommendations to the Government for any new regulations it thinks are necessary.

## The Health and Safety Executive

This has the job of making sure that the law is followed by employers. The Executive employs Inspectors. These can:

• enter premises such as factories, offices, building sites (if necessary they can get the support of the police to enter)
• investigate any possible breaches of the law – this includes examining machinery, taking photographs or seizing documents
• remove hazardous substances from premises

• require employers and employees to answer questions about working practices.

## Improvement Notices

Where the Inspectors find that there are breaches of the Health and Safety at Work Act they can issue Improvement Notices. Such a Notice will:
• state what part of the law has been breached
• indicate what improvements must be made
• set a time within which the improvements must be made.

## Prohibition Notices

Where there is risk of personal injury from a breach of the law, an Inspector can issue a Prohibition Notice. This type of notice forbids the activity until the risk is removed. An example could be that a particular piece of machinery must not be used until safety guards had been fitted.

## The 'six pack' regulations

There have been several regulations on health and safety at work. The main ones are aimed at:

- risk assessment
- maintenance of efficient and clean premises
- maintenance of plant and equipment
- maintenance of personal protection equipment
- manual handling
- safe use of Visual Display Units (VDUs) and work stations

## Risk assessment

These regulations require employers to carry out risk assessment of their working procedures, especially in relation to women of child-bearing age and to young people.

The employer must appoint safety officers at the premises and must establish procedures to be carried out in the case of a dangerous emergency.

Employees are under a legal duty to comply with all safety procedures.

## Maintenance of efficient and clean premises

There are several things that an employer must do to comply with the regulations on the maintenance of efficient and clean premises. The first point is that employers must maintain, repair and clean their premises effectively.

Another important point is that the employer must provide pure air, reasonable temperatures and adequate lighting in the workplace.

Other provisions are that an employer must:

- provide seats for employees where the work can be done sitting down
- control construction of doors and ladders and other methods of access to work
- provide adequate sanitary (toilet) arrangements for all employees

| Employer's common law duty to employees | Employer's duty under Health and Safety at Work Act 1974 |
|---|---|
| A duty to take reasonable care of the safety of his employees | A general duty to ensure, as far as is practicable, the health, safety and welfare at work of all his employees |
| This duty includes providing:<br>• safe competent working colleagues<br>• safe plant and equipment<br>• safe premises to work in<br>• safe system of work. | This includes:<br>• providing and maintaining a safe plant, systems of work and workplace<br>• ensuring safety in the handling, storage and transport of articles and substances<br>• providing such information, instruction, training and supervision as is necessary to ensure health and safety at work<br>• providing a safe working environment. |
|  | The Act is enforced by the Health and Safety Executive. |
|  | The Act also creates criminal liability. |

Figure 36.1 Chart comparing common law duty on safety and the Health and Safety at Work Act 1974

• provide facilities for changing clothes where this is necessary at work.

## Maintenance of plant and equipment

The main rule is that work equipment must be suitable and efficiently maintained. It must be kept in good order and must conform to European Union standards.

Employees must be given appropriate information on the equipment they have to use. There must also be effective steps taken to prevent access to dangerous parts of machinery.

In addition machines must have proper controls. These should include controls on access to the machinery, controls to stop it and to isolate any part where a problem occurs.

## Maintenance of personal protection equipment

Personal protection equipment (PPE) covers anything which has to be worn or held to protect employees from health and safety risks.

The equipment must be properly maintained and kept in good repair. Employers must also make sure that employees use it properly. So, if the area is one in which hard hats have to be worn, the employer must provide these hats and make sure that all employees know they have to wear them.

## Manual handling

An employer must reduce any manual handling which creates risks. Where employees have to manually handle items, the employer must do everything possible to minimise risk. This includes training employees on proper manual handling to avoid risk of injury.

## Safe use of Visual Display Units

Where staff are required to use VDU screens, the employer should provide free regular breaks or a change of activity.

The employer should also provide eye testing for employees who have to use VDUs.

---

**ACTIVITY**

### Activity 1

Explain how the employers of the following people may be in breach of health and safety laws.

1. Callum is employed as a paint sprayer in a car body workshop. He is supplied with a mask to use when he is spraying. The mask he is using at present has been damaged and there are large holes in it.

2. Dalvinder works as a ground maintenance man. One day he is told to use a chainsaw to cut down some small trees. Dalvinder has never operated a chainsaw before and has not been given any training in doing so.

3. Ellie operates a machine which has sharp cutting edges. There is no cover over these cutting edges.

4. Ferdinand has a very stressful job. In addition his line manager is particularly unpleasant to him and gives him extra work. Ferdinand has already been off work with a stress-related illness.

# Working time regulations

The basic working time provisions are:

- 48 hour week – this is worked out on an average over 17 weeks
- limits on night work with a maximum 8 hours in 24 hours
- each employee must have a minimum of 11 hours rest a day (the minimum is 12 for young workers)
- there must be a minimum of a 20-minute rest break after six hours work
- minimum paid holiday entitlement of four weeks a year.

## BRIEF SUMMARY OF CHAPTER

**Common law duty**

- An employer is under a duty to take reasonable care of the safety of his or her employees
- This duty includes providing:
  - safe competent working colleagues
  - safe plant and equipment
  - safe premises to work in
  - safe system of work.

**Health and Safety at Work Act 1974**

- An employer is under a general duty to ensure, as far as is practicable, the health, safety and welfare at work of all his or her employees

**The Health and Safety Executive**

- They enforce the Act and inspectors can issue Improvement Notices and Prohibition Notices

**The 'six pack' regulations**

- risk assessment
- maintenance of efficient and clean premises
- maintenance of plant and equipment
- maintenance of personal protection equipment

- manual handling
- safe use of Visual Display Units

**Working time regulations**

- limit the hours employees can work

## EXAMINATION QUESTION

In 1938 the House of Lords in *Wilson and Clyde Coal Co Ltd v English* first declared that an employer owes a personal duty of care to all his employees. At that time the court also identified that this duty was broken down into four specific duties.

Identify any **three** of those specific duties.

(3 marks)

*Part question, OCR Specimen Question B143*

# CHAPTER 37

# EMPLOYMENT LAW:
# TERMINATION OF EMPLOYMENT

The law accepts that there are occasions when an employer has to dismiss employees. However the law provides employees with protection from dismissal without a good reason.

Normally an employer must give an employee notice that the contract of employment will be terminated. The length of the period of notice is usually set out in the contract of employment.

If there is no agreed period of notice then the law states that the employer must give:

- at least one week's notice to anyone who has been employed between four weeks and two years
- an extra week for every year over two years that the employee has worked up to a maximum of 12 weeks.

There are different types of dismissal. These are:

- summary dismissal
- wrongful dismissal
- unfair dismissal
- constructive dismissal.

## Summary dismissal

Summary dismissal is where an employer dismisses someone on the spot. No notice is given and the employee is told to leave work immediately.

Summary dismissal can only be used where there has been gross misconduct by the employee. There must be a very good reason to dismiss the employee on the spot. Examples of gross misconduct include:

- using violence to another employee
- acts of dishonesty, for example stealing from the employer
- drunkenness – especially where the employee has to operate dangerous machinery or drive a vehicle.

## Wrongful dismissal

Wrongful dismissal is where an employer dismisses someone without giving them the correct notice they are entitled to under their contract of employment. Alternatively, it can be where an employee, who is on a fixed-term contract, is dismissed before the end of a fixed-term contract.

This type of dismissal is sometimes seen when a football manager has a contract for a fixed term, for example if the contract is for three years but the manager is dismissed after only two years.

Dismissing someone without the correct notice is a breach of the contract of employment. This means that the employee can claim for the amount of money he or she would have earned in the notice period or for the remainder of the fixed term.

So, in the example of a football manager being dismissed with one year still left on his fixed-term contract, he can claim the amount he would have earned in that final year.

An employee only has to work for four weeks to become entitled to the correct period of notice.

A claim for wrongful dismissal can be made in either an employment tribunal or in a court. It is also possible to make a claim for unfair dismissal in a tribunal at the same time.

## Pay in lieu of notice

If the employee agrees, then the employer can pay him the amount of money that he would have earned in the period of notice. Where this is done then it is not wrongful dismissal.

A claim for wrongful dismissal is most often made by:

- those on fixed-term contracts dismissed before the contract ends
- highly-paid employees, such as directors, where the amount of money they would have earned is above the limit paid for unfair dismissal
- employees who are excluded from claiming unfair dismissal, for example those who have not worked for the employer for one year.

### ACTIVITY

#### Activity 1

1. Assuming there is no agreed period for giving notice of termination of contract, how much notice must be given in the following situations?

   (a) John has worked for Sainsways plc for two months.

   (b) Antonia has worked for Dogbodies Ltd for five years.

2. Eddie, a newspaper editor on a salary of £160,000, has a contract under which he should be given six months' notice. The owner of the newspaper dismisses Eddie without giving him any notice.

   Advise Eddie as to what he can claim and where that claim can be made.

## Unfair dismissal

An employer must have good reason for dismissing an employee. The law protects employees from being unfairly dismissed. However, this protection only starts after the employee has been in continuous employment for one full year.

## Automatically unfair reasons for dismissal

There are some reasons for dismissal which are considered to be automatically unfair. These include:

- any reason connected with pregnancy or parental leave
- trade union membership or non-membership or legitimate trade union activities
- industrial action – unless the employer dismisses all those involved
- taking action about health and safety matters, for example being dismissed for refusing to operate an unsafe machine
- a dismissal that fails to comply with the statutory disciplinary and dismissal procedure (see below).

If the dismissal is for any of these reasons then an employment tribunal will declare it was an unfair dismissal.

## Potentially fair reasons for dismissal

The law recognises that an employer must have the right to dismiss employees in certain circumstances. So, there are certain reasons which are recognised as being potentially fair.

The main potentially fair reasons are:

- lack of capability or qualifications
- misconduct
- fair selection under a redundancy scheme

- dismissal because of a statutory restriction
- other substantial reason.

## Lack of capability and qualifications

Capability refers to:

- the skill
- aptitude
- health
- other mental or physical quality of the employee.

If the employee is incapable of carrying out the job then this may be a fair reason for dismissing him or her. However, if he or she has not been given adequate training by the employer then it will not be a fair reason.

In some cases lack of capability can even justify summary dismissal. This was seen in *Taylor v Alidair* (1978).

### CASE EXAMPLE

#### *Taylor v Alidair* (1978)

The complainant was a pilot who had crashed a plane on landing. The crash was because of his incompetence. The airline was justified in dismissing him. In addition the situation was one which justified a summary dismissal.

The employee may be incapable of work because of permanent illness. In this situation it would be unfair for the employer to have to pay him or her indefinitely, so it is a fair reason for dismissing. However, if the illness is temporary then the employer should give the employee a chance to return to work.

Qualifications refers to any academic, technical or professional qualification which is relevant to the position held.

Usually a dismissal for lack of qualifications will arise because the employee has lied about his or her qualifications in order to get the post. When the employer discovers that the employee has not got the qualifications he claimed then the employer is justified in dismissing the employee.

## Misconduct

This covers a wide range of misbehaviour. It includes such matters as persistent absenteeism, drunkenness at work, aggressive behaviour to others at work or refusing to obey lawful orders in relation to work.

Examples have included:

- using the Internet to look at pornographic sites during working time
- the employee has a history of insubordination (refusing to obey orders) and not responding to warnings
- the employee persists in engaging in unsafe practices despite warnings from the employer
- violence
- dishonesty.

If the misconduct is outside of working time and place then generally is not a reason for dismissal. However, there are some situations where it can be. For example if a bus driver is convicted of drink driving and disqualified from driving, the employer can dismiss him as he is no longer qualified to work as a driver. It does not matter that the drink driving occurred when driving his own car in his free time.

Where the employee is accused of misconduct then the employer must follow the correct disciplinary process.

## Redundancy

The employer may need to get rid of some employees because his business is reducing and there is less work to do. (see below for more detail on redundancy). Redundancy is a fair reason for dismissal.

| | Wrongful dismissal | Unfair dismissal |
|---|---|---|
| Definition | Dismissal with no notice or insufficient notice | Dismissal without a fair reason |
| Qualifying period of employment | Four weeks | One year |
| Where claim can be made | Court or employment tribunal | Employment tribunal |
| Time limit on claim | Six years for any claim made in a court | Three months from the date of dismissal |
| What can be claimed | The amount the employee would have earned in the notice period | An order for re-engagement or re-instatement Compensation but subject to current limits |

**Figure 37.1** Differences between wrongful dismissal and unfair dismissal

## Dismissal because of a statutory restriction

The law sets certain other rules in regard to employment. These restrict employers from employing certain people. For example, it is against the law to employ an illegal immigrant. So, if the employer has an employee and later finds out that this employee is an illegal immigrant, then the employer can dismiss him.

## Disciplinary and dismissal procedures

When an employer wishes to dismiss an employee, he should follow the Code of Practice set out by the Arbitration and Conciliation Service (ACAS). The main points are that employers should:

- carry out any necessary investigations to establish the facts of the case
- inform employees of the basis of the problem and give them an opportunity to put their case in response before any decisions are made
- allow employees to be accompanied at any formal disciplinary meeting

- allow an employee to appeal against a decision to dismiss him.

If an employer does not follow the Code of Practice then it is likely that an Employment Tribunal will rule that the dismissal was unfair.

## Constructive dismissal

This is where the employer has behaved in such a way that the employee feels forced to resign from their work. The employee is not actually dismissed by the employer.

The employer must have breached the contract in a fundamental way. This could be by harassment or victimisation, or because the employer has unilaterally (without consulting the employee) changed the working conditions.

An example of an employee resigning from work because of sexual harassment is *Porcelli v Strathclyde Regional Council* (1986). It was held that she was constructively dismissed.

## *Porcelli v Strathclyde Regional Council* (1986)

Mrs Porcelli was harassed by male employees working with her. They rubbed against her and made unpleasant remarks. Mrs Porcelli complained to her employers but they did nothing about it. Eventually she was so unhappy at work that she felt she had to resign.

## Redundancy

This is where the employer no longer has any work for the employee. In this situation the employer may lawfully dismiss the employee. This is known as being made redundant.

Employees have to have worked for at least two years to have rights to redundancy payments.

## Procedure

An employer must carry out the correct procedures when making redundancies. There must be:

- sufficient warning for the parties to consider alternatives
- proper and meaningful consultation with unions
- objective criteria for selection for redundancy with no bias.

In addition, where possible, the employer must identify reasonable alternative employment. For example, an employer may have several factories; if there is not enough work to keep all of the workforce at one of the factories, then the employer may be able to offer some employees work at another factory.

# Calculating redundancy payments

An employer has to pay anyone made redundant a redundancy payment. This is calculated by looking at the length of time the employee has worked for the employer and the level of the average week's pay.

The amount to be paid is:

- half a week's pay for each full year of service when aged 18–21
- one week's pay for each full year of service when aged 22–40
- one and a half week's pay for each full year of service when aged 41 and over.

If the employer making a person redundant does not pay them the correct amount, then a claim can be made to an employment tribunal who will work out the amount and order the employer to pay that amount.

**ACTIVITY**

### Activity 2

Advise the following people of their rights.

1. Ms Fogey, a receptionist aged 44, has worked for Gogetters Ltd for nine years. The managing director dismisses her, giving her nine weeks' notice, because he wants to establish a new image and employ younger and more glamorous staff.

2. Mr Sharp was employed as an accountant with the same firm for three years. His firm dismissed him without notice after hearing that he had run up large gambling debts.

3. Tom and Jerry are employed as machine operators. They join an official strike called by their union. After they have been on strike for 10 days, the company dismisses them.

## Claiming for unfair dismissal

A claim for unfair dismissal is made to an employment tribunal. The claim must be made within three months of the date of the termination of the contract.

The employee must fill in a claim form setting out details of employment from which he or she has been dismissed and the details of why it is claimed to be unfair. This has to be sent to the local Regional Tribunal Office.

The Office then sends the claim on to the employer, who can complete a form explaining his reasons for dismissal.

Following this ACAS will try to help the parties to reach a settlement of the claim. In fact, about 70 per cent of all claims are settled.

If the case goes to a hearing, this will be in front of a panel of three tribunal members. The chairman of the panel will be legally qualified; the other two will be one representing employers' organisations and one representing trade unions/employees associations. Neither of these will have any direct connection with the employer or employee.

The case will be heard in public.

## Remedies

There are three orders that an employment tribunal can make when they find that an employee has been unfairly dismissed. These are:

• reinstatement – where the employer is ordered to take the employee back in exactly the same job as though dismissal had never occurred
• re-engagement – where the employer is ordered to re-employ the employee. This will not be in the same position but must be one with substantially the same conditions of type of work, pay and hours of work
• an award of compensation.

The award of compensation is calculated as for redundancy. There is a limit on the amount that can be awarded. The Government sets this limit and increases it, usually each year.

### BRIEF SUMMARY OF CHAPTER

**Different types of dismissal**

■ summary dismissal
■ wrongful dismissal
■ unfair dismissal
■ constructive dismissal

**Summary dismissal**

■ on the spot for gross misconduct

**Wrongful dismissal**

■ without notice or insufficient notice

**Unfair dismissal**

■ **Automatically unfair reasons** for dismissing include pregnancy, union activities, health and safety and not following the correct dismissal procedures
■ **Potentially fair reasons** include reasons connected to lack of capability and qualifications, misconduct, fair selection under a redundancy scheme or other substantial reason

**Constructive dismissal**

■ The employer has breached the contract in a fundamental way so that the employee is justified in resigning from work

**Redundancy**

■ The employer no longer has any work for the employee

**Claims**

■ in respect of dismissals are made to an employment tribunal

## EXAMINATION QUESTION

1. There are four different types of dismissal:
   * summary dismissal
   * wrongful dismissal
   * unfair dismissal
   * constructive dismissal.

(a) Outline the ways in which **constructive** dismissal is different from the other types of dismissal.                    (3 marks)

(b) Chris has been dismissed half way through his working day, escorted from the premises, and told never to return (summary dismissal). His employer told Chris that this was because Chris refused to obey an instruction from his manager to stop reading the newspaper when he should be working, and when the manager repeated the instruction Chris punched the manager in the face.

Explain **three** reasons why summary dismissal may have been **appropriate**.      (3 marks)

*Part question, OCR Specimen Question B143*

# CHAPTER 38

# HUMAN RIGHTS: RIGHTS AND RESPONSIBILITIES AS A CITIZEN

In developed countries today the rights and freedoms of the individual are regarded as important. In Britain we say that we live in a free society, meaning by this that everyone has certain basic rights and freedoms. These include freedom of speech, freedom to practise one's chosen religion, freedom from discrimination because of race or sex and the right to liberty.

However, there are limitations on these rights. Some limitations are needed in order to protect other people's rights or to protect society as a whole. To illustrate this, consider the right to liberty; clearly it is important that ordinary people have freedom of the person, the right not to be held prisoner, but there are situations where it is necessary to imprison violent and dangerous criminals to protect society from them.

## Development of human rights

The horrors of the Second World War with the millions of people who were held in concentration camps and sent to the gas chambers made people aware that it was necessary to try to protect individual basic rights.

In 1948 the General Assembly of the United Nations made the Universal Declaration on Human Rights. Two years later, in 1950, the Council of Europe adopted the European Convention on Human Rights.

The Council of Europe is not part of the present European Union but a separate international

organisation formed in 1949 and with a bigger membership than the European Union. In 1950 there were 21 members and 20 of these, including the United Kingdom, signed the European Convention on Human Rights.

Since that date other European countries have joined the Council of Europe and signed the Convention. There are now over 50 countries that have signed the Convention.

## Convention rights

The European Convention on Human Rights sets out the rights and freedoms that the people of Europe should have. The most important ones are shown in Figure 38.1.

## The European Court of Human Rights

In order to protect the rights set out in the Convention, a Court of Human Rights was established in 1959. The procedure for applying to this court was simplified in 1994. A new permanent single European Court of Human Rights was established and individuals who feel their rights have been breached can apply direct to the Court. Member States can also report another Member State to the Court.

A Chamber of the Court will consider whether the complaint is admissible and if it decides that it is, the Government of the State concerned is asked for its comments. There is the possibility of coming to a friendly negotiated settlement, but if this is not successful then the Court will

| Article | Right |
|---------|-------|
| 2 | Everyone's right to life shall be protected by law |
| 3 | No one shall be subjected to torture, inhuman or degrading treatment or punishment |
| 4 | No one shall be held in slavery |
| 5 | Everyone has the right to liberty |
| 6 | Everyone is entitled to a fair trial |
| 8 | Everyone has the right to respect for his private and family life |
| 9 | Everyone has the right to freedom of thought, conscience and religion |
| 10 | Everyone has the right to freedom of expression |
| 11 | Everyone has the right to freedom of peaceful assembly and to freedom of association with others |
| 14 | The enjoyment of the rights and freedoms given by the Convention shall be secured without discrimination on any ground such as sex, race, colour, language, religion, political or other opinion, national or social origin |

**Figure 38.1** Rights given by the European Convention on Human Rights

hear the case in full and give a judgment. The European Court of Human Rights sits at Strasbourg.

## The Human Rights Act 1998

This Act incorporates the European Convention on Human Rights into British law. This means that anyone taking a court case in England or Wales can rely on the rights given in the Convention as part of their case.

The Act also makes it unlawful for a public authority to act in a way that is incompatible with a Convention right. Public authority includes any person who has some public function and also the courts. It does not, however, include Parliament or a person exercising functions in connection with proceedings in Parliament.

We will now go on to look at the various rights and freedoms. The basic rights of the right to life, the right not to be tortured, the right not to be held in slavery, the right to liberty and the right to a fair trial are considered in this chapter.

Freedom of communication is explained in Chapter 39 (including the tort of defamation). The right to privacy, freedom of association, freedom of religion and the right not to be discriminated against are in Chapter 40.

## Right to life

This is the most fundamental of human rights. Everyone's right to life is protected by law. If this is ignored then there is a breach of the Convention. This was seen in *McCann v United Kingdom* (1995).

### CASE EXAMPLE

*McCann v United Kingdom* (1995)

Three members of the Provisional IRA were shot and killed by Special Air Service soldiers in Gibraltar in 1988. Their families complained and it was held that this was a breach of Article 2 of the European Convention on Human Rights.

## Exceptions

However, there are some exceptions where depriving someone of life is not a breach of human rights. The first one is that States may execute convicted criminals. This means that countries are allowed to have the death penalty for serious crimes and to execute those convicted of such crimes.

In fact the death penalty was abolished in the United Kingdom in 1965.

The other situations where deprivation of life is not considered a breach of the Convention are set out in the Convention in Article 2.2 which states that:

> **66** Deprivation of life shall not be regarded as inflicted in contravention of this article when it results from the use of force which is no more than absolutely necessary:
> - in defence of any person from unlawful violence
> - in order to effect a lawful arrest or to prevent the escape of a person lawfully detained
> - in action lawfully taken for the purpose of quelling a riot or insurrection. **99**

All these are situations where there may be great danger to police or members of the public. It would be absurd if a gunman had to be allowed to keep shooting innocent people, because he had the right to life. If the only way of stopping him is to kill him, then this is not a breach of Article 2.

However, it is stressed in Article 2.2 that the use of force must be no more than absolutely necessary for the achievement of the purposes set out in the Convention.

## No one to be subjected to torture, inhuman and degrading treatment

Article 3 of the European Convention on Human Rights says that:

> **66** No one shall be subjected to torture or to inhuman or degrading treatment. **99**

Torture is defined as deliberate inhuman treatment causing very serious and cruel suffering.

Inhuman treatment is less severe but may include threats of torture, psychological harm, and physical assault.

In *Ireland v United Kingdom* (1978) it was held that there had been inhuman treatment in the way that suspected IRA terrorists were dealt with by the security forces in Northern Ireland.

### CASE EXAMPLE

**Ireland v United Kingdom** (1978)

Security forces used interrogation tactics on IRA suspects that included:
- forcing victims to stand against walls for long periods of time
- hooding suspects
- subjecting them to noise
- depriving them of sleep, food and drink.

It was held that this did not amount to torture, but that it was inhuman treatment and a breach of Article 3.

Degrading treatment is punishment arousing in the victim feelings of fear, anguish and inferiority. This includes behaviour which is capable of breaking the victim's moral resistance or making the victim feel debased. This was seen in *Price v United Kingdom* (2001).

### Price v United Kingdom (2001)

Ms Price, who was born with shortened limbs, was imprisoned for failure to pay a debt. She had to spend the first night in a police station cell where she had to sleep in her wheelchair and was unable to reach the call button or to use the toilet. She was then moved to a prison Health Care Centre with more suitable facilities. However, she complained that she was forced to allow male prison officers to assist her to clean herself after using the toilet and that on one occasion a female officer had exposed her to male officers when helping her to the toilet.

She claimed that this treatment was a breach of Article 3 as it was 'inhuman and degrading'. The European Court of Human Rights held that there was indeed a breach of Article 3.

## Right not to be held in slavery

Slavery is where one person owns another. Two hundred years ago this used to be legal in the United Kingdom. But it has been illegal ever since.

We no longer accept the idea that people can be owned and bought and sold. However, there are a few areas in the world where this does still occur.

## Right to liberty

Article 5 of the European Convention on Human Rights sets out that everyone has the right to liberty and that no one shall be deprived of his or her liberty except where the law allows arrest or detention. Even in these cases the arrested person has the right to be told of the reason for his or her arrest and brought before a court within a reasonable time.

In the English legal system this right to liberty has been important for centuries and was set out in the Magna Carta in 1215.

Today it is still very important. The right to liberty is the key reason why there has been so much opposition to allowing people to be held for long periods of time before being charged with a criminal offence.

In most criminal cases, the police only have the right to detain a person for 36 hours. After this time the police must either charge the suspect or release them. If the suspect is being held in relation to a serious offence, then the police can ask the magistrates to extend the detention time to 96 hours (4 days).

The exception to these rules is terrorism cases where a suspected terrorist can be held for up to 28 days without being charged. In 2007 and 2008 the Government proposed increasing this period from 28 days to 42 days. On each occasion Parliament voted not to extend the time. This was because the right to personal liberty is a key right and it was felt that detaining someone for 42 days would infringe the right.

## When detention is allowed

There are, as already pointed out, limitations on this right, but a person can only be detained on specific grounds set out in the law. The most widely used reasons for detaining people are:

(a) following a lawful arrest (see Chapter 6)
(b) on the order of a court while awaiting trial
(c) a sentence of imprisonment after being found guilty of a crime
(d) under the Mental Health Acts.

In these situations detention is generally necessary for the protection of the public.

Another reason for detention in the first two cases is that the person might fail to attend court. Where it is believed that the person will not attend for the next part of the case, our bail laws state that bail can be refused (see Chapter 3).

In the last situation, the mentally ill person may be a danger to the public, but detention may also be necessary for the person's own safety.

## Remedies

If a person has been unlawfully detained he may sue in the civil courts and claim damages for false imprisonment.

Where the person is still being detained there is a special writ (court order) that can be obtained; this is the writ of *habeas corpus*. An application for this writ is made to the High Court. The effect of the writ of *habeas corpus* is to order that the detained person be brought before the court immediately.

An application for a writ of *habeas corpus* takes priority over any other case in court on that day. It will be heard first. The court will decide whether the detention is lawful or not; if the court decides that there is no lawful reason for the detention it will order the immediate release of the prisoner.

Personal liberty is also protected by the law of tort. If there is a breach of the tort of false imprisonment, there is a right to claim damages (see Chapter 19 for more details on false imprisonment).

## Right to a fair trial

Article 6 says there is a right to a fair and public hearing within a reasonable time. This is so for both criminal and civil cases as shown by *Darnell v United Kingdom* (1993).

### CASE EXAMPLE

**Darnell v United Kingdom (1993)**

The European Court of Human Rights held that a case about the unfair dismissal of a doctor had taken so long to be decided that the United Kingdom was in breach of Article 6. The doctor had been dismissed in 1984 but the final decision of the Employment Appeal Tribunal had not been made until 1993.

The Convention states that the minimum rights for a fair trial are:

- to be informed promptly, in a language which he understands, of the nature of the accusation against him
- to have adequate time and facilities to prepare his defence
- to be capable of defending himself, or if not, to be given legal assistance with his defence – this assistance should be free if the defendant cannot afford to pay for legal help
- to be able to question the witnesses giving evidence against him
- to have the free assistance of an interpreter if he cannot understand or speak the language used in the court.

In *T and V v United Kingdom* (1999), the European Court of Human Rights ruled that there had been a breach of the right to a fair trial.

### CASE EXAMPLE

**T and V v United Kingdom (1999)**

The two defendants were ten-year-old boys charged with murder. Their trial had taken place in the Crown Court and, although the court day had been shortened to the length of a school day with a ten-minute break every hour, the court case was conducted in the same way as for adults. The trial had not been fair as the boys had been effectively unable to take part because 'the formality and ritual' of the proceedings 'must at times have seemed incomprehensible and intimidating' to the boys.

## BRIEF SUMMARY OF CHAPTER

**European Convention on Human Rights**

■ The **European Convention on Human Rights** sets out basic human rights that everyone should have

**Human Rights Act 1998**

■ The **Human Rights Act 1998** has incorporated the Convention into our law

**Basic human rights include:**

■ the right to life

■ the right not to be tortured or treated in a degrading way

■ the right not to be a slave

■ the right to liberty

■ the right to a fair trial

**Restrictions allowed on the right to liberty**

■ following a lawful arrest

■ on the order of a court while awaiting trial

■ a sentence of imprisonment after being found guilty of a crime

■ under the Mental Health Acts

**Right to a fair trial includes:**

■ to be informed of the accusation against him or her

■ to have adequate time/facilities to prepare a defence

■ to be given legal assistance with his or her defence if necessary

■ to question the witnesses giving evidence

■ to have the free assistance of an interpreter

# CHAPTER 39

# HUMAN RIGHTS: FREEDOM OF EXPRESSION

Article 10 of the European Convention on Human Rights states that everyone has the right to freedom of expression. This is the principle of freedom of speech and it is often regarded as being one of the key features of a democratic society.

## Freedom of expression

In this country it is possible to do such things as criticise the government and express opinions on current events.

People in a country which does not have freedom of speech may be imprisoned for such activities. In some countries newspapers, television and radio are controlled by the government and may only publish or broadcast material approved by that government.

In Britain the media are free to publish or broadcast almost any material or opinions; the Government does not interfere with the press.

## Limitations on rights

However, there are limitations, both on the freedom of individuals and on the media. These are designed to protect other people. The main restrictions are:

- national security
- obscenity laws
- contempt of court
- discrimination
- the law on defamation.

## National security

Publishing information that could put the security of the country at risk is forbidden. The Official Secrets Acts create various criminal offences which forbid disclosing information.

There is also the crime of treason which, among other things, prevents broadcasting enemy propaganda in times of war.

Another offence which restricts freedom of speech is sedition. A person saying or publishing material which would bring the government into hatred and contempt or encourage a rebellion could be prosecuted for sedition, although in practice prosecutions are very rare.

## Obscenity laws

It is a criminal offence to publish anything which is likely to 'deprave or corrupt' people. This law is aimed at preventing the worst type of pornographic material from being published. However there are very few successful prosecutions.

The law also forbids the taking or publishing of indecent pictures of young children under the Protection of Children Act 1978.

The law bans horror comics which are aimed at children and young persons from containing stories told mainly in pictures and showing violence, crimes, cruelty or incidents of a repulsive and horrible nature.

# Contempt of court

There are restrictions on reporting court proceedings; for example the names of children involved in court proceedings can only be published if the judge at the trial gives permission.

Jurors are not allowed to publish any details of discussions in the jury room.

There is also a general restriction on the press reporting of any material which might prejudice a fair trial. Newspapers have been fined very heavily for publishing such material in contempt of court.

# Discrimination

The Public Order Act 1986 makes it an offence to publish or distribute any written work which is intended to stir up racial hatred.

## Defamation

Defamation is making and publishing a false statement about another person which damages that person's reputation. Defamation has been defined as a statement which tends *'to lower a person in the estimation of right-thinking members of society'* or to cause those right-thinking members to 'shun or avoid' him or her.

Defamation can be either *libel* or *slander*.

## Libel

This is defamation in a permanent form. Obvious examples include articles published in a newspaper or magazine or any other written material, pictures, paintings and statues, films and videos, records, CDs and cassettes. In *Monson v Tussauds Ltd* (1894) it was even held that a waxwork model could be libel.

### CASE EXAMPLE

**Monson v Tussauds Ltd (1894)**

A model of the claimant that had been placed near models of convicted murderers in a 'Chamber of Horrors' was held to be defamation.

Broadcasting on television or radio is defined as a permanent medium. Also words spoken on a stage during a play are defined as a permanent form under the Theatres Act 1968. Articles on the Internet are also considered as 'permanent'.

Libel is another tort that is actionable *per se*, that is, without having to prove that there was actual damage. Libel may be a crime if it is likely to cause a breach of the peace or if it is obscene.

## Slander

This is defamation in a non-permanent form or a temporary form such as speech and gestures. Slander differs from libel in other ways as well: it cannot be a crime and it is not actionable *per se*. To prove slander the claimant must usually show that it has caused actual damage, for example that he lost his job as a result of what was said.

There are four exceptions where slander is actionable *per se* so that the claimant does not need to prove damage. These are where the slander implies that:

**(a)** a person has committed a crime punishable with imprisonment

**(b)** a person has an existing infectious disease which would cause other people to shun him or her (eg AIDS or VD)

**(c)** a woman is unchaste or has committed adultery

**(d)** a person is unfit to carry on his 'office, profession, calling, trade or business'.

# Defamation cases

A claim for defamation is heard in a civil court. This is normally the High Court but it is also possible for a case to be heard in the County Court.

Defamation is one of the few civil actions where a jury may be used. However, it does not have to be tried by jury: if the parties prefer, they can have a judge to decide the case.

Where a jury is used, the jury decides if the statement was defamatory and, if so, they also decide the amount of damages.

To establish defamation it is necessary to prove three points. These are that:

**(a)** the statement was defamatory
**(b)** the statement could reasonably be understood to refer to the claimant
**(c)** the statement was published.

It is necessary to consider each of these points in a little detail. Figure 39.1 on page 319 presents a flow chart for defamation.

## Statement must be defamatory

The statement must be untrue. A true statement cannot be defamatory. It must also, as we have already seen, tend to lower a person in the estimation of right-thinking members of society.

As public opinion changes, it can mean that different statements may become more or less likely to 'lower a person in the eyes of right-thinking members of society'. A statement that someone was illegitimate was very defamatory 50 years ago, but today it is unlikely to injure that person's reputation.

Consideration of the phrase 'right-thinking members of society' is shown in the case of *Byrne v Dean* (1937).

---

**CASE EXAMPLE**

### *Byrne v Dean* (1937)

Following a police raid on a golf club to remove an illegal gambling machine, a verse was put up on the club notice board. The verse included the lines:

> **❝** But he who gave the game away May he BYRNE in hell and rue the day. **❞**

Byrne sued for defamation, claiming that the verse suggested he had tipped off the police. The judge held that the words were not capable of being defamatory since they would not lower him in the estimation of 'right-thinking members of society'.

---

## Innuendo

The meaning of some statements is clear, for example saying that someone is a thief. However in other cases the statement appears to be innocent at first look, but it has a hidden meaning which is defamatory. This hidden meaning is called an *innuendo*. This happened in *Cassidy v Daily Mirror Newspapers* (1929).

---

**CASE EXAMPLE**

### *Cassidy v Daily Mirror Newspapers* (1929)

A newspaper published a photograph of a man and woman saying, wrongly, they were engaged to be married. On the face of it this did not appear to be defamatory, but the man was already married and his wife sued for defamation, claiming that there was an innuendo that she was living with him without being married to him.

---

Another case with a hidden meaning involved a cartoon of an amateur golfer and the mention of his name in an advertisement for chocolate.

The innuendo was that he had been paid for the advertisement and so broken his amateur status.

## Statement must refer to the claimant

Either the claimant must be named in the statement or else there must be a description which clearly identifies him or her. In the Cassidy case, the photograph of her husband was enough to identify Mrs Cassidy.

If a statement is not meant to refer to the claimant but the description fits the claimant, he will be able to sue for defamation. This happened in *Newstead v London Express Newspaper* (1939).

### CASE EXAMPLE

**Newstead v London Express Newspaper (1939)**

A statement that Harold Newstead, a 30-year-old Camberwell man, had been convicted of bigamy was published. This statement was true of one person called Harold Newstead, but not true of the claimant. Since the claimant was of the same name and age and lived in Camberwell it was held that the statement could reasonably be taken as referring to him.

Where a statement is made about a group of people, without mentioning specific names, it will depend on whether the group is so clearly defined that the statement could reasonably be taken as referring to the claimant. The larger the group is, the less likely that the claimant will be able to show that the statement could be taken as referring to him.

So saying that 'all lawyers are crooks' cannot be taken as referring to any particular lawyer. However saying that 'all the staff in the Law department at a certain college are drug addicts'

could be taken as referring to any one of the staff there.

A group cannot be defamed. In *Derbyshire County Council v Times Newspapers Ltd* (1993) the House of Lords decided that a County Council had no right to sue for defamation.

## Publication

The statement must be published to a third party. Published does not just mean that it must be printed in a book or paper. Published in this context also has the meaning of the libel being made known or communicated to another person. If the statement is made only to the person concerned, then it has not been published.

So, if Mr Green says to Mr Smith that Mr Smith is dishonest and has been stealing from him, that statement may be defamatory, but by saying it direct to Mr Smith and no-one else, it has not been published. But if one other person is present then it has been published.

Where the defamatory statement is in a letter written and addressed to the person concerned, the statement has not been published, even if someone else wrongly opens the letter and reads the statement. This was shown in *Huth v Huth* (1915).

### CASE EXAMPLE

**Huth v Huth (1915)**

A butler, without being authorised to do so, opened a letter addressed to his employer. The letter contained defamatory statements about the employer. It was held that it was not published as it was addressed to the person about whom the statements were made.

A postcard sent through the post is automatically assumed to be published. It is not necessary to show that anyone read it. The same is true of telegrams. Also where any libel is printed, for example in a book or paper, that is enough to show it was published. There is no need to prove that the book or paper was actually read by anyone.

There are two exceptions where a third party may be told without the statement being considered published:

**(a)** where the claimant himself publishes it
**(b)** where the defendant has told his own spouse.

## Dissemination

Every repetition of the defamatory statement is a new publication, so that the person defamed can sue for each publication. This could happen where a statement is originally made by one person and then repeated in a newspaper article. The repetition by the newspaper is a publication and the person defamed can sue both the original maker of the statement and the newspaper.

In *Godfrey v Demon Internet Ltd* (1999) it was decided that a defamatory article on the Internet was 'published' every time an Internet user accessed the web page which contained that article. It was also decided that once the service provider (Demon) knew that the article was defamatory and did not remove it from the web page, they could not use the defence of 'innocent dissemination'.

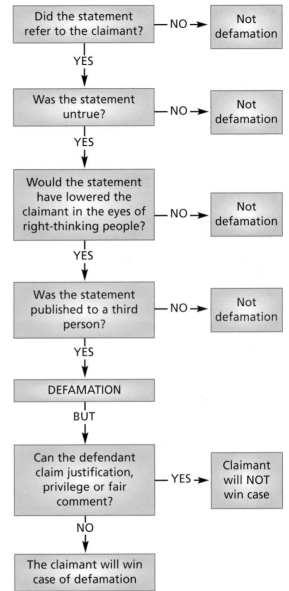

Figure 39.1 Flow chart for defamation

## Defences to defamation

The defendant in a defamation action can defend the case by:

**(a)** denying that the statement was defamatory, or
**(b)** denying that it referred to the claimant, or
**(c)** denying that it was published
**(d)** claiming innocent dissemination, where the person had no control over what was

published; it is a defence to printers, distributors and sellers of material because they cannot check every page of every book, paper, magazine etc; it is also a defence for broadcasters of live programmes, such as phone-ins or discussion programmes, in respect of statements made on air by people they have no control over.

Apart from these there are some special defences available to the defendant.

## Justification

Justification is a claim that the statement is true. To be a defence it is enough to show that the statement was substantially true. In other words if the facts said are mostly true then a small inaccuracy in one or two of the facts does not matter. This was what happened in *Alexander v North Eastern Railway Co* (1865).

---

**CASE EXAMPLE**

### *Alexander v North Eastern Railway Co (1865)*

A railway company, in an effort to stop people travelling without paying, published a sign which said that the claimant had been charged for 'riding in a train from Leeds for which his ticket was not available and refusing to pay the proper fare'. The sign went on to say that he had been convicted 'in the penalty of £9 1s 10d including costs, or three weeks' imprisonment'. This was inaccurate as it should have been 'two weeks' imprisonment', but the rest was accurate and true. The claimant sued for libel over the inaccurate statement of the number of weeks' imprisonment. The court held that the statement was substantially true and he lost his case.

---

## Absolute privilege

In some circumstances people are completely protected from being sued for defamation, regardless of what they have published. Absolute privilege means that the following people have a total defence to an action for defamation:

**(a)** Members of the House of Commons or the House of Lords for any statement made in Parliament

**(b)** reports of parliamentary proceedings which have been authorised by Parliament, for example in *Hansard*, or which are reproduced in full in a broadcast on radio or television or in any paper (if the original statements are not reproduced in full then the media can only claim qualified privilege – see below)

**(c)** people involved in court proceedings for anything said in the course of those proceedings; this includes judges, lawyers, the parties and witnesses

**(d)** fair, accurate and contemporaneous reports in newspapers or on radio or television of any court proceedings (this does not apply if the case is held in private)

**(e)** officers of State in any communication with each other about a matter of State; this category includes government ministers and very senior civil servants; it also includes military officers

**(f)** husbands and wives in respect of anything they say or write to each other.

The main reason for allowing the defence of absolute privilege is that public interest outweighs the rights of the person defamed.

## Qualified privilege

There are also situations where statements made will be privileged unless it is shown that the defendant acted out of malice or spite or some other improper motive. These are statements made:

**(a)** to protect an interest; this could occur where a shop manager reports to the managing director of the firm that he believes one of the employees is stealing. Provided this is not said out of malice the statement will be privileged. In such cases it is important that genuine suspicions are reported and investigated

**(b)** to perform a duty, for example supplying a reference for an employee. An employer will be protected by privilege for what he states provided that he does not do it maliciously

(c) as reports in media publications of any parliamentary or judicial proceedings; this covers situations where abbreviated versions of the proceedings are published. Reports on the meetings of other public bodies such as local councils are also protected by qualified privilege.

As with absolute privilege it is argued that qualified privilege is needed in the public interest.

# Fair comment

Fair comment applies to comments on matters which are of public interest. A statement will only be fair comment if it is a statement of opinion and not one of fact. The maker of the statement must honestly hold that opinion, although it does not mean that other people will agree with it. The test is: 'Was this an opinion, however exaggerated, obstinate or prejudiced, which was honestly held by the writer?'

However, if a statement is made maliciously then it cannot be fair comment.

# Apology

Where a defendant has unintentionally published a defamatory statement in a newspaper or periodical, then, under the Defamation Act 1996, he will have a defence if he offers to publish a suitable correction and an apology as soon as possible and offers to pay a sum of money by way of compensation. This is known as offer of amends. It cannot be used with any other defence.

## ACTIVITY

### Activity 1

Read the following extract from a newspaper article by Ben Hoyle in *The Times*, 2nd December 2008 and answer the questions below.

### Mother loses libel battle over 'Ugly' lawyer's misery memoir

The mother of a prominent barrister faces a legal bill of £500,000 after losing a High Court libel action against her daughter over allegations of abuse in *Ugly*, the best-selling memoir.

The jury took just over a day to find unanimously against Carmen Briscoe-Mitchell, 74, who had testified that her 11 children enjoyed a happy upbringing, contrary to the allegations in the book by her daughter, Constance Briscoe. The verdict is both a triumph and a relief for Miss Briscoe, a criminal barrister and one of Britain's first black part-time judges. Her career was at stake if she had lost.

Miss Briscoe defended her book as a true account of the suffering that she endured.

### Questions

The article above shows that Carmen Briscoe-Mitchell claimed for defamation against her daughter, Constance Briscoe, in the book *Ugly*.

1. What form of defamation was involved in the case – libel or slander?

2. Where was the case heard?

3. Who made the decision in the case?

4. Who won the case?

5. What defence was relevant in the case?

## BRIEF SUMMARY OF CHAPTER

**Freedom of expression**

■ is a right under the European Convention
  on Human Rights

**Limitations include:**

■ national security

■ obscenity laws

■ contempt of court

■ discrimination

■ the law on defamation

**Defamation**

■ Defamation is a tort

**Libel**

■ Libel is the permanent form

**Slander**

■ Slander is the temporary form

**Defamatory statement**

■ A statement is defamatory if:
  • it is untrue
  • it can reasonably be understood to refer to
    the claimant
  • it was published

**Special defences are:**

■ justification

■ absolute privilege

■ qualified privilege

■ fair comment

# CHAPTER 40

# HUMAN RIGHTS: OTHER FREEDOMS AND RIGHTS

## Right to privacy

Although many of the freedoms set out in the European Convention on Human Rights are recognised in our law, not all are. This is shown clearly by Article 8 which states that every person has a right to respect of his private and family life, his home and his correspondence. This right has not always been upheld in the English courts.

Let's start by looking at situations where the English courts have recognised the right to privacy. In *Malone v UK* (1984) the European Court of Human Rights ruled that there had been a breach of the right to privacy when the police tapped into telephone calls.

### CASE EXAMPLE

#### *Malone v UK* (1984)

Malone was an antiques dealer who had been convicted of receiving stolen goods. The police intercepted his phone calls. The Government at that time had not provided adequate law on when calls could be intercepted. It was held that this was a breach of the right to privacy.

Another area in which the European Court of Human Rights has ruled that the United Kingdom has breached the right to privacy is in relation to keeping DNA samples and fingerprints on a national database. This was decided in *S and Marper v United Kingdom* (2008).

### CASE EXAMPLE

#### *S and Marper v United Kingdom* (2008)

S was an 11-year-old boy who was charged with attempted robbery. He was acquitted of the offence. Marper was charged with harassment of his partner, but the case was later dropped. In both cases their fingerprints and DNA samples were taken when they were arrested. These remained on the national databases even though neither defendant was found guilty.

The European Court of Human Rights held that keeping information about fingerprints and DNA samples when the case against the person had been dropped or they had been found not guilty was a breach of the right to privacy.

However, the law in England has not protected a person's private life in other ways. There has been no rule against invasion of privacy. People in the public eye, such as the Royal family, film stars and sporting personalities have often suffered from the intrusion of the media into their private lives. This is now being changed by the Human Rights Act 1998 which brings Article 8 into our law.

An early case which recognised that there was a right to privacy was *Douglas and others v Hello! Ltd* (2001).

## CASE EXAMPLE

### Douglas and others v Hello! Ltd (2001)

The claimants tried to stop *Hello!* magazine from publishing unauthorised pictures of the wedding of Michael Douglas and Catherine Zeta-Jones. The court said there was a right to privacy but refused to order an injunction preventing *Hello!* from publishing the photos. This was mainly because Douglas and Zeta-Jones were prepared to allow publicity of their wedding and had made a contract with another magazine to publish photos.

In *Campbell v Mirror Group Newspapers* (2004) the House of Lords recognised that there was a right to privacy. It ruled that publishing photos taken without the celebrity knowing about it was a breach of the right to privacy in some circumstances.

## CASE EXAMPLE

### Campbell v Mirror Group Newspapers (2004)

A newspaper had published pictures of the model, Naomi Campbell, coming from a meeting of Narcotics Anonymous. It was held that the disclosure that the model was a drug addict and was receiving treatment for her addiction was justified in the public interest. However, publishing pictures (which had been taken secretly) of her coming out of a meeting of Narcotics Anonymous was a breach of her right to privacy.

## Balancing right to privacy and freedom of expression

There has to be a balance between the right to privacy and the right to freedom of expression. The test is whether it was information for which a person has a reasonable expectation of privacy. Even if it is, then there still may be a defence that the information published was of public interest. In other words that the person was a well-known figure and the public had a right to know the information.

However, where photographs have been taken secretly, especially when they show humiliating or embarrassing events, the publication of those photographs is likely to be difficult to justify. This decision gives some protection to celebrities' privacy.

## Freedom of religion

Under Article 9 everyone has the right to freedom of thought, conscience and religion. This includes the right to:

- change religion
- worship freely
- teach the religion
- keep the rules of a religion.

This freedom of religion can be limited if it is necessary to protect public order, health or morals. For example, if a religion encouraged men to have sexual intercourse with girls under the age of 12, then men who did so could still be convicted under our sex offences law because it is necessary to protect young girls.

In the United Kingdom individuals have the right to follow any religion they choose. The only exception to the principle of the freedom to worship is the Monarch who must be a member of the Church of England.

Generally today there is no discrimination against people because of their religion. The main area in which there have been cases is where religious dress has been banned in employment as the following two cases show.

### CASE EXAMPLE

#### *Azmi v Kirkless Metropolitan Council* (2007)

The complainant was a classroom assistant who was asked to remove her face veil while teaching. The Employment Appeal Tribunal found that this was potentially indirect discrimination. However, they held that in this case such a request was justified. This was because the complainant was helping children to speak English and it was important that they could see her lips.

A case in which the complainant made a successful claim was *Noah v Sarah Desrosiers* (2007).

### CASE EXAMPLE

#### *Noah v Sarah Desrosiers* (2007)

The complainant applied for a job as a hair stylist. She was not considered for it as she wore a headscarf because of her religion. The employment tribunal held that requiring her to work bare-headed was indirect discrimination.

## Freedom of association and freedom of assembly

Article 11 gives the right to freedom of peaceful assembly and to freedom of association with others, including the right to join trade unions.

## Association

In Britain most workers have the right to join a trade union, but there are some who have not. In 1984 the right to belong to a trade union was taken away from those working at the Government Communications Headquarters in Cheltenham. This limitation of rights was challenged in the English courts but it was held that the Government could withdraw trade union rights where national security was at risk.

There are also restrictions on associations where there is a crime involved; here the people concerned can be charged with the offence of conspiracy. Certain organisations are banned by laws aimed at the prevention of terrorism.

## Assembly

Meetings in private places are generally allowed, unless there is likely to be a crime. However there are a number of restrictions on meetings in public places. The main ones are:

1. The Highways Act 1980 makes it an offence to 'wilfully obstruct the free passage along the highway'. A police constable can arrest anyone who commits this offence.
2. The Public Order Act 1986 creates two different offences about people using violent conduct in both public and private places. These are:
   (a) riot: this is committed when 12 or more people present together use or threaten violence for a common purpose which would cause a person of reasonable firmness to fear for his or her personal safety

(b) *violent disorder:* this is committed if there are three or more persons present together using or threatening violence in such a way that a person of reasonable firmness would fear for his or her personal safety.

3. The Public Order Act 1936 makes it a criminal offence to wear political uniforms in public except for ceremonial or special occasions when the wearing of uniform is not likely to provoke a breach of the peace.

4. It is unlawful for 50 or more persons to meet within one mile of the Houses of Parliament when Parliament is sitting.

5. The Criminal Justice and Public Order Act 1994 gives the police powers to intervene where:

(a) two or more people are trespassing on land with the common purpose of residing there and either they have threatened the owner of the land or they have six or more vehicles on the land. This is aimed at New Age Travellers

(b) there is a gathering in the open air of 100 or more people at which amplified music is played during the night so loudly that it is likely to cause serious distress to local residents. This is aimed at so-called 'rave' parties.

In both these last two situations the police have powers to direct those involved to leave and if anyone refuses to leave the police may then arrest them.

## Processions

The Public Order Act 1986 makes several rules about processions. The organisers of a procession should give written notice to the local police of any intended procession at least seven days before it is due to take place. However annual processions such as local carnivals or May fairs are not included in this provision.

When a procession takes place, the most senior police officer present may impose any conditions necessary if he or she reasonably fears that serious public disorder is likely to result. So the police can change the proposed route of the procession.

Finally the Chief Constable for any area can apply to the district council for an order banning all (or certain types of) procession within a local area for up to three months.

## Freedom from discrimination

Article 14 of the European Convention on Human Rights says that all these rights and freedoms should exist without any discrimination on any grounds such as sex, race, colour, language, religion, political or other opinion, national or social origin, national minority, property, birth or status.

In this country the Sex Discrimination Acts and the Race Relations Act 1976 ban discrimination on the grounds of gender or race.

## Racial discrimination

The Race Relations Act 1976 forbids discrimination on the grounds of a person's race. This covers discrimination in public places such as hotels, restaurants, theatres and transport. It also forbids discrimination in the supply of goods and services and education as well as employment.

The Act set up the Commission for Racial Equality. The Commission gives guidance on avoiding discrimination and investigates possible breaches. It also can help a complainant to bring a case before the Race Relations Tribunal.

There is an exception where the law allows a person of a particular race to be employed. This is where race is a genuine occupational qualification: examples include an acting role, modelling or waiters in national restaurants.

## Public Order Act 1986

This Act creates various crimes for which people can be prosecuted. Such offences include committing acts or publishing material likely to stir up racial hatred.

## Sex discrimination

The Sex Discrimination Act 1975 makes it unlawful for employers to discriminate in any other way on the grounds of sex. This includes such areas as recruiting, promotion and training. A teenage girl was awarded over £24,000 compensation in 1994 because she was turned down for an apprenticeship as a motor mechanic because of her sex.

The Sex Discrimination Act 1975 set up the Equal Opportunities Commission which monitors equality. The Commission can help a complainant to bring a case. It can also bring cases itself when it believes there has been a breach of the law.

### BRIEF SUMMARY OF CHAPTER

**Right to privacy**
- Every person has a right to respect of his or her private and family life, his or her home and his or her correspondence

**Freedom of religion**
- Everyone has the right to freedom of thought, conscience and religion

**Freedom of association and freedom of assembly**
- Everyone has the right to freedom of peaceful assembly and to freedom of association with others, including the right to join trade unions

**Freedom from discrimination**
- The rights and freedoms given by the Convention should exist without any discrimination on any grounds

# TABLE OF ACTS OF PARLIAMENT

## Statutory Instruments

# European Legislation
## Conventions and Treaties

## Directives

# TABLE OF CASES

# INDEX